A Mirror for Magistrates and the Politics of the English Reformation

A volume in the series

Massachusetts Studies in Early Modern Culture

Edited by Arthur F. Kinney

A Mirror for Magistrates and the Politics of the English Reformation

SCOTT C. LUCAS

University of Massachusetts Press
Amherst

Printed in the United States of America

LC 2009017733
ISBN 978-1-55849-706-1

Designed by Jack Harrison
Set in Adobe Garamond Pro
Printed and bound by The Maple-Vail Book Manufacturing Group

Library of Congress Cataloging-in-Publication Data

Lucas, Scott (Scott C.), 1965–
A mirror for magistrates and the politics of the English Reformation / Scott Lucas.
p. cm. — (Massachusetts studies in early modern culture)
Includes bibliographical references and index.
ISBN 978-1-55849-706-1 (cloth : alk. paper)
1. Mirrour for magistrates. 2. English poetry—Early modern, 1500–1700—History and criticism.
3. Literature and history—Great Britain—History—16th century. 4. Reformation—England.
5. Great Britain—Politics and government—1485–1603. I. Title.
PR2199.M53L83 2009
821'.3—dc22
2009017733

British Library Cataloguing in Publication data are available.

Contents

Illustrations

Acknowledgments

Many of the arguments of this book found their first expression in a Duke University dissertation directed by Annabel Patterson. I owe an enduring debt of gratitude to Professor Patterson, who introduced me to *A Mirror for Magistrates*, encouraged me to investigate the fraught literary and political questions surrounding it, and provided through her scholarship a model of rigorous investigation into the intersections of early modern literature, politics, and culture. Among those at Duke with whom I worked I also thank Cynthia Herrup, who taught me much about the techniques of historical research and argument, and George Walton Williams, whose generous concern for me and for my project provided an important sustaining force during my time as a graduate student. George Williams's patient lessons in bibliographical analysis and in what he once termed "the art of fashioning the English sentence" enriched immensely both the content and the style first of my doctoral thesis and now of this book. I also thank Heather Hirschfeld for her valuable advice during the early stages of this project and Scott Jermyn, who for years has provided me both with great friendship and with unfailingly useful and careful responses to my arguments.

During the time I have worked on this book, many scholars and friends have extended their kind assistance and support. Chief among these is John N. King, to whom I am grateful not only for his friendship and constant encouragement but also for his trailblazing work in constituting the field of English Reformation literature as a specific area of scholarly investigation. Nearly every recent engagement with English literature circa 1530–1580 owes a great deal to King's comprehensive, groundbreaking scholarship, and my own monograph is no exception. Others to whom I am indebted for their help, encouragement, and goodwill include David Allen, Jeanie Brink, Yvonne Bruce, Ty Buckman, Jay Cahan, Derry Casey, Andrew Escobedo, Elizabeth Evenden, Tom Freeman, Alexandra Gillespie, Donna Hamilton,

Dale Hoak, Roger Kuin, Julie Lipovsky, Lisanne Lucas, Stephen Lucas, Tony and Anna Marie Martinovich, John McDiarmid, Susannah Brietz Monta, Sven Pierre Paret, Anne Lake Prescott, Ronald Schmidt, William Sessions, David Shields, Mona and Randy Shulman, Alzada Tipton, Edward Tucker, John Watkins, Robert White, Jessica Winston, and all my colleagues in The Citadel Department of English. Finally, I owe special thanks to George Deukmejian and Beth Quitslund, two dear friends whose support and good humor over the years have meant more to me than they may ever know.

For the financial and research assistance that made a project such as this one possible, I am grateful to a number of institutions, including The Citadel Foundation, the Keck Foundation, the Mellon Foundation, the National Endowment for the Humanities, Duke University, and the Huntington Library. Among members of The Citadel administration, I thank in particular Dean Alfred Finch, Provosts Harrison Carter and Samuel Hines, and Major General John S. Grinalds, emeritus president of The Citadel. I also thank the uniformly helpful and friendly staff of the Huntington Library, where much of the research for this book was undertaken. Sections of chapters 2 and 3 first appeared as part of "The Consolation of Tragedy: *A Mirror for Magistrates* and the Fall of the 'Good Duke' of Somerset," *Studies in Philology* 100, no. 1 (2003): 44–70. I thank the editor of *Studies in Philology* for allowing me to use this material and the Huntington Library for its permission to quote extensively from Lily B. Campbell's edition of the *Mirror*. For permission to reproduce images in their collection, I am grateful to the Bodleian Library, the British Library, the Folger Shakespeare Library, the John Rylands University Library, and the Victoria and Albert Museum. Finally, I thank Arthur Kinney, Bruce Wilcox, Carol Betsch, and Amanda Heller of the University of Massachusetts Press for helping to guide this study into print.

I dedicate this book to my mother, Elizabeth Lucas, to my daughters Charlotte and Caroline Lucas, and especially to my wife, Stephanie Lucas, without whose patient support this effort would not have been possible. The book is also dedicated to the memory of my late father, Justice Campbell M. Lucas, a model of probity, responsibility, and devotion to the highest of standards.

A Mirror for Magistrates and the Politics of the English Reformation

Introduction

In the opening scene of Ben Jonson's 1614 comedy *Bartholomew Fair*, several actors representing theater employees address the audience on how properly to view Jonson's play. One of these, the Scrivener, asks audience members to accept certain "Articles of Agreement" between themselves and the author before the play begins. Although this compact allows audiences generally to express opinions on the art of Jonson's comedy, it nevertheless strictly prohibits one particular method of interpretive analysis. The final article of Jonson's agreement demands that spectators promise "neither in themselves [to] conceal, nor suffer by them to be concealed, any state-decipherer, or politic picklock of the scene," that is, one who "will pretend to affirm, on his own inspired ignorance, what *mirror of magistrates* is meant by the Justice, what great lady by the pig-woman, what concealed statesman by the seller of mousetraps, and so of the rest."[1]

As Jonson's editors have noted, this prohibition against allusive interpretation is itself allusive: Jonson warns against expressing opinions on the topical significance of his character of the Justice by invoking the title of one of the best-known and most important literary works of his day, *A Mirror for Magistrates*.[2] Although it was first compiled and printed over sixty years before *Bartholomew Fair*, this collection of historical verse tragedies had remained widely read and influential throughout the Elizabethan and Jacobean periods.[3] In its original form, the *Mirror* presented a number of poetic narratives in the voices of fallen British political figures of the fourteenth and fifteenth centuries, stretching from the last years of Richard II's reign to the end of

1. Jonson, *Bartholomew Fair*, ed. Waith, 33; emphasis added.

2. Ibid., 190. *Mirror of Magistrates* was a common alternate title for the work. Sir Philip Sidney, for instance, speaks of it by this title in the *Apology for Poetry* (see G. G. Smith, *Elizabethan Critical Essays*, 1:196).

3. A new, expanded edition of the *Mirror*, in fact, had been issued in 1610, just four years before the first production of *Bartholomew Fair*.

Edward IV's (ca. 1387–1483). Its poems were originally composed and compiled in 1554 during the reign of Queen Mary I (1553–1558) under the title *A Memorial of suche Princes, as since the tyme of kyng Richard the seconde, haue been vnfortunate in the Realme of England.* The *Memorial* was to be joined to a new edition of *The Fall of Princes* by John Lydgate, the medieval *de casibus* tragedy compilation from which the poems of the *Memorial* took their literary form. All of *The Fall of Princes* and some or all of the *Memorial* had been printed when Queen Mary's Chancellor, Bishop Stephen Gardiner, ordered work halted and the *Memorial* suppressed. By order of the Privy Council, the whole printed *Memorial* was either destroyed or used as scrap, and its poems were never allowed to appear before the public during Mary's time in power. Only after Mary's death and the accession of Elizabeth I did the *Memorial* find its way before the public in the retitled and lightly revised form of *A Mirror for Magistrates* (1559).[4]

Upon publication, *A Mirror for Magistrates* became one of early modern England's most remarkable literary phenomena. For over six decades the *Mirror* remained almost constantly in print, appearing before the public in seven editions and six reissues between 1559 and 1621.[5] Several generations of Tudor and Stuart readers eagerly sought out the collection, making the *Mirror* perhaps the most widely read work of secular poetry of its time. Artists of all ranks and abilities set out to emulate in their own works the *de casibus* tragedy form of the *Mirror* poems; a number of these added their new creations directly to the *Mirror* itself, swelling the contents of the work over its lifetime to more than four times the size of the original collection.[6] Others eschewed the generic form of the *Mirror* but appropriated lines, themes, or

4. For the evidence that has led critics to accept that the 1559 *Mirror* is a lightly edited version of the 1554 *Memorial*, see the appendix to this book. William Baldwin served as editor for the 1554 *Memorial* and for the first two editions of the *Mirror*, those dated 1559 and 1563. For these volumes, see Pollard et al., *A Short Title Catalogue of Books Printed in England* [hereafter *STC*], at entries 1247 and 1248. All further references to *A Short Title Catalogue* are to this edition and are given by entry number. I use the title *A Mirror for Magistrates* to refer only to the editions edited by William Baldwin, except where noted. All page citations to *A Mirror for Magistrates* (and to Lily B. Campbell's introduction in her edition of it) refer to Campbell's *"The Mirror for Magistrates": Edited from Original Texts in the Huntington Library* and are given parenthetically in the text. For the sake of readability, I often present the titles of most *Mirror* tragedies in shortened form and with slightly modernized orthography (changing *u* to *v*, *v* to *u*, and *i* to *j* to accord with modern standards), usually after the initial appearance of each title. Following critical practice, I also modernize the spelling of noble titles, both in the short titles and in referring to characters in the poems.

5. New editions of the *Mirror* appeared in 1559, 1563, 1571, 1574, 1575 (reissue), 1578 (canceled and uncanceled variants), 1587, 1610, 1619 (two reissues), 1620 (two reissues), and 1621 (reissue). The last five issues of the *Mirror* differ from one another (and from the 1610 edition) only in the dates and booksellers named on their title pages. See *STC* 1246–1252.5, 13443–13448.7.

6. For the tragedies added to the *Mirror* after Baldwin's death, see Campbell, *Parts Added to "A Mirror for Magistrates"*; and Niccols, *A Mirour for Magistrates.*

images from its poems to enrich their own artistic creations. Finally, some of the best-known playwrights of the Elizabethan age seized upon the collection's historical narratives to present in a host of dramatic histories and tragedies their own portraits of the figures and events first portrayed in literary form in the *Mirror*. The collection was not only influential but highly esteemed as well. Numerous contemporaries lauded it as nothing less than a work of genius. Sir Philip Sidney is only the most famous of those who ranked the poems of *A Mirror for Magistrates* with some of the greatest works ever created in the English language.[7]

At first glance, Jonson's reference to the *Mirror* in *Bartholomew Fair* would seem out of place, given that it conjures up the title of a collection of historical verse tragedies in the introductory scene of a raucous contemporary comedy. Jonson's allusion, however, is not so much to the text of *A Mirror for Magistrates* as to a way of reading that text: to construe Justice Overdo in a topically referential manner is to fall into the sort of practice of reading invited by the poems of the *Mirror*.[8]

While Jonson's words stand as a warning against topical approaches to *Bartholomew Fair*, their allusive implication alerts modern readers to the significance of such interpretive practices for *A Mirror for Magistrates*. In this book I argue what Jonson's allusion implies: that many of the poems of *A Memorial of suche Princes* and *A Mirror for Magistrates* were created to be topically allusive in form and politically interventionary in purpose. Through these poems, the authors sought to address two primary audiences: evangelical Protestants suffering under the collapse of the Edwardian Reformation and Marian magistrates who were engaged in pursuing political courses of action to which the authors were opposed.[9] Their purpose was to shape readers' responses to recent and ongoing political acts of their time, and their method was the creation of topically applicable historical exempla, works crafted to evoke mid-Tudor events and figures even as they claimed only to speak about England's distant past.

The specific goals of these exempla are implied by the two successive titles their compiler, William Baldwin, chose for this collection, *A Memorial of suche Princes* (1554) and *A Mirror for Magistrates* (1559). For English evan-

7. Gary Waller suggests that among sixteenth-century English poetic works only Sternhold and Hopkins's metrical *Psalms* had more readers than *A Mirror for Magistrates* (Waller, *English Poetry of the Sixteenth Century*, 40). Insufficient work has been done on the influence of the *Mirror* on Elizabethan drama. For a survey of plays that handle events first dramatized in the poems of the *Mirror*, see Fleay, *Biographical Chronicle of the English Drama*, 1:17–20. For a selection of Elizabethan praise for the *Mirror*, see Trench, "*A Mirror for Magistrates*," 71–88.

8. Although she did not pursue its implications, Lily Campbell was the first to notice the interpretive significance of Jonson's allusion to the *Mirror* (*Mirror*, 55).

9. For the beliefs and culture of the mid-Tudor English evangelical community, see chapter 1.

gelicals, Baldwin and his fellows seek to guide readers to confront and to come to terms with the worst disasters of the previous reign (that of King Edward VI, 1547–1553). Their exemplary models guide readers to create new exculpatory "memorials" of lost evangelical Protestant heroes, men whose reputations and ideals—and, by extension, the reputations and ideals of their followers—had been tarnished by their personal downfalls and, later, by the complete collapse of the English Reformation on King Edward's death. The *Memorial-Mirror* authors craft these retrospectively topical exempla to lead readers to consolatory understandings of the recent past, understandings that stress the righteousness and unfulfilled promise of the Edwardian period and contest the dominant Marian interpretations of Edward's reign as one of misguided zeal ended providentially by God. For Marian magistrates, by contrast, the authors construct admonitory exempla displaying the "historically proven" tragic consequences of specific, ongoing political actions to which the authors are opposed. Their fictionally shaped, quasi-historical narratives thus offer exemplary "mirrors" in which certain officers may see the terrible results that will follow (so the poems claim) from the very actions in which those officers are engaged.

To read the poems of *A Mirror for Magistrates* in such a manner is to read them against the grain of most modern *Mirror* criticism. For over seventy years, critics have generally portrayed the *Mirror* as anything but politically controversial and locally engaged. Instead, most have treated the work as a serene, univocal storehouse of orthodox sixteenth-century political, philosophical, and literary "ideas," as a collection consciously designed to avoid specific political engagement and to display only uncontroversial, familiar, and universally acceptable "truths" to its readers.

This long-standing conception was created decades ago by three critics who remain guiding voices in *Mirror* criticism, Willard Farnham, Lily B. Campbell, and E. M. W. Tillyard. In 1926 Farnham inaugurated modern *Mirror* criticism with his article "The *Mirror for Magistrates* and Elizabethan Tragedy," which presented the *Mirror* to scholars as a "record of a maturing popular philosophy concerning man's misfortunes" useful as background material for studies of Elizabethan drama.[10] Selectively quoting from the twenty-seven tragedies and numerous prose passages of the 1559 and 1563

10. Farnham, "*Mirror for Magistrates* and Elizabethan Tragedy," 67. See also Farnham, *Medieval Heritage*, 271–303. Before Farnham, discussions of the *Mirror* had been confined almost solely to general literary histories (such as Courthope, *History of English Poetry*), to chiefly bibliographic investigations (such as Trench, *"A Mirror for Magistrates"*), and to individual appreciations of Sir Thomas Sackville's "Induction," a poem of the 1563 edition.

editions of the *Mirror*, Farnham argued in this article and, later, in his widely influential *Medieval Heritage of Elizabethan Tragedy* (1936) that the *Mirror* exemplified a shift from the medieval concept of blind fortune as the governor of worldly events to a new, Elizabethan idea that divine providence shaped human affairs. To Farnham, the *Mirror* was a sort of literary fossil, less an artistic achievement in its own right than an artifact preserving evidence of the evolution of tragic thought in the Tudor period. Farnham recommended the text to future scholars as a repository of philosophical statements easily transportable to the study of more worthy literary subjects, such as the dramas of Shakespeare and his contemporaries.

In the 1930s Lily B. Campbell took up Farnham's approach to the *Mirror* and adapted it to her own search for evidence of Tudor historical and political "beliefs." Campbell's interest in the *Mirror* was born from a larger theoretical project she pursued throughout the 1930s and 1940s. During those years Campbell argued for a new conception of historical literary criticism, one of an unique, philosophical kind.[11] Using Shakespeare as her chief subject, Campbell argued that a properly historical approach to Shakespeare's works (and, by extension, to those of his contemporaries) would not attempt to place the individual plays in the context of particular events or local concerns. Rather its purpose would be to discover in his plays the "dominant political pattern characteristic of the political philosophy of [Shakespeare's] age," a transcendent body of thought that lies behind and shapes the form of all of Shakespeare's political and historical dramas. The specific significances or roles of a text in the culture in which it was produced were not, she argued, valid subjects of study in themselves for a historically oriented literary critic. Instead, particulars (plots, characters, historical events, and the like) are important only when they are understood as "linked in meaning to the universal of which they are a representative part."[12] Campbell portrayed historicist literary study as properly a branch of the study of the history of ideas: its function, she argued, was the study of the imagining of universals in various cultures and times.

Campbell used this theoretical-historical method to elucidate *A Mirror for Magistrates*, describing the *Mirror* as a work designed to display just the sort of abstract, "universal" sixteenth-century political and philosophical ideas

11. See Campbell, *Collected Papers* and *Shakespeare's "Histories."*

12. Campbell, *Shakespeare's "Histories,"* 6–7. Thus, while Campbell acknowledged that Shakespeare presents individuated characters and plots and that his dramatic presentations were shaped by the thoughts and behaviors of his age, the important point for the literary scholar is to recognize that in each of his works Shakespeare "penetrates through experience to the meaning of experience" and reveals the "universal law" behind contingent events (7).

that she declared it was the task of the literary-historical scholar to uncover. Treating the words of various *Mirror* characters as objective representations of their authors' beliefs, Campbell argued that underlying the various narratives of the poems was a coherent, synthetic structure of Tudor political doctrine, a proto-Stuart theory of the divine right of kings that all the tragedies sought to exemplify. In the enormously influential introduction to her edition of the *Mirror*, Campbell wrote that "the political doctrine which it was the acknowledged purpose of the *Mirror* to teach was the orthodox Tudor doctrine," one "inculcated alike in the *Institutes* of Calvin, and in certain homilies appointed by the Tudor rulers to be read in all the churches, as well as in the addresses of the Tudor sovereigns to their people." This "Tudor doctrine" asserted that the king is God's vicegerent and responsible to God alone. The ruler's subjects may under no circumstances withdraw their obedience to him, for "to resist him is to resist God" (*Mirror*, 52–53). Like Farnham, Campbell did not recommend the *Mirror* to scholars as a literary text worthy of study in its own right. The importance of the work, she argued, lay not in its poems themselves but in the useful supply of doctrinal political and philosophic statements that could be extracted from it and used to uncover the belief "patterns" that gave shape to Shakespeare's dramas.[13]

In the 1940s and 1950s E. M. W. Tillyard popularized Campbell's "historical" literary criticism and raised her assertions about the political teachings of the *Mirror* to the level of dogma.[14] In a series of influential books and articles, Tillyard extracted from the *Mirror* passages that he claimed exemplified the "Elizabethan World Order," the "complete body of doctrine" that represented the ingrained belief of all people of the Elizabethan era in the importance of such matters as political order, obedience to the monarch, and the preservation of the hierarchical status quo. Following Campbell's lead, Tillyard read the *Mirror* as a work designed to teach an abstract body of "Elizabethan" thought, a collection of beliefs that "goes far beyond mere practical politics."[15] For Tillyard, the *Mirror* taught "the perfect orthodoxy of the time," displaying in its poems "current, conventional, yet heart-felt opinions on kingship and tyranny, on the sin of rebellion and the individual's ultimate responsibility, whatever the influence of the stars"[16] Though more sensitive to the literary merits of the text than had been Farnham and Campbell, Tillyard still joined these scholars in presenting the *Mirror* chiefly as a storehouse of Elizabethan "opinions," one whose passages could best be used

13. In the introduction to her edition Campbell herself noted that she devoted attention to the *Mirror* only in preparation for the study of Shakespeare's history plays (4).

14. Tillyard mentions Campbell's influence on him in *Shakespeare's History Plays*, vii.

15. Ibid., 10.

16. Tillyard, "*A Mirror for Magistrates* Revisited," 8.

to elucidate the thought that lay behind better-known literary works of the later Tudor period.

For decades scholars have chiefly followed the course these earlier critics laid out for study of the *Mirror*, approaching it primarily as a compendium of abstract ideas rather than as a collection of independent dramatic narratives worthy of analysis in their own right. In 1979 Jerry Leith Mills summarized the body of twentieth-century *Mirror* criticism as "predominantly concerned with the *Mirror* as an anticipation of things much greater than itself, as a medium through which medieval concepts of history and tragedy are both perpetuated and reshaped, as a repository of potentially brilliant ideas which matured in the age of Shakespeare."[17] Even many recent studies have continued to pursue projects similar to those of the past, investigating the collection chiefly for its presentation of Tudor "ideas" such as its musings on the idea of fortune, its displays of Renaissance "modes of perception," its presentation of Tudor concepts of history, or its exemplification of Calvinist political theory.[18]

If critics generally agree that the *Mirror* was designed to teach a clear body of doctrine, however, they have found remarkably little agreement on just what that doctrine is supposed to be. Over the years, numerous scholars have gathered evidence from the poems to support the Campbell-Tillyard thesis that the *Mirror* embodies a conservative politics, one that instructs readers to venerate the monarch and to abhor rebellion. Others, however, have drawn on equally extensive evidence from the collection to declare that the *Mirror* in fact seeks to undercut the exalted status of the ruler and even to lead readers to accept the idea that rebellion against the king is at times not a sin but a duty.[19] Some have gathered passages to support Farnham's thesis that the *Mirror* seeks to teach the manifest power of divine providence over human affairs. Others, by contrast, have drawn from different parts of the text to assert that the collection chiefly teaches the dominance of fortune in human life.[20] Even casual readers can identify a dizzying array of disparate and mutually exclusive political and philosophical "statements" in the text.

17. Mills, "Recent Studies," 349.

18. For a survey of *Mirror* criticism before 1980, see ibid., 343–52. More recent traditional studies include Green, "Modes of Perception"; Mosser, "L'Art de la poésie historique"; Kiefer, "*A Mirror for Magistrates*"; Budra, *"A Mirror for Magistrates" and the* de casibus *Tradition.*

19. Kinghorn, *Chorus of History*, 268–69; Waller, *English Poetry of the Sixteenth Century*, 40; Hadfield, *Literature, Politics and National Identity*, 81–107; R. S. White, *Natural Law*, 76–77. Hadfield's groundbreaking *Literature, Politics and National Identity* was the first study to argue at length for the politically contentious and even politically resistant nature of many of the poems of the *Mirror*.

20. *Mirror*, 52–54; Kiefer, *Fortune and Elizabethan Tragedy*, 30–59; Parry, *Protestant Vision*, 256; Mills, "Recent Studies," 345–46.

For instance, the *Mirror* seems to teach the lesson of strict obedience to the monarch in the tragedy "Thomas of Wudstocke," in which Wudstocke counsels magistrates "in that ye be Lyeges learne to obaye" even when the monarch does wrong (95). Later, however, the *Mirror* appears to overturn this lesson in the poem "John Earl of Worcester," whose protagonist urges "let none [high] office take, / Save he that can for right his prince forsake" (202). The *Mirror* appears to denounce rebellion (as in the tragedy of "Jack Cade" [176–77]) and yet also to celebrate it (as in the tragedy of "Robert Tresilian" [78–79]). Even the treatment of regicide in the *Mirror* seems self-contradictory: the killing of a king is portrayed as a crime in the tragedy of "Northumberland" but described as an entirely justifiable, even godly, act in "King James I" (134, 159).

Faced with the plethora of mutually exclusive, irreconcilable "statements" uttered by characters and authors alike in the collection, many have simply given up on making any final sense of the *Mirror*, declaring the work to be a literary failure for its refusal to articulate the clear body of Tudor "ideas" such scholars insist it was created to display. H. A. Kelly, for instance, execrates the *Mirror* for offering no univocal set of doctrinal statements concerning the roles of providence and fortune in human affairs. The typical *Mirror* character, Kelly complains, is "made to lament his fate and to draw universal morals or formulate universal laws of life, most of which are contradicted by the universal maxims arrived at by fellow unfortunates. . . . Counterexamples to the general law are usually ignored within each tragedy, though at times an effort is made to analyze the discrepancies involved in different kinds of tragedies. The effort is ordinarily not very successful."[21] Similarly, F. J. Levy describes the first poem of the collection, "The Fall of Robert Tresilian," as hopelessly contradictory in its lessons, arguing that "Richard II's chief justice, Tresilian, was certainly greedy and deserved his fate, but part of his crime had been a too-eager obedience of his master. . . . How was the lesson of obedience to rulers to be squared with that of responsibility to God?" According to Levy, this poem, like so many others in the collection, is simply unable to reconcile the doctrinal conflicts inherent in it. He blames such failure on the *Mirror* poets themselves, whom he describes as well-meaning men who were simply not up to the task of teaching the weighty political doctrine they had set out to convey.[22] Such denigrations of the text, coupled with C. S. Lewis's well-known dismissal of the *Mirror* as combining the worst of both "late medieval" and "drab" formal elements, have condemned the collection

21. Kelly, *Divine Providence*, 164–65.

22. Levy, *Tudor Historical Thought*, 214–17. For similar views, see also Peery, "Tragic Retribution" 123–25; Green, "Modes of Perception," 118–21; Kiefer, *"A Mirror for Magistrates,"* 121.

to a degree of critical neglect and even scorn remarkable for a text so eagerly read and so widely praised by many of the most important authors of the early modern period.[23]

The incoherence that scholars find in the collection has less to do with the *Mirror* itself, however, than with the misleading assumptions many critics bring to the work. First, although it has long been read as a work of Elizabethan literature, *A Mirror for Magistrates* is Marian in origin, not Elizabethan. The period of its composition was not the relatively stable time of Elizabeth's rule but that of the wrenching divisions and upheavals of Queen Mary's early reign, a time particularly indisposed to abstract reflection and detached meditation. The year of composition of *A Memorial of suche Princes* (1554) alone witnessed Wyatt's rebellion and its bloody aftermath, the reviled marriage of the English queen to the Prince of Spain, and the return of England to the Roman Catholic fold. From evangelical Protestant authors (a group to which all the known authors of the *Memorial* prominently belonged), such events elicited not works of serene meditation but texts of engaged political admonition, protest, and even opposition. The chief literary mode among evangelicals of this time was the polemical pamphlet. Despite the inhibiting strictures of Marian censorship, covert Protestant presses both in England and abroad issued a flood of texts decrying current governmental actions and, in many cases, admonishing the highest men and women of the land. Such works sought not to muse upon familiar doctrine but to engage with and to influence the most important religious and political actors of the day.[24] William Baldwin, the compiler and chief author of the poems of *A Memorial of suche Princes*, had himself pursued a career as an author of controversial evangelical literature before turning to the *Memorial* project. His two works composed prior to the *Memorial*, in fact, were so contentious in their evangelical, anti-Catholic content that they were unable to find publication until after Queen Mary's death. *A Memorial of suche Princes* was a product of this time and this author, and the collection must be read in its original context of production if one is clearly to understand its poems' controversial purposes, their intended audiences, and their rhetorical ends.[25]

23. C. S. Lewis, *English Literature in the Sixteenth Century*, 240–46. Two scholars have sought to argue that the contradictions in the text are intentional strategies of the authors: see Geller, "What History Really Teaches"; and Winston, "*A Mirror for Magistrates.*"

24. For a bibliography of Protestant polemical texts of this time, see Baskerville, *Chronological Bibliography*. For the censorship practices of Mary's government and the turn to political and religious polemic among evangelical authors, see Loades, *Politics, Censorship and the English Reformation*, 91–147; and Loach, "Pamphlets and Politics." For William Baldwin's own polemical writings and his troubles with Marian censors, see chapter 1.

25. See chapter 1.

Second, although it is often referred to as a single, unified poem in itself, the *Mirror* is in fact a collection of individual, independent tragedies.[26] In its original form (1559) the *Mirror* contained nineteen separate poems composed by nine different authors. Its second edition (1563) added five new poets and eight new tragedies. There is no evidence that these various authors collaborated or consulted with any others in creating their contributions, nor is there any evidence that they sought to produce a uniform body of doctrine in the work as a whole.[27] Since each of the poems was created as a separate, independent literary work in itself, it is a mistake to declare the collection as a whole failed or "confused" if different authors explain events differently, or if the same historical figure is cast in a different light in separate narratives.

Likewise there is no indication that the authors intended the seemingly universal statements offered at the beginnings and ends of their tragedies to apply to anything other than the specific poems in which they are found. Although *Mirror* critics have studied the aphoristic passages on divine providence, fortune, and political life in the poems as general expressions of sixteenth-century philosophy, these statements are always uttered in character and must always, therefore, be first and foremost judged in that context. Such generalized "statements" (which are, it should be noted, usually given only brief space compared to that devoted to the narrated events of the tragedies) are best interpreted solely in the context of the events or the personages of the tragedy in which they appear. Thus Thomas of Wudstocke's seemingly doctrinal "lesson" teaching obedience to the monarch should be applied only to *his* situation: that of a high-ranking officer who desired to have personal rule over his king (94–95). Similarly, John of Worcester's exhortation to disobey an erring monarch should be applied only to his own sort of situation: that of an officer asked to commit sinful acts (in Worcester's case, to murder the innocent children of Edward IV's political enemies) on behalf of his king. Rebellion is denounced in "Jack Cade" because Cade is ultimately motivated by pride, greed, and discontent with his social station. The revolt of the Lords Appellant that brings down Richard II's Chief Justice, however, is celebrated in "Robert Tresilian" because that action was undertaken to

26. Baldwin reports that nine authors composed the *Memorial* tragedies, eight men (himself and seven others) who met one night in 1554 and John Skelton (d. 1529), whose tragedy in the voice of Edward IV was used to conclude the volume (*Mirror*, 69, 235). Baldwin subsequently added eight more tragedies, some by *Memorial* authors and some by new men, to the 1563 edition.

27. *Mirror*, 69. See also the discussions of the composition and authorship of individual poems in the various prose passages of the collection (e.g., *Mirror*, 71, 81, 91).

rid the legal system of the corruption that Tresilian and King Richard had introduced into it.

Instead of seeking an elusive unity to this multivocal collection, scholars must examine its poems individually, judging each one for its individual purpose and specific function. Most important, critics must reintroduce the practice of looking for local resonance and topical meaning in the works, a method central to the reading practice of the authors' own time but one that until recently has not been pursued by modern *Mirror* scholars. That at least some of the poems of *A Mirror for Magistrates* are topical in form was first revealed by two early studies of the collection. In 1922 Eveline Feasey sought to explain the suppression of *A Memorial of suche Princes* by examining three tragedies thought to have been included in that collection, George Ferrers's "Humfrey Duke of Gloucester," "Edmund Duke of Somerset," and "Elianor Cobham."[28] Reading Ferrers's poems in the light of mid-Tudor politics, Feasey argued that these tragedies, each of which touched on the life and death of Henry VI's Lord Protector, Humfrey, Duke of Gloucester, were shaped allusively to portray the downfall of Edward Seymour, Duke of Somerset (d. 1552), King Edward VI's Protector of the Realm.[29] Feasey discerned in the Gloucester of the *Mirror* a covert representation of the recently deceased Seymour: both men had been Protectors of the Realm during the minority of their monarchs, both were uncles to their respective kings (Gloucester to Henry VI, Seymour to Edward VI), both were popular with the people and had been called "the good Duke," both engaged in long-running feuds with powerful noble opponents, and both were brought to "untimely," violent ends as a result of those feuds. Feasey detected as well in these tragedies an unflattering portrait of Bishop Stephen Gardiner in the character of Humfrey's most powerful enemy, the scheming Lord Chancellor, Cardinal Beauford (or Beaufort). In "Humfrey Duke of Gloucester" it is Beauford who brings down "the good Duke" Humfrey from his position of Protector. Since it was Lord Chancellor Gardiner himself who, according

28. The full titles of these tragedies are "How Dame Elianor Cobham Duchesse of Glocester for practising of witchcraft and Sorcery, suffred open penance, and after was banished the realme into the yle of Man," "How Hvmfrey Plantagenet Duke of Glocester Protector of England, during the minoritie of his Nephue kinge Henrye the sixt, (commenlye called the good Duke) by practise of enemies was brought to confusion," and "The tragedie of Edmund duke of Somerset, slayne at the first battayle at Saynct Albanes, in the tyme of Henrye the sixte." The last of these was included in the 1563 additions to the *Mirror*. The other two did not appear in the *Mirror* until the editions of 1578 (*STC* 1252, 1252.5).

29. Feasey, "Licensing of the *Mirror for Magistrates*." Throughout this book I refer to Edward Seymour, Duke of Somerset, as Seymour to avoid confusion with the *Mirror* character Edmund Beauford, Duke of Somerset, who shares Seymour's title.

to Baldwin, had ordered the *Memorial* suppressed, Feasey concluded that these poems that indicted Gardiner as the prime mover in Somerset's fall and death played an important role in Gardiner's decision to prohibit the work.[30]

Feasey's topical approach was taken up by only one other critic; surprisingly, that one critic was Lily B. Campbell. In her 1934 article "Humphrey Duke of Gloucester and Elianor Cobham His Wife in the *Mirror for Magistrates*," Campbell endorsed Feasey's discovery of a topical resonance to these poems. She presented further historical evidence to support Feasey's findings concerning the tie between Gloucester and Seymour and elucidated Ferrers's project of shaping and even altering the historical record of Gloucester's career in his poem in order to "mirror" more closely the events of Seymour's fall. Yet while affirming the topical function of the tragedies, Campbell sharply attacked Feasey's specific readings of them and dismissed Feasey's arguments about the poems' meaning and purpose. Campbell exposed numerous historical inaccuracies in Feasey's work; most damagingly, she pointed out that Bishop Gardiner had no hand in Edward Seymour's downfall: Gardiner was in prison during Seymour's troubles and could not have taken the guiding role against Seymour that Beauford takes against Gloucester. Setting the tone for much future *Mirror* criticism, Campbell concluded that there was no controversial purpose underlying Ferrers's covert references to Protector Somerset in his poems. When he alluded to Edwardian events, Campbell argued, Ferrers did so solely to give a contemporary context for the timeless lessons he sought to teach (such as the danger of high office and the sin of overweening ambition) and to reinforce the notion that certain political problems tend to repeat themselves over the years.[31]

Campbell's revelation of flaws in Feasey's scholarship (coupled with Campbell's incorporation of further historical errors into her own readings) helped to dissuade critics from building on Feasey's insights. More important, Campbell's complete rejection of topical criticism in the years following her own topical article served to banish this method of inquiry from studies of the *Mirror*. Although she suggested in her introduction to the *Mirror* that "identifying the persons and situations reflected in the *Mirror for Magistrates* was a favourite indoor sport, even as late as 1614," she refused to consider such readings of the text as worthy of serious pursuit. To study local resonances and topical allusions in literary texts, Campbell declared, is to engage in literary "gossip," and "into that gossip," she announced, "I do

30. Ibid., 184–85.
31. Campbell, "Humphrey Duke of Gloucester," 140–41.

not propose to go" (55). Campbell's has remained the dominant voice in *Mirror* criticism, and her prohibition on topical readings has been remarkably influential. Since Campbell's time, only one sustained topical reading of any *Mirror for Magistrates* tragedy has ever been published.[32]

The critical distaste for topical investigation that Campbell helped to create, however, is a modern phenomenon, not an early modern one. Leah Marcus notes that no matter in how poor a light some modern critics might hold topical or "local" readings, such readings were common practice for sixteenth-century audiences. In response to one critic's satiric labeling of topical criticism as "Fluellenism," Marcus suggests that an equally valid name would be "Elizabethism, since the queen and her subjects practiced it with as much zeal as the character in *Henry V.*" Richard Dutton's analysis of early modern censorship and licensing practices supports Marcus's claim. Far from an unusual practice, Dutton concludes, "politically charged analogical [i.e., topical] reading was *normal*, the *usual* condition of writing and reading in the [Tudor-Stuart] period, and not just something that happened when scandals such as those surrounding Chapman's *Byron* plays or *A Game at Chess* drew attention to it."[33]

Scholars such as Marcus, Dutton, David Norbrook, Annabel Patterson, and Greg Walker have profitably returned the attention of modern readers to the need for a suspicious, topical sensitivity for reading many English Renaissance texts.[34] A sixteenth-century English author seeking to release a public, printed work that touched on uncomfortable political or religious subjects composed his text under the constant threat of possible retribution for his writing—punishment that could come directly from censoring government officials or indirectly from offended private individuals with enough influence to cause the author difficulty. Many authors thus turned to the multivalent language and allusive structures of literary form to protect themselves, shaping their works to present those texts overtly to readers as innocent aesthetic endeavors even as they built in to them (in Marcus's words) "structural mechanisms by which a fierce desire for decoding is stimulated."[35] Such strategies for indirect communication allowed authors to convey elliptically to public audiences their controversial political or religious opinions

32. Lucas, "Consolation of Tragedy."

33. Marcus, *Puzzling Shakespeare*, 33; Dutton, *Licensing, Censorship and Authorship*, xi.

34. See, among other works by these authors, Norbrook, *Poetry and Politics*; Patterson, *Censorship and Interpretation*; Walker, *Plays of Persuasion*.

35. Marcus, *Puzzling Shakespeare*, 37. Indeed, Jonson's prohibition against topical interpretation of *Bartholomew Fair* is one such mechanism, drawing audiences' attention to the possibility of topical allusiveness in the play precisely by demanding that they not think about such a possibility. In fact Jonson does seem to have based his Justice Overdo on a contemporary English magistrate, the Lord Mayor of London, Thomas Hayes (Jonson, *Bartholomew Fair*, ed. Horsman, xx).

while preserving their ability to deny any such controversial content if called to account for their writings.[36]

Annabel Patterson, in fact, has detected just such mechanisms in the first piece in *A Mirror for Magistrates*, George Ferrers's tragedy "The fall of Robert Tresilian chiefe Iustice of Englande, and other his felowes, for misconstruing the lawes, and expounding them to serue the Princes affections" (composed 1554). In *Reading Holinshed's Chronicles*, Patterson briefly notes that the malfeasant behavior Ferrers unhistorically ascribes to Richard II's chief justices in this poem, namely the willful misinterpretation of statute law to satisfy the monarch's unjust desires, was precisely that employed by Queen Mary's own high justices in the notorious treason trial of Sir Nicholas Throckmorton (April 1554).[37] Patterson concludes that Ferrers's lengthy castigation in "Robert Tresilian" of the very crimes committed by Throckmorton's judges would make his angry exemplum "all too easily applicable to the events of 1554" for many mid-Tudor readers, even though the judges whom Ferrers claims to handle in this tragedy are men solely of Richard II's time, not Mary's. Furthermore, she continues, Ferrers then stimulates application of his poem's denunciations of judicial misbehavior to the actions of current legal officers by having Tresilian's now chastened ghost attack certain "sum in latter dayes" who emulated his and his fellows' corrupt "wresting of the ryght" in judicial proceedings (80). Of course, by including this allusion to unnamed latter-day judges, Ferrers spurs readers to ponder just who these men might be, to consider whether Tresilian's crimes match the actions of any contemporary jurists, and finally, to condemn those Marian judges whose practices are "mirrored" in the crimes of Ferrers's suffering protagonists.[38] The sort of topically evocative mechanisms that Patterson detects in "Robert Tresilian" pervade many of the poems of *A Mirror for Magistrates*. It is the *Memorial* and *Mirror* authors' use of such elements in their tragedies, the purposes to which they put them, and the indirect, allusive, and often politically controversial content they seek to convey that form the chief focus of this study.

To open such a project, chapter 1 of this book examines the creation of *A Memorial of suche Princes*, offering a survey of its origin, construction, and

36. For the strategies available to mid-Tudor authors used in one politically contentious series of poems (a series to which William Baldwin is thought to have contributed), see Lucas, "Diggon Davie and Davy Dicar."

37. For "The Fall of Robert Tresilian" and its relation to Throckmorton's trial, see chapter 5.

38. Patterson, *Reading Holinshed's Chronicles*, 160. William Baldwin's comment in the prose link following "Tresilian" that Ferrers's denunciatory poem is "not vnfyt for the persons touched in the same" also serves as a prompt for topical application, moving readers to ponder just which men Ferrers sought to "touch" in this allusive tragedy (81). For Baldwin's use of the verb "touch" specifically to indicate the practice of referring indirectly to contemporary figures in allusive verse, see *Mirror*, 347.

suppression. In addition, it recovers the communities—political, religious, and literary—in which the *Memorial* authors wrote and in which they expected their poems to be received. The known authors of *A Memorial of suche Princes* were members of a specific group—the shaken, defeated, and generally silenced evangelical community living in England in the first years of Mary I's reign. To varying extents, the known *Memorial* authors shared in the desperation of this group's members at the time—their fear of the future under Mary and their almost compulsive need to make sense of the sudden, traumatic loss of their once confident power and authority under the previous monarch, Edward VI. It was the prompting of such desperation that spurred the *Memorial* authors to hijack a printer's plan for a continuation of Lydgate's medieval *Fall of Princes* and to turn it into a work of topically engaged political admonition and historical revision. The chapter ends with a reading of William Baldwin's artful construction of the framing pieces of the *Memorial*, which render even the seemingly extraneous prefatory matter of the collection into communicative devices meant to deflect the initial suspicions of hostile readers while simultaneously signaling to those who would be sympathetic to Baldwin's project the politically contentious nature of the collection.

The second and third chapters engage with several of the retrospectively topical poems included in or intended for *A Memorial of suche Princes*, tragedies that seek to return readers to the worst moments of the reign of Edward VI. The purpose of these works is to urge readers still suffering from the collapse of Edwardian England to confront, come to terms with, and find comforting explanations for the series of stunning disasters that destroyed the authors' great Edwardian heroes and cast into doubt the ideals of the English Reformation. The exempla that evoke memories of Edward Seymour, Duke of Somerset, are directed at a specific audience: those men and women who had once revered the fallen Protector and who still suffered because of the tragic manner in which his career and life had ended. George Ferrers's "Edmund Duke of Somerset," "Humfrey Duke of Gloucester," and "Thomas of Wudstocke" seek through their narratives to evoke in readers memories of the worst tragedies of Seymour's last years. Then, through their moralization of those narrated events (that is, in their causal and moral explanations of how and why those tragic events occurred), they provide models for interpreting the tragedies of Seymour's final years in ways that could free the late Protector from the widespread charges of sinfulness and divine disfavor that so pained his partisans.

Chapter 4 explicates the *Mirror* tragedies that champion the lost nationalistic ethos and the imperialistic foreign policies of King Henry VIII and of

Edward Seymour, Protector Somerset. Through poems portraying the initial glory and subsequent failures of the fifteenth-century French campaigns of King Henry VI's time, the authors lament the collapse of the aggressively expansionist designs of Henry VIII and Protector Somerset on Scotland and France. Furthermore, they urge readers to indict those whom the authors hold responsible for Seymour's deposition and execution, and protest the pacifistic, internationalist foreign policies pursued by the officers of Mary's early reign. The chapter also highlights the poets' admonition to Queen Mary, which warns that if she allows herself to be dominated politically by her new, powerful foreign spouse (Prince Philip of Spain), she runs the risk of igniting a civil conflict akin to that of the Wars of the Roses.

Chapter 5 focuses on the use of the *Memorial* tragedies as "mirrors" for contemporary Marian magistrates. In a series of poems claiming to portray the political crimes of King Richard II's reign, the authors protest specific instances of Marian officers' abuse of English law on the queen's behalf. These historical narratives both reflect on and extrapolate from the actions of contemporary magistrates, working to persuade England's highest officers that allowing Queen Mary to "transcend the lymittes of [her] lawe" will only result in a renewal of the tragic events of the last years of Richard II: violent revolt and, ultimately, the "miserable falls" of the monarch and those officers who thought to gain the most from their misdeeds.

The last chapter reveals how Baldwin uses the poem "Collingbourne the Poet" in the 1563 edition of the *Mirror* to persuade Elizabethan magistrates to allow the literary realm to be an unfettered discursive space for political critique. The discussion reconstructs the unique literary theory of the *Mirror*, including the specific rules it formulates for the proper composition and reception of political literature. It further shows how the authors define the "perfect Poete" as nothing less than a quasi-governmental "officer," one whose official duties are to supervise and correct the moral and political behavior of the rulers of the nation. The tragedy of "Collingbourne" insists that the well-being of the commonwealth depends on the ability of poets to admonish their governors, and it issues a demand to the magistrates of the new Elizabethan regime to permit without restriction the multiply interpretable, allusive form of literary expression as an untroubled conduit for political comment and even political protest. Following this chapter is a conclusion tracing the legacy of the *Mirror* in Tudor and Stuart literary and political culture and an appendix handling the thorny bibliographical questions surrounding the development of this text from *A Memorial of suche Princes* (1554) through William Baldwin's last gathering of *Mirror* poems in 1563.

It is my aim in this book to reconstitute the poems of *A Memorial of suche Princes* and *A Mirror for Magistrates* not as reflections of Tudor political "ideas" but as political acts in themselves, uniquely effective—because affective—attempts to rewrite the recent political past and to alter the political future. Through a revisionary analysis of *Mirror* poems in the context of the events that gave rise to them, I seek to reveal the interventionary purpose of the poems of *A Mirror for Magistrates* and thereby return this remarkable but long-neglected collection to its rightful place as one of the most important works of sixteenth-century English political literature.

CHAPTER ONE

A Memorial of suche Princes: Creation and Contexts

From the beginning, the work that would become known as *A Mirror for Magistrates* was a product of English Reformation politics. Only the change from Edward VI's evangelical Protestant government to Mary I's Anglo-Catholic (or Henrician Protestant) one brought together a Catholic printer with the initial idea for a new work of *de casibus* tragedies and an evangelical editor who shaped the project as an allusive memorial of fallen leaders and a mirror for contemporary magistrates.[1]

England's evangelical Protestant monarch Edward VI passed away on July 6, 1553. In the wake of his death, those who had been outspoken in support of evangelical reform under Edward's rule fearfully anticipated reprisals from the government of England's new queen, Mary, a monarch strongly opposed to her brother's religious innovations. One of these fearful men was the printer Edward Whitchurch, who in the Edwardian period had been a leading producer of evangelical literature. Within weeks of King Edward's death, Whitchurch closed his shop and retired from the print trade. Several months later he sublet or sold his former business to a scrivener named John Wayland, a religious conservative who enjoyed the favor of Mary's government. In early 1554 Wayland took control of Whitchurch's printing house, his presses, and his employees, including Whitchurch's well-known "servant," the author, printer, and compositor William Baldwin.[2]

1. I use the terms "Anglo-Catholic" and "religious conservative" to denote those Englishmen and women who accepted (at least overtly) the royal supremacy but who adhered, against evangelical opposition, to the traditional Catholic doctrines and practices preserved by Henry VIII's church. Mary's government remained nominally Anglo-Catholic until January 3, 1555, when Parliament abolished the title "Supreme Head of the Church of England" (Loades, *Reign of Mary Tudor*, 270).

2. Blayney, "Site of the Sign of the Sun," 13. So hostile was the new Marian government to Whitchurch that it specifically excluded him from the general pardon issued at the queen's coronation (October 1553).

It was in Wayland's newly acquired shop that *A Memorial of suche Princes*, the first version of *A Mirror for Magistrates*, was printed. Wayland had embarked on the print trade in Mary's reign solely in order to publish the new Marian primer, the officially sanctioned text of private devotion that would replace the evangelically tinged primer of Edward's time.[3] By October 1553, even before Convocation and Parliament had decreed a return to pre-Edwardian religious practices, Wayland had secured letters patent awarding him sole right to print the uniform Marian primer as soon as it was prepared. Since the primer was the best-seller of devotional books, a text that even in normal years constituted the stock-in-trade of many printers, Wayland anticipated a huge nationwide demand for this new work.[4]

Wayland, however, did not expect the new Marian clergy to write, review, and authorize the final text of this primer in any brief period of time. Therefore, with both presses and employees standing idle, he conceived of a plan to release a series of venerable "notable" and worthy literary works to generate income and to keep his shop employed until the copy of the new primer was available (*Mirror*, 6).[5] One of the works he chose to print was John Lydgate's fifteenth-century collection of *de casibus* tragedies, *The Fall of Princes* (ca. 1431–1439). In a printer's note included on the verso of the title page of his edition Wayland explained his decision:

> While I attended [i.e., awaited] the quenes highnes plesure in setting fourth an vniforme Primer to be vsed of her Subjectes, for the Printynge wherof it pleased her highnes (which I besech god long to preserue) to geue me a Priuilege vnder her letters Patentes, I thought it good to employ and occupy my Print & seruaunts for that purpose prouided, about sum necessary & profitable worke. And because that sundry gentlemen very wel lerned, commended much the workes of Lydgate, chefely the fall of Prynces, which he drew out of Bochas [Boccaccio], whereof none were to be got, after that I knew the Counsayles pleasure & aduice therein, I determined to print it. (5)

Wayland further decided to append to *The Fall of Princes* a new work, "a continuacion of that Argument, concernynge the chefe Prynces of thys Iland, penned by the best clearkes in such kinde of matters that be thys day lyuing, not vnworthy to be matched with maister Lydgate" (6). Following Lydgate's example, the *Memorial* would present ghosts of famous past figures who suf-

3. For Wayland's career, see Byrom, "John Wayland."

4. Trench, *"A Mirror for Magistrates,"* 13; Birchenough, "Prymer in English," 177, 179; Byrom, "John Wayland," 345. The best discussion of Wayland's Marian primer is Eamon Duffy's in *Stripping of the Altars*, 537–43.

5. Wayland was not able to publish the primer until June 1555, almost two years after he secured the letters patent (*Mirror*, 6).

fered untimely deaths. Each specifically British ghost would relate the details of his tragic fall, and each would present readers with lessons to be derived from his suffering.

Wayland assigned this project to one of his new employees, the accomplished literary author, printer, and, unknown to Wayland, evangelical polemicist William Baldwin.[6] Baldwin accepted the project and gathered seven men to assist him in composing historical verse tragedies in the voices of figures spanning from the end of Richard II's reign to that of Edward IV. Printing of *The Fall of Princes* and its new continuation, titled *A Memorial of suche Princes, as since the tyme of king Richard the seconde, haue been vnfortunate in the Realme of England*, began in summer 1554. Wayland's shop had printed all of *The Fall of Princes* and some or all of the *Memorial* when Mary's Lord Chancellor, Stephen Gardiner, suddenly ordered production of the work stopped. While he eventually allowed Wayland to publish his edition of the *Fall*, Gardiner suppressed Baldwin's *Memorial.* The initial leaves of the *Memorial* had to be cut from those of *The Fall of Princes* to which they were cognate, and a new title page for the *Fall* had to be printed to remove any mention of the *Memorial.* The whole printed *Memorial* was either destroyed or used as scrap, and its poems were never allowed to appear before the public in Mary's reign.[7] Only after Mary's death and the accession of Elizabeth I did the *Memorial* find its way before the public in the retitled and lightly revised form of *A Mirror for Magistrates* (1559).

While it is unknown how the *Memorial* came to Gardiner's attention, the presence alone of the three men certainly identified as authors of its poems—William Baldwin, George Ferrers, and Sir Thomas Chaloner—may have been enough to raise questions about the project among Marian observers. Each of the known authors of the *Memorial* had come to prominence as a member of the evangelical Protestant community under Edward VI, and each had played an important role in the literary and/or political circles of King Edward's time. George Ferrers and Thomas Chaloner in particular would not have been unknown to supporters of Mary's Anglo-Catholic government. Under Edward, Ferrers had produced scandalously anti-Catholic performances at court, while under Henry VIII, Chaloner had accused

6. For Baldwin's covert and unreleased anti-Catholic and evangelical writings, see the discussion later in this chapter.

7. For the complicated printing history of the *Memorial* and the date of its suppression, see the appendix and Lucas, "Suppressed Edition." On the basis of the contents of the 1559 *Mirror*, it has been estimated that between twenty-five and thirty folio leaves would have had to be excised from *The Fall of Princes* after the Council's order to suppress the *Memorial* (Jackson, *Carl H. Pforzheimer Library*, 1:87).

Gardiner of receiving secret messages from papal agents.[8] Furthermore, as we have seen, the very first piece in the collection, George Ferrers's tragedy "The Fall of Robert Tresilian," seems to signal its own topical applicability when it urges readers to apply its condemnation of judicial malfeasance to their current queen's own chief legal officers, those unnamed "sum in latter dayes" who had emulated the poem's protagonists' willful misinterpretation of English laws "to serue the Princes affections" (73).[9]

Whatever prompted an unknown observer or observers to bring the collection to the attention of Mary's Lord Chancellor, circumstantial evidence suggests that it was one *Memorial* poem in particular, Ferrers's "Humfrey Duke of Gloucester," that moved Gardiner to suppress the *Memorial* as a whole. "Gloucester" is the only tragedy mentioned in the table of contents of the first edition of *A Mirror for Magistrates* (the lightly edited 1559 version of *A Memorial of suche Princes*) that does not actually appear in that collection (523). In the prose link preceding the place where (according to the table of contents) it should have appeared, Baldwin presents Ferrers as remarking on "how the cardinal Bewford maligneth the estate of good duke Humfrey the kinges vncle & protector of the realme, & by what driftes he first banisheth his wife from him. And lastly howe the good duke is murderously made away through conspiracy of Quene Margaret and other: both whose tragedies [those of Gloucester and his wife] I entend at leasure to declare" (161). Ferrers's words in this passage point out to readers the absence of "Humfrey Duke of Gloucester" from the 1559 *Mirror for Magistrates*, despite Ferrers's stated intention to tell Humfrey's and his duchess's tale. The fact that "Gloucester" was announced in the 1559 *Mirror* text and appeared in its table of contents (under the title "Good duke Humfrey murdered, and Elianor Cobham his wife banished") but did not appear in the collection itself suggests that this may have been the specific tragedy that Gardiner found so intolerable that Baldwin excised it even from the copy of *A Memorial of suche Princes* which he preserved for himself in the wake of the suppression. That "Gloucester" attracted Gardiner's particular attention would not be surprising, since the prose link preceding it in the *Memorial*, its title in the table of contents, and the tragedy itself all evoke memories of the fallen evangelical leader Edward Seymour, Duke of Somerset, who, like Humfrey of Gloucester, was "the kinges vncle & protector of the realme," who was called "the good Duke," and who during his time as Protector of the Realm often

8. See the discussion later in this chapter.

9. Patterson, *Reading Holinshed's Chronicles*, 160–61. See also the introduction and chapter 5 of this book.

used Duke Humfrey's protectorship in Henry VI's reign as a point of reference for his own.[10] Also, as Gardiner (who had known both Seymour and his enemies intimately) would have recognized, Ferrers consciously shaped "Gloucester" to evoke in readers both sympathetic memories of Edward Seymour and hostile recollections of Seymour's Anglo-Catholic opponents, including, prominently, Queen Mary herself. The allusive implications of such a poem (championing the evangelical hero Seymour and offering indirect condemnation of Mary Tudor's actions in the previous reign) would alone be sufficient grounds to have Queen Mary's Chancellor forbid the whole of Baldwin's collection. The harsh if indirect criticism of Mary that the poem offers, furthermore, likely made it still too controversial in Baldwin's mind to risk inclusion even in the months after Mary's death, when he sought a long-denied license from the new government of Mary's sister, Elizabeth, to print this already prohibited, controversial text.[11]

That the authors of the collection risked official disfavor and even personal retribution in order to release *A Memorial of suche Princes* speaks to the depth of the need they felt to address their chosen audiences on the subjects that their poems allusively handle: the recent Edwardian political past and the uncertain Marian political future. To understand the authors' need to confront these subjects, one must first understand the unique mental situation of the religious and cultural community to which all the known *Memorial* authors belonged, that of the community of reform-minded Protestants known as English evangelicals. The *Memorial* authors experienced the often wrenching events of the Edwardian and Marian periods as members of this formerly triumphant and, under Mary, subsequently silenced and suffering community. The fierce desire the authors felt to speak out in print was shared with other evangelicals and was born of an almost compulsive need to make sense of the recent tragic past—including the traumatic collapse of Edwardian England in general and the haunting fall of Protector Somerset in particular—and to ward off what they feared would be an even more tragic future for the nation. It was for these purposes that Baldwin and his fellows dared to create *A Memorial of suche Princes*, and it is only through the eyes of the evangelical

10. Campbell, "Humphrey Duke of Gloucester," 126–28; Brigden, *London and the Reformation*, 489; Alford, *Kingship and Politics*, 49, 95. Furthermore, Gardiner would have recognized the epithet "the good Duke" in the full title of "Humfrey Duke of Gloucester" (and in the prose link preceding the tragedy) as precisely that applied by his admirers to Edward Seymour during the time of his Protectorate (*Mirror*, 445).

11. Despite being mentioned once again in the table of contents of the 1571 edition, Ferrers's "Humfrey Duke of Gloucester" did not finally appear in the *Mirror* until 1578, long after Baldwin's death. For the composition and printing of this poem (and of Ferrers's later tragedy "Elianor Cobham"), see the appendix.

Protestant community of Mary's early reign that one might understand the powerful impetus that spurred the *Memorial* authors to pursue, even at the risk of personal danger, their two goals.

Evangelicals and English Politics, 1534–1554

England's evangelical community came to prominence at the time of King Henry VIII's break from the Roman Catholic Church. While all Protestants celebrated Henry's repudiation of papal authority, many held strong reservations about the traditionalist doctrines and practices of the king's new English church. Henry modeled his church in great measure on the Roman Catholic one, preserving numerous of its rituals and beliefs. Many English Protestants objected to the retention of such traditional elements and called for continued ecclesiastical reform based on scriptural principles. These reformers identified themselves by a variety of names, including gospellers, the godly, and of course "true Christians." Modern scholars, however, have come to call these dissenting men and women evangelicals. While embracing no single body of doctrine, English evangelicals found unity in their shared support for the dissemination of scripture in the vernacular and in their fervent opposition to key elements of the Henrician church, such as its Latin service, the restriction of Bible reading, the practice of clerical celibacy, and the sacramental nature of the Mass.

In the 1530s evangelicals enjoyed limited protection under Henry's vicegerent for spiritual affairs, Thomas Cromwell. By 1540, however, Cromwell had fallen, and those opposed to further radical church reform began to exercise renewed influence over the developing English church. In the wake of Cromwell's fall, conservative religious and political leaders vigorously enforced conformity to prescribed church practices, arresting, imprisoning, and in some cases even executing the most visible Henrician evangelicals. The program of evangelicalism suffered setbacks in the last years of Henry's rule, as religious traditionalism rather than religious innovation dominated the practices of the late Henrician church.

While finding itself stymied in influencing church doctrine and discipline, evangelicalism nevertheless spread rapidly in the political world of Henry's court. In the early 1540s a number of reform-minded young men began to enter royal service and to occupy places in key centers of influence in the realm. Some of them had served Cromwell before his arrest and execution in 1540. Others came to Henry's court from Cambridge University, where they had received an education both reformist and humanist in character. Several gained employment as tutors in the household of the young Prince Edward;

their influence ensured that Edward would himself embrace evangelicalism as king. Even Henry's own Privy Chamber, overseen by the evangelical Sir Anthony Denny, became filled with men who sympathized with religious reform. The presence of such men around Henry angered conservatives and resulted in a number of acrimonious "heresy hunts" at court, sparked both by both religious differences and by political factionalism. Despite the attempts of conservatives such as Bishop Stephen Gardiner and Chancellor Thomas Wriothesley to purge evangelicals from the court, however, the king protected many of his personal servants from harm, and by the last year of Henry's reign, evangelicals at court had gained premier influence in both the Privy Council and the royal chamber.[12] Between their growing importance at court and their guidance of Prince Edward's education, evangelical reformers looked to the accession of Edward VI with great hope, anticipating a time when persecution might be lifted and many of their dreams of a renewed, far-reaching reformation could be fulfilled.

Edward's accession came in January 1547, when the new king was but nine years old. In his will King Henry had directed that during Edward's minority a regency council composed of his will's executors should rule England. At their first meeting, however, Henry's executors moved to modify the terms of the late king's will by creating two new paramount offices, Protector of the Realm and Governor of the King's Person. They awarded both these high offices to the evangelical Protestant leader Edward Seymour, Earl of Hertford, the new king's maternal uncle. Despite initial opposition from Chancellor Wriothesley, Seymour took up both offices in early 1547 and, soon after, assumed the title Duke of Somerset. Seymour's rise to power began his remarkable three-year period of personal domination of the English government, one whose initial promise and shocking failure would haunt English evangelicals and become, as we shall see, one of the chief catalysts for the creation of *A Memorial of suche Princes*.

Seymour had been a powerful figure in English politics even before his elevation to the protectorship. Though a "new man" by traditional standards, Seymour had come quickly to prominence under Henry by means of his personal charisma, his numerous military victories in Scotland and France, and his status as the brother of Henry's beloved wife Jane Seymour. At the time of Henry's death Seymour was a high noble, a Privy Councilor, and the Great Chamberlain of Henry's household. Beyond the court he enjoyed great popularity among the people of England in general, who revered him as the country's most successful military commander, and among English

12. Brigden, "Thomas Cromwell and the 'Brethren'"; Brigden, *London and the Reformation*, 326–27; Loades, *Tudor Court*, 122; Jordan, *Edward VI: The Young King*, 40–50.

evangelicals in particular, who looked to him as their most important political ally.[13]

Seymour's assumption of power in 1547 created a climate of fierce admiration and hopeful expectation among his numerous supporters, one perhaps unmatched in the Tudor period. Seymour's admirers looked upon their hero as nothing less than a paragon of wisdom, bravery, kindness, patriotism, and piety.[14] Many knew him simply as "the good Duke," a man zealous in religion, solicitous of the poor, and strongly committed to the establishment of economic and social justice in England, and they championed Seymour as the ideal leader of the Protestant English nation. Seymour's followers ascribed all manner of laudable traits to him, construing their hero (seemingly paradoxically) as England's powerful, confident governor and yet also as a man of gentle, naïve innocence; as a fierce military leader and yet also as one whose natural inclination was never to do harm; and as a high and glorious noble whose mind constantly dwelled on the plight of the poor of the nation.[15] This public image of the Protector gained wide dissemination in Edwardian England after Seymour's loosening of Henrician restrictions on public religious and political comment (1547). In response to their newfound freedom of expression, numerous of Seymour's supporters rushed to issue paeans of praise for England's new leader, his "glorious" rule, and his "godly" government policies.

Seymour's most important base of support was the evangelical Protestant community. Over the course of the Protectorate, Seymour drove the already fervent devotion of his evangelical followers to all but feverish heights through his adoption of a rhetoric of divine sanction for his rule. At the beginning of the Protectorate, Seymour claimed that he had been "caused by Providence to rule" and described himself as the "shepherd" of God's flock in England and the "sword-bearer" of divine justice on earth. Evangelicals responded eagerly to such claims, and many declared Seymour's accession to be nothing less than the Lord's long-awaited deliverance of them and "true religion" in England. They adopted Seymour's providentialist language and used it to justify not merely his sweeping reforms in the English church but even such secular actions as his invasion of Scotland and his agrarian economic policies.[16] In a flood of writings that poured from the presses in 1547 and 1548,

13. Jordan, *Edward VI: The Young King*, 33–36, 46.

14. Shagan, "Protector Somerset," 47–53.

15. For a concise summary of such adulatory beliefs, see John Foxe's description of the former Protector in *The First Volume of the Ecclesiastical History, contayning the Actes and Monuments of thinges passed in euery kinges time* [hereafter Foxe, *Actes and Monuments*], 1323.

16. Strype, *Ecclesiastical Memorials*, vol. 2, pt. 2, 311–12; Bush, *Government Policy*, 41–126; Stephen and Lee, *Dictionary of National Biography*, s.v. "Edward Seymour, Duke of Somerset (1506?–1552)"; Edward Seymour, *Edward, Duke of Somerset*; Edward Seymour, *Epistle or Exhortacion*.

evangelical authors identified Seymour as the Lord's appointed "instrument" or "messenger" on earth. Others spoke of him as the new builder of the Holy Temple, and even as the apostle Peter. In particular, Seymour's decision in July 1547 to permit universal reading of the Bible in the vernacular made him in the eyes of many nothing less than the first true "presenter of Christ" to the English people, a man whose work on behalf of the gospel was akin to that of the earliest apostles. Evangelicals, who had spent long years suffering under Henry's VIII's opposition to continuing reform, joyously greeted the far-reaching ecclesiastical innovations over which Seymour presided, including the adoption by the English church of the doctrine of sole faith, the establishment of communion in two kinds, the permitting of clerical marriage, the creation of a vernacular service, and the abolition of the doctrine of the real presence and of many traditional ceremonies of the Mass. Characteristically, many evangelicals construed Seymour's success in implementing such religious reforms providentially, interpreting that success as proof positive that God himself was guiding the "good Duke" and sanctioning his godly policies of reform.[17]

Evangelical Protestants were not Seymour's sole source of support. He also enjoyed the particular devotion of the poor, who embraced his widely publicized domestic programs seeking economic amelioration for the lowest members of English society. As Protector, Seymour spoke constantly the language of social justice, even to the point of alienating many valuable upper-class allies. He engaged in several well-publicized attempts to redress the economic woes of the nation, including disparking royal lands for use by the commons, hearing the complaints of poor men in his own residence and helping their causes in courts of law, denouncing oppressive landowners, and appointing several controversial enclosure commissions to explore rural laborers' complaints about loss of commons land.[18] In response, England's poor lionized Seymour as an agent of revolutionary change and as their greatest protector. The "poor commons," it was said, expected nothing less than a new golden age of justice and plenty to be brought about by the "loving" policies of the heroic Lord Protector.[19]

17. See, for instance, Ochino, *A Tragoedie or Dialoge of the Vniuste Primacie*, sig. Y1r; Hooper, *A Declaracion of Christe*, sigs. A4v–A5r; Bullinger, *An Holsome Antidotus*, sigs. A7r–A8v; Ayre, *Prayers and Other Devotional Writings of Thomas Becon*, 3–11; Robinson, *Original Letters Relative to the English Reformation*, 2:733–34. In *A Tragoedie*, Ochino actually presents a heavenly dialogue in which Christ explains to the angel Gabriel his plan behind making Seymour England's "Christian protectour" (sig. Y1r). For a list of the religious reforms of Seymour's Protectorate, see Bush, *Government Policy*, 100.

18. Bush, *Government Policy*, 55–56; Brigden, *London and the Reformation*, 490–92.

19. Strype, *Ecclesiastical Memorials*, vol. 2, pt. 2, 430; Tytler, *England under the Reigns of Edward VI and Mary*, 1:114.

Leading evangelicals, too, praised Seymour's commitment to social reform and interpreted that commitment in the same providentialist terms in which they construed his ecclesiastical reforms. Many evangelical authors saw Seymour's policies as fulfilling their own dreams for a truly equitable Christian commonwealth. These men, often called "commonwealth men," urged the shaping of England into a polity based on fraternal love and mutual devotion among all classes. To achieve this goal, these writers urged a complete revolution in social behavior in England. In the godly commonwealth, men and women would eschew greed, embrace charity, love their neighbors as themselves, and dedicate their lives to being good stewards of God's gifts. All men and women would follow Christ's teachings (as interpreted by the commonwealth writers) and work selflessly on behalf of one another, from the lowest laborer to the monarch himself, whom the commonwealth writers construed as one more officer of the realm rather than as a figure different from and naturally above all others. The fervent commonwealth beliefs of Edward's time energized preachers and laymen alike to counsel and admonish England's political leaders on the subject of godly social and political reform. They justified their outspoken behavior by asserting that every member of the commonwealth shared a duty to exhort all others to the sort of proper behavior that could bring the truly godly commonwealth into being. Such men looked to Seymour as a kindred spirit, and their social ideals would influence both the rhetoric of Seymour's Protectorate and, later, that of the poems of *A Memorial of suche Princes*.[20]

Finally, Seymour also earned wide admiration from a large cross-section of Englishmen and women through his wildly popular expansionist foreign policies and his "glorious" victory over the Scots at the battle of Pinkie Clough. In September 1547, during his first year in power, Seymour marched on Scotland in an attempt to compel the Scots to honor an English-dictated marriage contract by which the infant Mary, Queen of Scots, was to be wed to England's King Edward VI. In pressing for this marriage, which had been arranged by Henry VIII, Seymour sought to join the two crowns of England and Scotland in order to create a new nation to be called Britain. Seymour engaged Scottish forces near Edinburgh and, in a crushing victory, devastated the Scottish army marshaled against him. As was his wont, Seymour construed his victory as a sign of God's favor for his expansionist foreign policies. His partisans echoed Seymour's providentialist rhetoric in printed works, publicly declaring the victory over his Catholic foes to be a

20. On the origin of evangelical commonwealth thought under Henry VIII, see Brigden, *London and the Reformation*, 318–20, 408. For an overview of Edwardian commonwealth thought, see Davies, *Religion of the Word*, 140–76.

manifest sign of God's favor for the evangelical cause. Seymour's supporters further understood the victory at Pinkie Clough as a *national* victory, one that proclaimed the strength not merely of the English monarch but of the English people as a whole. In the wake of Seymour's invasion, a strong sense of patriotic nationalism seized the country: many Englishmen and women, already inspired by Henry VIII's capture of French Boulogne in 1544, looked to Seymour to bring Scotland quickly into the English fold and then to turn his attention to Henry VIII's dream of reclaiming the English lands in France lost under Henry VI. Patriotic English subjects looked with anticipation to the time when Seymour might lead the nation to become one of Europe's most important imperial powers.[21]

It was precisely the air of intense hope and fervent admiration surrounding Seymour's Protectorate that made the "good Duke's" sudden fall from power so shocking. The rapid series of political disasters that led to Seymour's deposition began in early 1549, when he permitted the execution of his younger brother, Lord Admiral Thomas Seymour, on a charge of treason. Thomas's death in March of that year horrified the nation, for many believed him to have been innocent of the charges against him and suspected that Thomas's condemnation may have resulted not from impartial justice but from a fit of jealousy on the Protector's part.[22] Soon after Thomas's death, a series of widespread, ferocious rebellions engulfed the English countryside—uprisings which spread so quickly that by July the central government itself seemed in danger of collapse. In dealing with these revolts, Seymour chose to negotiate and to offer pardons to the rioters rather than to suppress the uprisings militarily. While this approach preserved his popularity among the common people, it failed to quell the revolts, and it outraged his fellow Privy Councilors, who came to believe that Seymour was sympathetic to the rebels' cause and hostile to the upper classes. Soon after the rebellions were suppressed, a group of powerful Privy Councilors met in London to discuss bringing Edward Seymour's government to an end. Suspecting an imminent coup d'état, Seymour publicly called for men to repair to Hampton Court in order to defend him and the young King Edward against a "most dangerous conspiracy." An armed standoff between the London Lords (as the coup leaders came to be called) and the Protector ensued, with an army commanded by Privy Councilor John Dudley, Earl of Warwick, challeng-

21. Jordan, *Edward VI: The Young King*, 259–60; Richard Grafton, *Grafton's Chronicle*, 2:504; Patten, *Expedition into Scotland*, 57–77, 156; Hooper, *A Declaracion of Christe*, sigs. A2r–A4v. At Pinkie Clough the English lost about 250 men and the Scots at least 10,000.

22. See chapter 2.

ing the four thousand "peasants" who came to aid Seymour after his call for assistance.[23]

Over the next several days the coup leaders publicly denounced Seymour and his "evel government." In a widely disseminated proclamation the London Lords declared that Seymour's rule had created nothing but a series of "calamities, losses, and displeasures" for England. Despite his rhetoric of concern for the commonwealth, the London Lords charged, Seymour had used his supreme power not on behalf of the people but to pursue his own "devilyshe and evill purposes," including secret schemes to enrich himself at the expense of the realm, to subvert law and justice, and to sow disorder and class conflict. Ultimately, the proclamation warned, Seymour sought nothing less than to seize supreme power for himself and "to destroy his Soveryne Lord," King Edward.[24]

In the wake of the year's disasters, many came to support, or at least not to oppose, the coup leaders' bid against the once revered Lord Protector. Religious conservatives welcomed the coup in the hope that the prominent Anglo-Catholics who had taken a leading role in organizing opposition to Seymour would turn back the hated religious reforms over which Seymour had presided. The leaders also gained the sympathy of many members of England's propertied classes, who had been stunned by the destructive rural risings and angered by Seymour's reluctance to use military force to quell them. Even strong English nationalists came to question their support for the Lord Protector, as the coup leaders laid recent losses of English possessions in France squarely at the feet of Edward Seymour, who they claimed had willfully neglected the English holdings near Boulogne that previous forces had fought and died to protect. Even many of Seymour's longtime admirers found themselves consumed with doubts about their hero's recent actions and the justice of the London Lords' cause, as Seymour's celebrated policies of social justice at home and expansionism abroad seemed ultimately to have produced only riot and failure. Some of his most fervent supporters came to lose faith in the Lord Protector, while others distanced themselves from him at this troubled and confusing time, preferring to wait and see the result of the coup and to find out the truth of the charges against him.

With little support among England's powerful and only unarmed "peasants" to protect him, Seymour eventually surrendered himself to his

23. Jordan, *Edward VI: The Young King*, 441–43, 506; Bush, *Government Policy*, 47, 84–85; Bergenroth et al., *Calendar of State Papers, Spanish* [hereafter *CSP, Span.*], 9:395.

24. *A Proclamacion . . . Conteinyng the Very Trouth of the Duke of Somerset's Evel Government, and False and Detestable Procedinges*, in Nicholas Pocock, *Troubles*, 95–100.

opponents, who imprisoned him as a traitor in the Tower of London. To Edwardian observers Seymour's downfall could not have been more stunning. In the words of one contemporary, over the course of a few short days England witnessed its glorious Lord Protector topple from his place as the virtual "king of the king" to a new, abject role as "a miserable prisoner universally despised."[25]

Seymour's humiliation did not end with his fall from office. In December the victorious coup leaders, who now held key positions of power on the Council and in Edward's household, drew up a list of twenty-nine articles of accusation against the former Protector, charging him with a host of crimes including abuse of office, subversion of English laws, loss of English-held lands in France, and even covert support for the recently defeated rural rioters. In a bid to save his own life, Seymour quickly confessed to all twenty-nine of these charges and threw himself on the mercy of the king and the Privy Council. Seymour's two "confessions" indeed saved him from the executioner's block, but only by dealing a grave blow to the idealized image his supporters had constructed for him. Seymour's confessions turned all the laudatory narratives by which his admirers had understood their hero completely on their heads. The man whom the nation had revered as England's glorious agent of imperial expansionism now declared himself to be the true cause of English losses abroad. The charismatic leader who had promised to bring equal justice and peaceful order to all England now painted himself as England's worst criminal and as the very cause of the gravest outbreak of disorder (the popular riots) since the Wars of the Roses. Seymour even repudiated his own carefully cultivated reputation for wisdom and virtue, declaring in a desperate bid for mercy that his confessed "offences, faults, and crymes" as Protector were the products not of malice but of his congenital "ignoraunce, negligence, follie, wilfulnesse, and . . . lacke of good consideration."[26]

To the sorrow of his admirers, Seymour became forever enrolled in government records as an ambitious villain, one whose time as Protector had been little more than a secret and systematic assault on the realm. For years after, those who gained power in the wake of Seymour's deposition made him a convenient scapegoat for all the nation's problems. As late as March 1553, for instance, the authors of a parliamentary subsidy bill justified the need for a new subsidy on the grounds that the effects of Edward Seymour's "wilfull mysgov[er]naunce" and "insaciate ambicion" continued even at that late date to afflict the realm. Opponents of Seymour's religious policies similarly seized on the language of articles and Seymour's confessions, using

25. Jordan, *Edward VI: The Young King*, 507, 515; Robinson, *Original Letters*, 2:734–35.
26. Stow, *Annales* (1592), 1014–19.

them to execrate the evangelicals' greatest political hero and to celebrate his removal from power.[27]

Seymour's submissions allowed him to avoid execution and, eventually, won him release from the Tower (February 1550). Despite winning back many of his admirers and returning to the Privy Council, however, Seymour found himself unable to regain his former place as chief subject of the realm. Instead he was forced to watch his former ally John Dudley, Earl of Warwick, and his supporters abandon many of his most cherished economic reform programs and expansionist foreign policies. Seymour resented his loss of place and Dudley's assumption of supreme power, and within months of Seymour's release, Dudley and his allies on the Council began to receive evidence that the increasingly frustrated Edward Seymour was actively plotting against them.[28] Finally, in October 1551, after what appeared to have been an aborted plot to attack members of the Privy Council, Seymour was arrested once more and accused of seeking the deaths of England's chief officers. After a controversial trial, he was judged a felon in December and executed for his crimes two months later.

Despite the boundless optimism and rhetoric of divine sanction with which the Protectorate had begun, both Seymour and his celebrated domestic and foreign policies ended in failure. The events that brought him down forced a crisis in the evangelical community. After Seymour's second arrest many evangelicals simply abandoned their fallen leader, denouncing what they came to see as his desperate bids for power and his all-consuming desire for personal revenge against his successors.[29] Others were left to wrestle with a host of disturbing, seemingly unanswerable questions about the man whom they had long regarded as God's glorious lieutenant in England. What role did Edward Seymour play in Thomas's execution, and why did he allow his own brother to die? Why did the common people, whom he loved and who loved him, rise against him? Why did nearly every member of England's Privy Council (men Seymour himself had personally selected for that body) turn against him in 1549 and support his deposition from office? Had Seymour really been from the beginning an ambitious and conspiratorial criminal, as so many both in and out of government had charged? If not, how could one explain his alienation of the Council and his conviction for conspiratorial plotting? Finally, and most disturbing of all, if Seymour and

27. Tomlin, Taunton, and Raithby, *Statutes of the Realm*, vol. 4, pt. 1, 176; Dickens, "Robert Parkyn's Narrative," 300; Nichols, *Chronicle of the Grey Friars*, 64.

28. For an analysis of Seymour's highly suspicious actions at this time, see Brigden, *London and the Reformation*, 506–16.

29. For some of these, see Beer, *Northumberland*, 120.

his reformist policies had been divinely favored as so many had believed, how could God have allowed both the man and his cherished programs of social reform to be destroyed so tragically? After all, by the providential logic with which they had construed Seymour's triumphs as proof of divine sanction for the Protector and his ideals, Seymour should have been maintained in his glory, not driven from it. In the wake of his political failure and ignominious execution, the painstakingly constructed master narrative of wisdom, divine sanction, and glorious progress that evangelicals built around Seymour's rule now lay in ruins. To the dismay of his admirers, its chief replacement was the widely disseminated, damning official account that cast Seymour as an incompetent villain and his followers as, at best, blinded dupes.

Seymour's former supporters wrestled with such doubts in a culture increasingly marked by cynicism and fear. Despite the rhetoric of concern for the commonwealth by which he and the other coup leaders had justified the Protector's deposition, Seymour's successor, John Dudley, was soon widely suspected of being precisely the sort of ambitious criminal that Dudley and his former allies had claimed Seymour to be. Dudley's government abandoned Seymour's popular programs of social amelioration, ended the relative freedom of speech enjoyed under the Protectorate, disastrously devalued the coinage, and, to the horror of many, surrendered all the French holdings captured under Henry VIII—the very possessions that Dudley and his fellow coup leaders had once execrated Seymour for not properly protecting. While they initially praised Dudley for embracing their cause in the wake of Seymour's fall, even evangelicals began to lose faith in their most powerful secular ally, suspecting him and his associates in government of using the rhetoric of reform to plunder covertly the riches of the English church. Many evangelicals had grave doubts about Dudley and began to suspect his motives in deposing Edward Seymour. With no evangelical noble powerful enough to replace Dudley, many dreamed of a time when their idealized young monarch, Edward VI, would himself turn Dudley out of power and rule England in his own name.

That dream was never to be realized. On July 6, 1553, King Edward passed away, taking with him the reformers' greatest hopes for the future. After Dudley's abortive and unpopular attempt to place his own daughter-in-law Jane Grey on the throne, Mary I acceded to the crown. To the sorrow of English evangelicals, Mary and her officers quickly began a process of reversing the Edwardian religious reforms. Upon Mary's accession, traditional practices long banned under Edward revived. Mary herself heard Mass in Latin almost immediately after taking power and even held a Mass for the soul of her evangelical brother, who had opposed that ritual. Leading religious conservatives such as Norfolk, Gardiner, and Bonner were freed from the Tower and restored to positions of influence, while reformers such as Cranmer, Becon, Veron, and Bradford were imprisoned. Within months of her accession, Mary issued a series of proclamations that curtailed preaching and tightened restrictions on the press; later her government specifically excluded many evangelicals from the general pardon issued at her coronation, thus forcing them into hiding, exile, or prison. In December 1553 all of the Edwardian religious reforms were officially swept away, and by the early months of 1554 it was clear that England soon would return to the Roman Catholic fold.[30]

If her religious policies created fear and anger among English evangelicals, Mary's announced wedding plans created similar emotions among nearly all of her subjects. By fall 1553 it became clear that Mary sought to wed the widely hated Prince Philip of Spain, a man whom she had never met and whose reputation in England was that of a bloodthirsty tyrant. Many feared that Philip would turn the rule of England over to "strangers" and seek to reduce the once proud English nation to at best a petty holding of the Habsburg Empire and at worst an oppressed Spanish colony.[31] The queen's marriage plans—and her refusal to hear any words against it, even from Parliament—sparked a rising led by the evangelical Protestant knight Sir Thomas Wyatt (January–February 1554). Despite the popularity of its cause, Wyatt's rebellion failed in the streets of London when a general hatred for rebellion and the queen's promise never to marry Philip without the consent of her subjects spurred even evangelical Londoners to rally against the rebels.

Despite their assistance in suppressing Wyatt's revolt, Mary's evangelical subjects soon endured renewed persecution in the wake of Wyatt's failure. An angry queen and Council, suspicious of all Protestants after Wyatt's uprising, moved quickly to enforce strict religious conformity and to remove potential enemies, often with less than full respect for English law. Wyatt was beheaded soon after his trial, while about fifty of his followers were hanged at various locations throughout London as "a terror to the common sort." To the "great griefe of good citezens," Mary's government kept these gallows, with the executed rebels' remains still on them, standing in the London streets throughout the spring. One pair, in fact, stood in Fleet Street, close to the print shop in which William Baldwin worked and in which the *Memorial*

30. Prescott, *Mary Tudor*, 195–98; Brigden, *London and the Reformation*, 527–28.

31. Brigden, *London and the Reformation*, 555; Prescott, *Mary Tudor*, 232, 240; for a survey of the various fears concerning the rule of the Spaniards, see Loach, *Parliament and the Crown*, 182–92.

was compiled.[32] Mary and her officers moved even against subjects who did not take part in Wyatt's revolt. Lady Jane Grey, whom Mary had spared in 1553, was executed with her husband, Guilford Dudley, within days of Wyatt's failure, despite having played no part in the rising. Princess Elizabeth, suspected of being Wyatt's choice for queen in place of Mary, was brought to the Tower and forced to make a frightened, submissive appeal for protection from her sister. Friends of all three known *Memorial* authors suffered arrest and, in some cases, execution. Even Sir Nicholas Throckmorton, the evangelical gentleman who had daringly sent Mary word of Edward VI's death when the Council had kept it secret from her, was arrested merely for having spoken with Wyatt and his supporters before their rising. Throckmorton became the subject of a notoriously illegal treason trial in which the jury that exonerated him was itself punished by Mary's vindictive government.[33] It was on February 11, 1554, evangelicals could recall, that Chancellor Gardiner had preached a sermon in which he demanded that the "hurtfull members" of the commonwealth be "cutt off and consumed," from which, as one observer noted, "all the audyence dyd gather ther should shortly followe sharpe and cruel execution."[34] By summer such fears seemed confirmed, and evangelicals foresaw only more arrests, more convictions, and more executions to come as Mary and her officers capitalized on their triumph over Wyatt, the arrival of Prince Philip in England, and the advance of their religious cause.

By the spring and summer of 1554, when the *Memorial* poems were being composed, it was clear that the power of the English evangelical community had been shattered and that the guiding ideals of England were now in many ways the exact opposite of all those for which its members had striven in the previous reign. In their demoralized state, evangelicals were left to wrestle with how, after their triumphs of Edward's reign, the Reformation could have failed and they themselves could have fallen into such misery. In Tom Engelhardt's terms, the collapse of the Edwardian reformation was the end of "victory culture" for English Protestants.[35] The Edwardian period had been for many evangelicals a time of confident triumph and hope for the future. Its sudden failure traumatized evangelicals and left them desperately searching for means to explain the sudden reversal of all to which they had devoted themselves in the previous reign. Marian Catholics, of course, supplied their own explanations, employing the evangelicals' rhetoric of manifest providentialism to declare the failure of the Edwardian regime to be clear proof

32. Grafton, *Chronicle*, 2:543; Loades, *Reign of Mary Tudor*, 82.
33. Brigden, *London and the Reformation*, 551–54. See also chapter 5.
34. Nichols, *Chronicle of Queen Jane*, 54.
35. See Engelhardt, *End of Victory Culture*.

of God's hatred for the supposedly "godly" evangelical movement.[36] Just as the fall of Seymour had done earlier, the collapse of the Edwardian reformation called into doubt fundamental assumptions, principles, and beliefs by which evangelicals had long interpreted God's will and their own lives. If their evangelical beliefs had been divinely favored, as they had believed, why did God destroy the reformation and its greatest leaders? If Catholicism was not the true faith, why did the Lord allow it gradually to be restored in England? Was their defeat and subsequent oppression under Mary divine punishment for their rejection of the Catholic Church? Had they and their fellow evangelicals, who had striven mightily to serve the Lord, in fact all along been unwitting sinners and heretics? At the time of the *Memorial*, many evangelicals found themselves trapped in a painful cognitive limbo, wrestling with both the lingering questions and doubts surrounding the tragedies of Edward's reign and their increasingly miserable condition under their new Catholic queen.[37]

As evangelical Protestants who had come to prominence in the Edwardian period, the three known *Memorial* authors wrestled with such questions just as others did. Furthermore, as men who had begun Edward's reign devoted to Edward Seymour, Duke of Somerset, they struggled particularly acutely with the questions surrounding that fallen leader's baffling actions in his last years in power and, later, in his last months of life. Finally, as men deeply involved with shaping the course of politics and religion in Edward VI's time (either as government officials or as "articulate citizens"), they felt particularly concerned with what they saw as the growing political corruption and disorder created by Queen Mary's chief officers. It was these questions and these concerns that prompted the *Memorial* authors to risk censorship and even personal punishment in order to craft a work of allusive political comment that might communicate their beliefs to the two audiences—suffering evangelicals and erring magistrates—whom they keenly sought to address.

The Known Authors of *A Memorial of suche Princes*

Over the years a number of men have been proposed as members of the group who composed the tragedies of *A Memorial of suche Princes*; the names of only three *Memorial* authors are known for certain, however: William

36. See, for instance, MacCulloch, "*Vita Mariae Angliae Reginae,*" 276–77; Loach, *Parliament and the Crown*, 110.

37. For some attempts by evangelicals to come to terms with the disturbing implications of what seemed the failure of the English Reformation, see Lucas, "Coping with Providentialism"; and Shakespeare, "Plague and Punishment."

Baldwin, George Ferrers, and Sir Thomas Chaloner.[38] Each of these men was a leading light of mid-Tudor literary endeavor; each, too, had been closely connected with the rule of Edward Seymour, Duke of Somerset, and committed to the ends of the evangelical governments of King Edward VI. Finally, each had suffered either materially or mentally under the new government of Mary I, and each had reason to fear for the future under the rule of the new queen and her magistrates.

William Baldwin

Perhaps no other mid-Tudor author was more suited for the task of compiling *A Memorial of suche Princes* than William Baldwin, the well-known poet, translator, editor, and covert evangelical controversialist. The details of Baldwin's early life are unknown. Though he claims in the *Mirror* to be of Welsh ancestry, there is no certain record of his origins or activities until the first year of Edward's reign, when he is found in the employ of the evangelical printer Edward Whitchurch.[39] Under Edward VI, Whitchurch was one of the most prolific printers of reformist literature; employment in Whitchurch's shop allowed the zealously evangelical Baldwin to interact with a host of important Edwardian reformers, including John Hooper, William Turner,

38. Baldwin and Ferrers are the only living authors identified by name in the 1559 edition of *A Mirror for Magistrates.* Chaloner is designated as the author of the Richard II tragedy in the one surviving leaf of the suppressed *Memorial of suche Princes* (*Mirror*, 119). Evidence suggests that these three men were the guiding spirits behind the *Memorial.* As John King notes, John Bale groups Baldwin, Ferrers, and Chaloner as a literary circle in his *Scriptorum Illustrium maioris Brytanniae . . . Catalogus* (King, *English Reformation Literature*, 425). Notably, the next author whom Bale lists is Edward Seymour, Duke of Somerset (Bale, *Scriptorum Illustrium*, 2:108). Although numerous *Mirror* scholars, following Lily B. Campbell, identify Thomas Phaer as the author of the *Memorial-Mirror* tragedy "Owen Glendower," there is no reliable evidence to link him to this poem or to any other tragedy in Baldwin's collection. There is no mention of Phaer in any of the *Memorial-Mirror* editions edited by Baldwin. Phaer's name only becomes connected with the *Mirror* fifteen years after Baldwin's death, when the editor of the 1578 edition of the *Mirror* (probably John Higgins, a man unconnected to the original group of poets) ascribed to Phaer authorship of the tragedy "Owen Glendower" (120). Since all previous editions of the collection, including the sole surviving leaf from *A Memorial of suche Princes*, clearly ascribe "Owen Glendower" to William Baldwin, there is no compelling reason for scholars to adopt the 1578 edition's late and unique ascription of "Owen Glendower" to Phaer (indeed, the editor of the next edition of the *Mirror*, that of 1587, dropped the 1578 ascription of the poem to Phaer and returned credit for the poem to Baldwin) (119). Furthermore, the 1578 text proves unreliable in its other ascriptions of tragedies in the collection. Most notably, this text ascribes the poem "Kyng Richarde the Seconde" to the pen of George Ferrers, when we know from the surviving leaf of *A Memorial of suche Princes* that Sir Thomas Chaloner wrote this work (119). This is not to say that Phaer, who had been a close friend of both Ferrers and Chaloner in the mid-Tudor period, could not have been an author of one or more of the anonymous poems in the original *Memorial-Mirror* collection. In the absence of reliable evidence linking him to any specific tragedy, however, Phaer cannot be described as a certain author of the text.

39. *Mirror*, 119; see also Gutierrez, "William Baldwin," 19–20.

Thomas Sternhold, John Rogers, and Baldwin's fellow print employee John Olde. Service to Whitchurch also allowed Baldwin to advance the political and religious ends of Edward Seymour, Protector Somerset. During the Protectorate, Seymour used Whitchurch's house as a quasi-official government press; on Seymour's behalf, Whitchurch and his employees produced numerous works expressing and advancing the ideals of Seymour's government.[40] Baldwin found such work highly congenial, and he dedicated his early career as an author to promoting the beliefs he shared with the new Protector and to praising Edward Seymour and the ends of his godly government.

Baldwin's first known literary work was a commendatory sonnet—the first English sonnet ever to be printed—which he appended to a medical text dedicated to England's new Protector (1547).[41] In January 1548 Baldwin released his first substantial creation, a collection of classical proverbs and aphorisms titled *A Treatise of Morall Phylosophie*. He dedicated this work to Protector Somerset's young son Edward Beauchamp, Earl of Hertford, and used its dedicatory epistle to proclaim his deep admiration for Hertford's father. In his dedication Baldwin praised the elder Seymour for his wisdom and virtue and publicly declared that God himself had called Seymour to rule the nation.[42] Indeed, Baldwin used the *Treatise* as a whole to promote ideals associated with Seymour and his government, particularly those values expressed by the "commonwealth men" whom Seymour was known to patronize. Using loose translations and long contextualizing prefaces, Baldwin marshaled pagan philosophers to support Christian "commonwealth" ideals such as love of one's neighbor, the need to labor in one's vocation, the need for private property to be put into use for others, and the reformation of English society within the boundaries of traditional social hierarchy.[43] Baldwin's *Treatise* quickly became one of the early modern period's great successes. His work appeared in four editions in Edward's reign alone and in an astonishing twenty subsequent editions over the next one hundred years. The *Treatise* further brought him to the attention of the most important evangeli-

40. King, *English Reformation Literature*, 94.

41. Langton, *A Very Brefe Treatise . . . of Physick*, sig. A1v.

42. Baldwin, *Treatise of Morall Phylosophie*, sig. A3r.

43. According to Baldwin, the ancients teach above all that we should "endeuour oure selues euery man in his vocation, to vse suche morall vertues, and vertuous behauyours one to wardes an other, that oure loue and charitie vsed towardes our brotherne, maye testify our fayth and loue towardes god" (Baldwin, *Treatise*, sig. A7r). To support this assertion, Baldwin rewrites maxims by Plato, Pythagoras, and other pre-Christian authors in order to reconcile them with Christian teachings, to make them champion the holding of private property, to allege classical support for the Christian social concept of laboring in one's vocation, and to make Plato's political teachings compatible with a hereditary monarchy. See, for instance, Baldwin, *Treatise*, sigs. A5v–A7r, I1v, N3v. See also Maslen, "William Baldwin," 34–35.

cal authors of the Edwardian period; it was on the basis of the *Treatise* that John Bale celebrated Baldwin as a man of "much learning and wisdom" who "shined forth in the same manner as Cato himself."[44]

Baldwin's next work continued to advance programs associated with Seymour's Protectorate, this time Seymour's push for a universal dissemination of scripture in English. In 1549 Baldwin published a verse translation of the Song of Songs, titled *The Canticles or Balades of Salomon.* In his preface to King Edward, Baldwin declared his zeal for the publication of biblical texts in the vernacular. He insisted, however, that he composed his metrical *Canticles* not only as a contribution to scriptural translation but also as a means to shape the moral health of those at the center of English power. Baldwin desired that his *Song of Songs* should play the sort of ameliorative role at Edward's court that his acquaintance Thomas Sternhold had sought for his metrical psalms, providing godly substitutes for the "baudy balades of lecherous love that commonly are indited and song of idle courtyers in princes and noble mens houses."[45] Although he was still a "servant" to Edward Whitchurch, Baldwin proved himself with the *Canticles* to be an accomplished and independent printer in his own right; using Whitchurch's presses, Baldwin personally supervised the production of the *Canticles* and published the text under his own name and printer's device.

In the years after the collapse of Seymour's Protectorate, Baldwin's writings became increasingly controversial.[46] In 1551 Baldwin is thought to have contributed to one of the most celebrated exchanges of poems of the mid-Tudor period, the heated war of words that arose over the publication of Thomas Churchyard's poem *Davy Dycars Dreame.* Churchyard's poem was a putative dream vision that allusively indicted the Dudley regime and called for Edward VI to rule England in his own name. In response to this work,

44. King, *English Reformation Literature*, 358. On the creation and reception of the *Treatise*, see Gresham, "William Baldwin."

45. King, *English Reformation Literature*, 368.

46. Even after both Seymour's ignominious fall from power in 1549 and his execution in 1552, Baldwin continued to use his *Treatise of Morall Phylosophie* to express his admiration for the fallen Protector and his family. After Seymour's fall, Baldwin continued to dedicate new issues and editions of his work to the younger Edward Seymour, and he persisted in praising Hertford's "vertuous parentes," the Duke and Duchess of Somerset. Even after Seymour's execution, when Parliament stripped the Seymour children of their noble standing, Baldwin stubbornly persisted in addressing the late Protector's son by his lost courtesy title, Earl of Hertford, in each new printing of the *Treatise* (1552, 1553, 1556), despite the fact that the younger Edward Seymour did not regain that title until 1559 (William Seymour, *Ordeal by Ambition*, 365–66). In all of his post-execution versions of the *Treatise*, Baldwin boldly continued to offer praise for both the late Protector and Seymour's much-maligned wife, Anne Seymour, long after many others had turned away in silence from these widely discredited figures.

one Thomas Camell wrote a poetic reply rebuking Churchyard and challenging the authority of any commoner poet to speak on the affairs of England's leaders. Numerous poets came to Churchyard's defense, arguing that his poem was a work of literature—a fictional representation of a "dark" dream vision—and thus could not be determined to express any certain political commentary, no matter what allusive import suspicious readers might claim to perceive in the work. One of the most sophisticated of Churchyard's defenders was the pseudonymous "Western Wyll," an author whom the editors of the *Short Title Catalogue* tentatively identify as William Baldwin. If Western Wyll's two poems on the controversy are in fact by Baldwin, they reflect his growing penchant for (anonymous) participation in public controversy, his early opposition to the Dudley regime, and, most important, his intense interest in the use of literary form as a means to protect authors eager to comment publicly on political affairs—each a key interest that would shape Baldwin's *Memorial of suche Princes*.[47]

Baldwin's next work was an anonymous translation of the ferociously anti-papal satire *Wonderfull Newes of the Death of Paul the Third* (ca. 1552).[48] In the preface to this piece, Baldwin revealed not only his commitment to the anti-Catholic, evangelical cause but also to another of his chief interests, the use of literary form to communicate potentially dangerous opinions. Baldwin begins his preface with a celebration of the many methods of indirect communication available to polemical authors. It is "wonderfull," Baldwin declares, to consider the variety of strategies open to men who wish "to declare & publishe suche thynges as they thinke necessary to be knowe[n]." Some do so, he observes, "vnder the colour of fayned histories, some vnder the persons of specheles beastes, and some vnder [the] shadow of dreames and visions."

47. Western Wyll, *Westerne Wyll, Vpon the Debate betwyxte Churchyarde and Camell* and *Westerne Will to Camell*, are both included in the Elizabethan compilation of the *Davy Dicar* poems, *The Contention bettwyxte Churchyeard and Camell, vpon Dauid Dycers Dreame* (London, 1560) (*STC* 5225). For the *Davy Dicar* controversy and its display of the power of literary form to protect politically engaged authors, see Lucas, "Diggon Davie and Davy Dicar." It was almost certainly for this exchange of poems, John N. King notes, that Churchyard was "troubled before the Lords of the Counsell" in 1551; Churchyard escaped punishment at this time only through the intervention of Edward Seymour (King, *English Reformation Literature*, 106, 246).

48. Publius Esquillus [pseud.], *Wonderfull Newes of the Death of Paul the .iii.* The Latin original of *Wonderfull Newes*, *Epistola de Morte Pauli Tertii* (Basel, 1549), purports to be the work of "P. Aesquillius," a pseudonym designed to evoke the name of Pasquillo (or Pasquil), the famous Roman statue associated with satires. Many scholars ascribe the *Epistola* to the Croatian Reformer Matthias Flacius Illyricus, who published a German translation of the work. In a preface to his translation, however, Flacius claims only to be the translator of the *Epistola*, and he suggests that the pasquinade is in fact Italian in origin. See P. Aesquillius [pseud.], *Ein Sendbrieff P. Aesquillii von dem tode Pauli*, sigs. A3v, B2r.

In the years after compiling this list, Baldwin was to adopt every one of the literary techniques he laid out in his preface, using them as means to advance covertly his own controversial views on matters of religion and politics.[49]

After *Wonderfull Newes*, Baldwin could release no new work under his own name until Elizabeth's reign.[50] Each of the subsequent writings certainly ascribed to him was either suppressed or deemed by its author too dangerous to publish. Baldwin composed his *Beware the Cat*, an anti-Catholic satire cast as a beast fable, in the early part of 1553, but it did not appear in print until 1570. Baldwin dedicated this work to John Young, a reformist member of Parliament and former servant of Edward Seymour. The preface to its second edition (by the anonymous T.K.) notes that in Mary's reign the book was "exiled because . . . it showed the toys and drifts / Of such as then, by wiles and wills, / maintained Popish shifts."[51] Baldwin's next work, *The Funeralles of King Edward the Sixt*, faced similar impediments to publication under Mary. Writing in 1560, Baldwin recalled that this verse narrative was "penned before his [the king's] corse was buryed [1553], & endevoured since by many meanes to have had been printed: but such was the time, that it could not be brought to passe." Its inability to be printed under Marian censorship is not surprising, since the work offered a strongly evangelical view of Edward's death and insisted that only further religious reform could save England from God's wrath.[52] In 1554, of course, the *Memorial of suche Princes* was "hyndred" by Chancellor Stephen Gardiner and suppressed before it was allowed to come before the public. Baldwin's last known work of the Marian period was a three-hour moralistic drama that he sought in 1556 to present before the queen. It was never allowed to be performed at court.[53]

49. Publius Esquillus [pseud.], *Wonderfull Newes*, sig. A1v. "Fayned histories," of course, is the method of all the *Memorial* poems with the exception of "Richard Duke of York," which is presented as a dream vision (*Mirror*, 181). Furthermore, Baldwin presented much of the anti-Catholic commentary of his satire *Beware the Cat* "vnder the persons of specheles beastes" (see discussion later in this chapter). On the *Wonderfull Newes*, see King, *English Reformation Literature*, 371–87.

50. His sole published output between 1552 and 1559 under his own name was one new issue and one revised edition of the *Treatise of Morall Phylosophie* (1553, 1556). Under Edward, Baldwin is also thought to have produced two court dramas, but their texts have not survived. Robert Maslen has gathered persuasive circumstantial evidence to suggest that Baldwin is the author of the *The Image of Idleness* (London, 1556?), an anonymous work of prose fiction published by the evangelical bookseller William Seres. See Maslen, "William Baldwin."

51. Baldwin, *Beware the Cat*, 1; Bindoff, *History of Parliament*, 3:684–85. John Young had ties as well to George Ferrers: Young had served with Ferrers in Henry VIII's household and was apparently one of Ferrers's distant kinsmen (Bindoff, *History of Parliament*, 3:684–85).

52. Baldwin, *Funeralles of King Edward the Sixt*, sigs. A1v, B2v.

53. While there is a letter of Baldwin's preserved in the Revels accounts offering this play to Mary's Master of Revels Sir Thomas Cawarden, there is no record of its ever being performed or of any money paid out for materials for it. See Feuillerat, *Documents Relating to the Revels*, 215–17; and Baldwin, *Beware the Cat*, xx.

Although stymied as an author under Mary, Baldwin continued to work as a printer, first in John Wayland's house and, later, in the house of Thomas Marshe. Baldwin may have been involved in the shadowy affair that prompted Mary's government to search Marshe's shop in July 1558 for works that "impugne the Catholyke Faith."[54] Under Mary, Baldwin continued to gather tragedies for an expanded manuscript version of the *Memorial* project. Though prohibited from printing the original poems of the *Memorial*, he planned one day to attempt to print these later, less controversial tragedies covering chiefly the reigns of Edward V and Richard III. Even these relatively benign poems, however, could not gain publication until after Mary's death.[55]

Upon Elizabeth's accession, Baldwin finally gained the opportunity to bring his Marian works before the public. In 1559 he released a lightly edited new version of the suppressed *Memorial of suche Princes*, which he titled *A Mirror for Magistrates.* Soon after, Baldwin published his Marian *Funeralles of King Edward the Sixt* (adding to it a newly composed Elizabethan piece of admonitory verse), and in 1563 he agreed to work with John Stow on a new English chronicle. Baldwin's last publication was an expanded edition of *A Mirror for Magistrates*, which added to the tragedies of the original volume both the Marian poems Baldwin had gathered subsequent to the suppression of *A Memorial* and a set of more recent Elizabethan tragedies (1563).[56] Still a zealous reformer, Baldwin took orders in 1560 but succumbed to the plague within three years of beginning his clerical career (September 1563). His last known words were a demand that Mary's surviving bishops be hanged.[57]

George Ferrers

After Baldwin, George Ferrers (ca. 1510–1579) is the most prolific known author of *Memorial* tragedies, contributing to the collection poems in the voices of Sir Robert Tresilian; Humfrey, Duke of Gloucester; Thomas of Wudstocke; and (in the wake of the suppression of the *Memorial*) Edmund, Duke of Somerset. Ferrers was a close acquaintance of Baldwin, and he brought to Baldwin's project not only literary expertise but also extensive personal experience in law, history, and the intricate moves and countermoves of mid-Tudor politics.

Ferrers was born in St. Albans about 1510. He attended Cambridge University and received a degree in canon law in 1531. In 1534 he began a career in London as a common lawyer and legal historian, joining Lincoln's

54. Metzger, "Failure and Success," 143; Loades, *Politics, Censorship and the English Reformation*, 117; Metzger, "Controversy and 'Correctness,'" 441.

55. *Mirror*, 387, 421.

56. See chapter 6.

57. Baldwin, *Beware the Cat*, xx.

Inn and publishing in that year his first printed work, a translation of the Magna Carta and several other historical statutes.[58] By 1538 Ferrers entered the world of politics, joining the service of Thomas Cromwell, Henry VIII's most important government officer. At the time of Ferrers's employment, Cromwell's household was a locus of political life in Henrician England. Ferrers's time in Cromwell's household allowed him to observe at firsthand some of the most important reforms of the Henrician period: the year 1538 alone witnessed Cromwell's September Injunctions, which swept away many traditional practices in the English church; the publication of the vernacular Great Bible under Cromwell's patronage; and Cromwell's order that the scripture be made available in English to worshippers in every parish church.[59] Ferrers's service to Cromwell also placed him at a center of intellectual ferment in mid-Tudor England, bringing him into contact with the numerous young men who flocked to Cromwell's residence to debate matters of religion and government and to present Cromwell with their often radical calls for reforms in church and state. Cromwell's encouragement of evangelicals gave his household a distinctly reforming air; the reformist views of many of the younger Cromwellians, including, it is likely, Ferrers, were forged during their years as Cromwell's servants. Ferrers was marked by his service in Cromwell's household, and for years after he remained in close contact with many of those who, like him, had begun their careers with Henry's once powerful officer.[60]

In 1539 Ferrers moved from Cromwell's service to the royal household, joining Henry's court first as a member of the king's "new bodyguard" and then, in 1542, as a page in Henry's chamber.[61] As a page of the chamber, Ferrers gained daily access to the king and with it a necessarily unvarnished,

58. Ferrers, *Boke of Magna Carta with diuers other statutes . . . translated into Englyshe* (*STC* 9272). A second, "newly corrected" edition appeared in 1541 (*STC* 9275). Ferrers may also have been the translator and editor of the *Great Boke of Statutes . . . from the Fyrst Yere of Edwarde the thyrd tyll .xxv. Henry the .viii.* (*STC* 9286). The *STC* gives the date of this work as "1533?" There is no record of Ferrers's early career as a lawyer; in his Latin elegy "Ad Georgium Ferrarium," however, John Leland highly praised Ferrers's skill as a lawyer and legal historian. Leland composed his poem around 1546, but it was not published until many years later, in the collection *Principum, ac Illustrium Aliquot & Eruditorum in Anglia Virorum, Encomia, Trophaea, Genethliaca & Epithalamia* (London, 1589) (*STC* 15447), 99. Receiving poetic praise from Leland put Ferrers in the company of the major young intellectual and political figures of the day; among the others whom Leland celebrates in verse are Thomas Lupset, Sir Thomas Smith, John Cheke, William Cecil, Sir Anthony Denny, Sir Thomas Elyot, and Roger Ascham (Binns, *Intellectual Culture*, 18–26).

59. Brigden, *London and the Reformation*, 286–88.

60. Brigden, "Thomas Cromwell," 31–50. In his Edwardian encomium to Ferrers, Leland specifically praises Cromwell for having had the foresight to include Ferrers among his servants (*Principum*, 99).

61. Bindoff, *History of Parliament*, 2:129–30; *Mirror*, 25.

demystified view of the king and kingship. Furthermore, Ferrers became an eyewitness to the personal conflicts, factional infighting, and changes of royal favor that marked the intimate political culture of the Tudor court. It was in the chamber, finally, that he became acquainted with numerous of the king's gentlemen who soon would dominate the political life of King Edward's reign, among them the future Protector Edward Seymour, his brother Thomas Seymour, and John Dudley, Viscount Lisle, the very men, in other words, who would later figure prominently in Ferrers's topical poems in *A Memorial of suche Princes*.[62] Upon joining Henry's chamber Ferrers also added his own voice to affairs of state, beginning a lengthy parliamentary career that led him to a seat in all but one of the Parliaments held between 1542 and 1555.[63]

After Edward VI's accession, Ferrers seems to have won patronage from both Protector Somerset and his brother, Lord Admiral Thomas Seymour. In 1547 it was almost certainly with the help of Thomas Seymour that Ferrers gained his seat in King Edward's first Parliament. Ferrers accompanied Edward Seymour on his 1547 invasion of Scotland and was identified soon after by William Patten as "a gentleman of my Lord Protector's" in Patten's account of Seymour's victory. After the invasion Ferrers remained in Seymour's good graces. In 1548 Ferrers received a gift of over two hundred acres of land from the crown. The wording of the grant identified him as a man enjoying the high favor of both the Protector and the king himself.[64]

There is no record of Ferrers's activities at the time of Seymour's deposition; shortly after Seymour's release from the Tower, however, Ferrers became embroiled in a controversy involving an attack on the government of Seymour's successor, John Dudley. In March 1550 a number of anonymous letters critical of the Dudley-led Privy Council began to circulate at court. In response the Council interrogated several of the "ffyne wytted yong men" who it suspected were responsible for their content. Among those whom the Council suspected was George Ferrers. No lesser a personage than John Dudley himself ordered Ferrers's arrest "upon suspycyon to be a counsell with the makyng of the sklaunderous letters ageynst the counsell" and held

62. See chapters 2 and 3.

63. Ferrers's arrest for another man's debt while on the way to Parliament sparked a celebrated decision in favor of parliamentary liberties which became known as "Ferrers's case." King Henry himself intervened on behalf of Ferrers, using the occasion to utter his famous declaration that "we at no time stand so highly in our estate royal as in the time of Parliament." For Holinshed's account of the affair, see Elton, *Tudor Constitution*, 267–70.

64. Bindoff, *History of Parliament*, 2.130, Patten, *Expedition into Scotland*, 97; *Calendar of the Patent Rolls Preserved in the Public Records Office*, 1:314; *Mirror*, 27. The wording of Leland's "Ad Georgium Ferrarium" suggests that Ferrers took part in Seymour's 1545 expedition into Scotland in addition to his 1547 one.

him for an unknown period of time at the Dudley residence in Greenwich.[65] Several other suspects were arrested and/or interrogated as well, including Seymour's fervent admirer William Patten, author of the *Expedition into Scotland*, and *Memorial* author Sir Thomas Chaloner's two younger brothers, Francis and John. Although Richard Scudamore, the chief source for this episode, does not detail what made the bills so offensive, it appears likely that they expressed support for the former Protector, who had by now been released from the Tower but remained under house arrest and was excluded from the Council. Seymour's political status was the chief question of the day, and—to the discomfort of the Councilors—many of his followers were making vocal their support for him and his bid to return to the Council.[66] Even if he was innocent of participation in the affair of the letters, Ferrers's arrest earned him a reputation as someone outspoken on the highest affairs of state and as a suspected active opponent of the current Dudley regime.

If Dudley held any lingering animosity toward George Ferrers, however, his young king did not share it. At Christmastime 1551–52 Edward VI personally appointed Ferrers his holiday Lord of Misrule. In fulfilling this office Ferrers developed an elaborate entertainment with which to please the king, making an impressive royal entrance as a foreign potentate who would take over Edward's court and rule it for the period of the Christmas holiday. Ferrers revealed the depth of his evangelical commitment in the choice of entertainments he devised for the Christmas holiday, presenting several anti-Catholic performances before the king, including an outrageous performance mocking the veneration of the host which angered a number of foreign observers.[67] King Edward was delighted by such spectacles and invited Ferrers back to reprise his role the next year. When Ferrers returned as Lord of Misrule for the Christmas season of 1552–53, he brought with him as his assistant for these revels his future collaborator on *A Memorial of suche Princes*, William Baldwin.[68]

There is no record of Ferrers at Mary's court. In the first year of Mary's reign Ferrers was reappointed a justice of the peace for Hertfordshire and sat in Mary's 1553 and two 1554 Parliaments. During Wyatt's rebellion Ferrers

65. Brigden, "Letters of Richard Scudamore," 125, 127.

66. Ibid., 125; Jordan, *Edward VI: The Threshold of Power*, 71–72.

67. Feuillerat, *Documents Relating to the Revels*, 56; Billington, *Mock Kings*, 38–39; *CSP Span.*, 10:443–44. Furthermore, the account books show that costumes for friars and for a "serpente with sevin heddes called Hidra" were ordered, all props for the sort of anti-Catholic performances that delighted Edward (Paul White, *Theatre and Reformation*, 54).

68. For praise of Ferrers's performance, see Grafton, *Chronicle*, 2:526–27. Numerous modern critics have followed Grafton's suspicion that these revels were a plot by Dudley to distract an allegedly heavy-hearted King Edward while Dudley brought Seymour to his death. In fact, King

joined other evangelicals in defending London against Wyatt's men, acting on the oft-displayed abhorrence for rebellion by private subjects and support for the rule of law that he shared with many of his fellow *Mirror* authors.[69] He may also have been the same "George Ferys" who reported John Dee's casting of King Philip's, Queen Mary's, and Princess Elizabeth's horoscopes.[70] After 1555 Ferrers abandoned participation in Marian public affairs. It is unknown whether he suffered as a result of his poems in *A Memorial of suche Princes*; he was, however, not reappointed justice of the peace for Hertfordshire after 1554, and he did not sit in the 1558 Parliament. It is likely that he confined himself chiefly to his estates until Mary's demise.[71]

After Elizabeth's accession Ferrers remained friends with both Baldwin and Chaloner and continued to work as a lawyer in London. Later he seems to have become attached to Robert, Earl of Leicester, the evangelical patron who had entered Elizabeth's reign untainted by the black reputation of his father, John Dudley. In the 1560s Ferrers apparently became involved in Leicester's plan to make Mary, Queen of Scots, Elizabeth's heir, and he continued to support Mary's claim even as a member of Elizabeth's 1571 Parliament.[72]

Edward showed no signs of sadness over Seymour's death, despite what Seymour's admirers such as Grafton wished to believe. See Lucas, "Conspiracy and Court Revels." See also chapter 3. There is no indication of how Ferrers and Baldwin met, though one likely connection is Thomas Sternhold, a friend and possible political patron of Ferrers. Sternhold would have known Baldwin through Edward Whitchurch, one of Sternhold's closest friends.

69. His work during the rebellion is recorded by Edward Underhill, the self-styled "hot gospeller" who encountered George Ferrers (and who describes Ferrers as his friend and fellow Protestant) at the time Ferrers was conveying a message from the Privy Council to the defenders of London (Nichols, "Autobiographical Anecdotes," 163). By the time of the composition of the *Memorial*, of course, Ferrers's attitude toward rebellion had changed enough that he could present in a celebratory light the corporate rising of the English people against monarchical injustice in his poem "Robert Tresilian." See chapter 5.

70. Hole, *Witchcraft in England*, 130–31. There was at least one other George Ferrers (or Ferys) of the gentry class during this time.

71. Bindoff, *History of Parliament*, 2:130. While his *History of Parliament* biographer suggests that Ferrers may have fled abroad after 1555, he was certainly in London in 1556 or 1557 to pass on to Baldwin Thomas Churchyard's poem "Shore's Wife" and his own "Edmund Duke of Somerset" (see the appendix). Furthermore, in the last year of Mary's reign Ferrers was involved in a dispute over lands in Hertfordshire granted him in 1552 by King Edward. See Page, *Victoria History*, 2:195.

72. Murdin, *A Collection of State Papers*, 30, 43, 48. For Leicester's work to make Mary both Queen Elizabeth's heir and the wife of the Duke of Norfolk, see McCaffrey, *Shaping of the Elizabethan Regime*, 296, 308, 352–57, 384, 450. Although McCaffrey lists Ferrers with men connected chiefly with Norfolk, surviving evidence points to a connection with Leicester. Ferrers's stepdaughter Elizabeth, in fact, married one of Leicester's servants in 1573 (albeit without Ferrers's approval), and two years later Ferrers participated in Leicester's Kenilworth entertainment for the queen (Hasler, *History of Parliament*, 2:113–14). Ferrers may have been won over to Mary's cause by Sir Nicholas Throckmorton, who served as Leicester's right-hand man in the succession and Norfolk marriage schemes (Williams, *Thomas Howard*, 149–52). Under Mary, Throckmorton had been the allusive subject of Ferrers's *Memorial* poem "Sir Robert Tresilian" (see chapter 5).

According to John Stow, Ferrers also composed under Elizabeth a history of Mary's reign that Richard Grafton took from him and printed as his own in *A Chronicle at Large* (1569).[73] Ferrers's last known literary endeavor was on behalf of Leicester's famous Kenilworth pageant for Queen Elizabeth (1575), for which he composed the oration delivered by the Lady of the Lake.[74] He died in 1579.

Sir Thomas Chaloner

Like Ferrers, Sir Thomas Chaloner was a valuable choice for Baldwin's politically interventionary *Memorial* project. By Mary's reign, Chaloner (1521–1565) had proved himself both an accomplished author and an important figure at court, in Parliament, and in the humanist circles of mid-Tudor England. Chaloner was born in London in 1521. He received his education at Cambridge University at a time when it had become dominated by reform-minded humanists such as Sir John Cheke and Sir Thomas Smith, men who would remain his lifelong friends. Upon receiving his degree, Chaloner returned to London and was picked by Thomas Cromwell as a young man worthy of service in the royal household. In the early 1540s Chaloner earned a post as secretary to Henry Knevyt on a diplomatic mission to the Holy Roman Emperor at Regensburg. Bishop Stephen Gardiner also took part in this embassy, and Chaloner's charge that Gardiner had been in contact with papal agents while abroad may have caused the trouble Chaloner would later face from Queen Mary's government. At the time, however, Chaloner enjoyed political favor, moving into royal service first as a teller of the exchequer and then, in 1545, as a junior clerk of the Privy Council.[75] As clerk Chaloner became immersed in the day-to-day politics of Henry's and Edward's governments. It was the duty of the clerks to write all the Council's letters, warrants, and similar documents, to keep "minutes" of all incoming letters, to poll individual Councilors on issues of importance, and to organize the Council's business by drawing up the agendas for its meetings.[76] His time as clerk thus gave Chaloner a deep understanding of how policy was made and how political maneuvers were accomplished in the Privy Council, the center of national power in both the Edwardian and Marian periods. Furthermore, as a clerk of the Council, Chaloner came to know intimately the most important leaders of both Henry's and Edward's governments and witnessed at first-

73. Stow, *Annales* (1605), 1070. See also Stow, *Survey of London*, 1:liii.

74. *Mirror*, 30.

75. Bindoff, *History of Parliament*, 1:611.

76. The Privy Council met about fifteen times a month during this period. For more on Chaloner's duties as clerk, see Hoak, *The King's Council*, 156–63, and Clarence Miller, *The Praise of Folie by Sir Thomas Chaloner*, xxxii–xxxiii.

hand their clashes and their struggles—conflicts that would be reflected in the details of the allusive tragedies of the *Memorial* and *Mirror*. In addition to his duties as clerk, Chaloner became in the 1540s an accomplished author, composing, translating, or editing several works, including the first English translation of Erasmus's *Praise of Folly* (1549). He remained intimate with many of the humanist-trained Cambridge men who came to court during Henry's and Edward's reigns, including Sir Thomas Smith, Sir John Cheke, Walter Haddon, and William Cecil.

Like Ferrers, Chaloner took part in the political life of mid-Tudor England as a member of Parliament. Chaloner served as a member of at least three of Henry's, Edward's, and Mary's Parliaments, and thus made himself part of some of the most important and contentious political actions of the period. Like Ferrers as well, Chaloner from early on won the trust and favor of Edward Seymour. Under Edward, the Seymour-led Council retained Chaloner in his post as clerk, and in September 1547 Seymour made Chaloner his "Chief Secretary" on his expedition into Scotland. So pleased was Seymour with Chaloner's service there that he personally knighted Chaloner on the field.[77] In 1548 Chaloner became the Council's chief clerk and thus performed numerous formal and informal duties on behalf of Edward Seymour and Seymour's personal secretary, William Cecil.

Despite his earlier service to the Lord Protector, Chaloner remained in his post of chief clerk during Seymour's October 1549 standoff with the London Lords, even fulfilling his duty of reading aloud before Londoners one of the Lords' proclamations against Seymour.[78] In this he emulated many others who distanced themselves from Seymour at this troubling time, and it may have been that regret at abandoning the beleaguered Lord Protector in 1549 helped spur him later to join a project seeking to rehabilitate the fallen Protector's reputation.[79]

In the wake of Seymour's fall, Chaloner remained clerk of the Council and took part in the 1551–52 Christmastime festivities presided over by Ferrers at Edward's court, presenting a witty dialogue between figures representing Youth and Riches. He spent much of the rest of Edward's reign on diplomatic missions, first in Scotland and then as an ambassador to France. Upon

77. Patten, *Expedition into Scotland*, 110, 149. Seymour's wife also highly favored Chaloner, giving him a gift of a jewel upon his return from Scotland.

78. Wriothesley, *Chronicle of England*, 2:26.

79. Chaloner's position in 1549 was similar to that of Richard Grafton, the royal printer who had worked closely with Seymour but who nevertheless printed the London Lords' proclamation denouncing the Lord Protector. Later Grafton would work to rehabilitate the memory of the man he had once followed through adulatory passages in chronicle works such as his *Chronicle at Large*.

Mary's accession, however, Chaloner was quickly recalled from his ambassadorial post. He was specifically excluded from the general pardon issued at Mary's coronation and was forced to sue out an individual pardon. His troubles were likely the work of Chancellor Stephen Gardiner, who could easily recall Chaloner's testimony against him concerning the Regensburg matter during his 1550 trial. The disfavor that Mary's government showed Chaloner seems never fully to have dissipated; there is no evidence that Chaloner was ever permitted at Mary's court, and his only regular crown employment was far outside of London on the semiautonomous Council of the North.[80]

If Chaloner had been angered by his treatment at the hands of Mary's government in 1553, the queen's decision early in the next year to execute Lady Jane Grey caused any animosity Chaloner harbored to flare into hot rage. Jane Grey had been long beloved by English evangelicals for her precocious learning and fervent piety. Although she was technically a usurper of Mary's throne for nine days after Edward's death, few condemned Jane herself for her role in the attempt at the crown; most excused her and blamed instead John Dudley, her father-in-law, for forcing an innocent young girl into a crime she did not want to commit. Mary's decision to execute Jane and her husband, Guilford Dudley, in the wake of Wyatt's rebellion—a rising in which they took no part—thus horrified many. Chaloner was outraged by Jane's death. Shortly after Elizabeth's accession he composed a remarkably bitter Latin elegy on the subject and devoted many of its lines to an angry attack on Mary and her officers for slaying the virtuous Jane. In the poem Chaloner denounces Mary for cruelly destroying this young, accomplished, and pregnant girl, an innocent whose only crime was to have been the pawn of conspiratorial nobles (many of whom, Chaloner ruefully notes, Mary had earlier pardoned for their own part in making Jane queen). According to Chaloner, Jane's death was nothing less than an affront to God himself. Mary's brief reign, her painful, lingering sickness in the last days of her life, and the miserable deaths of many of her officers, Chaloner insists, were providential punishments administered by an outraged God.[81] Chaloner's fury, which still burned hot years after Jane's death, was likely a chief goad

80. *Calendar of the Patent Rolls, Philip and Mary*, 410; Bindoff, *History of Parliament*, 1:611. Even Chaloner's place on the Council of the North came to him not through the favor of Mary's government but through the specific request of the Earl of Shrewsbury, president of the Council of the North. Attendance at meetings was not required of council members, and many attended no meetings other than that of the opening day. Despite joining the council in September 1553, Chaloner thus served both in Parliament and as a justice of the peace for Middlesex in 1554 (Reid, *King's Council*, 181, 155–57).

81. Chaloner, "Deploratio acerbae necis heroidis praestantissimae D. Janae Grayae," sigs. T4v–T6r. I thank John McDiarmid for his assistance in translating Chaloner's difficult Latin.

prodding this normally circumspect diplomat to join Baldwin and Ferrers in their project of engaged admonition and complaint against Mary and her officers. Indeed Chaloner seems to have composed the one poem in the collection certainly ascribed to him, his account of the fall of the foolish tyrant King Richard II, as a warning specifically to Queen Mary herself.[82] In later years, Chaloner may have come to regret his open participation in the *Memorial* project. By 1559 he appears to have wished to distance himself from the controversial collection, since his name, which had been attached to the poem on Richard II in the 1554 *Memorial*, was removed completely from the 1559 *Mirror for Magistrates*.

With Elizabeth's accession Chaloner once again enjoyed royal favor, becoming one of the new queen's earliest and most trusted advisors. Elizabeth soon made Chaloner her ambassador to Spain, where his evangelical Protestant views sometimes created conflict with his Catholic hosts. Under Elizabeth, Chaloner turned his hand once more to literary endeavor, composing several poems on subjects such as the rule of England and the life and career of King Henry VIII. He remained close with George Ferrers and with Thomas Sackville, who had sought to continue Baldwin's *Memorial* project after its suppression. After Chaloner's death in 1565, his close friend William Cecil commissioned a memorial volume of Chaloner's Latin verse and wrote an emotional, laudatory dedication to his memory. Through the praise of Cecil and numerous others, Chaloner's name remained for decades a byword in England for probity, dutifulness, and artistic achievement.[83]

Creating Contexts: The Prefatory Material of the *Fall* and the *Memorial*

As evangelicals, Baldwin, Ferrers, and Chaloner had suffered from the collapse of the Edwardian regime and from the ongoing policies of Mary's officers. Like many other evangelicals in 1554, they wrestled with the haunting questions surrounding the collapse of the Edwardian regime and sought means by which they could reconcile the tragedies of the Edwardian period with their beliefs about the rectitude of the evangelical faith and its lost heroes. Chief among these heroes was Edward Seymour, Duke of Somerset, whose glorious, promising beginning and sudden, disturbing failure seemed in retrospect a harbinger of the traumatic course of the Edwardian reforma-

82. See chapter 5.

83. The most complete account of Chaloner's Elizabethan career is Blazer, "Life of Sir Thomas Chaloner." For Chaloner's relations with Ferrers and Sackville under Elizabeth, see *Calendar of State Papers, Foreign Series*, 5:108, 325, 583; 6:62, 358, 498.

tion as a whole. Furthermore, like so many other Marian Protestants, each of the *Memorial* authors sought to ward off what seemed a certain future of increased persecution and arbitrary government in the coming years of Mary's reign. The authors were loyal subjects of the English crown who nevertheless were strongly opposed to specific courses of action taken by their governors. As men outspoken on religious and political affairs in the previous reign, the *Memorial* authors found it impossible to stand idly by and watch the country fall into what they feared would be danger and ruin; they thus strove for means to persuade the queen and her officers to abandon those practices the authors saw as most pernicious.

Both to come to terms with the tragedies of the Edwardian past and to intervene in the politics of the Marian present, Baldwin, Ferrers, Chaloner, and other unnamed sympathizers seized on the allusive communicative potential of Wayland's exemplary *Memorial* project and turned it to their own politically contentious ends. The literary form of the *Memorial* project promised them what the openly polemical style of other evangelical writing under Mary could not: the possibility of conveying controversial opinions to the English public without inciting the immediate wrath of their queen's censoring officers. In composing the allusive tragedies of the *Memorial*, the authors set out to create an aboveground, widely disseminated work of consolation and counsel, a work that could avoid immediate disfavor only by handling recent events allusively and by conveying its admonitory message in such a manner as to deflect the immediate hostility of their targeted magisterial audience.

It was thus the complex task of its editor, William Baldwin, to deflect the suspicions of a potentially hostile audience while simultaneously alerting sympathetic readers to the allusive nature of his project. To do so, Baldwin carefully built in to the prefatory material of the *Fall* and the *Memorial* matter that established separate interpretive contexts for those who would encounter the new poems of the volume. In both written and iconographical prefatory material, Baldwin worked to establish two contexts for reading the *Memorial* tragedies, one overt but actually deflecting and misleading, and the second much less widely interpretable but highly significant for the intended audience to whom it spoke. Through the first of these contexts Baldwin sought to attract readers (in particular, Marian officers) who likely would be hostile to his messages of political rebuke. Through the second he signaled to members of the evangelical Protestant community (especially those involved in the writing and printing of controversial literature) the resistant nature of the collection, its authors' commitment to the nationalist and "godly" ideals celebrated so fervently during Edward's rule, and finally his support for free expression of potentially uncomfortable political commentary in print. It is to the *Fall* and the *Memorial* themselves and to these materials that we now turn.

Deflecting Suspicions

As Baldwin well knew, the most difficult problem for a writer of unsolicited political counsel was persuading those in power to read his works. In 1553 Roger Ascham noted that officers frequently refuse to read straightforward works of beneficial advice simply because they assume such writings will be offensive and insulting: too often officials "are so ware [in receiving such works], that commonly they will complaine of theyr hurt before they feele harme."[84] For evangelical authors, Ascham's observation seemed resoundingly confirmed in Mary's reign. Under Edward VI printers and writers had enjoyed an unprecedented period of free speech. The print trade had flourished, and works on social, religious, and even political issues appeared in print with an outspokenness unheard of in earlier times. Many were addressed specifically to Edward or to his officers and sought to convince those in power to adopt their authors' views. Even after Protector Somerset's deposition (October 1549), when the government was less tolerant of critics of its reforms, writers and printers still enjoyed a relatively large amount of freedom for their works.[85]

Such freedom of speech was sharply curtailed in the Marian period. Mary's reign opened with a proclamation banning any discussion of religion in print except that authorized by her government. This was followed in early 1554 by a ban on "seditious" writings. The threat of punishment for works that had been acceptable and even encouraged during the previous reign demoralized the Marian print community, particularly those who under Edward had made evangelical religious and social commentary virtually their stock-in-trade. Whereas Edward's government had not only permitted relatively open discussion of religious and social matters but also at least appeared sometimes to hear the counsel of "articulate citizens," Mary's officers tended to seize and to destroy rather than to tolerate the numerous works that dared to advise them on religious and political policy.[86]

In this climate Baldwin could well expect that his and his fellow authors' attempts to offer admonition to those in power would experience a similar reception. He thus shaped the *Fall-Memorial* volume to deflect any initial suspicions of controversial matter in the text of the new *Memorial* tragedies.

84. Ascham, *Report of the Affaires and State of Germany*, 160.

85. King, *English Reformation Literature*, 84–85; Ferguson, *Articulate Citizen*; Loades, *Politics, Censorship and the English Reformation*, 114–15.

86. Hughes and Larkin, *Tudor Royal Proclamations*, 2:5–8, 41–42; Loades, *Politics, Censorship and the English Reformation*, 103; Loach, "Pamphlets and Politics," 39–40.

In constructing the prefatory matter of the collection, Baldwin drew on techniques recommended by contemporary oratorical theory. In the *Arte of Rhetorique* (1553), Thomas Wilson counseled those who would address hostile audiences to abandon plain speaking and to seek "prively to get favour" through an indirect introduction of their subject: "a privy begynnyng, or crepyng in, otherwyse called Insinuation must then, and not els be used," Wilson advised, "when the judge is greaved with us, and our cause hated of the hearers."[87]

It is precisely this strategy that guides Baldwin in choosing the wording of the *Fall* and *Memorial* titles. In the 1559 edition of the *Mirror*, Baldwin highlights for readers the presence of tragedies in the collection that serve as warnings to erring magistrates, pointing out on the title page of the collection that the *Mirror* would show "with howe greuous plages" the vices of English officers are punished (62). The titles in the *Fall-Memorial* volume, by contrast, call no attention to the politically admonitory function of the tragedies the volume contains. The title chosen for Lydgate's work in the suppressed edition merely identifies it as *The Fall of Princes*, giving no indication of a corrective moral purpose, unlike, for instance, the title chosen for Richard Tottel's edition of the same year, which calls attention to the fatal "detestable & wicked vices" of the rulers whom Lydgate portrays. Similarly, the title Baldwin gave to his continuation of Lydgate, *A Memorial of suche princes, as since the tyme of king Richard the seconde, haue been vnfortunate in the Realme of England*, makes no mention of sinful rulers, "vices," or divine retribution. The *Memorial* will portray, the title page suggests, only "unfortunate" princes, not specifically vicious ones. The effect is to suggest misleadingly that the *Fall* and its "continuation" are presented chiefly as *de contemptu mundi* meditations on the vicissitudes of fortune rather than as works of often pointed political admonition.[88]

Elsewhere in the volume Baldwin arranges introductory materials to suggest an aura of official sanction for the *Memorial* that the text in fact does not

87. Wilson, *Arte of Rhetorique*, 210.

88. The full title of Wayland's edition is *The Fall of Prynces. Gathered by Iohn Bochas, fro[m] the begynnyng of the world vntyll his time, translated into English by Iohn Lidgate Monke of Burye. wherunto is added the fall of al such as since that time were notable in Englande: diligently collected out of the Chronicles* (*STC* 3177.5). The full title on the internal title page is *A Memorial of suche princes, as since the tyme of king Richard the seconde, haue been vnfortunate in the Realme of England* (*STC* 1246). After the suppression of the *Fall-Memorial* volume, Wayland reissued the *Fall* by itself, with a new title page that stressed the morally admonitory function of Lydgate's work, which the original title left unmentioned: *The tragedies, gathered by Ihon Bochas, of all such Princes as fell from theyr estates throughe the mutability of Fortune since the creacion of Adam, vntil his time: wherin may be seen what vices bring menne to destruccion, wyth notable warninges howe the like may be auoyded. Translated into Englysh by Ihon Lidgate, Monke of Burye* (*STC* 3178).

deserve. The note on the verso of the *Fall* title page declares to readers that Wayland would not print the *Fall* until he "knew the Counsayles pleasure & aduice therein." Since the *Fall* and the *Memorial* were printed as a single continuous volume (with the *Memorial* beginning in the middle of a gathering), and since the note describes the *Memorial* merely as a "continuacion" of Lydgate's work, the suggestion of Council approval that greets readers on the first page after the title would imply a sense of approval for the *Fall-Memorial* volume as a whole, rather than just for its first section. In fact the Council's approval refers solely to *The Fall of Princes* and has nothing to do with the *Memorial* (68).

It is for similar effect that Baldwin prefaces the *Memorial* itself with Wayland's letters patent.[89] These take the form of an address from Mary herself to all readers. They speak of the queen's "especial grace" toward Wayland, and they demand that "as ye tendre oure pleasure," none must disregard the special protection she has extended to Wayland, her "welbeloued Subiect." Yet, like the Council's blessing for the printing of *The Fall of Princes*, the letters patent so prominently displayed have nothing to do with the *Memorial* itself. They do not sanction all works from Wayland's press but refer only to the new primer.[90] Their effect, however, would be to reinforce a general sense of approval for the work they preface, and thus they help to allay initial suspicions of unorthodox or critical material in a collection of poems on fallen English rulers.

Baldwin uses his prose introduction to the *Memorial* (titled "William Baldwin to the Reader") further to deflect suspicions concerning the work. First, he employs this preface to hide his guiding role in the conception and creation of the *Memorial*, shifting responsibility for the collection from him and his fellow authors to the more trustworthy Wayland. In the Elizabethan dedication to the 1559 edition, Baldwin openly reveals his preeminent role in creating the *Memorial* and his shaping of it as an admonitory "loking glas" for the officers of his time. He confesses that he designed it as a work of admonition and sought through its poems to move contemporary officers to "the soner amendment" of behaviors to which he and his fellow authors were opposed (65–66). The preface of the *Memorial* carries no such declarations;

89. See *Mirror*, plate 5.

90. It should be noted that in works by Wayland in which such deflecting maneuvers would not be needed, the letters patent appear at the *end* of the volumes and not at the beginning. This is the case, for instance, for Wayland's edition of James Cancellar's *The Pathe of Obedience, Righte Necessarye for all the King and Quenes Maiesties Louing Subiectes* (London, 1556) (*STC* 4564), a work strongly supportive of Mary's government whose sentiments could in no way be misconstrued. The title page of the *Fall of Princes* that eventually appeared after the suppression of the *Memorial* includes neither Wayland's note nor his letters patent. Its verso is completely blank.

instead it works to draw attention away from Baldwin's influence and from the urgent political project of his exemplary tragedies. In the *Memorial* Baldwin presents himself as a reluctant author and editor. He asserts that it was neither his idea to write new tragedies (rather, unnamed "dyuers" gentlemen suggested the idea to Wayland) nor his desire to take on the project Wayland assigned to him. At first, he claims, he "refused vtterly to vndertake it," and after Wayland reiterated his demand that Baldwin create for him a continuation of the *Fall*, Baldwin claims to have searched for any way to "shift [his] handes" from it (68). Only when Wayland found other men to help him, Baldwin declares, did he give in and take up the unwanted task.

In fact, all evidence suggests that Baldwin himself was the printer as well as the editor and chief author of this work, and it was certainly he who revived and continued this supposedly unwanted project in Elizabeth's reign. Furthermore, despite Baldwin's suggestion that Wayland found and brought together the company of authors, none of the known writers of *Memorial* tragedies had any ties to Wayland; instead, they had ties only to one another. By suggesting that Baldwin and his fellow authors were only literary workmen assigned to a specific poetic task (expanding Lydgate's collection), Baldwin once again seeks to deflect suspicions about the collaborative nature of the project, its contributors' status as a group of like-minded evangelical authors, and their reasons for gathering to write in the months after Wyatt's rebellion on the sensitive topics of revolts, depositions, civil broils, and the falls of princes.

Baldwin's introduction also plays fast and loose with the reason for beginning the *Memorial* at the end of Richard II's reign. In the preface George Ferrers claims that the authors begin with fallen figures of the fourteenth century solely on Wayland's orders. Briefly noting the stories of Richard I and King John, Ferrers remarks, "But seinge the printers mynde is to haue vs followe where *Lidgate* left . . . , I wyll begin at the tyme of Rycharde the second, a tyme as vnfortunate as the ruler therein." If Wayland had actually ordered them to begin where Lydgate had ended, the authors would have begun with the reign of Edward III, not Richard II (69–71). Nor would they have begun only in the last twelve years of Richard's reign, a choice that entailed skipping over the many important political events of its early period. As readers would learn only after embarking on the tragedies themselves, the logic of the authors' chronology lies not in their overtly claimed reasons but in their covert project. In beginning the *Memorial* at the end of Richard II's reign, the authors chose a time that was much more than "unfortunate": it was exactly the period that best allowed them to foreground narratives which display opposition to an English monarch who would not hear good counsel and who was allowed to rule "above the law." As we shall see, Richard's faults were among those the *Memorial* authors feared most greatly in their own monarch, and thus they offered prime matter for the authors' admonitory purpose. Finally, starting at the end of Richard's reign rather than at its beginning allows them the opportunity to commence seemingly by chance with the poem "The Fall of Robert Tresilian," a tragedy that, readers soon would learn, is one of the most angry, urgent, and pointedly allusive works in the collection.

Through the suggestions of orthodoxy built into his *Fall-Memorial* volume, its presentation of itself to readers as merely a literary continuation of an old, venerable work, and the misleading, deflecting rhetoric of his preface to the *Memorial*, Baldwin effects the "privy creeping in" he sought for his collection. It was Baldwin's hope that Marian officers would have little reason to suspect this poetic collection of being a text of complaint and rebuke until they were already engaged in reading and learning from the tragedies that asserted the dangerous consequences of precisely their own actions.

Signaling Covert Content

For certain other readers there would be an introductory message quite different from the overtly misleading one displayed by various of the prefatory materials. Upon opening the *Fall-Memorial* volume, those familiar with the evangelical book trade would be immediately struck by one important fact: the title page—including the printer's device displayed on it—is not Wayland's at all but John Day's. While it was not unheard of for new printers to borrow the title page compartments of others, such an act would seem odd in this case, for Wayland had inherited several of his own woodcut title page compartments from Edward Whitchurch and had adapted them to signify his own name. Thus in his first known Marian production (and the only one known to have preceded the *Fall-Memorial* volume), a reissue of Hawes's *Pastime of Pleasure* (1554), the title page contained one of Whitchurch's old compartments with Whitchurch's initials, "E. W.," altered to read "I. W." (that is, John Wayland). The *Fall-Memorial* title pages, however, were printed with a distinctive woodcut compartment designed specifically for Day and which symbolically evoked his name through a rebus showing a young man waking another with the motto "Arise, for it is Day" at the bottom (see figures 1, 2, 3).

Its presence on the title pages of the *Fall-Memorial* volume would seem to be the work of William Baldwin, not John Wayland. While there is no known connection between Wayland and Day, Baldwin had been closely connected to Day in Edward's reign and had even made Day's own residence one of the settings of his *Beware the Cat.*[91] Day had been forced from the legitimate print trade upon Mary's accession, and it seems likely that he passed his unique, highly personalized title page compartment directly to Baldwin after he quit publishing.[92]

The use of this title page at the time of the printing of the *Memorial* would be highly significant for those familiar with reformist religious literature. Before he was forced from the trade, Day had been perhaps the most prolific and zealous Protestant printer of the late 1540s and early 1550s. Both in partnership with William Seres and on his own, Day produced many important religious and political controversial works; in particular, as John N. King notes, he was "the most innovative and industrious popularizer of the Bible" in Edward's reign.[93] Day had commissioned the highly symbolic title page compartment of the *Fall-Memorial* volume specifically for his 1551 folio edition of the Matthew Bible, a conflation of Tyndale's and Coverdale's Bible translations that had been banned by Henry VIII (see figure 4).[94] It had not reappeared in print until Edmund Becke revised it for Day in 1549. Day's three editions of the Matthew Bible were among the most important Bibles produced under Edward, and Day viewed Becke's version of it as a work of great importance, releasing Becke's Bible (as it is often called) both in complete folio editions and in a series of octavo volumes for "the commoditie of these pore" who could not afford a full book of scripture.

In 1551 Day produced his third edition of Becke's Bible, introducing it with a new iconographical title page compartment. This version contained a preface by Becke himself, which directed kings and magistrates in particular to the study of scripture for its many words of counsel pertaining to their duties in office. Magistrates must read the Bible "as they haue bene vsed to do in Cronicles & Canterbury tales," diligently studying holy scripture for its

91. Baldwin, *Beware the Cat*, 9–10; Elizabeth Evenden suggests that under Edward VI, Baldwin regularly proofread for Day's press in addition to working for Whitchurch. On his return to the print trade in 1556, furthermore, Day became an "assign" of John Wayland and printed on Wayland's behalf copies of the Marian primer. This was a position to which Baldwin rather than Wayland likely helped Day (Evenden, "The Fleeing Dutchmen," 68, 74). It is also noteworthy that Thomas Chaloner chose Day as his own printer in Elizabeth's reign. See *STC* 4938.5 and 4939.

92. This could explain how the compartment returned to Day in 1560, after Wayland had been imprisoned for debt and had left the print trade. It is noteworthy that neither Wayland nor any other printer was to use Day's compartment again in Mary's reign after Wayland's *Fall of Princes* and the new, benign replacement for the *Memorial* appended to it, Roger Bieston's *The Bayte and Snare of Fortune*, appeared (McKerrow and Ferguson, *Title-Page Borders*, 79–82).

93. King, *English Reformation Literature*, 128. Among those whose works Day published were Tyndale, Latimer, Bale, Simon Fish, Luke Shepherd, and Robert Crowley.

94. C. S. Lewis discusses the contents of the Matthew Bible in *English Literature in the Sixteenth Century*, 209–10. Its first printing (Antwerp, 1537) was superintended by Edward Whitchurch.

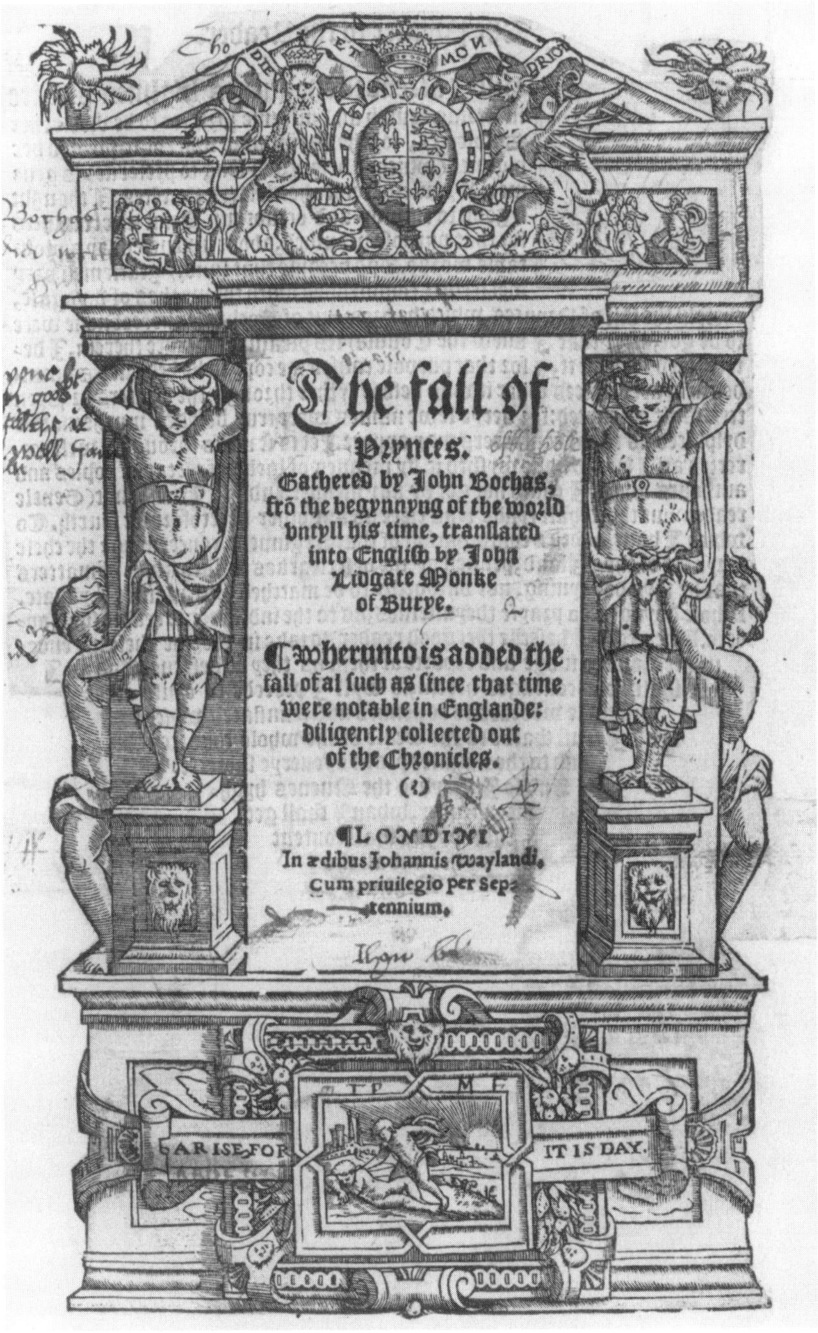

DIEU ET MON DROIT

The fall of Prynces.

Gathered by John Bochas, frō the begynnyng of the world vntyll his time, translated into Englissh by John Lidgate Monke of Burye.

¶ Wherunto is added the fall of al such as since that time were notable in Englande: diligently collected out of the Chronicles.

(∴)

¶ LONDINI

In ædibus Johannis Waylandi.

Cum priuilegio per Septennium.

FIGURE 1. Title page of the prohibited volume of *Fall of Princes/Memorial of suche Princes*, sig. [+1r] (London: John Wayland, 1554) (*STC* 3177.5). *Reproduced by permission of V&A Images/Victoria and Albert Museum, London.*

DIEU ET MON DRIOT

A memorial of suche Princes, as since the tyme of King Richard the seconde, haue been vnfortunate in the Realme of England.

¶LONDINI In ædibus Johannis Waylandi, cum priuilegio per Septennium.

ARISE, FOR IT IS DAY.

FIGURE 2. Internal title page of the suppressed *A Memorial of suche Princes*, sig. [2G4r] (London: John Wayland, 1554) (*STC* 1246). *Reproduced by permission of the Folger Shakespeare Library.*

The trage-
dies, gathered by Jhon
Bochas, of all such Princes as
fell from theyr estates throughe
the mutability of Fortune since
the creacion of Adam, vntil his
time: wherin may be seen what
vices bring menne to destrucci-
on, wyth notable warninges
howe the like may be auoyded.
Translated into Englysh by
John Lidgate, Monke
of Burye.

Imprinted at London, by
John Wayland, at the signe
of the Sunne ouer against
the Conduite in Flete-
strete.

Cum priuilegio per Sep-
tennium.

FIGURE 3. Title page of Wayland's allowed edition of *The Fall of Princes*, sig. +1r (London: John Wayland, 1554) (*STC* 3178). *Reproduced by permission of the Folger Shakespeare Library.*

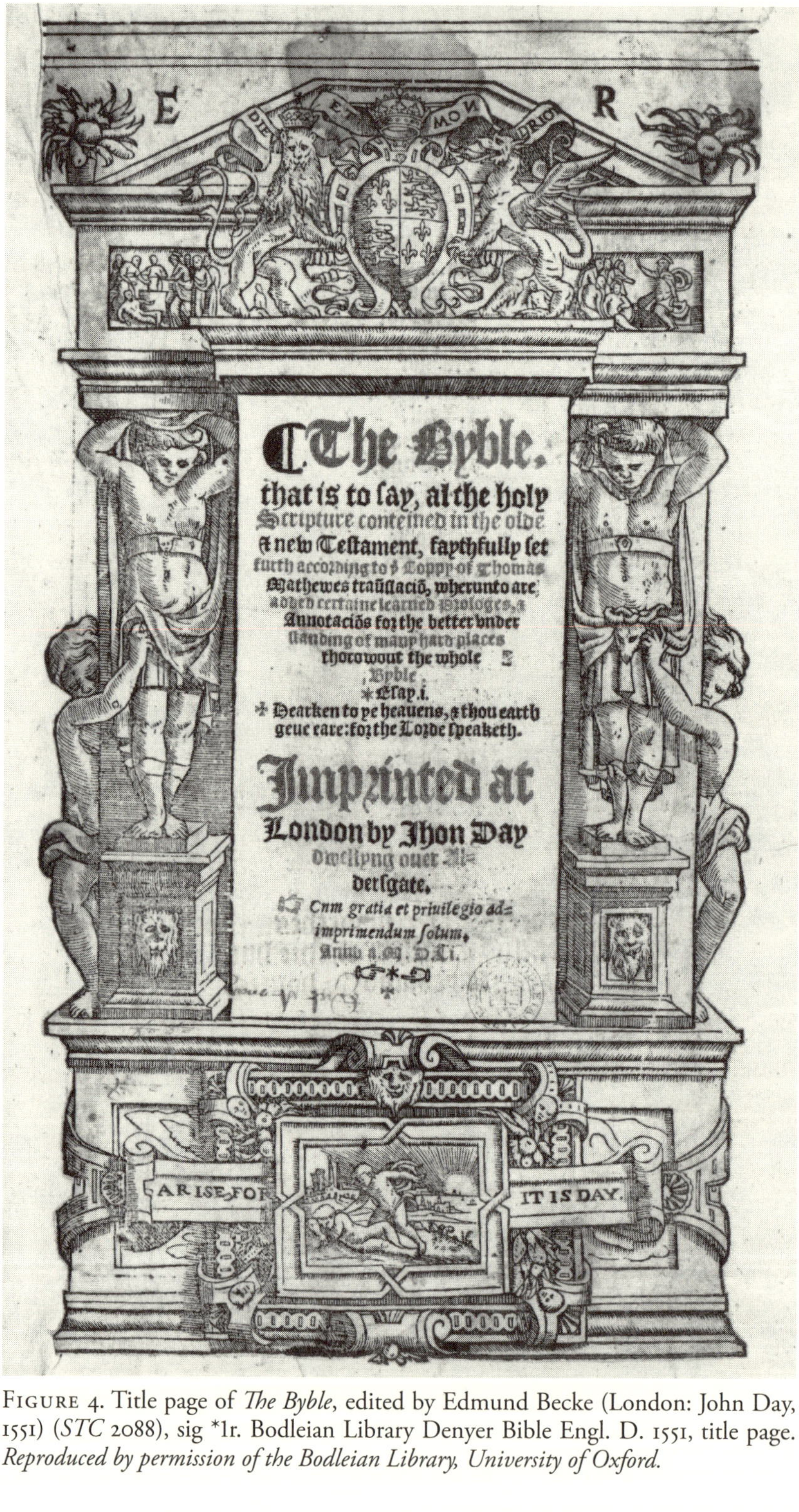
E R

DIEU ET MON DROIT

The Byble, that is to say, al the holy Scripture conteined in the olde & new Testament, faythfully set furth according to ỹ Coppy of Thomas Mathewes traũslaciõ, wherunto are added certaine learned Prologes, & Annotaciõs for the better vnderstanding of many hard places thorowout the whole Byble.

Esay.i.

Hearken to ye heauens, & thou earth geue eare: for the Lorde speaketh.

Imprinted at London by Jhon Day dwellyng ouer Aldersgate.

Cum gratia et priuilegio ad imprimendum solum.

Anno .M.D.LI.

FIGURE 4. Title page of *The Byble*, edited by Edmund Becke (London: John Day, 1551) (*STC* 2088), sig *1r. Bodleian Library Denyer Bible Engl. D. 1551, title page. *Reproduced by permission of the Bodleian Library, University of Oxford.*

moral teachings. If officers would only read the Bible with the zeal they have reserved for history and literature, Becke apostrophized King Edward, "oh what a florishyng co[m]mune wealth should your grace enjoy & haue."[95]

Baldwin's prominent use of Day's title page compartment reminds evangelicals familiar with Becke's Bible of the ends of the original work for which it was created.[96] Whereas Becke had exhorted rulers to devote to the Bible the time they had previously spent with "Cronicles and Canterbury tales," Baldwin offers the *Memorial*, a work filled with matter designed to be "to all princes a ryght notable and wurthy instruction," as a sort of redemption of these genres (119). Whereas chronicles often contain merely records of past events, and fictional "tales" are frequently designed solely for entertainment, a chief function of Baldwin's collection is the moral correction of its readers. A major goal of its "tales" is to present historical narratives mirroring transgressions of contemporary magistrates, so that reading of the work may "be a good occasion to move [magistrates] to the soner amendment" of similar vices (65–66). The vices with which the *Memorial* is chiefly concerned are those associated with rulers and government men: injustice, ambition, cruelty, and corruption. Day's title page compartment is a particularly apt choice for a text offering exemplary works designed to rescue England's rulers from the specific sins most common to their station.

Not only is the Day title page compartment meant to recall Becke's Bible, but also its iconography is meant to be "read" in and of itself. As Margery Corbett and Ronald Lightbown note, printed iconographical title page compartments such as Day's had originated as a specifically Protestant form of communication: the German Lutherans of the 1520s had begun the practice "as a means of pictorial propaganda for their religious beliefs," and it is "in their tracts and in Reformation Bibles that we find the first title-pages whose iconography bears more than an illustrative relation to the text." In Reformation England this means of communication had remained closely associated with works by Protestant authors and printers. Its first English example, in fact, was the Great Bible of 1539, printed jointly by Richard Grafton and Baldwin's printmaster, Edward Whitchurch.[97]

95. *The Byble, that is to say, al the holy Scripture*, sigs. *3v–*4v; see also King, *English Reformation Literature*, 129–30. Becke originally wrote this preface for Day's first folio Bible (London, 1549) (*STC* 2077).

96. Baldwin reinforced the mnemonic effect of the compartment by placing it both on the title page of the *Fall-Memorial* volume and on the internal title page introducing solely the *Memorial* (sig. 2G4r). Its use on pages dividing a single, continuously printed volume into separate sections would also recall Becke's Bible, which Day divided into five sections, each with its own title page featuring his ornate compartment.

97. Corbett and Lightbown, *Comely Frontispiece*, 3.

Day's title page was created according to the traditions of this reformist mode of communication, and its ability to communicate relied on the interpretive practices which a Protestant audience could employ to tease out its full significance. Day had been a fierce supporter of Edward VI and his religious reforms, and John King calls Day's 1551 Becke Bible "the best example of the use of the printed Bible as a royal emblem." As King notes, the most important emblematic piece of this Bible is its title page compartment, whose images suggest symbolically that the advancement of Protestant reform and the rule of the Tudors are inseparable:

> The illustration [of the title page] symbolizes divine revelation through the agency of the crown; at the same time it contains a rebus on Day's name, trade, and faith. The upper compartment contains the royal arms supported by the British griffin and crowned lion. The two small side compartments, which portray the raising of Lazarus and the Resurrection, link the royal monogram and heraldry to God's word. At the bottom, Day's motto "ARISE, FOR IT IS DAY" and his device, which depicts one naked man waking another at the sun's rising, continue the symbolism of resurrection and revelation. Like Donne's "Goodfriday, 1613, Riding Westward," the woodcut alludes to the conceit of Christ as the rising sun. To the elect Christian reader, the emblematic motto and device identify the text as the source of salvation by means of allusion to 1 Thessalonians 5:5: "For you are all sons of light and sons of the day; we are not of the night or of darkness." Day sold books at the sign of the Resurrection.[98]

Not only are familiar symbols of the English monarchy combined in it with symbolic renderings of Protestant doctrine, but also placed above all is the highly charged image of the English crown imperial. As Dale Hoak has shown, the crown had become by Edward's reign a symbol among evangelical Protestants of the superiority of the English king's supremacy in religious affairs and of England's independence from any foreign authority (whether religious or secular). This sense of imperial iconography went back at least to the Act of Appeals (1533), which declared that "this realm of England is an empire" and not subject to the pope's authority. By the time of the Edwardian radical reformation, the image of the imperial crown had become for many the very "*impresa* of protestant imperialism."[99]

Day was one of the chief architects of this symbolism. In 1549 (two years before he had commissioned the Becke Bible title page compartment), Day had adopted as a printer's device an allegorical representation of the imperial crown (see figure 5). Day "set the Garter and Edward VI's crown imperial and

98. King, *English Reformation Literature*, 187; see also Mumby, *Publishing and Bookselling*, 72–73.

99. Hoak, "Iconography of the Crown Imperial," 90, 87.

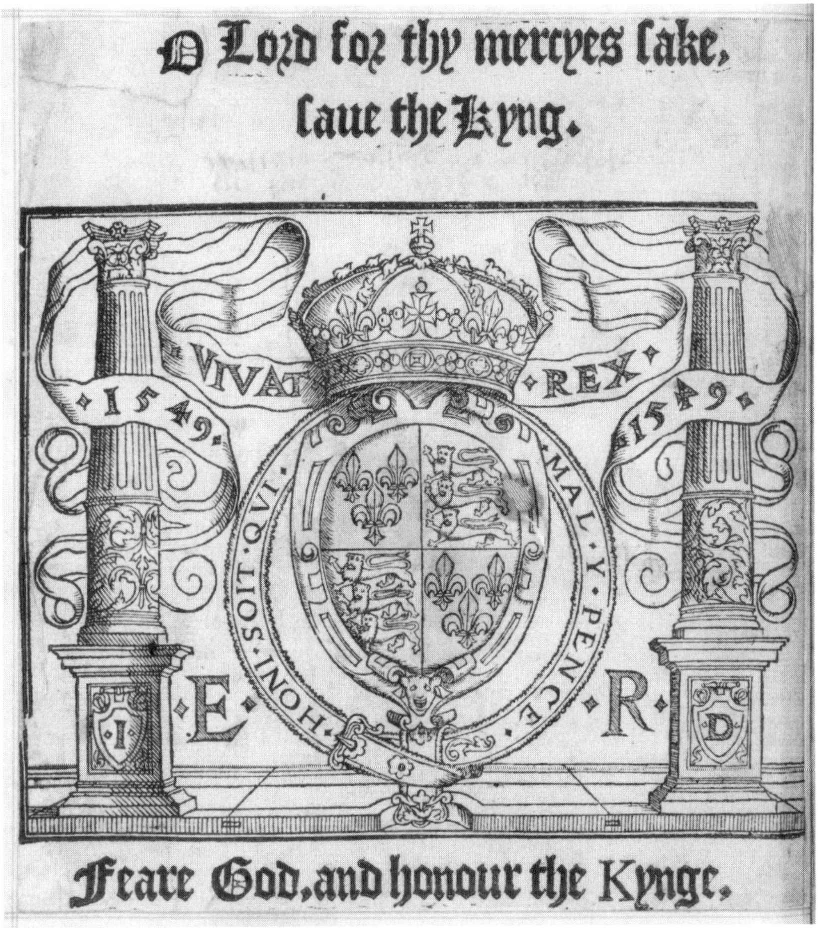

FIGURE 5. John Day's columnar printer's device. From *The Byble,* ed. Edmund Becke (London: John Day, 1551) (*STC* 2088), unsigned leaf facing title page. *Reproduced by courtesy of the University Librarian and Director, The John Rylands Library, The University of Manchester.*

arms between a pair of columns, a composition based on the internationally recognizable personal device of Emperor Charles V [see figure 6]. . . . For zealous reformists at the courts of Edward VI and Elizabeth I, Daye's mark became the patriotic emblem of Protestant Tudor imperialism, a silent but assertive English response, as it were, to the mark and motto of international Catholic (Hapsburg) imperialism."[100]

100. Ibid., 90. See also John N. King's chapter "The Crown versus the Tiara," in *Tudor Royal Iconography,* 116–81.

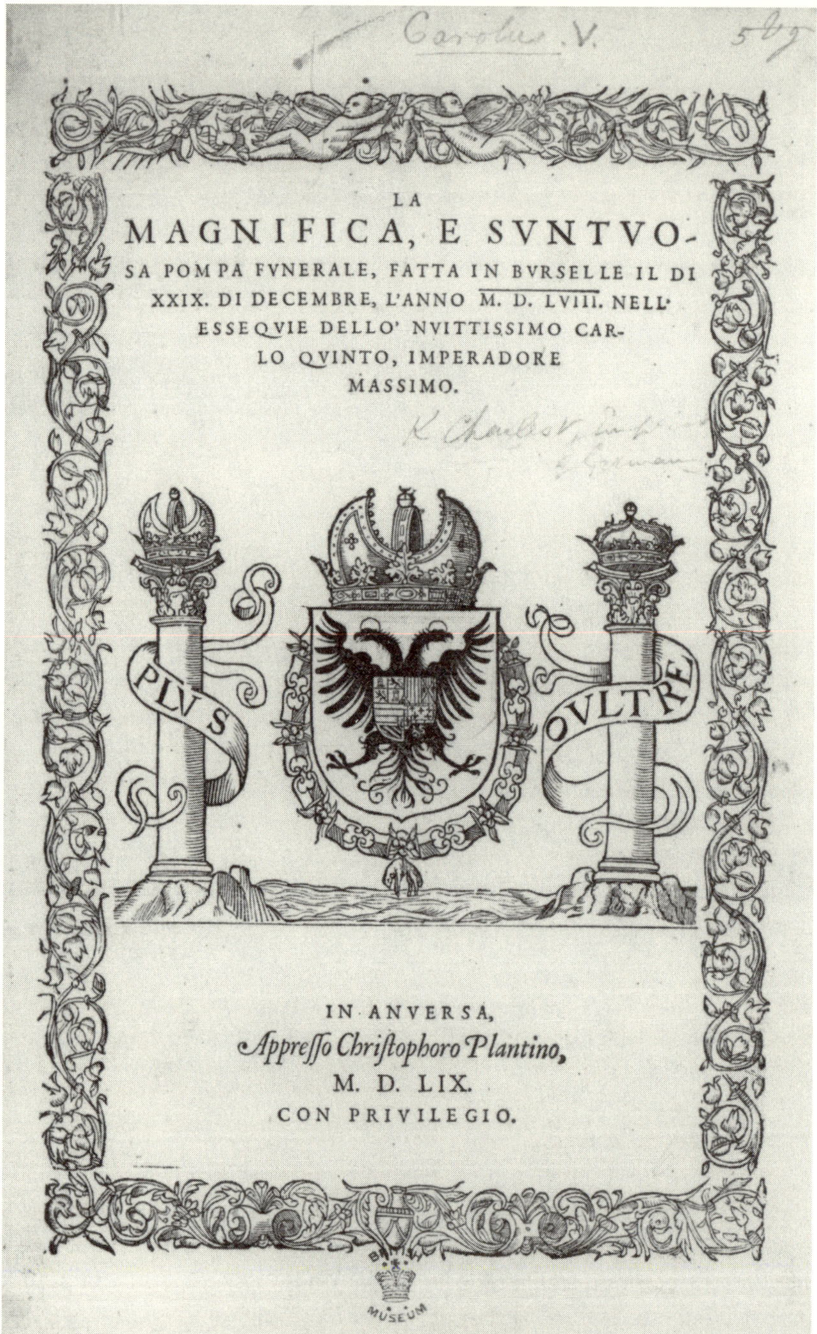

LA
MAGNIFICA, E SVNTVO-
SA POMPA FVNERALE, FATTA IN BVRSELLE IL DI
XXIX. DI DECEMBRE, L'ANNO M. D. LVIII. NELL'
ESSEQVIE DELLO' NVITTISSIMO CAR-
LO QVINTO, IMPERADORE
MASSIMO.

PLVS OVLTRE

IN ANVERSA,
Appresso Christophoro Plantino,
M. D. LIX.
CON PRIVILEGIO.

FIGURE 6. Columnar device of Emperor Charles V. From *La Magnifica, E Svntvosa Pompa Fvnerale* (Antwerp: Plantin, 1559), title page. Reproduced by permission of the British Library.

The iconography of the *Fall-Memorial* title pages would invoke, for those who could read it, the memory of the abandoned political and religious policies of Edward's regime and the political leaders who had championed them. To the interpretive community of strongly nationalistic Protestants (of which all the known *Memorial* authors were a part), it evokes memories specifically of Edward Seymour, Duke of Somerset, the evangelical political leader whose government had championed religious reform and aggressive English expansionism (see chapters 2, 3, and 4). By 1554 both the looming reintroduction of Roman Catholicism and Mary's new Habsburg king consort threatened the fragile national cohesion with which Mary's reign had begun. In particular, Wyatt's rebellion had been a protest against both the feared loss of English sovereignty in England and the Marian religious reaction—a cause with which many evangelicals strongly sympathized even if they could not condone Wyatt's open rebellion. The title page compartment of the *Fall-Memorial* volume would alert those familiar with Day's iconography and evangelical thought to the controversial nature of what would seem at first glance an uncontroversial literary-historical text.

Finally, in addition to all these implications, there was for men and women connected with the Protestant print trade yet another local significance to be read in these title pages, a personal one tied to the career and misfortunes of Day himself. Shortly after Mary's accession, Day (along with Whitchurch) was specifically exempted from Mary's general pardon for printers. Day disappeared from the aboveground printing world. In October 1553, however, three months after Mary's accession, a series of controversial evangelical pamphlets began to appear in London. All were printed from the same type and purported to come from "Roane" (Rouen), from the house of "Michael Wood." We know them now to be the work of John Day.[101] These pamphlets (ten between October 1553 and May 1554) contained direct attacks on Chancellor Gardiner, letters sent by evangelical ministers abroad to Protestants in England, a letter written by Lady Jane Grey, and, most gallingly for Mary's Lord Chancellor, two translations of Gardiner's own *De Vera Obedientia*, a piece of propaganda Gardiner wrote on Henry's orders to defend the king's break from Rome.

For those aware of the ongoing production of evangelical protest literature, Baldwin's title page stands as something of a testimonial to Day and his beliefs, which had been forced underground but not silenced. There would also have been added significance by the end of 1554, for in October of that

101. Evenden, "Michael Wood Mystery."

year Day was caught and sent to the Tower for "pryntyng of noythy [naughty] bokes."[102] We do not know precisely when in 1554 Baldwin printed these title pages; in any event, whether or not Baldwin knew of Day's arrest, the title page would have accrued a further testimonial significance in light of the troubles Day incurred for printing the voices of Protestant opposition. For those aware of his role as "Michael Wood" and his link to Baldwin, it would align the purpose of Baldwin's new collection of verse tragedies to the voices of protest against Marian policies in the works Day had been producing surreptitiously.

Baldwin expected Day's title page compartment to be read as a text in itself. Through the covert symbolic resonances of the title page, Baldwin signaled simultaneously opposition to the reestablishment of Roman Catholicism, support for the government policies of Edward's reign in general and Edward Seymour's Protectorate in particular, and protest against the silencing of those such as Day who opposed Mary's policies.[103] Of course it is impossible to say if Marian magistrates were fully ignorant of the significance of the *Fall-Memorial* title page. It is noteworthy however, that when the *Memorial* was suppressed, the *Fall* itself was released with the same Day title page compartment as before, allowing this work to speak something of Baldwin's prohibited message to a Marian audience. It alone escaped the suppression of the *Memorial* in Mary's reign to tell its ingenious tale.

102. On October 16, 1554, in the month Parliament met to discuss full reconciliation with Rome, Henry Machyn wrote, "Cam rydyng owt of Northfolke on[e] John Day prynter and ys servand, and a prest, and an odur prynter, for pryntyng of noythy bokes to the Towre" (Nichols, *Diary of Henry Machyn*, 72).

103. This would be the only opportunity Baldwin would have to signal his views on religious issues. He carefully avoids any direct engagement with religious concerns in the narratives or prose links of the *Memorial*, no doubt in order to ensure that this work of aboveground literature would not be immediately condemned as heretical.

CHAPTER TWO

The Consolation of Tragedy: "Edmund Duke of Somerset," "Humfrey Duke of Gloucester," and the Fall of the "Good Duke" of Somerset

In the *Memorial-Mirror* tragedy "How Thomas Montague the earle of Salysbury in the middes of his glory, was chaunceably slayne with a piece of ordinaunce," Salisbury's ghost begins his narrative with a lengthy execration of the way the world typically remembers well-intentioned but unsuccessful men. "A goodly thing is surely good reporte," he declares; too often, however, "we find opprest / By foule defame those that deserve it best" (143). "How many shall we find," he continues,

> For vertues sake with infamy opprest?
> How many agayn through helpe of fortune blind,
> For yll attemptes atchiued, with honour blest?
> Succes is wurst ofttimes whan cause is best,
> Therefore say I: god send them sory happes,
> That iudge the causes by their after clappes. (144)

Salisbury directs Baldwin's attention specifically to the case of his father, John, Lord Montague (or Montacute), a man whose condemnation for treason still torments Salisbury even in the afterlife.[1] Montague, Salisbury explains, undertook in the wake of King Richard II's deposition to slay Richard's supplanter, "erle Henry [Henry IV], king agaynst all lawes." His attempt, however, was betrayed before it could be undertaken, and Montague

1. By agreement of the authors, all but one of the ghosts of the *Memorial* and 1559 *Mirror* address their complaints directly to Baldwin. The exception is John Skelton's Edward IV, whose poem was composed decades before the *Memorial* was compiled.

was executed for plotting treason. Despite his condemnation, Salisbury insists, his father was never a traitor to his king. In opposing "erle Henry," Montague sought only virtuous, laudable ends: to save the life of the lawful ruler, Richard II, and to return England's "true heires to right." Yet while Montague's noble "cause doth clayme eternal fame," the failure of that cause (and Montague's execution for treason) ensured that Montague's memory would be ever after unjustly relegated to "the dounghill of defame." One must therefore never judge a man's worth by his ultimate success or failure in life, Salisbury concludes, for success is solely in the hands of blind fortune, the "cause of all distresse." Instead, "the cause and not the casual spede, / Is to be wayed in euery kinde of dede," and a man's intentions and not his actual achievements must be the only bases on which one should establish his posthumous "reporte" (144–46).

Nevertheless, even in insisting that readers dwell on his father's good intentions and ascribe the ultimate outcomes of all human endeavors to "fortune blind," Salisbury reveals that he cannot fully free himself from the doubts generated by his father's untimely, ignominious demise (144). In confronting his father's end, Salisbury finds himself forced to admit that Montague planned to use illegitimate, violent means ("rigor") to accomplish his laudable goals and that "God hateth rigor though it furder right." "Who furdereth right is not therby excused," Salisbury continues, "If through the same he do sum other wrong: / To every vice due guerdon doth belong" (145). It is for this reason that Salisbury is unable to dismiss from his mind the melancholy suspicion that God himself allowed Montague's death as punishment for the violent methods by which he sought to pursue his cause. Still, such doubts about the rectitude of Montague's means, Salisbury insists, should not blind readers to the virtue of his undertaking. Salisbury thus beseeches Baldwin to "waye the cause, / And prayse my father as he doth deserue." No matter what his faults or failings, Lord Montague must always be remembered as a good man, one worthy of veneration for his fierce and unwavering devotion to his monarch and to "right" (144).

Salisbury's lengthy consideration of his father's legacy accomplishes several purposes. It reminds readers that worldly success or failure often bears no relation to the virtue of the action attempted or of the person attempting that action. It urges readers to judge the men and women of the past not on their actual achievements, which are ever in the hands of "fortune blind," but on the intentions with which they undertook their acts. Finally, and most important, this revisionary account of his father's tarnished legacy allows Salisbury, still suffering from his father's shameful end, to contest the legacy with which Montague's memory had been burdened, to exonerate his father from the charges of malice and treason laid against him, and even to supply means by which readers might come to laud this well-intentioned but unjustly maligned man. Such attempts to rehabilitate his father's reputation cannot, of course, change the manner of Montague's death or erase the painful knowledge that he employed desperate means to achieve his laudable ends; it can, however, offer Salisbury a sense of personal comfort in proving to at least one man, William Baldwin, that his beloved father was never the villain the world holds him to be but a good man ever devoted to the service of "right."

Salisbury's attempt to rehabilitate his father's reputation, even in the face of his own troubling doubts about Montague's end, displays in microcosm the rehabilitative project of many of the most important poems of *A Memorial of suche Princes*, which seek to provide readers with models for coming to terms with the troubling, even traumatic career of the fallen evangelical hero Edward Seymour, Duke of Somerset. The goal of the authors is to exonerate Seymour, as much as possible, from the charges of crime, incompetence, and even sin laid against him during his life; to "rewrite" the dismal legacy of his time in power; and to lead readers to indict those men and women whom the authors hold to be truly to blame for the manifest disasters that afflicted the "good Duke" of Somerset. Like Salisbury's, the *Memorial* authors' project in these poems is above all to offer psychological consolation to those who were still in anguish over the loss of the once glorious Protector and who desperately sought means to explain the painful series of events that led to their former hero's fall from power and, later, to his untimely, humiliating death.

This chapter examines two such poems, each by *Memorial* author George Ferrers and each thought to have been included in or intended for *A Memorial of suche Princes*, "The tragedie of Edmund duke of Somerset, slayne at the first battayle at Saynct Albanes, in the tyme of Henrye the sixte" and "How Hvmfrey Plantagenet Duke of Glocester Protector of England, during the minoritie of his Nephue kinge Henrye the sixt, (commenlye called the good Duke) by practise of enemies was brought to confusion."[2] Through these fictionally shaped, topically applicable exemplary tragedies, Ferrers creates consolatory models for interpreting some of the most troubling occurrences of Edward Seymour's career. By evoking readers' memories of the

2. "Humfrey Duke of Gloucester" appears to have been part of the suppressed 1554 *Memorial.* "Edmund Duke of Somerset," by contrast, was intended for the *Memorial* but not completed until after its prohibition. At some point in Mary's reign, Baldwin preserved this poem in a manuscript comprising tragedies that he had gathered in the wake of his first collection's suppression, with the intention of placing it among the original gathering of *Memorial* poems at some future date (244, 387). For the complicated composition and printing history of these two works, see the appendix.

worst tragedies of Seymour's last years, Ferrers seeks to suggest comforting explanations for the tragic setbacks that plagued the "good Duke" in 1549 and after, explanations that could account for the failure of Seymour as England's leader and of his celebrated, supposedly divinely sanctioned reformist policies. Ferrers pursues two goals in shaping these poems as he does. First, he aims to rehabilitate the tarnished reputation of the fallen Lord Protector and revalidate his former admirers' faith in him and in his ideals, thereby rebuilding the confidence that had become shaken by the disturbing implications of Seymour's loss and the world's seeming repudiation of all for which he stood. Second, Ferrers guides Seymour's former followers to place blame on those who, he suggests, were truly responsible for Seymour's suffering. Through the allusive, exemplary content of "Edmund Duke of Somerset" and "Humfrey Duke of Gloucester," Ferrers urges readers to recall the fallen Protector not as a failure or a criminal but above all as a well-meaning yet tragically afflicted man, one under whose rule justice, godliness, and "glory might have growen" had he not unjustly fallen victim to "yll Fortune" and the undeserved malice of others (401, 388).

"Edmund Duke of Somerset"

In Ferrers's "The Tragedie of Edmund Duke of Somerset," Edmund Beauford (or Beaufort), Duke of Somerset (d. 1455), returns from the dead to offer an anguished account of his role in the series of disastrous events that occurred during the middle period of King Henry VI's reign (ca. 1447–1455).[3] Somerset begins by ruefully acknowledging that during his life ill fortune dogged all his actions. Despite his good intentions and his rise to chief subject in the realm, all that he attempted ultimately resulted in tragedy. His most costly decision was his consent in the death of his cousin Humfrey, Duke of Gloucester (d. 1447), the king's uncle, the victim of a conspiracy of ambitious foes. To gain Somerset's consent, the devious plotter William Delapole, Marquess of Suffolk, persuaded Somerset that the innocent Humfrey was a traitor. Only later did Somerset come to realize that the former "faythful frende" whose death he permitted had in fact been guilty of no crime, a realization that continues to torture him even now in his ghostly state (400).

3. Although "Somerset" was the last of Ferrers's three such tragedies to be composed, I attend to it first, because its content focuses allusively on the earliest of the great disasters that afflicted Edward Seymour in King Edward's reign, namely, the controversial execution of his brother Thomas. Ferrers's other two tragedies touching on Edward Seymour, "Humfrey Duke of Gloucester" and "Syr Thomas of Wudstocke," allude chiefly to the later travails of the former Lord Protector and thus are considered after "Somerset."

After Gloucester's fall, Somerset became Henry VI's chief officer. He was opposed, however, by the Duke of York and several co-conspirators who sought supreme power in the realm. The conspirators put into motion an elaborate plot designed to drive Somerset from his high place near the king. Claiming that Somerset had misgoverned the country, the Yorkists provoked a popular uprising (Jack Cade's rebellion) in order to weaken Somerset's rule. At the same time, York and his allies spread lies about Somerset's governance, painting his rule as corrupt and pernicious. Until Cade's revolt Somerset had been strong enough to counter the conspirators' opposition; so powerful did Cade's rebels prove to be, however, that to appease them, the king was forced to send Somerset to the Tower. After the rebellion was put down, Henry quickly freed Somerset, an act that provoked the Yorkists to use "open force" against the government. Joining with the powerful Earl of Warwick, York assembled an army and engaged the king's supporters at the town of St. Albans. There Somerset met Warwick "face to face" in battle and was cut down. Somerset's death spelled tragedy for King Henry and his loyal supporters. In the wake of St. Albans, Henry VI was "made a pray vnto his enemies handes." The Duke of York obtained personal rule over the weak, "childysh" monarch, and he and his fellow "traytours" eventually usurped all power in England, a move that allowed them to pillage the country and to oppress England's rightful leader (388–401).

In constructing this account of Somerset's life, Ferrers extensively alters his historical source, Edward Hall's *Vnion of the Two Noble and Illustre Fameliesof Lancastre & Yorke*, in order to parallel more closely the travails of Edward Seymour. Hall relates that the fifteenth-century Edmund of Somerset spent much of his adult life fighting in France; Ferrers, by contrast, barely acknowledges his protagonist's foreign career and mentions only in passing the most politically consequential event in the historical Somerset's life, his loss of English-held Normandy (389).[4] Instead Ferrers exaggerates the importance of Somerset's domestic career, completely omitting Queen Margaret's and the Duke of Suffolk's period of ascendancy in English politics (1447–1450) in order to suggest falsely that Somerset lost supreme power in Henry's government almost immediately after Gloucester's death (394).[5] Elsewhere Ferrers asserts that King Henry sent Somerset to the Tower during Cade's

4. Hall, "Henry VI," in *Vnion of the Two Noble and Illustre Families*, fol. 74r. Since Hall begins new foliation in his chronicle at the beginning of each new king's reign, passages in Hall's work are cited both by section name (e.g., "Henry VI") and by folio number.

5. In fact Somerset spent almost all of the first three years after Gloucester's death fighting in France.

rebellion, when in fact the historical Somerset was not even in England during the revolt (June–July 1450).[6] Likewise Ferrers refers to the middle years of Henry VI's reign, when the king was in his mid-twenties, as if they were a period of a king's minority and as if the Duke of Somerset and not King Henry had been England's chief leader.[7] Finally, Ferrers compresses and alters the chronology of the political setbacks Somerset experienced between 1447 and 1455. He presents the death of the king's uncle, the popular rebellion, the dissemination of slanderous complaints against Somerset's government, Somerset's removal from power, his imprisonment, and, after his release, his death brought about by his enemy the Earl of Warwick (Richard Neville) as if they occurred successively during a brief period of time and not over a period of several years.

In its highly altered details Ferrers's "historical" narrative conjures up thoughts not of Henry VI's reign but of the period of King Edward VI's minority, when the sixteenth-century Duke of Somerset (Edward Seymour), like Ferrers's fifteenth-century Duke of Somerset (Edmund Beauford), faced a popular rebellion, the opposition of powerful nobles, charges of corruption and misrule, imprisonment in the Tower, and, finally, death at the hands—so it was believed—of the Earl of Warwick (John Dudley).

Similarly, Ferrers adapts the Gloucester of Hall's chronicle to evoke strong memories of the last years of Edward Seymour's brother Thomas. In "Somerset," Humfrey of Gloucester (who, like Thomas Seymour, was the king's uncle and a near kinsman of the Duke of Somerset) is accused of treason, a charge unprecedented in Ferrers's source but the very accusation brought against Thomas Seymour in 1549.[8] Furthermore, the poem insists on an unhistorical friendship between Gloucester and Somerset and falsely claims

6. Hall, "Henry VI," fols. 77r–79r (Cade's rebellion), 85v–86r (Somerset sent to the Tower; his release provokes York to assemble an army). Ferrers also draws on Hall, "Henry VI," fol. 81r–v, for events that he unhistorically conflates with those of Cade's revolt. See also Wolffe, *Henry VI*, 240, 276. Furthermore, as Hall notes, Henry VI was "sicke" (i.e., insane) at the time of Somerset's crucial arrest and thus had no hand in it (Hall, "Henry VI," fol. 85v; Wolffe, *Henry VI*, 276).

7. Ferrers misapplies the biblical text "Ve terrae illi cuius rex est puer" ("Woe to the land whereof a chylde is head") to this time and describes Henry as "childysh" in order to speak of this period of Henry's reign as if it were that of a minor (*Mirror*, 391). Ferrers further downplays the importance of Queen Margaret's continuing influence in the ruling of the country during Somerset's ascendancy in order to make Somerset appear more powerful.

8. According to Hall, Gloucester's enemies accused him of enriching himself at the king's expense and of showing too much leniency to condemned criminals—but not of treason (Hall, "Henry VI," fol. 69r). Furthermore, Hall makes it clear that Gloucester died under suspicious circumstances during the time he was held prisoner by his enemies. However, to suggest better Thomas Seymour's execution, Ferrers speaks of Gloucester's death almost as if it were an official government action, one to which Somerset gave his consent not as a co-conspirator but as a government official who needed to be consulted (*Mirror*, 401).

that Somerset took no active part in bringing Humfrey to his death, when in fact the historical Somerset was a member of the Beauford (or Beaufort) family, the clan whose members were among Gloucester's most ferocious enemies. Far from having no active hand in Gloucester's downfall, Somerset was among those who arrested Gloucester at Bury and brought him to the confinement in which he was shortly after found dead.[9] By these means, Ferrers's Gloucester recalls not the historical Humfrey but the popular image of Thomas Seymour, a noble who had been a close ally of his brother in Henry VIII's reign and whose attainder and execution were arranged (at least overtly) by men other than Protector Somerset. Likewise, Ferrers's claim that Gloucester's death had an immediate and decisive impact on Somerset's career is inapplicable to the historical Somerset, although it does suggest the widely held mid-Tudor belief that there was a causal relation between Thomas's troubles and those suffered shortly thereafter by Edward Seymour.[10]

Just as Ferrers shapes the narrative details of "Somerset" to suggest Edward Seymour's last years, so he shapes the moral commentary on his protagonist's career to suggest new, exculpatory explanations for Seymour's troubling actions and setbacks in the *annus horribilis* of 1549. The questions that the ghostly Edmund Beauford seeks to answer about his own life are those Edward Seymour's former followers wished to answer about their hero's: How could such a good man have permitted the death of his innocent, virtuous kinsman? Why did his government collapse so quickly, and why, despite all his efforts, was his king "conquered" by his worst enemy (in Beauford's case, the Duke of York; in Edward Seymour's case, John Dudley)? Why did his well-intentioned political actions end only in failure? Ferrers's exemplary poem allows Seymour's pained followers to revisit the time of Seymour's first troubles, to confront them in displaced form, and to begin to lay to rest the doubts that had plagued them for so long.

Edward Seymour and the Death of Thomas Seymour

Much of Ferrers's poem is dedicated to one seemingly small event in Edmund Beauford's career, his mistaken consent to the death of the king's uncle, Humfrey Duke of Gloucester. Through his account of Somerset's relations with his cousin Humfrey, Ferrers evokes for readers the first and, for many of

9. Wolffe, *Henry VI*, 131. In fact Ferrers identifies Edmund Beauford as one of Humfrey's *enemies* in the poem "Humfrey Duke of Gloucester" (identifying him by his earlier title, Marquess of Dorset), since it suited no allusive purpose in that poem to alter the historical record (*Mirror*, 456, l. 352).

10. Stow, *Summarie of Englyshe Chronicles*, fol. 210v; Thomas Cooper, *Coopers Chronicle*, fol. 344r; Grafton, *Grafton's Chronicle*, 2:506; Foxe, *Actes and Monuments*, 1317, 1323.

Edward Seymour's partisans, the most troubling of all the disastrous events of 1549, the arrest, attainder, and execution for treason of the Protector's brother, Lord Admiral Thomas Seymour (ca. 1509–1549).

In the last years of his life Thomas Seymour was a charismatic, popular, but extremely ambitious and frustrated man. At the beginning of his nephew King Edward's reign (January 1547), Thomas had expected to receive the position of Governor of the King's Body, one of the two chief offices in a minor king's government. Instead, both that position and the office of Protector of the Realm were given to Edward Seymour. Envious of his elder brother's power, Thomas worked over the next two years to undermine Edward's authority and to strengthen his own. Matters came to a head in late 1548, when the Privy Council learned that Thomas was fortifying Holt Castle in what seemed to be preparation for a bid to wrest control over King Edward from the Protector. On January 17, 1549, Edward Seymour and the Council ordered Thomas's arrest on a charge of treason. Privy Councilors Thomas Wriothesley and Sir Richard Rich constructed a case against the younger Seymour that moved the Council to enter against him a bill of attainder. In February the House of Lords voted unanimously to attaint Thomas Seymour, while the House of Commons, less certain of his guilt, "very much debated and argued" the charges before they too, after instruction by the chief legal men of the realm, voted to condemn him. Thomas Seymour was executed less than a month after his attainder.[11]

Modern studies have shown that Thomas Seymour was indeed plotting against his brother. Nevertheless, the case brought against him was legally weak, and many at the time found his condemnation by attainder rather than by trial to be highly suspicious.[12] Most mid-Tudor observers could not believe that Thomas, a military hero who had been the husband of Henry VIII's widow, the pious Queen Catherine Parr, and who was understood to be well loved by King Edward, could ever contemplate the death of his "dear" nephew. Furthermore, people were horrified by the penalty the Lord Admiral received. For many, Protector Somerset's permitting his own brother's execution was an act of profoundly troubling severity.[13]

11.Bernard, "Downfall of Thomas Seymour," 217–28; Jordan, *Edward VI: The Young King*, 374–77; Bindoff, *History of Parliament*, 3:301.

12. Jordan, *Edward VI: The Young King*, 377, 381; Dasent et al., *Acts of the Privy Council*, 2:252. Judgment by bill of attainder rather than by open trial meant that Thomas Seymour was never heard in his own defense—a fact that disturbed many observers.

13. See, for instance, Crowley, *Epitome of Cronicles*, sig. 4D4v; Jordan, *Edward VI: The Young King*, 381. Most of the Protestants who had revered Edward Seymour for his religious reforms had also revered Thomas Seymour and his wife, Catherine Parr, for their important patronage of Protestant writers and preachers. See Robinson, *Original Letters*, 1:477.

In this climate of confusion and anger, many blamed not Thomas for his downfall but his brother the Protector. During and after Thomas's troubles, Edward Seymour was accused of "extreme hatred" for his brother, a hatred fanned by several public instances of acrimony between the two men and their wives that flared during the Protectorate. People observed that it was the Protector's rule that Thomas had been accused of challenging, that the case against Thomas had been legally weak, and that it was only with Protector Somerset's full permission that Thomas could have been executed.[14] Despite Edward Seymour's attempts to distance himself publicly from the proceedings against his brother, Thomas's execution resulted in "grave, perhaps irreparable, damage to Somerset's reputation and position." To the consternation of the Protector's followers, many in England proclaimed the execution a sin and labeled the Protector a fratricide, accusing him of one of the most horrible crimes in the Tudor imagination.[15] Writing toward the end of Edward's reign, the Catholic poet George Cavendish described Thomas Seymour as an innocent man made martyr to his own brother's "ambycyous disdayn." Out of "malice and dispight," Cavendish charged, Edward Seymour had falsely accused the virtuous Thomas of a treasonous attempt to seize control of the government, "hyme self well knowyng / it was not so."[16] Similarly, John Foxe identified the former Protector, otherwise one of his greatest heroes, as the man responsible for his brother's execution. In his *Actes and Monuments*, John Foxe declared that Edward Seymour had "blotted" or "darkened" his soul with a terrible "spot of vice" when he allowed his brother to be executed. Like many other Protestant observers, Foxe felt constrained to interpret Edward Seymour's own death three years later as divine punishment for Thomas's execution: "credible it is," wrote Foxe, "that the sayd duke, in suffryng or procuring this death of his brother, not onely endamaged hym self, & weakened his own power, but also prouoked [the] chastisement of Gods scourge and rod, which dyd so light vpon hym."[17]

As a man with ties of patronage and perhaps even friendship to both Seymour brothers, Ferrers was touched personally by Thomas's fall and Edward

14. Many writers noted the "extreme hatred" that flared between the brothers. See, among others, Foxe, *Actes and Monuments*, 1317; Stow, *Summarie of Englyshe Chronicles*, fol. 210v; Thomas Cooper, *Coopers Chronicle*, fol. 344r; Grafton, *Abridgement of Chronicles*, sig. S8v.

15. Jordan, *Edward VI: The Young King*, 381; Robinson, *Original Letters*, 2:735.

16. Cavendish, *Metrical Visions*, 97, 99, 107.

17. Foxe, *Actes and Monuments*, 132[2] (page 1322 is misprinted as 1323 in the copy owned by the Huntington Library); see also Robinson, *Original Letters*, 2:735; Thomas Cooper, *Coopers Chronicle*, fol. 353v.

Seymour's role in it.[18] Furthermore, as a member of the Parliament charged with voting on Thomas's attainder, Ferrers must have wrestled deeply with the same questions surrounding Thomas's execution that for long after haunted Edward Seymour's supporters. Both for his own and for others' psychological well-being, Ferrers needed to return to this traumatic time, to renarrate and "remoralize" the recent past in order to offer convincing, psychologically acceptable explanations for Thomas's death and for Edward Seymour's baffling actions.

In examining "Edward Duke of Somerset," it is important to note first what Ferrers does *not* suggest in this poem's narrative. In offering reasons for Somerset's role in Gloucester's death, Ferrers excludes any that might evoke the dominant Marian explanations for Thomas Seymour's execution, those widely circulated accounts that identified either Thomas's attempted treason or his brother's "extreme hatred" as the cause of Thomas's death. "Somerset" makes it clear that the executed Duke Humfrey was never a traitor: Gloucester was all along, the poem relates, "the duke innocent" and the very "proppe" of, not enemy to, Henry VI's government (390). Likewise, "Somerset" excludes "extreme hatred" between Somerset and Gloucester as a cause for Gloucester's demise. Far from expressing hostility to his kinsman, Somerset speaks of Gloucester in loving terms, calling him "my cosyn my refuge and staye" and a "faythful frende" whose loss still tortures his memory (390, 400).[19]

Instead Ferrers shows how Edward Seymour's admirers might acknowledge the Protector's undeniable hand in Thomas's demise yet still preserve their hero's reputation for rectitude. In the poem, the grieving Duke of Somerset admits that he played a role in Gloucester's death, but he ascribes all

18. Ferrers became acquainted with Thomas Seymour at least as early as their time together in Henry VIII's household (Ferrers as a page of the chamber, Seymour as a gentleman of the Privy Chamber; see Bindoff, *History of Parliament*, 3:297, 2:130). Ferrers seems to have been on good terms with Thomas Seymour in Edward's reign, for it was almost certainly through Thomas's assistance that Ferrers gained a seat in Edward VI's first Parliament (November 1547–April 1552). Ferrers represented the borough of Cirencester (Gloucestershire), a moribund franchise that had been revived specifically for Thomas Seymour, who was the most important landowner in the area. Cirencester had not sent representatives to Parliament since the fourteenth century and, after Thomas Seymour's death, was to send no more until Elizabeth's reign (Bindoff, *History of Parliament*, 1:95, 2:130, 3:300).

19. A single line about Somerset's possibly being "held" at one time by "priuie spite" is the only suggestion of the animosity the two brothers had felt toward each other, and Ferrers phrases this reference only to dismiss it as a motivating force in Somerset's consent (*Mirror*, 401). The conditional clause "If priuie spyte at any time me helde" permits readers neither to fix a particular time when Somerset was supposedly filled with spite nor even to be certain that Somerset was ever in that condition at all.

guilt for that role to another—the crafty and malicious Marquess of Suffolk, who falsely accused Gloucester of treason and who led Somerset, through a series of lies, tragically to permit Gloucester's death:

> And so I was abusde and other moe
> By Suffolkes sleyghtes, who sought to please the quene,
> Forecasting not the miserye and woe
> Whych thereof came, and soone was after sene:
> With glosing tonge he made vs fooles to weene,
> That Humfrey dyd to Englandes crowne aspyre,
> Which to prevent, his death they dyd conspyre. (400–401)

No matter what events might otherwise have suggested, Somerset insists, he was an innocent party in the moves against Gloucester. Somerset never acted with malice toward his cousin; instead he ascribes all evil intentions to Suffolk and declares himself to have been in fact one of Suffolk's chief *victims*, a man preyed upon by that devious villain just as Gloucester was.

Through his description of the "glosing" Suffolk, Ferrers leads readers to identify a figure other than Seymour as the true guilty party in the matter of Thomas's execution, namely, Thomas Wriothesley, Earl of Southampton, the prominent Anglo-Catholic noble who convinced England's leaders that Thomas sought to harm King Edward and seize the crown. Wriothesley took an active, highly visible role in Thomas Seymour's condemnation. He supplied personal evidence of Thomas's alleged treason, led the investigation into Thomas's actions on behalf of the Council, and constructed the notorious, widely discounted formal case that led to Thomas's execution.[20] With Ferrers's prompting, readers could quickly come to suspect Wriothesley of dealing falsely in the matter of Thomas Seymour. Even before his investigation into Thomas's actions, Wriothesley had been widely vilified as a malicious, duplicitous, and bloodthirsty man, one well known to be a fierce enemy of the Seymours and their evangelical beliefs. Under Henry VIII, Wriothesley clashed numerous times with Edward Seymour. In fact Wriothesley undertook his most notorious act, the racking of Anne Askew in 1546, in part to compel Askew to implicate Edward Seymour's wife in her heresy. Upon Henry's death, Thomas Seymour called for Wriothesley to "be carried off at once to the Tower," and his demand must have seemed justified when, just days later, Wriothesley alone openly opposed Edward Seymour's

20. Jordan, *Edward VI: The Young King*, 382; Hoak, *King's Council*, 50, 239; Gibbons, *Political Career of Thomas Wriothesley*, 224–25, 230–31.

elevation to the office of Protector.[21] Two years later (and within months of Thomas's death), Wriothesley took a leading role in the coup that deposed Edward Seymour from office. Given Wriothesley's well-known animosity toward both Seymour brothers, his reputation for malice and plotting, the widespread popular rejection of his charges of treason against Thomas, and his later move against Edward Seymour, the Protector's former supporters could accept that the treason case created by Wriothesley was, as so many already believed, a tissue of lies, and that its author, and not the innocent, deceived Edward Seymour, was the true malefactor in the Thomas Seymour affair.

In leading readers to ascribe the fateful decision to attaint Thomas to the machinations of one of the Seymours' chief enemies, Ferrers's poem shares in the conspiratorial logic of other mid-Tudor accounts of Thomas Seymour's troubles, which blamed the lies and provocations of various covert foes for the Seymour brothers' sudden explosion of mutual enmity and suspicion.[22] Yet in echoing the logic of existing English beliefs about "conspiracies" against Edward and Thomas Seymour, Ferrers does not merely endorse such accounts but builds on and refines them. Most mid-Tudor narratives blaming others for creating the animosity between Thomas and Edward Seymour still execrated Edward for acting upon that animosity by maliciously executing his brother.[23] By contrast, Ferrers's narrative shows readers how to shift the blame for Thomas's execution entirely onto others and to construe Edward Seymour as but a passive bystander in his brother's demise. According to the poem, Somerset held no malice toward Gloucester nor did he ever raise a hand against him. Instead Somerset's "fault only consisted in

21. William Seymour, *Ordeal by Ambition*, 237; Gibbons, *Political Career of Thomas Wriothesley*, 8–9, 230; Jordan, *Edward VI: The Young King*, 70; *CSP, Span.*, 9:340. See also the discussion of Wriothesley in the section of this chapter on "Humfrey Duke of Gloucester." Wriothesley's partner in the racking of Anne Askew was Sir Richard Rich, who later would join Wriothesley in creating the treason case against Thomas Seymour. For Wriothesley's several clashes with Edward Seymour in Henry's and Edward's reigns, see Slavin, "Fall of Lord Chancellor Wriothesley," 270, 278, 284; Foxe, *Actes and Monuments*, 1209; *CSP, Span.*, 8:556, 9:100, 340; Brewer et al., *Letters and Papers*, vol. 21, pt. 2, 387; Scarisbrick, *Henry VIII*, 478.

22. Most of these conspiracy theories centered on Edward Seymour's seeming ally John Dudley, Earl of Warwick, and his alleged covert creation of divisions between the two brothers (Hoak, *King's Council*, 239–40). For the centrality of conspiracy beliefs to the thinking of mid-Tudor evangelicals, see Riordan and Ryrie, "Stephen Gardiner." See also Brigden, *London and the Reformation*, 352–55.

23. See, for instance, Cavendish, *Metrical Visions*, 99, 107. See also the comments contained in the anonymous Elizabethan historical narrative "A 'Journall' of Matters of State" (BL Add. MS 48023, fols. 350–69) and in the anonymous account of Seymour's travails titled "Certayne brife notes of the controversy between the dukes [sic] of Somerset and the duke of Nor[t]humberland" (BL Add. MS 48126, fols. 6–16), printed in *Religion, Politics, and Society in Sixteenth-Century England*, ed. Archer et al., 52–136, esp. 52–67, 123–25.

consent": a deceived Somerset permitted Suffolk to pursue Gloucester's life, but he took no active part in that pursuit himself (400).[24] The poem further suggests that Somerset's "fault" arose not from malice but from his characteristic *virtue*. According to "Somerset," Duke Edmund made his decision to permit Gloucester's death only with the most admirable of intentions. Somerset honestly feared that "Humfrey dyd to Englandes crowne aspyre," and for that reason alone he consented not to stand in Suffolk's way. Somerset's chief concern during his life was the safety of Henry VI: "Constant I was in my Prynces quarell," Somerset recalls, "To dye or lyve and [I] spared for no parell" (401). In permitting Gloucester's death, Somerset believed that he was pursuing his highest duty, the protection of his king. Such was his dedication that he pursued that duty even at the personal cost of losing a kinsman and former "faythful frende."

In applying this account to the similar events of Edward Seymour's last year in office, readers are meant to understand Seymour's part in his brother's death as one of mere "consent" to the actions of others, and they are likewise to construe the ethical nature of Seymour's decision as they do Somerset's: as an expression of Seymour's loyalty to his nephew King Edward and thus as more evidence of the virtue that his followers so fervently believed composed the core of his character. In fact this interpretation would be particularly attractive to Seymour's followers precisely because it would present itself to them not as speculative rationalization but as recent memory. Somerset's rhetoric of passive consent, many would have recalled, was Edward Seymour's own during Thomas's travails. Privately the Protector had played a major role in arranging Thomas's attainder; publicly, however, Seymour presented himself as a grieving man who had been driven reluctantly to assent to the fatal decisions of others. Thus, when he appeared before King Edward with the Privy Council to ask for the bill of attainder against Thomas, Seymour claimed that he came to King Edward with the other Councilors only because he "coulde not resist nor wolde not be against the Lordes [of the Privy Council's] request."[25] He had played no role in the decision to request an attainder bill, his rhetoric implied; rather it was other Privy Councilors who had decided Thomas's fate.

Similarly, Somerset's virtuous placing of duty over familial affection in the poem recalls Seymour's rhetoric in explaining why he had allowed the bill of attainder to be brought against his brother. Seymour declared in 1549 that he

24. Cf. Grafton, *Grafton's Chronicle*, 2:529.

25. Dasent et al., *Acts of the Privy Council*, 2:257. Seymour similarly managed to avoid taking an overt part in parliamentary deliberations over Thomas's fate by playing the role of the reluctant, grieving brother (ibid., 2:260, 261).

had done so only because he did "rather regarde his bounden dewtie to the Kinges majestie and the Crowne of Englande [more] than his owne sonne or brother, and did wey more his allegiaunce then his bloode."[26] At that time, so strong were the imputations of jealousy between the two brothers that few were able to accept this justification. Revisited five years later, however, and inserted into a believable conspiracy narrative, Seymour's words could be recalled, reevaluated, and accepted by his former partisans as the most "reasonable" explanations for Seymour's heretofore disturbingly inexplicable behavior.[27] Using Ferrers's exemplary narrative as a guide, Seymour's admirers could derive consolation from exonerating their late hero in their own minds from the terrible charge of malicious fratricide that had so long haunted his legacy.

The 1549 Risings and the End of the Protectorate

"Somerset" further provides readers with means to exonerate Seymour from guilt in the next great matter for which he was widely condemned, the ferocious rural risings that spread quickly in the months after Thomas Seymour's death. If Thomas's execution dealt a crippling blow to Edward Seymour's personal reputation, these outbreaks of spring and summer 1549 caused equally extensive damage to Seymour's political standing. The first stirrings of revolt occurred within a month of Thomas Seymour's death; by May, counties all across England were experiencing violent unrest. Virtually every shire suffered some sort of upset, with the most organized incidents afflicting Devon, Cornwall, and Norfolk. The ferocity of these disturbances caught the government completely off guard. England's leaders watched in horror as

26. Ibid., 2:257.

27. Even the poem's admissions that Somerset suffered from "want of foresight" and other flaws that led him into his fatal consent, can be construed by readers in a positive light. In the poem, Somerset castigates the "folly" of his characteristic "overlight credence," yet he also castigates the "noughty time" of Henry's reign that turned this single character trait into such a deadly liability (390, 401). When Somerset describes himself as a "simple" man prone to be too easily deceived, his words recall the explanation for Seymour's "deception" by his political enemies later taken up by admirers such as John Foxe. Somerset's character here evokes Seymour's reputation as a man of simple goodness, a man, in Foxe's characterization, so well meaning and innocent that he was "vtterly ignorant of al craft and deceit." To Seymour's admirers, it was his supposedly unworldly piety and sympathetic heart that led him to his godly reforms in the church and his solicitous care for the poor, yet these same qualities were said to have made him ever "more apt and ready to be deceyued than to deceiue." In the matter of Thomas's death, Foxe laments that Seymour had not been worldly enough to reject the lies of those "certayne, who soeuer they were," who led him eventually to hate his brother (Foxe, *Actes and Monuments*, 132[2]). For Foxe, Seymour was neither malicious nor incompetent but rather too purely innocent for this fallen world. Those reading of Somerset's "simple" nature and his tragic deception are to apply this poem's lessons to the fallen Edward Seymour. They are to construe Seymour's alleged gulling by Wriothesley as they do Somerset's "overlight credence": as a sign of the Protector's famous simple purity, a sign not of incompetence but of praiseworthy moral virtue.

rebels captured important towns and even appeared to encroach on London itself. By July matters had come to such a point that many in power feared it would be only days before they witnessed the complete dissolution of central authority in England.[28]

Modern scholars point to a host of causes for these rebellions. In the west (chiefly Devon and Cornwall), popular hostility to the new Edwardian prayer book provoked men and women of all classes to rise in protest. In all parts of England, hatred of enclosed lands, high rents, and the perception that local justices of the peace were unwilling to mete out justice equally to all spurred rioters. Various local feuds and personal grievances further fanned the flames.[29]

Despite this myriad of causes, the English government in 1549 charged a single man with creating *all* of the numerous and heterogeneous risings in England: Edward Seymour, Duke of Somerset. In the wake of Seymour's deposition, the Privy Council claimed that Seymour's divisive agrarian reform policies were the true catalysts of the rural revolts. Furthermore, it declared that Seymour's alleged public denunciations of England's nobles and gentlemen as "the only causes of the derth of things" directly spurred rioters to seek to "reform things the[m]selues." As the rebellions raged, the Council's charges continued, Seymour offered encouragement to the rebels by speaking in favor of their demands, by denouncing the landowning classes of England, and by restraining England's nobles from taking effective action to subdue the riots. Finally, and most damagingly, the articles declared that while pretending to oppose the risings, Seymour actually "did comfort and encourage diuers of the said rebels, by giuing to them diuers summes of [his] own money, and by promising to diuers of them fees, rewards, and seruices."[30]

When, to save his own life, Seymour subscribed to these damning charges, he ensured that they would forever remain a part of parliamentary and Council records. Seymour's acceptance of the articles officially recast his supposedly just and compassionate policies of economic reform as in reality covert mechanisms for encouraging popular revolution. The formerly celebratory accounts of Seymour's Protectorate as dedicated to bringing England to a new, godly order of peace and fraternal love between the classes were now undercut by Seymour's "confession" that his government's policies had been in truth devoted to sowing seeds of class hatred and to destroying altogether the peaceful order of the realm. The rebellions and Seymour's forced submis-

28. Jordan, *Edward VI: The Young King*, 440–41.
29. Bush, *Government Policy*, 84–99; J. P. Cooper, *Propaganda and the Tudor State*, 58–68.
30. See articles 10–17 and article 20 in Stow, *Annales* (1592), 1015–16.

sion severely damaged the former Protector's long-cultivated reputation as a wise and altruistic governor. Among his former admirers, the riots and the events surrounding Seymour's deposition called into question both the man they had once so venerated and the political ideals they had so fervently shared with him.

Through his account of Cade's rebellion and its aftermath, Ferrers urges readers to confront once more Seymour's tarnished political legacy. As with his handling of Gloucester's death, Ferrers excludes from his account of Cade's rising in "Somerset" anything that might lead readers to embrace the official charge that Seymour himself had brought the 1549 revolts upon England, thereby undermining his own government. As we have seen, Ferrers portrays Somerset throughout the poem as a well-meaning, virtuous leader, a man who did nothing in his governance of England that would have caused the people to rise against his rule of their own accord. The poem explains Cade's rebellion by identifying it as neither spontaneous nor popular in origin at all. Rather, "Somerset" insists, it was but one part of a calculated, far-reaching plot by the ambitious Duke of York to purge Somerset from power. As Somerset ruefully describes York's plan:

> So for the fyshe casting forth his net,
> The next point was in dryuing out his plat,
> Common doltes to cause furiously to fret,
> And to rebel, I can not tel for what,
> Requyring redres of this and of that:
> Who yf they speede, [York] standing at receyt,
> Graspe would the pray that he long dyd awayte. (395)

While the people who rose with Cade did have grievances (they required "redress of this and that"), none of those concerns, according to the poem, was coherent or pressing enough to justify a rebellion ("I can not tel for what" the people followed Cade, Somerset complains). Rather, the decision to rebel was made by malicious conspirators who whipped ignorant "doltes" into an irrational fury to serve their own ambitious ends.

Ferrers's unhistorical placement of Cade's revolt during Somerset's ascendancy and his insistence that this revolt was the product of a secret plot against England's chief officer provide a model by which readers might interpret anew the similar rebellion faced by Edward Seymour in 1549. It urges readers to accept a sinister conspiracy narrative in place of those painful official accounts that blamed the rebellions on Seymour's own conspiracies and misgovernment. As with his explanation of the Protector's role in Thomas Seymour's death, Ferrers does not ask readers to accept new, seemingly ad hoc arguments. Instead he builds his version of events on Seymour's and his supporters' own beliefs about the disturbances. Throughout the period of the 1549 risings, readers of "Somerset" would recall, Seymour and numerous others had publicly insisted that the revolts were neither popular nor spontaneous in origin but were the work of secret agitators, a cabal of "ranke Traytors" and "sedicious papists" who manipulated the people into serving their own malign ends. The commoners in revolt were "wonderfully abused," Seymour asserted, by "certen popyshe prests, whiche color all theyr doyngs with . . . sedytyous rumors" about the government in order to create rebellion. While these agents provacateurs spoke the language of economic redress and conservative Protestantism to the commons, their real purpose, Seymour and others warned, was "nothing ells but to subdue the people to the pope."[31] As the revolts spread, the existence of Roman Catholic conspirators behind the risings became for Seymour's supporters the dominant explanation for the unrest. In sermons, pamphlets, and other documents, men such as Thomas Cranmer and Philip Nichols decried the machinations of covert Catholic agitators in the west and the north and denounced the plot they perceived against Seymour's godly rule. Such conspiracy thinking guided Seymour even after the rebellions were suppressed, as his government continued in their wake to conduct searches for the Catholic agents it believed had been behind the recent revolts.[32]

Furthermore, like Somerset in the poem, Seymour and his partisans detected the hand of upper-class opponents behind these supposedly popular risings. Both during and after the disturbances, Seymour and various of his supporters charged several prominent religious conservatives with manipulating the rebels for their own ends, among them Sir Robert Southwell, Bishop Rugge of Norwich, Bishop Bonner of London, and the powerful Cornish magnates Sir Thomas and Sir John Arundell.[33] As the rebellions spread, Seymour's greatest fears of upper-class machinations centered on the most powerful religious conservative (and perceived Roman Catholic) of them all, Lady Mary Tudor. Seymour well knew that as sister to the king and heir to the throne, Mary was the most likely candidate to assume power

31. Grafton, *Grafton's Chronicle*, 2:517; Nicholas Pocock, *Troubles*, 16; Shagan, "Protector Somerset," 56. Somerset's rhetoric of "common doltes" foolishly tricked into rebellion recalls the Edwardian government's own frequent assertion that the commons were "by error seduced" and "ignorauntly led" into doing the bidding of lying papists and traitors. See, for instance, the government's address to the western rebels in Grafton, *Grafton's Chronicle*, 2:515–19.

32. Loach, *Edward VI*, 76–77; MacCullough, *Thomas Cranmer*, 436; Nichols, *Chronicle of the Grey Friars*, 61; Brigden, "Letters of Richard Scudamore," 87.

33. Rose-Troup, *Western Rebellion*, 351–52; Nicholas Pocock, *Troubles*, 26, 29, 38–39; "A 'Journall' of Matters of State," 58–59; Brigden, "Letters of Richard Scudamore," 90–91; Foxe, *Actes and Monuments*, 1273–[75] (the page numbers 1274 and 1275 are misprinted as 1318 and 1319 in the copy owned by the Huntington Library).

if the rebels were to bring down the Protectorate. Seymour was thus highly disturbed by the suspicious actions of Mary and those closely associated with her during the period of the revolts. He and others of the Privy Council could not help but note that Mary remained at her residence in the rebel center of Norfolk during the risings, despite the fury of the rioters around her, and that the rebels appeared consciously to spare her and her property from destruction. The fact that Mary openly defied the Edwardian Act of Uniformity, declaring it to be no law, and that she held several highly visible celebrations of the prohibited Mass each day during the risings seemed to the Council bids to signal her support for the rebels' challenge to the Protector's authority. Most worrisome of all were reports from the field that identified members of Mary's household and their servants as "chief in these commotions" against Seymour's government. When the Council demanded to question those accused, Mary allowed none of her servants to be interrogated and instead challenged the authority of the Council to have any say in her affairs. The suspicion that Mary and her supporters were behind the rapidly spreading risings was intense. Sir Thomas Smith, for one, described himself at the height of the risings as almost "destroyed" by his fear that Mary and "the Marians" were the real forces behind these stunningly successful revolts.[34] In the wake of Seymour's deposition, such plot narratives became obscured by the charge that Edward Seymour himself had been the catalyst and mainstay of the risings. Ferrers's poem, however, works to recall to readers these earlier conspiracy narratives, to revive them, and to move Seymour's former supporters to accept such beliefs once again as the best way to explain the baffling riots and thus to dismiss Seymour's responsibility for them, the charge that had so long troubled those who revered him.[35]

34. Knighton, *Calendar of State Papers, Domestic Series*, 126; *CSP, Span.*, 9:405, 407–8, 444; Loades, *Mary Tudor: A Life*, 145–49; Foxe, *Actes and Monuments*, 1289–90; Tytler, *England under the Reigns of Edward VI and Mary*, 1:188; Bindoff, *Ket's Rebellion*, 11. For Edwardian charges of a Catholic conspiracy behind both the western and northern risings in general and charges against Lady Mary and the "Marians" in particular, see Nicholas Pocock, *Troubles*, 146, 150–51; Foxe, *Actes and Monuments*, 1271; MacCulloch, "Kett's Rebellion in Context," 60–61, and "Kett's Rebellion in Context: A Rejoinder," 74–75; MacCulloch, *Thomas Cranmer*, 436–38, 451–52; *CSP, Span.*, 9:406–8, 444; Prescott, *Mary Tudor*, 121; Brigden, "Letters of Richard Scudamore," 87, 90–91. Tom Betteridge discusses the logic behind evangelicals' ascription of these risings to "papists" in *Literature and Politics in the English Reformation*, 95–96.

35. In Elizabeth's reign a plot narrative similar to that suggested by Ferrers became the basis of many evangelical authors' accounts of the 1549 risings. See, for instance, Foxe, *Actes and Monuments*, 1268; and Whetstone, *Censure of a Loyall Subiect*, 30. This interpretation even achieved official sanction through the 1570 "Homelie Against Rebellion," which taught that "the Byshop of Rome" himself planned the seemingly spontaneous 1549 risings (Bond, *"Certain Sermons or Homilies" (1547) and "A Homily Against Disobedience and Wilful Rebellion" (1570)*, 244).

The Deposition of Protector Somerset

Ferrers's poem further supplies means to explain the final and, to Seymour's supporters, the most stunning disaster of Seymour's Protectorate, the arrest, imprisonment, and deposition of the Lord Protector in October 1549. As we have seen, Seymour was driven from power on charges of misrule and corruption in office. Through its detailed description of York's conspiracy against Somerset, Ferrers's poem provides a model by which readers could contest those charges, condemn the supposedly upright officers who overthrew Seymour, and assert once more the rectitude and innocence of the long-maligned Lord Protector.

Ferrers has Somerset bitterly describe the Yorkist party's plot to undermine Somerset's authority by coupling Cade's rebellion with open, public denunciations of Somerset's alleged misgovernment. If these means indeed proved able to weaken his rule, Somerset recalls, the Yorkists planned

> by surmyse of sumthing pretended
> Such [men] to displace as they may well suspect
> Lyke to wythstand theyr practices entended,
> And in theyr roomes theyr banders to elect.
> The adverse party proudly to reiect.
> And then wyth reportes the simple to abuse,
> And when these helpes fayle, open force to vse. (395)

The Yorkists would justify their purge of Somerset and his allies from Henry VI's household by falsely claiming that the expelled men were "counsayle corrupt" about the king (394). With the last men around King Henry "lyke to wythstand" their machinations purged, the Yorkists could then freely pursue their bid to usurp the crown. Perhaps most gallingly, Somerset recalls, at each step in their scheme York and his allies would cloak their treachery in a pious rhetoric of concern for king and country, putting a "goodly face" on their corrupt bid for absolute power:

> So this Dukes traynes were covert and not seene,
> Which nought lesse meant, then he most pretended.
> Lyke to a serpent covert vnder greene,
> To the weale publycke seemed wholly bended:
> Zelous he was, and would have all thing mended,
> But by that mendment nothyng els he ment,
> But to be kyng, to that marke was his bent. (395–96)

This plot worked magnificently, as the virtuous Somerset was made an object of hate among the people, forced with his allies from power, imprisoned by the king, and ultimately killed by the Yorkist party.

By portraying Cade's revolt, the public charges of misrule, and Somerset's purge from power as all part of a single conspiracy, Ferrers leads readers to blame a similarly complex single plot for the disasters Edward Seymour endured in his last months in office. Readers are to see the coup leaders' actions in the wake of the rural risings not as the spontaneous response of virtuous officers outraged by the Protector's misrule but as the key step in a long-planned conspiracy against him.

Once again, Ferrers builds his suggested counternarrative on a foundation of Seymour's and his followers' own early beliefs. During his standoff with the London Lords, Seymour insisted both publicly and privately that the coup attempt was not a justifiable political act but a "most dangerous conspiracy," one constructed, like that of the Yorkists against Somerset, chiefly from "vayne l[ett]res and fals tales" maliciously designed to make him a hated figure.[36] "Somerset" urges readers to recall and accept such conspiratorial logic, to link it to the charges of conspiracy behind the rural revolts, and to use it to create a seamless plot narrative that could explain all of the opposition Seymour faced in his last months in power. Indeed, readers could discern many points of contact between the "conspiracy" behind the rural risings and the coup that drove Edward Seymour from power. Many observers at the time of the coup had understood the move to depose Seymour as the work of precisely the same sort of men who had fomented the recent rural risings—crypto-Catholic zealots who sought above all to return England to the papal fold.[37] Among the chief leaders of the October coup, in fact, were several of the same upper-class religious conservatives accused of assisting the rural rebels on behalf of Lady Mary. The Norfolk landowner Sir Robert Southwell, a Privy Councilor and prominent gentleman servant of Mary Tudor, had been accused of acting as a covert "author" of the Norfolk rebellions on the orders of "Lady Marie and her counsell."[38] Just months later Southwell took his place as one of the chief figures behind Seymour's deposition. The powerful Cornish gentleman Sir Thomas Arundell, cousin to the rebel leader Humphrey Arundell and the "Marian" most deeply suspected

36. Hughes and Larkin, *Tudor Royal Proclamations*, 1:483; Nicholas Pocock, *Troubles*, 82–83 (see also 79). In Mary's reign, John Ponet similarly revived Seymour's conspiracy charges as he indicted the coup leaders for "forgeing a great meany of false lettres a[n]d lies to make the Protectour hated" during the coup (Ponet, *Shorte Treatise*, sig. I3r).

37. While the chief coup leaders were likely Anglo-Catholic in sympathies, many evangelicals saw them as covert papists. For detailed discussions of the religiously conservative nature of the coup, see Hoak, *King's Council*, 241–58; and Loades, "Thomas Cranmer and John Dudley." For contemporary interpretations of the coup as a "popish" plot in particular, see Loach, *Edward VI*, 92–93; Robinson, *Original Letters*, 1:69–73, 2:464–65; Tytler, *England under the Reigns of Edward VI and Mary*, 1:209; Brigden, "Letters of Richard Scudamore," 97, 114.

38. "A 'Journall' of Matters of State," 58; MacCulloch, *Thomas Cranmer*, 451–52.

of active participation in the western risings, assumed a similar commanding role in Seymour's deposition, serving, it was said, as "cheafe councellor" to the coup leaders and as the man who allegedly united Dudley and the conservatives in the bid to depose the Protector.[39] Many understood even John Dudley to have been a Roman Catholic at the time of the revolt against Seymour, and some may have known that at the height of the risings Dudley joined with several of England's most powerful religious conservatives to approach Mary with a plan to overthrow the Protector.[40] Certainly readers could recall that it was the rural risings which allowed Dudley to gather the army he and the other coup leaders subsequently used to challenge Seymour. Most important, Seymour himself had publicly declared that the immediate goal of the October "conspirators" was precisely that of the perceived Marian plot behind the rural risings, "to make the lady Mary regent and pulle downe me from the protectorshipp." His replacement by Mary, Seymour warned his followers, was not an end in itself but a step by the conspirators toward their ultimate aim: the murder of the king and the seizing of complete power for themselves. "Thei do not seeke me but the king," Seymour warned, "for if he were in their ha[n]des and shode miscary, thei had that thei seeke."[41]

Though they were obscured in later years by Seymour's confessions and Dudley's decision to continue evangelical rule, Ferrers's poem urges readers to recall such earlier plot narratives surrounding the rural revolts and Seymour's deposition, to shape them into a single, coherent conspiracy, and to accept that account as the most believable explanation of how the revered Lord Protector suffered such a stunning, sudden loss of authority among the people, an almost universal loss of allegiance among the nobility, and, finally, complete loss of power and freedom in the wake of the coup.

John Dudley and the "Plot" against Edward Seymour

As we shall see, Ferrers uses the poem "Humfrey Duke of Gloucester" to lead readers to condemn primarily Edward Seymour's Anglo-Catholic enemies

39. For Southwell's alleged part in the summer risings and his leading role in the October coup, see MacCulloch, "Kett's Rebellion in Context: A Rejoinder," 74; MacCulloch, *Thomas Cranmer*, 437, 451–52; Ponet, *Shorte Treatise*, sig. I3r–v; Hoak, *King's Council*, 242. For the roles of Sir Thomas Arundell, his brother Sir John Arundell (another participant in the October coup), and their servants in the summer rebellions and in Seymour's deposition, see Bindoff, *History of Parliament*, 1:335–38; Rose-Troup, *Western Rebellion*, 351–52; Nicholas Pocock, *Troubles*, 26, 29, 38–39; *CSP, Span.*, 9:470; Ponet, *Shorte Treatise*, sig. I3v; Cavendish, *Metrical Visions*, 111 (for "cheafe councellor"), 210; Brigden, "Letters of Richard Scudamore," 89, 107, 114, 117; Jordan, *Chronicle* 19.

40. Brigden, *London and the Reformation*, 502–3. On the July communication concerning Seymour's deposition between Lady Mary and Dudley, Wriothesley, Fitzalan, and Paulet, see *CSP, Span.*, 9:445; and Berkman, "Van der Delft's Message."

41. "Certyane brife notes," 129–30.

for the Protector's deposition from office. He crafts "Somerset," by contrast, to direct readers chiefly to indict John Dudley for his role in arranging Seymour's deposition and death. Ferrers designs his Duke of York, the mastermind and chief beneficiary of Somerset's downfall, to evoke thoughts of Dudley, who, in the same manner as Ferrers's York in the wake of Somerset's fall, became England's preeminent leader after the deposition of his rival, who arranged the death of the Duke of Somerset, and who was popularly believed to have subsequently stolen from the land and the king and to have sought the crown for his own.[42] By the time of Mary's reign, John Dudley had become almost universally vilified. The "black legend" that grew up around him painted him as a bloodthirsty, devious climber, allowing mid-Tudor men and women to ascribe almost any crime to him. Ferrers builds on Dudley's dark reputation in "Somerset," urging readers to embrace beliefs about Dudley's conspiracies during Edward's reign and to use them to interpret all of Dudley's further moves against the fallen Protector and his allies in the wake of Seymour's fall from power.

Thus Ferrers shapes York's plan to "displace" Somerset's allies in Henry VI's household so as to recall the similar purge by Dudley and his fellow coup leaders of Seymour's chief adherents in the royal household following Seymour's deposition. The coup leaders justified their actions against Seymour's men by declaring that the expelled officers had served as Seymour's malign "instruments" of "yll gouernement" around the king. "Somerset," by contrast, seeks to rehabilitate the reputations of Seymour's supporters who were humiliatingly expelled from office, arrested, and sent to the Tower in the wake of his deposition. Readers are to understand the expulsion of Seymour's men in precisely the same way they understand York's purge of Somerset's men: not as a salutary bid to remove "counsayle corrupt from place about the kyng," as the official justification would have it, but instead as a devious scheme to remove the last honest men around the king, the only ones left "lyke to wythstand" the coup leaders' intended abuse of their monarch (394–95).[43]

42. See chapter 1.

43. Dasent et al., *Acts of the Privy Council*, 2:343, 344. For the replacement of Seymour's men with men loyal chiefly to John Dudley, see Hoak, "The King's Privy Chamber," 96–103; Hoak, "Rehabilitating the Duke of Northumberland," 36–39. Those of Seymour's partisans expelled from the household and imprisoned were William Grey, Edward Wolfe, and Sir Michael Stanhope, First Gentleman of the Privy Chamber. Recent studies have concluded that these men indeed had been Seymour's "pryncipall instrumentes and counsailors" in his last months in office in their roles as members of the hated "new council" of personal advisors who guided Seymour in place of Seymour's fellow Privy Councilors (*Acts of the Privy Council*, 2:342–43; Hoak, "Rehabilitating the Duke of Northumberland," 35; Bindoff, *History of Parliament*, 2:256–57).

Similarly, Ferrers alludes to York's employment of "open force" against Somerset on the latter's release from the Tower in order to guide readers' understanding of Dudley's arming of his and his allies' adherents in the wake of Seymour's release from the Tower in February 1550 (395). Shortly after Seymour's release, Dudley and his allies on the Privy Council made several moves to arm their adherents. On the very day of the former Protector's readmission to the royal household, Dudley and his allies quadrupled the standing guard around the young king, installing four hundred armed men under their own command and using them to greet Seymour upon his arrival at court.[44] They later created their own private military forces, establishing a new personal cavalry of about 850 "gendarmes" under their own rather than the king's command. To outside observers this seemed to be nothing less than a revival of the practice of maintaining personal armed retainers, something that had not been seen on such a large scale since the Wars of the Roses. Tellingly, these forces were used to secure London on the day of Seymour's arrest, and the Councilors displayed these men before Londoners in an elaborate parade shortly after Seymour's trial, in what appeared to be a show of military might against the former Protector's supporters.[45] It was in the context of this martial show of force, the poem leads readers to recall, that John Dudley presided over the condemnation of Seymour at his trial. In reading of York's declaration of "open warre" and of the Earl of Warwick's murder of Somerset, the poem's readers would remember that it was the modern-day "Earl of Warwick," the title by which Dudley was known until just days before Seymour's arrest in 1551, who, through a questionable felony conviction, brought Seymour to his violent end (396-97).[46] Ferrers's account of Somerset's murder at St. Albans allusively urges readers to confirm in their own minds what so many already believed, that Seymour's execution was not an act of legal justice but one of malicious violence, a crime long plotted and prepared for by a power-hungry villain bent on removing all impediments to his personal rule.

Ferrers is able to embrace such thinking precisely because of what followed Seymour's execution: Dudley's supposed "reuing and robbing" of both the king and the realm, his marrying of his son Guilford to Jane Grey, and his subsequent armed attempt to place his son and daughter-in-law on the

44. Hoak, "The King's Privy Chamber," 92–94, 104–5.

45. Ibid., 92; Jordan, *Edward VI: The Threshold of Power*, 97–98, 435–36. Readers could recall that Dudley and his allies disbanded these forces within months of Seymour's execution, further suggesting that these forces were indeed created only to use against Seymour.

46. Hoak, "Rehabilitating the Duke of Northumberland," 48; Jordan, *Edward VI: The Threshold of Power*, 96.

English throne.[47] Ferrers urges readers to see Dudley's crowning of Jane as but the last step in a long and intricate conspiracy, and to use that belief in imagining a far-reaching plot that would explain every troubling aspect of Edward Seymour's career in 1549 and beyond.

By applying Ferrers's narrative of multiple conspiracies against Edmund Beauford, Duke of Somerset, to the suffering of Edward Seymour, Duke of Somerset, Seymour's former supporters might find means to lay to rest the troubling questions surrounding Seymour's travails. By embracing such a plot narrative, Seymour's former followers could believe that, despite appearances, his deposition was never deserved, no matter what the London Lords, the majority of Seymour's fellow Privy Councilors, Parliament, and even Seymour himself in his forced confession all seemed to confirm. Ferrers's poem provides guidance for placing the blame for the rural risings, and the deposition that followed them, not on Edward Seymour, as the official accounts would have it, but on the men who overthrew Seymour, men who whipped up the rural risings in order to use them to justify their attack on Seymour. Most important, it allows readers to reject the troubling claims of the London Lords as mere lies promulgated to serve the ambitions of the men whose action against Seymour in 1549 ensured his downfall and the black reputation which had besmirched his memory since his expulsion from office. Even though a reinterpretation of Seymour's downfall would not bring the lost Protector back, it could afford readers the comfort of believing that Seymour was never the evil or incompetent ruler of official and popular accounts but rather an innocent victim of the malice of others. Freed from the doubts and imputations that had stained Seymour's memory, his supporters might embrace once more their laudatory image of Seymour as the virtuous and godly Lord Protector, a victim of others' malice but never a criminal himself.[48]

"Humfrey Duke of Gloucester"

Ferrers's "Humfrey Duke of Gloucester" shares the exculpatory ends of "Edmund Duke of Somerset." Through this poem Ferrers returns readers to Sey-

47. On the widespread beliefs that Dudley secretly nursed plots to seize the crown and that he and his allies robbed both the realm and its monarch, see Jordan, *Edward VI: The Threshold of Power*, 430–31; *CSP, Span.*, 11:46–49; Brigden, *London and the Reformation*, 503–5, 515–16; and Crowley, "Philargyrie of greate Britayn." For Dudley's almost universal vilification in the mid-Tudor period, and for a concise modern defense of Dudley against those charges, see Hoak, "Rehabilitating the Duke of Northumberland," 29–51.

48. While in the poem Ferrers has Somerset admit that he indeed had "faultes" as England's governor, he insists that Somerset's flaws were never crimes worthy of expulsion from power and

mour's deposition, leading them to identify and condemn what he sees as the other great cause of Seymour's fall from power, in addition to the ambition of John Dudley: the hatred of Seymour's religious conservative enemies.

In "Humfrey Duke of Gloucester," Duke Humfrey returns from the grave to present his life as an exemplary "mirrour" in which to see the dangers that face good men in high office. At the beginning of his infant nephew Henry VI's reign, Humfrey became Protector of the Realm, while his brother John, Duke of Bedford, took charge of English "affayres Martiall" in France (445, 451). Unfortunately, Bishop Henry Beauford, Henry VI's Lord Chancellor, envied Humfrey's authority and challenged his rule. The quarrel between Gloucester and Beauford quickly escalated into an open and bitter feud. Only when John of Bedford returned from France to come to his brother's aid was peace made between the two men. Chancellor Beauford, however, only pretended amity toward Gloucester; secretly he persisted in his hatred and merely waited for a new opportunity to strike.

After John of Bedford's death several years later, Beauford reopened his campaign against Humfrey by disseminating bills and rumors charging the Protector with indiscretions in both his public and private life. Nevertheless, it was not until Gloucester's wife, Elianor Cobham, was charged with witchcraft that Beauford and the Protector's other enemies could make inroads against him. Elianor's public shaming was a calculated "preparatiue" to bringing down her husband (455). In its wake, Henry—now Cardinal—Beauford and the Marquess of Suffolk formed a conspiracy against Protector Gloucester. The devious Duke of York joined these two men in an alliance against Humfrey, as did Henry VI's ambitious wife, Queen Margaret, whom the conspirators won over by persuading her that she and not the Protector should rule in King Henry's name. The plotters laid their trap for Gloucester at Parliament in Bury St. Edmunds. Upon Gloucester's arrival, the conspirators arrested him on a charge of high treason and, soon after, murdered him while holding him under arrest.

As Lily Campbell first noted, Ferrers's contemporaries found many points of comparison between Humfrey, Duke of Gloucester, and Edward Seymour,

imprisonment. Rather the Yorkists used them as "cloakes theyr practise to conceale," casting minor failings as crimes in order to justify their purge of the one man powerful enough to prevent their ambitious schemes from being realized (394). Ferrers's wording gives readers a model by which they could admit any manifest failing they might have noted in Seymour's rule but also categorize such failings as minor, excusable "faultes" rather than as malicious crimes. Seymour himself, in fact, adopted such rhetoric during the coup attempt, when he sought to acknowledge some errors in office without having to accept the London Lords' charges of malicious intent. During the coup Seymour admitted in a letter to the London Lords (written in the king's name) that he had "faults" as Protector, but not ones deserving to be treated with the "crueltye" he believed the Lords were plotting for him (Nicholas Pocock, *Troubles*, 103).

Duke of Somerset. Both men had been Protectors of the Realm, both were uncles to their respective kings, both were revered by the people and had been called "the good Duke," both had suffered politically from the actions of their wives, both had engaged in feuds with powerful noble opponents, and both were brought to a violent end as a result of those feuds.[49] In his poem Ferrers works to strengthen such points of contact by altering the account of Duke Humfrey's career found in his historical source, Hall's *Union*, so that it might be applied more readily to the career of Edward Seymour. In his chronicle Hall is highly equivocal in his portrait of Duke Humfrey. To Hall, Gloucester was generally a good man, but one tragically susceptible to the temptations of ambition, greed, and lust. In particular, Hall condemns Gloucester for his bigamous marriage to Jaquet of Hainault, estranged wife of John of Brabant. He blames Gloucester's rash union solely on disreputable motives, identifying either Gloucester's blind desire for this "wanton" woman or his greed for her vast wealth and lands as the impetus for this marriage, which engendered numerous political problems for England. By contrast, Ferrers presents Gloucester in his poem as a man of absolute virtue and describes the Jaquet affair as at worst one of Gloucester's "*Delicta Iuuentutis,*" a minor incident of Gloucester's youth that had no lasting consequences (452).[50] Similarly, Hall casts doubts on the motives of both Gloucester and Beauford in his account of the two men's feud of 1424–25, suggesting that Gloucester's "disdain" for Beauford was as likely to have started the battle between the two men as Beauford's envy of Gloucester. In Hall's account, furthermore, it was Chancellor Beauford who summoned John of Bedford for aid against Gloucester. When he helped to settle the dispute between the two, Hall notes, Bedford upbraided both Gloucester and Beauford (and all the English lords) for allowing this foolish quarrel to develop.[51] Ferrers, however, presents Beauford as unquestionably the author of the feud, and he portrays Bedford as intervening in it in order to protect his brother from

49. Campbell, " Humphrey Duke of Gloucester." See also Alford, *Kingship and Politics*, 49, 95. According to the author of "Certayne brife notes" (a text of which Campbell was not aware), Seymour himself justified his taking of the protectorship and governorship together by arguing that the concentration of their power in a single man's hands might allow Edwardian England to avoid conflicts between two equally powerful political figures such as those that arose between Duke Humfrey and Bishop Beauford during Henry VI's minority ("Certayne brife notes," 123–24).

50. Hall, "Henry VI," fols. 2v, 10v–11v. The claim that this was an act of Gloucester's youth is Ferrers's invention. In fact the historical Gloucester was thirty-two years old at the time of this union and, as Hall notes, already Henry VI's Protector of the Realm.

51. Ibid., fol. 12r–v. Hall also notes that it was Parliament that ended the feud between the two men after hearing their complaints; Ferrers, by contrast, mentions only John's role in ending the open conflict.

Beauford's persecution. Gloucester's claim that Bedford's death left him exposed to his enemies has no source in Hall's narrative, nor does the poem's assertion that Beauford secretly disseminated "rumours false" in "letters and bylles" against Gloucester's government (452).

Later in the poem Ferrers offers an account of the conspiracy that destroyed Gloucester which differs noticeably from that of Hall. Hall blames Queen Margaret for creating the scheme to replace Gloucester with herself as chief subject in the realm. Margaret and her co-conspirators Suffolk and Buckingham accuse Gloucester of mishandling the king's finances and of illegally commuting criminal sentences. In Ferrers's telling, by contrast, it is not Margaret but other of Humfrey's enemies who conceive of the plot against him. Only later do these men bring Queen Margaret to their side. Furthermore, Ferrers's conspirators indict Gloucester not with Hall's charges but with a charge of high treason (seeking the crown). Finally, Ferrers prominently portrays Cardinal Beauford and the Duke of York as key conspirators in the plot to murder Gloucester; Hall, in contrast, casts Beauford as only a minor figure in the conspiracy and does not mention York as a plotter at all.[52]

Ferrers shapes his poem's protagonist, Humfrey of Gloucester, to evoke memories of Edward Seymour, who (unlike the historical Humfrey) did have a somewhat scandalous yet politically inconsequential first marriage in his youth, who was widely understood to have been weakened by his brother's death, who had "rumours" and "letters and bills" spread against his rule, and who was arrested by his enemies on multiple charges of high treason. Likewise, Ferrers shapes his portrait of Gloucester's first enemy, Chancellor Henry, Cardinal Beauford, to evoke memories of Edward Seymour's own initial and most ferocious opponent, Chancellor Thomas Wriothesley, who, in the manner of Ferrers's Beauford, opposed England's new Protector in the earliest days of the Protectorate, seemed thereafter to reconcile with him, but later publicly condemned him in bills and letters and took a leading role in driving him from power.[53]

Ferrers stimulates such memories to suggest ways of understanding the events surrounding Seymour's ignominious expulsion from office that could serve to exonerate Seymour from the charges that his own ambition and corruption caused his fall from power. Ferrers also shapes this narrative to lead readers to identify a cabal of Seymour's foes as the true agents behind Seymour's downfall in 1549. As we have seen, in "Somerset," Ferrers em-

52. Ibid., fols. 68v–70r.

53. Lily Campbell was the first to suggest a connection between the poem's Chancellor Beauford and Thomas Wriothesley. See Campbell, "Humphrey Duke of Gloucester," 141.

phasizes John Dudley's role in deposing Seymour from the protectorship. In "Gloucester," by contrast, Ferrers seeks to indict Seymour's two greatest religious conservative opponents for their own parts in the coup, namely, Thomas Wriothesley, Earl of Southampton, and the current monarch herself, Mary Tudor.

Chancellor Wriothesley and the Creation of the Protectorship

The prominent religious conservative Thomas Wriothesley was Edward Seymour's earliest rival for power under Edward VI. In the last years of Henry VIII's reign, Wriothesley had wielded extensive authority as Chancellor of England. By virtue of his office, Wriothesley presided over Henry's Privy Council meetings, controlled the Court of Chancery, and was looked upon by England's Anglo-Catholics as their most influential political leader.[54] Upon Henry's death, Wriothesley was reappointed to the chancellorship, and he expected to have a dominant voice in the new regency council composed of Henry VIII's executors, which, according to the terms of the king's will, would rule England during Edward VI's minority. It was therefore with shock that Wriothesley greeted a motion by the majority of the regency council's members, made at their very first gathering (January 31, 1547), to create new supreme offices of Protector of the Realm and Governor of the King's Person and to bestow those offices on the evangelical leader Edward Seymour, a man with whom Wriothesley had clashed numerous times in the previous reign. In the meeting at which this move was proposed, Wriothesley openly declared himself "sore against" Seymour's elevation and the altering of the provisions of Henry's will, which directed that a council and not a Protector should rule during Edward VI's youth. Even after the councilors confirmed their decision to appoint Seymour to the new supreme offices (February 1, 1547), an outraged Wriothesley continued in his complaints, "ouermuch repugnyng" Seymour's elevation and, it appears, protesting as well the sudden and unprecedented addition of Edward Seymour's brother Thomas to the ruling council (February 2, 1547).[55]

Any attempt Wriothesley might have mounted in the ensuing weeks to thwart Seymour's elevation (which had yet to receive royal confirmation) was cut short by unexpected charges of abuse of office lodged against him by a group of prominent common lawyers. In late February 1547 several leading legal men accused Wriothesley of a host of misdeeds as Chancellor, including

54. Gibbons, *Political Career of Thomas Wriothesley*, 155–209.

55. Ibid., 206, 215–16; "Certayne brife notes," 134–35; Hoak, *King's Council*, 43–44, 236; *CSP, Span.*, 9:100; Grafton, *Grafton's Chronicle*, 2:499–500.

deciding cases in Chancery on private conscience, illegally dispossessing men of goods, and exceeding his authority by sealing a commission to delegate some of his official responsibilities without permission of the crown and Privy Council. After examining Wriothesley on the charge of acting *ultra vires*, Wriothesley's fellow Councilors (led by Edward Seymour) condemned him for "abuses sundry wayes in his office," most notably for unauthorized use of the Great Seal. On March 4, 1547, the Council forced Wriothesley both from his office of Chancellor and from the Privy Council, confined him to house arrest, and levied against him a heavy fine. Seymour had his elevation to Protector confirmed by letters patent shortly after Wriothesley's fall.[56]

Two months after his expulsion Wriothesley told the imperial ambassador that he had opposed Seymour's elevation out of a principled refusal to countenance any changes to King Henry's will. Furthermore, he claimed that it was Seymour's long-standing enmity to him, rather than the actual offense of exceeding his authority, that led the Seymour-dominated Council to expel him.[57] Nevertheless, Wriothesley and Seymour soon seemed to reconcile, and in 1548 Seymour returned Wriothesley to the Privy Council. By 1549, however, Wriothesley stood against Seymour once more, taking a leading position among the October coup leaders and composing several of their caustic letters and proclamations against Seymour's government. By the time of the coup, many of those who had voted to create the protectorship had come to consider Wriothesley's early opposition to Seymour's elevation prescient. Both during and after the coup, the executors among the London Lords declared several times that Seymour had made a mockery of the rules they had laid down for his office. Despite promising to follow their counsel in any matters involving the governance of the realm, they complained, Seymour almost immediately abandoned his pledge to confer with them and began instead a program of personal rule. So angry were these men at Seymour's autocratic style of government that they listed Seymour's refusal to seek "the assent of the late kings executors" for his government actions as their very first article of accusation against him. To those who gathered to depose the Protector, Seymour had clearly used the high offices granted him chiefly to feed his own ambition and to aid in his enrichment. Only by deposing him from office, the coup leaders claimed, could they restore justice

56. Dasent et al., *Acts of the Privy Council*, 2:56; Slavin, "Fall of Lord Chancellor Wriothesley," 265, 276–79.

57. *CSP, Span.*, 9:91, 100.

and good governance to the realm and protect the young monarch from his power-hungry uncle.[58]

Of course, Seymour's acceptance of the articles against him in December 1549 ensured that their damning charges would become forever a key part of both official and unofficial accounts of his rule. Over a year after his death, for instance, a parliamentary subsidy bill included a public denunciation of the late Protector's "insaciate ambicion," which had led him to seize "by pretence" supreme power in the realm contrary to the wishes of King Henry VIII.[59] The poet George Cavendish enshrined similar charges in his private volume of *de casibus* poetry, portraying Edward Seymour himself as acknowledging that he had taken the office of Protector primarily so that he might have no opposition to his ambitious schemes. "With great presumcion / whan the noble kyng [Henry VIII] was gon," Cavendish's Seymour admits,

> To be than the protector / I presumed to it anon
> And banysshed all theme / that had prerogatyfe.
> By [Henry VIII's] pryncely . will / to avoyd all stryfe /[60]

It was precisely Seymour's "banishing" of Henry's executors from the day-to-day rule of the nation, Cavendish continues, that led to the worst disasters of Edward's reign. Such accounts, of course, completely rewrote the legacy of the once celebrated Protectorate in the wake of Seymour's fall. The man whose wisdom, virtue, and "loving" government policies had been so widely lauded was now portrayed as a grasping villain whose rhetoric of godliness and social justice was but a means to achieve his own self-aggrandizement. To the further pain of Seymour's followers, such accounts struck at the reputation not only of the Lord Protector but of all those who had supported him as well, casting Seymour's former supporters in the process as at best dupes of the duplicitous Lord Protector and at worst his very partners in crime.

Seymour's Elevation and the Origin of the 1549 Coup

In "Humfrey Duke of Gloucester," Ferrers leads readers to confront the damning accounts of Seymour's rule, to contest them, and to replace them with interpretations of his career as Protector that could serve once more

58. Stow, *Annales* (1592), 1015; Nicholas Pocock, *Troubles*, 95–101.

59. See, for instance, Pocock, *Troubles*, 95–101; Slavin, "Fall of Lord Chancellor Wriothesley," 284; Tomlin, Taunton, and Raithby, *Statutes of the Realm*, vol. 4, pt. 1, 176.

60. Cavendish, *Metrical Visions*, 105. All punctuation is Cavendish's own.

to validate the virtue and wisdom of this fallen former hero. Ferrers first encourages readers to champion Seymour's assumption of the Protectorate and to impugn Thomas Wriothesley's motives for opposing it. He then urges them to accept Wriothesley's lingering bitterness over Seymour's elevation as the true catalyst for the 1549 coup and to blame the deposition of the Lord Protector not on magisterial outrage at his misgovernment but on a conspiracy sparked by Wriothesley's malice and motivated by the individual ambitions of Seymour's most powerful enemies.

To guide readers to such conclusions, Ferrers excludes from "Gloucester" all of the moral ambiguity with which his source, Edward Hall, endows his portraits of Duke Humfrey and Chancellor Beauford. In Ferrers's poem, Protector Gloucester is a uniformly dutiful and upright servant of his king; Beauford, by contrast, is a thoroughly corrupt, malicious schemer, a "proude prelate" who, "beeng made high Chauncellour of the Realme, / Not like a Priest, but like a prince did reigne, / Nothing wanting which might his pride mainteine" (450). It is clearly the malicious Beauford who began the feud with Gloucester, and Beauford's determination to cause Gloucester "dishonour and dispite" both during this feud and after arose solely from a host of wicked motives (451): Beauford's "great mallice" toward the Protector (450), his anger over Humfrey's thwarting of his desire to comport himself as "his Princes peere" (451), his envy of Gloucester's elevation to high office (451–52), and his perverse hatred of Gloucester's rule of "the state by lawes" (452).

Ferrers shapes his account of the early struggle between these two men as an exemplary model for interpreting the later struggle their conflict allusively suggests: the contention between Edward Seymour and Thomas Wriothesley that arose over Seymour's rise to the protectorship. Ferrers's narrative leads readers to interpret the struggle surrounding Seymour's bid for supremacy at the beginning of Edward VI's reign in terms of Gloucester's struggle with Beauford at the beginning of Henry VI's—as a clash between a virtuous and good governor eager to serve his king and a corrupt and proud climber eager to seize supreme power for himself. When Gloucester insists that he exercised the authority of his office in pursuit of his "bounden dutie" to defend the king and the nation from overmighty subjects such as Chancellor Beauford, just so, readers are to think, did Seymour accept the power of Protector as a means to defend his vulnerable young nephew the king from dangerous rivals such as Chancellor Wriothesley (451). In turn, Wriothesley's opposition to Seymour's assumption of the protectorship is to be seen, like Beauford's enmity toward Gloucester, as the act of a malicious climber spurred in his opposition to England's Protector solely by the condemnable motives Ferrers ascribes to Beauford.[61]

Ferrers could count on evangelical readers to embrace such an account of Wriothesley's opposition to Seymour precisely because he built it on beliefs about the former Lord Chancellor already widely shared by English reformers. Beauford's motives for opposing Gloucester—his congenital malice, his desire for supreme power in the realm, his particular hatred of the new Protector, and his contempt for the rule of law—all reflect assumptions about Wriothesley held by Edwardian evangelicals in general and by Seymour's supporters in particular. As we have seen, mid-Tudor evangelicals understood Wriothesley to be an ambitious, malicious, and duplicitous man. In their writings they branded him a "tyrant," the "picture of pride," and a man whose "vengeable witte" and "ambissious mynde" ever moved him to acts of malicious "conspir[ing] and practis[ing]."[62] Wriothesley's several clashes with Edward Seymour over the course of his career identified him as one who bore particular "malice" toward England's Protector, while his "illegal" moves under Henry against court evangelicals and his later purge from office on the charge of misusing the Great Seal of England confirmed for many his status as someone who hated the "rule [of] the state by lawes" (452).[63] Those who already held Wriothesley to be a malicious, corrupt officer could readily accept that it was precisely the malign causes Ferrers suggests and not a

61. Furthermore, by having Gloucester receive his office "by Testament," and by presenting Gloucester's work against Beauford as a direct continuation of that of Henry VI's father, Henry V, Ferrers obliquely sidesteps the chief charge by which Wriothesley challenged Edward Seymour's elevation to Protector, namely, that the creation of the protectorship violated the wishes of Henry VIII (450–51). Mention of Henry V's efforts to thwart Bishop Beauford's corrupt attempt to use religious advancement for political gain evokes memories of Edward VI's father, Henry VIII, and his thwarting of Thomas Wriothesley's use of religious matters against his political enemies in the last year of Henry's reign (Gibbons, *Political Career of Thomas Wriothesley*, 175–76, 186; Ryrie, *The Gospel and Henry VIII*, 53–57). By the logic of Ferrers's allusive model, Seymour did not violate Henry's wishes when he accepted a supreme office not named in Henry's will but instead sought best to fulfill those wishes by gaining the power necessary to continue the late king's work against the ambitious Lord Chancellor.

62. Christmas, *Select Works of John Bale*, 241; George Blagge, "Of Lord Wrythesley," in Hughey, *Arundel Harington Manuscript*, 1:344; Ponet, *Shorte Treatise*, sig. I4r; "Certayne brife notes," 136. For further contemporary testaments to Wriothesley's reputedly malign and conspiratorial character, see Gibbons, *Political Career of Thomas Wriothesley*, 8–9; Jordan *Edward VI: The Young King*, 70.

63. For Wriothesley's clashes with Seymour in the last months of Henry's reign, see note 21. For the several charges of abuse of the law lodged against Wriothesley during his lifetime, see Gibbons, *Political Career of Thomas Wriothesley*, 175–81; Stephen and Lee, *Dictionary of National Biography*, s.v. "Sir Thomas Wriothesley (1505–1550)"; Dasent et al., *Acts of the Privy Council*, 2:48–57. As a common lawyer and member of Lincoln's Inn, Ferrers would have been well informed about the charges of corruption lodged by his fellow common lawyers against Wriothesley.

principled devotion to King Henry's wishes that led Wriothesley to contest Seymour's rise to power.[64]

After leading readers to discover base motives behind Wriothesley's opposition to Seymour's elevation, "Gloucester" then urges them to see those same motives as the catalysts for the coup that drove Seymour from office. Ferrers links the feud between Gloucester and Beauford with Gloucester's arrest twenty years later by asserting (unhistorically) that Beauford had only pretended to reconcile with Gloucester in the wake of their initial clash. In reality, according to Ferrers's poem, Beauford continued to harbor a secret hatred for Protector Gloucester, and it was just that hatred which led Beauford later to distribute lying rumors, letters, and bills against Gloucester's rule; to attack Humfrey's foolish wife; and, when the time was right, to gather a diverse cabal of Gloucester's enemies to plot his overthrow. As with his account of the feud between Gloucester and Beauford, Ferrers shapes his description of the aftermath of the two men's early struggle as a model for interpreting the events that followed Wriothesely's loss of office in 1547. Guided by the poem's exemplary narrative, readers are to understand that Wriothesley continued to hate Seymour in the wake of their dispute over the latter's elevation, and that he used his seeming amity with Seymour to lull the innocent Protector into a false sense of security as he and others plot-

64. In addition, by having Gloucester's brother John come to Gloucester's aid against Beauford, Ferrers uses "Gloucester" to celebrate the memory of Thomas Seymour and to insist on Thomas's support for his brother at this time of crisis. Like John of Bedford in Ferrers's poem, Thomas Seymour was the brother of England's Protector and a man devoted to "affairs martial" (in Bedford's case, as regent in France; in Thomas's case, as Lord Admiral). In reading of John's sudden appearance in England to support his brother against Beauford, courtly readers (at the least) are to recall Thomas Seymour's similarly sudden and surprising appearance on the ruling council at the very time of Wriothesley's challenge to Edward Seymour's elevation (Hoak, *King's Council*, 41–43). Recent work on Edward's reign suggests that Edward Seymour probably added Thomas to the Council as a way to compensate his angry brother for not bestowing on him the position of Governor of the King's Person, the high office that Thomas had expected to receive at Edward's accession (ibid., 234). Ferrers's poem, by contrast, urges readers to construe Thomas's sudden appearance in the new government as they do Bedford's return to London in the poem: as the act of a loving kinsman intent on protecting his brother from a malicious enemy. To reinforce this view, readers could recall that Thomas was known to have strongly opposed Wriothesley in the last days of Henry VIII's reign and that, on Wriothesley's deposition, it was Thomas Seymour who led the party that stripped Wriothesley of the Great Seal (*CSP, Span.*, 9:340; Dasent et al., *Acts of the Privy Council*, 2:57–58). Similarly, Ferrers asks readers to draw a causal link between the loss of Thomas's "protection" and Edward Seymour's later deposition. When Ferrers has Gloucester lament that "if God had lent a longer life [to Bedford], / Our house [would] haue [been] kept from stormes of inward strife," he obliquely insists on Thomas's support for his brother and asserts a causal link, similarly suggested in "Edmund Duke of Somerset," between Thomas's death and Edward Seymour's fall (*Mirror*, 447).

ted Seymour's overthrow.[65] Similarly, readers are to construe the numerous damning rumors and documents denouncing Seymour's government in the days leading up to his deposition in precisely the same terms as the "letters and bylles" against Gloucester: as lies and exaggerations created by Seymour's enemies solely to turn the Protector into an object of hate (452).[66]

In place of accounts stressing Seymour's misrule as the cause of his deposition, readers are to accept that it was the malice and personal ambition of the various coup leaders themselves that led to Seymour's overthrow. Ferrers shapes his poem to indict specific men and women for the "crime" of unjustly deposing the innocent Lord Protector. In particular, by making Bishop Beauford the creator of the plot and by emphasizing Beauford's use of his position as cardinal to advance his secular power, Ferrers seeks to revive memories of the "Catholic" origins of the October coup. As a result of the "black legend" that grew around John Dudley during his years of ascendancy, partisans of the Lord Protector even as early as Mary's reign tended to ascribe Seymour's political downfall almost solely to its ultimate beneficiary, Dudley. In response, Ferrers uses "Gloucester" to revive memories of the roles of Seymour's Anglo-Catholic rivals in the "plot" against the Protector and to lead readers to indict them for causing misery not only to the innocent Lord Protector but also to the king, to the nation, and even to themselves.[67] Thus Ferrers unhistorically casts Chancellor Beauford as the originator of the plot and the author of the "letters and bylles" against Gloucester in order to recall to readers Thomas Wriothesley's key roles in fomenting the coup and in composing many of the condemnatory documents through which the London Lords' justified their defiance of Seymour's authority (452). His identification of the Marquess of Suffolk as the "maister

65. See Gloucester's bitter execration of the false sense of safety in which he had naïvely existed during the period leading up to his arrest (446). For Ferrers's elliptical condemnation of Wriothesley's seeming amity with Edward Seymour as the chief catalyst for Thomas Seymour's execution, see my earlier discussion of "Edmund Duke of Somerset"; for the attacks by Seymour's enemies on Anne Seymour, the Protector's wife, see the tract "Agaynst Edwarde duke of Somerset falsely vsurpinge the name of Protectour," in Historical Manuscripts Commission, *Seventh Report*, 607. The view that Anne Seymour's faults contributed to Edward Seymour's deposition was shared even by many of the Protector's supporters; see *CSP, Span.*, 9:429, 457.

66. The charges these letters, bills, and rumors lodged against Seymour ranged from accusations of incompetence in office to active plotting against the king's life. See my earlier discussion of "Somerset" and also Nicholas Pocock, *Troubles*, 80–118; Campbell, "Humphrey Duke of Gloucester," 131. At least two of the documents impugning Seymour are in Wriothesley's hand. For the malicious rumors Seymour believed to have been spread against him by the coup leaders, see Jordan, *Edward VI: The Young King*, 509; and Gammon, *Statesman and Schemer*, 162.

67. In later years John Ponet and the author of "Certyane brife notes" would also pursue such a project in their own works. See Ponet, *Shorte Treatise*, sig. I3v; and "Certayne brife notes," 128–36.

of this myne," as the "contriuer chiefe of this conspiracie," and as Beauford's most important advisor evokes memories of Sir Thomas Arundell, the powerful conservative magnate who served as who served as "cheafe councellor" in Seymour's deposition and who successfully united the Protector's Anglo-Catholic enemies to ensure that Seymour's expulsion might take place (456, 457).[68] Similarly, Ferrers's unhistorical inclusion of "the Duke of Yorke, and other of his bloud," among those who joined with Beauford and Margaret to destroy Gloucester is meant to evoke thoughts of John and Andrew Dudley, the evangelical brothers who, in the manner of York and his kinsmen in the poem, joined with their "former foes" among England's religious conservatives to ensure the deposition of Edward Seymour but who, again like the Yorkists of "Gloucester," turned on their erstwhile allies soon after in order to seize power for themselves (457).

Most daringly, Ferrers uses the figure of Queen Margaret to guide readers to criticize the current queen herself, Mary I, for her alleged part in the deposition of the Lord Protector. In the poem Gloucester recalls how Cardinal Beauford and his allies approached Queen Margaret, Henry VI's wife, to persuade her to join their plot against the Protector. Although the conspirators presented Margaret with a variety of political arguments to win her support, it was not concern for the state that compelled Margaret to join the growing conspiracy but base personal motives, namely, her jealous hatred of the Lord Protector and her ambitious desire "to rule . . . the king and al the state" on her own (456). The wily Duke of York encouraged Margaret in her illicit desire for power. "Other there were, that this il humour fed," Gloucester bitterly reveals,

> To neither part, which had good wil or minde,
> The Duke of Yorke, our cousin most vnkinde,
> Who keeping close a tytle to the crowne,
> Lancasters house did labour to pul downe.
>
> . . . .
>
> This hope made [York] against me to conspyre
> With those which foes were to ech other late,
> The Queene did weene, to win her whole desire
> Which was to rule, the king and al the state
> If I were ryd, whom therefore shee did hate:
> Forecasting not, when that was brought to passe
> How weake of frendes, the King her husband was. (456)

68. Cavendish, *Metrical Visions*, 111; *CSP, Span.*, 9:470.

The queen's support allowed the conspirators to strike against Gloucester, yet Margaret's time in power was brief, cut short by the duplicitous York, who quickly turned on his erstwhile allies in an attempt to seize the crown for himself. Far from securing her the chief place in England, Margaret's assistance to the plotters brought only misery to herself, her allies, and the long-suffering king whom she had so ambitiously sought to control.

This unhistorical account of the plot against Gloucester recalls key assumptions about the 1549 coup held by Seymour and his supporters during the time the events against the Protector were unfolding. As we have seen, even months before the coup Seymour had come to believe that Mary Tudor and her followers were working covertly to oppose his rule. Later, as the coup attempt unfolded, Seymour publicly insisted that the king's sister was its key figure and that its immediate purpose was nothing less than "to make the lady Mary regent and pulle downe me from the protectorshipp."[69] Ferrers's exemplary narrative urges readers to see once more Mary's hand in the 1549 coup and to accept Queen Margaret's base motives for joining an attempt against England's Protector as Mary Tudor's own. If Thomas Wriothesley conceived of the coup against Seymour and Sir Thomas Arundell planned that coup's course, it was Mary's status as sister to the king and heir to the throne that gave the coup legitimacy and a positive goal to accomplish beyond the mere expulsion of Seymour from office.[70] Readers are to conclude that personal ambition blinded Mary to the danger that would occur if the powerful Edward Seymour were to be driven from power.[71] When it declares that Margaret and "the King, with all their lyne and race, / Depriued were of honour, lyfe, and place," the poem recalls Dudley's destruction of the bid for a Marian regency in the months after Seymour's deposition, his alleged oppression of both Edward and Mary during his time in power, and finally his exclusion of Mary Tudor from the succession and his bid to bestow the crown on a member of his own family.

Recent work on John Dudley's break with his former religious conservative allies in the wake of Seymour's fall argues that their expulsion from

69. "Certyane brife notes," 130. For a detailed account of the evidence suggesting that the coup leaders indeed sought to make Mary regent, see Hoak, *King's Council*, 246–58.

70. Hoak, *King's Council*, 250–51.

71. Mary's misery became so acute in the months after Dudley gained ascendancy that she sought to flee England altogether. For Mary's struggles with the Dudley-led Council and the anguish they brought her, see Prescott, *Mary Tudor*, 132–66; Loach, *Edward VI*, 130–34. For Mary's expressions of regret that the coup ever took place, see *CSP, Span.*, 10:6. Ferrers's surprisingly harsh description of Margaret as "wilful as a Mule" echoes the judgments of other evangelicals about Mary's indomitable personality and how her unyielding single-mindedness often led her into grave fault (456). John Foxe, for instance, describes Mary in *Actes and Monuments* as "stiffe and obstinate" and as a woman of "great stubburness" (1338, 1336).

power by Dudley was the culmination of a series of contingent reactions to their own machinations, including Wriothesley's and his allies' bid to dominate the Council and, later, to arrest Dudley as an accomplice in Seymour's crimes.[72] Ferrers, by contrast, shapes "Gloucester" to suggest that Dudley's move against his Anglo-Catholic fellow coup leaders was plotted well before the coup attempt even began. In reading of York encouraging Margaret's desire for sole rule in the realm, readers are to see Dudley as similarly seducing Mary to join with him against Seymour, while all along he planned the overthrow of her and her allies when the time was ripe for his own open bid for supremacy in the realm.[73] When Gloucester laments that Margaret and King Henry were left fatally "weake of frendes" in the wake of his fall, his words allusively suggest that only the powerful political and military leader Seymour had the strength to withstand the machinations of the similarly powerful political and military leader John Dudley (456).

Thus if "Somerset" suggests that Dudley must bear the greatest blame for the miseries suffered by Seymour and the realm in 1549 and after, "Gloucester" leads readers to accept that Mary and her religious conservative allies too must be condemned for removing the Tudor family's one sure bulwark against Dudley's ruthless drive for power. The tragic result of Mary's ambition to control her brother (and thus the crown) is the allusive theme of Gloucester's lengthy digression on the subject of Henry II and his rebellious sons. Early in the poem Gloucester bewails the miseries of the Plantagenet family, ruefully lamenting the fact that "deadly discord which Kingdomes great doth spill / Bred by desire of high Dominacion, / Brought our whole house to playne desolation" (447). In the midst of describing how Henry II's children preyed on their family members solely out of a desire for supremacy in the realm, Gloucester suddenly exclaims,

> Let him peruse the stories throughout
> Of English kinges, whom practise did oppresse,
> And he shal fynde the cause of their distresse
> From first to last, vnkindly to beginne,
> Alwayes by those that next were of the kynne. (449)

It is noteworthy that Gloucester's words here echo Edward Seymour's own about Mary Tudor. At the height of the rural risings, as reports poured in of Mary's servants leading the commons in revolt, and as Mary herself openly

72. Hoak, "Rehabilitating," 36–39.

73. Compare "Certayne brife notes," which asserts that Dudley led his rivals among England's religious conservatives foolishly to join with him "vpon a pretence that Quene Mary sholde be requent" if Seymour were to fall (128).

engaged in tactics that seemed to be designed to encourage the rebels, Seymour bitterly declared that "the chronicles of the time would give evidence that all the mischief in the kingdom came from the differences between him who wore the crown and those who were nearest to him."[74] Ferrers recalls such sentiments in this passage, and he uses both the story of Henry II and his children and the story of Henry VI and his queen as models for interpreting the disastrous year 1549 not as the product of Seymour's political failings but as the tragic result of the jealousy and ambition that so often grows in those closest to the crown. In this way Ferrers ultimately urges familial and dynastic readings of the conflicts of Seymour's time in power, presenting Seymour's travails not chiefly in the context of stories of papists against the godly but in the same interpretive framework through which Edward Hall presented the tragedies of the Wars of the Roses, as the products of private ambition, lust for power, personal grudges, and the dangers that arise when a weak, vulnerable king wears the crown. If, for Hall, Henry VIII was the monarch whose accession joined the rival houses of England and ended its civil conflicts, Ferrers's poem, written from the vantage point of Mary's rule, suggests that Henry's reign was but a break in the action. The power vacuum created by a minor king, exacerbated by the selfishness and duplicity of the most powerful subjects in the realm, allowed dynastic conflicts to rise once again, as a powerful new noble "house," that of the Dudleys, arose to challenge the rule of the Tudors. If the Tudors survived Dudley's brief capture of the crown of England, readers are to believe, it was only after the loss of their one great protector, Edward Seymour, after much suffering at Dudley's hands, and with the tragic knowledge that the foolish ambition of one of the family's chief members created the very conditions by which Dudley was able to make his bid for the crown.

To those still suffering from the ignominious end of Seymour's Protectorate, Ferrers's plot narrative provides comforting means by which to reject the dominant accounts that blamed Seymour's own malice and misrule for his political downfall. It also allows the satisfaction of "discovering" the parties that were truly guilty in the matter of Seymour's deposition, and it offers the consolation that, despite his humiliating purge and his abject confessions, Seymour was never the duplicitous criminal he was made out to be. Indeed, by applying the model of "Gloucester" to the dismal events of October 1549, readers could even celebrate this failed leader as the sole high magistrate of the Protectorate who lived only for righteousness and duty. With Ferrers's

74. *CSP, Span.*, 9:407.

guidance, Seymour's erstwhile admirers might rehabilitate the tarnished reputation of their former hero and view him anew as a figure deserving of the world's pity, not its scorn, as one more of those maligned but ever laudable souls whose memories remain tragically "for virtues sake with infamy opprest" (144).

CHAPTER THREE

"Syr Thomas of Wudstocke" and the "Unfortunate" Death of Edward Seymour, Duke of Somerset

In "Somerset" and "Gloucester," George Ferrers provides models by which readers might exonerate Edward Seymour from the damning charge that it was his own corrupt incompetence that led to his fall from power. In yet another *Memorial* tragedy touching on the career of the fallen Protector, "Howe syr Thomas of Wudstocke Duke of Glocester, vncle to king Richarde the seconde, was vnlawfully murdred," Ferrers turns his revisionary project to the last years of Seymour's life, leading readers to confront once more the final and most painful set of charges lodged against Seymour, those that painted the former Protector as a desperate conspirator whose schemes to seize power for himself in 1551 justly brought him to his ignominious execution.[1] "Thomas of Wudstocke" is the most emotionally complex of all of Ferrers's tragedies in *A Memorial of suche Princes* and *A Mirror for Magistrates*. If the tone of "Somerset" and "Gloucester" is one of sorrow for the loss of all that was promised by Seymour's rule over the nation, that of "Wudstocke" is a mix of fierce anger and bitterness—anger directed at those who Ferrers believes unjustly drove Seymour to his death and bitterness over Ferrers's haunting knowledge that Seymour's own personal failings in the wake of his deposition helped to hasten his destruction. Through "Wudstocke," Ferrers guides Seymour's former admirers to acknowledge the personal flaws and foolish scheming that marked their fallen hero's career in the wake of his

1. To avoid confusion with the protagonist of "Humfrey Duke of Gloucester," in this chapter I refer to Thomas, Duke of Gloucester (d. 1397), as "Wudstocke," the name by which Thomas of Gloucester identifies himself in the poem (92). The historical Thomas Plantagenet was often called by his contemporaries Thomas of Wudstocke (or Woodstock), a name derived from his place of birth.

fall from power. Yet in the midst of this painful project, Ferrers simultaneously seeks to offer such readers a modicum of consolation, urging them to remember their lost leader, despite all the faults and failings of his last years, not as a villain but as a tragic figure, a man more worthy of the world's pity than of its anger.

The Second Fall of Edward Seymour

As we have seen, Edward Seymour was deposed from power in October 1549. The subsequent struggle between John Dudley and his religious conservative former allies late that year led Dudley, in a bid to win support from Seymour's evangelical admirers, to protect Seymour from execution for the crimes charged against him. In February 1550 Seymour received a royal pardon and was released from the Tower. Far from showing gratitude to Dudley for preserving his life, the newly freed Seymour almost immediately began to search out means to challenge the power of his newly ascendant rival. Over the months following Seymour's deposition, Dudley had stocked both the Privy Council and the royal household with his supporters; Seymour thus cast his net widely for anyone who might join with him in opposition to Dudley, courting both evangelicals and Anglo-Catholics alike in an obsessive drive to regain supreme authority. By the fall of 1550 Seymour (who had returned to the Privy Council in April) was making open attempts both to win fellow Council members to his cause and "to engage the deep loyalty which the commons always reposed in him." Rumors claimed that Seymour and his adherents planned to use the next meeting of Parliament to denounce the Dudley-led government and to open the way for Seymour to return to his lost office of Protector of the Realm.[2]

In the following year Seymour's actions became increasingly suspicious. In February 1551 the Council learned that Seymour's adherent Richard Whalley was urging members of Parliament to agitate for Seymour's return to the protectorship whenever the next session of Parliament might be held. In April, Dudley and Seymour openly quarreled at the Council board, and rumors spread through London of an imminent popular rising designed to bring Seymour back to power. It was not until October, however, that Dudley's government moved against the former Protector, arresting him on charges of plotting to raise a popular revolt and planning to assassinate Dudley and "divers" other members of Edward's Privy Council.[3]

2. Jordan, *Edward VI: The Threshold of Power*, 48, 78.
3. Ibid., 79–83; Brigden, *London and the Reformation*, 508–11; Jordan, *Chronicle*, 86–89.

During the months of October and November the Council interrogated a number of men accused of conspiring with the former Protector, gleaning from them varying accounts of Seymour's alleged conspiracies. Sir Thomas Palmer, the man who first brought word to John Dudley of Seymour's schemes, insisted that Seymour had sought to raise the people on Saint George's Day (April 23) and to slaughter Dudley and several other Councilors at a banquet. Palmer also described a plan to attack the Councilors' gendarmes with a mixed band of Seymour's own horsemen and common supporters. Meanwhile, another alleged conspirator, William Crane, declared that Seymour in fact had not discussed a plan to kill his rivals but only to apprehend them. After the imprisonment of Dudley and his supporters, Crane attested, Seymour and the influential nobleman (and Dudley opponent) Henry Fitzalan, Earl of Arundel, would "have a Parliament" in which they would seek to reorder the government and to lay the legal basis for Seymour's return to power. Both Crane and, in his own interrogation, Arundel denied that any of these schemes was ever put into action. Seymour had indeed spoken of moving against his enemies on the Council, both men suggested, but his plots had remained only words.[4]

Despite Crane's repeated insistence that Seymour had never actively pursued his designs, and despite the fact that those sent to interrogate Seymour questioned him only about a plot to apprehend Dudley and his Council allies and not about a plot to murder them, the formal indictments handed down against the former Protector accused him of actively attempting (in both April and May 1551) to assassinate members of the Privy Council, to spark a popular revolt, and "to seize the King's person . . . and, at his, the Duke's will and pleasure to exercise royal authority." On December 1, 1551, Seymour was tried in the court of the Lord High Steward. During the course of his hearing Seymour vigorously denied the charges brought against him and challenged the veracity of his accusers. After hearing all the evidence, a jury composed of Seymour's peers determined that the former Protector's actions did not rise to the definition of treason; its members did, however, convict Seymour of feloniously gathering men for the purpose of seizing or murdering a Privy Councilor. This offense was a capital crime, and Seymour was duly executed on January 22, 1552.[5]

4. Jordan, *Chronicle*, 92–93; Brigden, *London and the Reformation*, 513–14; Jordan, *Edward VI: The Threshold of Power*, 88–90; Tytler, *England under the Reigns of Edward VI and Mary*, 2:38–45. Cf. Edward VI's account of Crane's confession, supplied to him by John Dudley, in which Crane supposedly confirmed Palmer's assertion of an assassination attempt (Jordan, *Chronicle*, 92–93).

5. Tytler, *England under the Reigns of Edward VI and Mary*, 2:48–50; Jordan, *Edward VI: The Threshold of Power*, 93–94; Loades, *John Dudley*, 187–88.

The responses of mid-Tudor observers to Seymour's arrest and conviction were widely divergent. Some, including a number of Seymour's most important former supporters, fully accepted Seymour's guilt and lost faith in the fallen Lord Protector once and for all. Others, by contrast, simply could not believe the truth of the charges lodged against Seymour or the justice of the verdict against him. Indeed, supporters and detractors of the former Protector alike noted with discomfort the many troubling questions that swirled around Seymour's arrest, trial, and conviction. It seemed suspicious, for instance, that Seymour's chief enemy, John Dudley, was the first to bring the Protector's alleged plot to light, claiming as he did that Sir Thomas Palmer had confessed the conspiracy directly to him in the course of visiting his home on another matter. Others found it strange that several of the men accused of crimes by Seymour's alleged co-conspirators were never prosecuted or, in some cases, even interrogated. The assassin supposedly suborned by Seymour to kill his fellow Councilors was even rewarded by the Dudley-led government shortly after Seymour's death. Parliamentarians and legal men noted further that the statute under which Seymour was tried had been created to apply not to nobles but to rebellious commoners, and that the specific charge on which Seymour was convicted, the gathering of the twelve men for the purpose of attacking a member of the Council, was alleged by only two of the witnesses against Seymour but denied by four others. Finally, the presence on Seymour's jury of the very men Seymour was specifically accused of seeking to murder, John Dudley, William Parr, and William Herbert, cast great doubt on the impartiality of the jury's verdict. Many insisted that Seymour's felony conviction was nothing more than a naked attempt by Dudley to ensure the execution of an innocent man for whom he had conceived a dislike.[6]

Edward Seymour and His Plots

Ferrers uses his tragedy "Howe syr Thomas of Wudstocke Duke of Glocester . . . was vnlawfully murdred" to return readers to the events surrounding Seymour's final months of life. In Ferrers's poem the fourteenth-century nobleman Thomas of Wudstocke, Duke of Gloucester, returns from his grave to complain to Baldwin "in the forlorne hope of the Englysh flocke" (92).

6. Jordan, *Chronicle*, 86–87; Jordan, *Edward VI: The Threshold of Power*, 96; William Seymour, *Ordeal by Ambition*, 344; Loades, *John Dudley*, 187–88; Brigden, *London and the Reformation*, 514. Even as steadfast an opponent of the former Protector as George Cavendish could not believe that Seymour and his associates were guilty of the crimes with which they were charged. See Cavendish, *Metrical Visions*, 107–13.

Wudstocke recalls how from his earliest days of adulthood he had shown himself to be marked for greatness. Even as a young man Thomas enjoyed “bewty, strength, high fauour and fame,” while his skill in warfare abroad helped him to glorious “honoure and triumph.” Under his nephew King Richard II, Wudstocke found rapid advancement, first to the “Glocester Dukedome” and then to the premier political office, High Constable of England (92–93).

Despite Wudstocke’s position as “chiefe officer in the realme,” King Richard preferred to take counsel from men other than his uncle. Upset with Richard’s choice of counselors, Wudstocke tried to force his royal nephew to expel those around him, foolishly “presumyng,” the ghostly Wudstocke confesses, “so far vpon my high state / That dread set aparte, my prince I would mate” (94). To achieve this goal, Wudstocke and several noble allies armed themselves, gathered supporters from among the common people, and mounted a show of force against those about the king. After a battle at Ratcote Bridge, Wudstocke and the other so-called Lords Appellant put “to flyght” Richard’s chief familiar, Robert Vere, Duke of Ireland (96). After defeating Vere, Wudstocke exercised his power as High Constable to call a Parliament, “where not in roabes, but with bastardes bright, / We cam for to parle of the Publyke weale” (96). Wudstocke and his allies used this Parliament to purge Richard’s counselors and to force the king “the Rule of his realme wholy to resygne, / To the order of those, whom we dyd assygne” (96).

Instead of permanently reducing the king to their control, however, Wudstocke and his allies merely earned Richard’s silent enmity, which Wudstocke further enflamed through subsequent confrontations with the king over matters of financial irregularity (97). The tragically unwary Wudstocke had no inkling of his sovereign’s well-dissembled hatred for him. He was therefore caught by surprise when Richard suddenly struck, ordering a “bande” to seize him and, soon after, to murder him (98). Wudstocke’s spirit ends his narrative with a bitter execration of his violent death, of his enemies’ mendacious attempts to present his murder as an act of justice, and, most of all, of his own nephew’s undeniable hand in arranging his slaughter. Indeed, in the most passionate stanza of the poem, Wudstocke declares to all readers that Richard’s assassination two years later was nothing less than divine retribution for the illicit, unnatural murder of his own uncle (99).

As he does in “Somerset” and “Gloucester,” Ferrers offers in “Wudstocke” telling points of similarity between his tragedy’s protagonist and the recently deceased Edward Seymour, Duke of Somerset. Both men, mid-Tudor readers could note, were uncles to their kings, both won fame and honor as military heroes, both were made dukes by their royal nephews, both served as "chiefe officer in the realme," and both met violent, untimely ends that were widely construed as acts of murder rather than of justice. Ferrers works to strengthen these points of identification by shaping his account of Wudstocke's armed rising of 1387, the historical event to which he devotes the greatest attention in his poem, specifically to conjure up memories of Seymour's planned rising of 1551. To reveal Ferrers's allusive strategy, it is fruitful to compare his narrative of the uprising of the Lords Appellant in "Wudstocke" with his account of the very same event in an earlier poem in the *Memorial-Mirror* collection, "Robert Tresilian."[7] There Ferrers describes the Lords' rising as a spontaneous movement conceived of and executed corporately by the whole "Baronye of Englande" (78). Far from portraying Wudstocke in "Tresilian" as the mastermind behind this event, as he does in Wudstocke's own poem, Ferrers never mentions Duke Thomas at all. In "Tresilian," furthermore, Ferrers specifically names eight of King Richard's men as those who earned the Lords Appellant's wrath through their corruption and malign influence on the king. Indeed in "Tresilian," Ferrers ascribes the origin of the Appellants' rising solely to the outrage brought about by these pernicious officers (75, 79). Finally, Ferrers praises the Appellants' Parliament in this poem as a free and beneficial gathering designed to reverse the corruption that Richard and his associates had brought to the land. Under the Lords' protection, Ferrers claims in "Tresilian," the Parliament called by the Appellants remained "francke and free for all men without checke to debate / As well for weale publyke, as for the princes state" (78).

Ferrers's portrait in "Wudstocke" of this rising differs radically from that in "Tresilian." In "Wudstocke," Ferrers portrays Duke Thomas as the sole genius behind the Lords' revolt, and instead of eight men, Ferrers identifies only one of the king's familiars, Robert Vere, Duke of Ireland, as the focus of the Lords' ire. Furthermore, Ferrers offers no indication in "Wudstocke" that Vere or any of his fellows was corrupt in his rule, despite making the misgovernment of Richard's officers the sole impetus for the Appellants' rising in "Tresilian" (96). Finally, far from casting the Appellants' Parliament

7. Though much of "Wudstocke" is his own invention, Ferrers adapts details from a variety of historical sources for use in his poem. For his account of the Lords Appellant's rising, including the spelling of several characters' names, Ferrers draws on the rolls of Parliament, a source to which he calls attention in the middle stanzas of "Wudstocke" (96). Ferrers also loosely follows Fabyan's chronicle for his poem's anecdote concerning the unpaid soldiers of Brest and Froissart's chronicle for its account of the Londoners' desire for a reckoning of the realm's revenue (97). See Fabyan, *Chronicle of Fabyan*, sigs. 3C3v–3C4r; and Froissart, *Here Begynneth the Thirde and Fourthe Boke*, fols. 105v–107r. For "Tresilian," Ferrers draws solely on the Parliament rolls.

as an assembly devoted to "francke and free" debate, Ferrers describes it in "Wudstocke" as one held in an atmosphere of threat and coercion. Its members met "not in roabes, but with bastardes bright," Wudstocke recalls, and it was "with swurdes and no wurdes" that Wudstocke and his allies carried their motions (96).

The differences between Ferrers's two accounts of the Appellants' uprising in the *Memorial* are a direct result of the two different topical purposes to which Ferrers puts these poems.[8] In "Wudstocke," Ferrers specifically shapes his account of Thomas of Gloucester's revolt to suggest particular details of the rising planned by Edward Seymour in 1551, a rising, like Wudstocke's in the poem, concocted by the king's uncle, mounted primarily against a single high-ranking counselor who "ruled alway" the king (Robert Vere, Duke of Ireland, in the case of Wudstocke, John Dudley, Duke of Northumberland, in the case of Edward Seymour), and whose immediate goal was the expulsion of the nation's most powerful officers from their places of influence about the monarch.

Ferrers presents his matter-of-fact, topically evocative account of the Lords' rising in "Wudstocke" in order to spur readers to accept as equally a matter of fact what so many of Seymour's admirers had wished to deny: Seymour's plots against his political enemies. Ferrers further chooses the specific details he bestows on Wudstocke's revolt to suggest which of the numerous charges lodged against Edward Seymour in the wake of his arrest should be accepted as true. Thus Ferrers shapes "Wudstocke" so as to suggest that Seymour, in the manner of Duke Thomas, indeed plotted to rise, with the support of both upper-class allies and members of "the Commons," in order to overthrow the king's most important officers, even if he, unlike the fourteenth-century Duke of Gloucester, never put his schemes into action. The poem also suggests that Seymour, had he acted on his plots, would have forced a meeting of Parliament in order to establish legal sanction for his political ends. Finally, it indicates that, like Wudstocke, Seymour sought far more from his planned coup than merely to depose his political enemies. Instead his ultimate goal was to seize once more the supreme authority he had lost at his fall from power and to "haue his owne waye" in the governance of the king and the realm (95). By leading readers to admit Seymour's plotting and his contemplation of violent, disorderly means to achieve his ends, Ferrers abandons the consolatory strategies of exculpation that inform "Somerset" and "Gloucester," poems that guide readers to judge Edward Seymour innocent of all the charges lodged against him during his time as Protector.

8. For Ferrers's use of "Tresilian" as a warning to Marian justices, see chapter 5.

If Ferrers offers to readers any sort of consolation at all in the details of Wudstocke's rising, it is solely through the oblique suggestion that Seymour planned not to *kill* his chief enemy, John Dudley, as the indictments against him charged, but only to put him, as Ferrers's Wudstocke did his own chief foe Robert Vere, "to flyght" (96).[9]

Not only does Ferrers force Seymour's admirers to accept that their hero had contemplated illegal means to achieve his political ends, but also in so doing he refuses them even the luxury of believing that Seymour was motivated by altruistic concerns in his contemplation of an armed revolt. Ferrers's Wudstocke forthrightly admits that selfish personal motives were the true cause of his decision to rise against Richard and his men. "I beyng a Duke descended of Kinges," Wudstocke confesses,

> Constable of Englande, chiefe officer in the realme,
> Abused with esperaunce in these vaine thinges,
> I went without feete, and flewe without winges:
> Presumyng so far vpon my high state
> That dread set aparte, my prince I would mate.
>
> For where as al kings haue counsel of their choyse,
> To whom they refer the rule of theyr lande,
> With certayne famyliers in whom to reioyce,
> For pleasure or profyt, as the case shall stande,
> I not bearyng this, would nedes take in hande,
> Maulgree his wyll those persons to dysgrace,
> And such as I thought fyt to appoynt in their place. (94)

It was not Richard's counselors themselves whom Wudstocke found unbearable, Duke Thomas's words suggest, but his king's independent choice of them. As "chiefe officer in the realme," Wudstocke believed that he and not his "yong king" should select those to whom Richard would "refer the rule of [his] lande" (93, 94). It was for this reason that Wudstocke struck against Richard's officers, and it was for this same reason that Wudstocke and his allies did not stop at expelling Vere and his fellows but presumed soon after to usurp Richard's authority and to force their king "the Rule of his realme wholy to resygne, / To the order of those, whom we dyd assygne" (96).

Ferrers designs this account of the motives behind Wudstocke's 1387 rising to provide a guide for construing the impulses behind Edward Seymour's

9. Following the historical record, Ferrers does note that some of those around the king were "executed with capytall payne"; nevertheless, the only man mentioned in the poem as specifically acted against, Robert Vere, is merely put "to flyght," and Wudstocke's general description of his action against the king's counselors speaks only of deposition, not destruction ("whom so we knewe with the kyng in good grace / Playnely we depriued him of power and of place" [96]).

concoction of similar plots in 1551. From the model offered in "Wudstocke," readers are to conclude that Seymour's motives in plotting to expel Dudley and his allies were the very same as Wudstocke's in his own rising: jealousy of his rivals' influence and a presumptuous belief that he and not his "yong king" should choose those who would rule the realm (93). With Ferrers's prompting, readers could recall that just such an explanation, as painful as it was, was one even many of Seymour's admirers in 1550 and 1551 found themselves forced to accept in light of Seymour's reckless bid to regain his lost offices. Edwardian observers recognized a marked change in Edward Seymour in the last months of his life. Gone, according to many, was the zeal with which he had pursued the religious and social ideals that guided him during the Protectorate, replaced instead by a burning desire to resume his former authority by any means necessary.[10] A single-minded devotion to his own advancement, in fact, seemed the only way possible to explain the "good Duke's" increasingly unprincipled actions in the wake of his release from the Tower. How else could Seymour's supporters explain their hero's open courting of hated religious conservatives in his bid to return to power? How otherwise could they make sense of Seymour's conspiring with the Earl of Arundel and Sir Thomas Arundell, two former opponents who helped to arrange his first downfall in 1549? Finally, how else could they explain how Seymour, a man lauded by his supporters as a paragon of justice and devotion to young King Edward, could ever have contemplated the illegal and violent means of an armed rising and popular revolt to achieve his political ends? To avoid such unpalatable questions, many of Seymour's admirers by the time of Mary's reign attempted simply to suppress all thoughts of their hero's disturbing behavior in his last years.[11] Ferrers, by contrast, returns his readers to memories of those troubling times and leads them to accept the painful proposition that Seymour indeed contemplated violent actions against the king's chief officers, and that jealousy, pride, and desire for personal power alone spurred him to such schemes.[12]

10. See, for instance, Jordan, *Edward VI: The Threshold of Power*, 104; Hoak, *King's Council*, 74–75; Robinson, *Original Letters*, 2:734–37.

11. See, for example, Foxe, *Actes and Monuments*, 1321; Ponet, *Shorte Treatise*, sig. E1v; Thomas Becon, *A Comfortable Epistle to the Afflicted people of God* [1554], in Ayre, *Prayers and Other Pieces of Thomas Becon*, 205.

12. The reasons behind Ferrers's decision to lead readers to accept Seymour's failings in "Wudstocke"—despite the great lengths to which he goes in "Somerset" and "Gloucester" to get them to reject charges of similar failings made during Seymour's time as Protector—will, of course, never be known with certainty. It may well be, however, that Ferrers had little choice in this matter. As we have seen, during the Protectorate Ferrers had served as "a gentleman of my Lord Protector's" and had been close enough to Seymour to receive from him rewards and expressions of approval. Even after Seymour's deposition, Ferrers was suspected of continuing to serve the

Fortune, Folly, and the Decline of Edward Seymour

In its narrative details, Ferrers's exemplary account of Wudstocke's plots and personal failings offers remarkably little in the way of consolation to Seymour's troubled former followers. What comfort he does seek to provide these readers comes not in an attempt to lead them to deny Seymour's faults in his last years but in an attempt to lead them, as much as possible, to pity rather than to condemn Seymour for those faults. Ferrers seeks to move his readers to remember Seymour as at bottom a good man, one whose errors in the last months of his life should be the subject of their compassion, not their contempt.

To this end Ferrers crafts the opening of his poem to elicit from readers initial thoughts of sympathy for Thomas of Wudstocke, before revealing to them Wudstocke's later fall into error. In the first nine stanzas of the poem Ferrers paints Wudstocke solely as a tragic innocent, an unjustly afflicted man fallen victim to "frowarde Fortune" and "Fortunes blast" (91). There is no hint in these early lines of Wudstocke's later crimes; instead Ferrers has Wudstocke dwell solely on his own suffering, including the "treason" he endured at the hands of those whom he had trusted, the fatal blindness that led him unwittingly into entrapment, and his unjust "murder" by his enemies (93, 98). To strengthen readers' sympathy for his protagonist, Ferrers also portrays Wudstocke in his opening stanzas as an entirely admirable and dutiful figure, a hero who during his life stood "seconde to none in glory and fame" in England. Wudstocke enjoyed all the "sundry graces" nature and fortune could offer, including "bewty, strength, high fauour and fame" (92). He served his prince faithfully as well, risking life and limb to win King Richard "glory and honors encrease" by fighting on his behalf in France. As a result of these deeds, the poem relates, Richard loved his glorious uncle, joining the nation in celebrating him with great "honoure and triumph" upon his return from France and raising Wudstocke to the highest of all the noble ranks (93).

---

former Protector's interests by helping in early 1550 to compose "sklaunderous letters" against the Dudley-led Council. Ferrers was a member of Parliament during the years in which Seymour sought parliamentary support for his drive to regain his lost offices, and it thus seems likely that this former "gentleman of my Lord Protector's" was one of those very parliamentarians whom Seymour and his adherents courted in their bid to return Seymour to power. Ferrers's indirect assertion of the reality of Seymour's plotting and of the unprincipled motives behind it may well have arisen from an uncomfortably close personal familiarity with Seymour's obsessive thirst for power in his last years of life. If this was indeed the case, it could go a long way toward explaining why not even Ferrers, otherwise one of Seymour's great apologists in the *Memorial*, could find a way to avoid accepting the painful fact that selfish motives alone led Seymour to contemplate the criminal schemes that so troubled his admirers and ultimately cost him his life.

When he does reveal to readers Wudstocke's later failings, Ferrers presents them as faults not inborn within this heroic and good man but tragically imposed upon him. Wudstocke's fatal personal flaws came to him only after he had risen to unprecedented heights of rank, office, and favor. "Thus hoysted so high on Fortunes wheele," Wudstocke relates,

> As one on a stage attendyng a playe,
> Seeth not on whiche syde the scaffolde doth reele,
> Tyll tymber and poales, and all flee awaye:
> So fared it by mee, for day by daye,
> As honour encreased I loked styll hyer,
> Not seying the daunger of my fonde desyer.
>
> For whan Fortunes flud ran with full streame,
> I beyng a Duke descended of Kinges,
> Constable of Englande, chiefe officer in the realme,
> Abused with esperaunce in these vaine thinges,
> I went without feete, and flewe without winges:
> Presumyng so far vpon my high state
> That dread set aparte, my prince I would mate. (94)

Wudstocke confesses that ambition and presumption led him to instigate his rising; he shapes his confession to insist, however, that these failings were not part of his natural character but afflictions imposed by "frowarde Fortune" and its seeming gifts of worldly success (91). It was fortune that "hoysted" him to the "high state" in which his desire for further advancement first emerged, and it was just that "high state," he continues, that created within him the presumptuous expectations ("esperaunce") that "abused" him into believing that he and not his monarch should order the government of the realm. In relating his faults, Wudstocke paints for himself a remarkably passive, pitiable role in their development. Thus in revealing the growth of his ambition, Wudstocke asks readers to think of him as they would of a victimized spectator, an innocent, helpless playgoer imperiled by an act of misfortune that he could not foresee, that he could not prevent, and, crucially, for which he was in no way to blame. Wudstocke was a man "abused," Ferrers tells his readers, and thus a figure worthy of their compassion (91, 94).

In fact Ferrers goes so far as to suggest that Wudstocke's ambition, pride, and envy should not be seen as ambition, pride, and envy at all. Instead, his flaws should be seen solely in terms of a single, less pejorative personal failing, a temporary but tragically all-consuming folly. Wudstocke's thirst for advancement, the poem suggests, was not the sort of ambition that marked Beauford's malicious plotting in "Gloucester" or York's lust for supremacy in

"Somerset." Rather it was an instance of "fonde desyer," a foolish, irrational longing that led Wudstocke into tragic blindness and acts of fatal presumption. Wudstocke's tone is one of bitter self-mockery as he relates to readers his thoughts and actions at the time of his rising; he employs sarcasm ("I went without feete, and flewe without winges"), mocking understatement (he "would nedes take in hande" a rebellion against his king, as if such a move were merely an irksome task he thought it necessary to perform), and rueful irony (he calls his illicit acts of usurpation "myracles") to register his deeply felt chagrin at the lengths to which his newly acquired folly led him. In presenting Wudstocke's sense of grim discomfiture in this section, Ferrers seeks to draw from readers not responses of horror at Wudstocke's crimes or even expressions of forgiveness for his faults but chiefly pity for his fallen protagonist, as Ferrers reveals the strong sense of bitterness and shame this proud and once glorious man must endure whenever he recalls the shocking deeds into which folly's overwhelming force swept him.

Ferrers confirms the justness of such a response through his lengthy account of Duke Thomas's demise. As *Mirror* critics have noted (at times with expressions of surprise and even of distaste), Ferrers refuses to moralize Wudstocke's death in this poem as it would seem to deserve, as either providential retribution for the sin of disobedience or as just recompense for Wudstocke's manifest crimes.[13] Instead, Ferrers accounts for the tragic end of Wudstocke's rising in the same manner that he accounts for the rising's origin, by pointing to the malign workings of a fatal, all-consuming folly. In planning his revolt, Wudstocke completely misjudged his monarch's probable response to an attempt to wrest from him his royal power. Wudstocke assumed that King Richard would simply submit to his assertion of mastery over him, and it was the blinding nature of this foolhardy belief that led Wudstocke in the wake of his rising never to suspect that his nephew planned revenge against him until it was too late to prevent it. Wudstocke's part in engineering his own downfall, the poem suggests, arose chiefly from his foolish lack of foresight, and it is for this reason that the sole lesson Wudstocke draws from the tragic end of his rising is a practical rather than a doctrinal one, a warning that subjects should refrain from attempting to overrule their princes, simply because rulers usually have the power to repay such presumption with vicious acts of revenge. Drawing on the politically allusive debate on belling a cat held by a mouse and "the Rat of renoune" in *Piers Plowman*, Wudstocke warns readers that

13. For a particularly bitter attack on Ferrers for his handling of Wudstocke's death, see Kelly, *Divine Providence*, 168–69.

who so wyll assaye,
Aboute the Cats necke to hang on a bell,
Had fyrst nede to cut the Cats clawes awaye,
Least yf the Cat be curst, or not tamed well,
She haply with her nayles may clawe him to the fell:
For doyng on the bell about the cats necke,
By beyng to busy I caught a sore checke.

. . . .

But in that ye be Lyeges learne to obaye,
Submytting your wylles to your princes lawes,
It fytteth not a subiecte to haue his owne waye,
Remember this bywurde of the Cats clawes:
For princes lyke Lyons haue long and large pawes
That reache at raundon, and whom they once twitch,
They clawe to the bone before the skyn itch. (94–95)

Wudstocke's rising ended in tragedy not because of God's hatred for rebellion but because its author never stopped to consider the anger his action would stir in his monarch. Even here, while warning readers not to follow Wudstocke's example, Ferrers still presents his fallen protagonist as a figure worthy of sympathy. Muting in these stanzas readers' sense of the enormity of Wudstocke's actions (he speaks of Wudstocke's crime here in the mild metaphoric form of "beyng to busy" in belling a cat), Ferrers focuses their attention instead on the tragic consequences of the rising for Wudstocke himself. As he does in his account of the growth of Wudstocke's ambition, Ferrers speaks of his protagonist in the aftermath of his revolt as if he were a passive victim, presenting him in terms of a helpless mouse caught by a cat and a defenseless man mauled "at raundon" by a lion. The compassion with which he narrates Wudstocke's death becomes even greater as the poem advances. In the final section Ferrers leaves behind any sense of possible wrongdoing on Wudstocke's part in order to present Wudstocke's "murder" as an unjust, undeserved, and even sinful act against an innocent man (98). In his closing stanzas Ferrers portrays Wudstocke just as he did in the opening lines of the poem, as an innocent and pitiable figure tragically afflicted by "frowarde Fortune" and the "treason" of those who brought him to his violent demise, a figure deserving of readers' sympathy and sorrow, even in the midst of all his confessed failings and faults.

Of course, Ferrers's refusal to condemn Wudstocke for his manifest acts of treason makes little sense in the context of the narrated action. It does make sense, however, in the context of the allusive dimension to which the poem points its readers, the actions and schemes of Edward Seymour in the last two years of his life. Unlike Wudstocke, Seymour never actually led a rising against his prince's chief officers, and most construed Seymour's death precisely as Ferrers presents Wudstocke's own, as an act of cruel injustice. By leading readers to pity Wudstocke even while they acknowledge his failings, Ferrers's exemplary poem suggests that they remember Seymour in similar terms, as a good man whose rise to "high state" tragically swept him in the last years of his life into uncharacteristic folly and rash schemes, and ultimately to his death. Ferrers's account of Wudstocke's admirable qualities and service to his prince recalls Seymour's own celebrated personal "graces" and (what his followers understood to be) his fierce devotion to his "yong king," Edward, during the time of the Protectorate. Wudstocke's description of his high birth, high rank, and high office recall Seymour's honors in Edward's early reign, when he stood as the king's most powerful blood relation, as the only man of ducal rank in the English government, and as the "chiefe officer in the realme" (94). In reading of Wudstocke's unfortunate development of his tragic traits, readers are to construe Seymour's sudden display of ambition, jealousy, and presumption in precisely the same light as they do Wudstocke's, as the product of Seymour's tragic acquisition of folly and not (as his enemies would have it) of malice. Such folly was imposed on him by the ill effects of his rise to unprecedented heights of worldly power. The very same "vaine thinges" that led Wudstocke into error, readers are to conclude, were those that "abused" Seymour with the presumptuous belief that, because of his "high state," he and not his young nephew should rule the realm and choose the officers who would guide the nation during Edward's minority.

To Seymour, a return to the office of Protector seemed entirely appropriate. He had, after all, been appointed to that office by the executors of King Henry's will and had been confirmed in it by royal letters patent. Furthermore, he had lost that position through an illegal and, to his mind, unjust rising against him. In the first months after his release from the Tower, many had expected him to resume his old offices, and even up to the point of his arrest his closest adherents continued to encourage him in this dream. Finally, Seymour saw Dudley as nothing less than a criminal, one whose malfeasance harmed both King Edward and the realm. To his mind only a return to power could right the wrong caused by his deposition, salvage those beloved social and foreign policies that Dudley had overturned, and protect both the nation and his young king from the depredations of his current officers.[14]

14. It is this view of Seymour as principled in his opposition to Dudley's government that the "Salisbury" poet suggests in his reminiscence of John, Lord Montague, whose plotting was undertaken solely to "furder right" (145). It is also the view of the author of the *Memorial* tragedy "How Lorde William Delapole Duke of Suffolke was worthily punished for abusing his Kyng and causing the destruction of good Duke Humfrey," though the "Suffolk" poet, unlike Ferrers and the author of "Salisbury," allows no hint of Seymour's troubling schemes in the last months of his life. For "Suffolk," see chapter 4.

For others, however, blinding folly was simply the least painful way to account for Seymour's reckless thirst for power in his last months of freedom. Much had changed at court since Seymour's expulsion from office in 1549, and he and his co-conspirators alone seemed unable to see it. The helpless boy whom Seymour had dominated during the Protectorate was now a teenager who played a growing part in the governance of his nation. By 1551 Edward was happily attending meetings of his Privy Councilors; reading and, at times, altering Council documents; and keeping personal notes, agendas, and memoranda on the day-to-day workings of the government. By the time of Seymour's arrest, Edward had begun to adopt a rhetoric of personal rule in his political communications and had shown himself to be strongly determined to impose his royal will upon others, particularly in matters of religion.[15] While Edward was heavily influenced in all his royal decisions by the counsel of John Dudley and his allies, and while many of Dudley's opponents (including, as we have seen in "Somerset," George Ferrers) lamented the fact that the allegedly corrupt and scheming Dudley "ruled alway" the king, Edward was entirely content with Dudley and his adherents. Whether "for pleasure or profyt," Ferrers's poem reminds readers, it was King Edward who had chosen Dudley and those associated with him to be his royal servants, and it was these men whom Edward desired to have as his "famyliers" and chief counselors as he looked toward the day when he would reach his majority.[16] For Seymour to believe that this confident young prince would sit idly by while his deposed uncle rose against his government, purged his handpicked counselors, and seized from him the royal prerogative seemed to many evidence of utter senselessness. No king would willingly accept such presumption, particularly not the proud son of King Henry VIII. For those who acknowledged Seymour's desperate conspiring but sought to reject the government's charge that malice and ambition had motivated such schemes, a belief in a sudden onset of blind, irrational folly was the most acceptable (because least painful) explanation at which they could arrive to account for the "good Duke's" actions at this time.

15. Jordan, *Edward VI: The Threshold of Power*, 410–11, 420–22; MacCulloch, *The Boy King*, 35–39; Murphy, "Illusion of Decline," 128–31, 139–40; Alford, *Kingship and Politics*, 160–61.

16. Murphy, "Illusion of Decline," 128–29. The men Edward appointed to the Privy Chamber and Council were those suggested to him by John Dudley or others associated with him (such as Thomas Cranmer). Whereas Seymour merely called upon his nephew to ratify Seymour's own previously made choices, Dudley and his allies presented their men to Edward as suggestions for his consideration rather than as foregone conclusions, an act of deference that highly pleased the young monarch. Dudley was also careful to recommend men whom Edward was likely to approve; all of those he suggested for the Privy Chamber, for instance, were evangelicals, and several had been childhood friends of the king. On Dudley's influence over Edward (and Edward's over Dudley), see Hoak, "Rehabilitating," 43–45; Hoak, *King's Council*, 123–24, 249; Murphy, "Illusion of Decline," 127–40.

Thus while Ferrers cannot deny either Seymour's plotting in 1551 or the defects of character that spurred it, he can at least hope through "Wudstocke" to offer Seymour's former followers a modicum of comfort in recalling their lost leader, despite his conspiring, his flaws, and his ignominious death, as at bottom a good man temporarily and tragically led into error, as a victim of "frowarde Fortune" and, in his suffering, a man worthy of sympathy, not condemnation.[17]

Edward VI and the "Murder" of Edward Seymour

Ferrers uses "Wudstocke" to identify not Edward Seymour but those who brought him to his death as the true malefactors in the events of the former Protector's last months. Ferrers shapes his account of Wudstocke's "execucion" to suggest precisely what so many of his readers already believed, that Seymour's death was nothing less than an act of legally sanctioned murder. In the poem Wudstocke recalls how, in the wake of his rising, he was seized by a "bande" of Richard's royal servants, who carried him to Calais and, soon after, put him cruelly to death. Upon their return to England, these men attempted to excuse their crime as an act of legitimate execution by having Wudstocke posthumously convicted of treason. Their "rygour to cloke in habyte of reason," Wudstocke angrily declares,

> By crafty compas deuise they can,
> Articles nyne of ryght haynous treason:
> But doome after death is sure out of season,
> For who euer sawe so straunge a presydent,
> As execucion doen before iudgement. (98)

Although Wudstocke's enemies claimed an air of legal sanction for Wudstocke's death, their posthumous conviction of the man they had already

17. The temporary nature of this folly would seem to be confirmed for those who wished to believe it by Seymour's own stunning change of attitude evinced in his moving, widely reported scaffold speech (January 1552). In this speech, Seymour displayed nothing of the man who had spent his last months of freedom consumed by jealousy, ambition, and plotting. Instead he protested his innocence of the charge for which he had been convicted, declared his unwavering loyalty and long service to his royal nephew, and even asked the people to pray with him both for the king and for his ministers. He begged forgiveness from any he might have offended throughout his life, and he several times declared his firm adherence to the reformed faith. Those who had witnessed his desperate, troubling state of mind in 1550 and 1551 could well believe that by the time of this speech Seymour had recovered, in the same manner as Wudstocke's ghost in the poem, from an attack of temporary blindness and returned to the virtue and dutifulness that had previously been the hallmark of his character. For Seymour's words from the scaffold, see Foxe, *Actes and Monuments*, 1321–[22].

killed, the poem insists, was nothing more than an empty "cloke" devised to hide the true nature of their murderous act.[18]

Wudstocke's execration of the unjust nature of his supposedly legal "execucion" returns readers to Edward Seymour's own legally sanctioned but highly controversial death in 1552. As we have seen, his trial was so thoroughly compromised by legal and evidentiary irregularities that even many of Seymour's detractors construed the former Protector's unexpected conviction for felony as merely a ploy by Dudley and his allies to justify their murder of a hated political rival.[19] In reading of Wudstocke's death and the false legal sanction granted to it, readers are to recall Seymour's own widely discounted conviction and to construe it as they do Wudstocke's conviction in the poem, as a cynical attempt by a band of murderers to authorize the "vniust" slaughter of an innocent man (98).

Nevertheless, it is not the members of Seymour's jury whom Ferrers urges readers to hold chiefly responsible. Rather, Ferrers, virtually alone among evangelical authors, leads them to indict above all Seymour's nephew, King Edward VI, for his guiding role in his uncle's death. Toward this end Ferrers casts Wudstocke's nephew, King Richard, as the chief agent behind Wudstocke's arrest and "execucion." In Ferrers's telling it was Richard who burned with hatred for his presumptuous uncle and who, in the wake of Wudstocke's rising, began to study "nought els but howe that he myght / Be highly reuenged of his high dispight" (96). It was Richard, furthermore, who conceived of the plot that resulted in Wudstocke's capture, and it was Richard who ensured that plot's success by lulling Wudstocke into a false sense of security shortly before setting his royal servants upon him. Finally, although others performed the physical act of Wudstocke's murder, it was King Rich-

18. Ferrers reshapes the historical accounts of Wudstocke's capture and demise to reflect more closely events of Edward VI's reign. Neither the major chroniclers nor the Parliament rolls suggest that Richard's government presented Wudstocke's death as punishment meted out to a traitor; rather, Wudstocke's keeper in Calais, Thomas Mowbray, Earl of Nottingham, declared that Wudstocke had died of natural causes while in captivity. Likewise, the chroniclers and parliamentary records alike show that the historical Wudstocke was arrested at his residence not for actions undertaken in 1387 but for a second conspiracy he was said to be creating in 1397. By referring to Wudstocke's death as an "execucion" and by describing that death as a direct consequence of Wudstocke's rising against Vere and his men, Ferrers seeks to remind readers not of the death of the historical Thomas, Duke of Gloucester, but of the trial and execution of their contemporary, Edward Seymour. See Strachey, *Rotuli Parliamentorum*, 3:374–79; Froissart, *Here Begynneth the Thirde and Fourthe Boke*, fols. 286r–v, 294r; and Fabyan, *Chronicle*, sigs. 3c4r–v.

19. For a survey of the irregularities surrounding Seymour's arrest and trial, see Loades, *John Dudley*, 182–88. George Cavendish, a man who had little love for Edward Seymour, nevertheless insisted that Seymour's felony conviction was nothing but a desperate plot by Dudley and his allies to destroy Seymour, hastily concocted after the former Protector's peers had properly refused to find Seymour guilty of treason. For Cavendish's outraged attack on the perceived plot behind Seymour's conviction, see *Metrical Visions*, 108, 121.

ard who ordered that deed accomplished, and it was thus Richard, the poem insists, who bore ultimate blame in the eyes of both God and man for the spilling of his innocent uncle's blood (98).

Ferrers's exemplary account of Richard's vengeful response to Wudstocke's presumption moves readers to reconsider the events of their own recent past, urging them to entertain and to accept as fact the melancholy, even traumatic assumption that King Edward so despised his uncle during the last months of Seymour's life that he willingly sought to bring Seymour to his death. By advancing such an assertion, Ferrers sets himself forcefully against what W. K. Jordan has described as the "almost maudlin contemporary idealization of the young King," that fervent and widespread tendency among Tudor evangelicals to portray their like-minded monarch as an almost otherworldly paragon of virtue, wisdom, and piety.[20] As John N. King notes, such an idealized image of Edward VI caused later evangelical authors profound discomfort when they sought to understand the king's role in the demise of his similarly idealized uncle.[21] Many simply avoided this troubling question altogether; those few who did confront it wished desperately to explain why Edward, who held the power to pardon Edward Seymour, never acted to do so. In 1559 Robert Crowley accounted for the king's inaction by asserting that he had been brainwashed by Seymour's enemies. According to Crowley, during the Christmas season Seymour's opponents created sinister spectacles and entertainments for the young monarch that twisted Edward's mind and led him, against his better nature, "to forgette, yea rather to hate, hys good uncle." The chroniclers Thomas Cooper and Richard Grafton soon after took up Crowley's account and shaped it into a narrative even more favorable to the young king. Both men insisted that Edward had not hated his uncle in the wake of Seymour's conviction but in reality grieved for him. This innocent boy, however, was deviously distracted from thoughts of Seymour's peril by the holiday entertainments mounted for him at the command of Seymour's foes. The tragically manipulated young king did not recall his uncle's plight until it was too late to save him from destruction. These Christmas revels were, of course, those overseen by George Ferrers, and it was Ferrers who bore implicit blame in these narratives for helping Seymour's enemies ensure the former Protector's destruction.[22]

20. Jordan, *Edward VI: The Threshold of Power*, 534.

21. On the idealized image of Edward in the mid-Tudor period, see King, *English Reformation Literature*, 161–206; MacCulloch, *The Boy King*, 1–56; Alford, *Kingship and Politics*, 5–15.

22. Crowley, *Epitome of Cronicles*, sig. 4E3r; Thomas Cooper, *Coopers Chronicle*, fol. 353r; Grafton, *Grafton's Chronicle*, 2:526–27; King, *English Reformation Literature*, 182. For the influence of Crowley's, Cooper's, and Grafton's assertions on modern scholarship, see Lucas, "Conspiracy and Court Revels."

Such attempts to detect sinister motives behind Ferrers's Christmas entertainments were the wishful thinking of Elizabethan authors determined to preserve an idealized image of their lost evangelical monarch.[23] Unlike these writers, Ferrers was present at court in the crucial months of December 1551 and January 1552 and for many days of this period was in constant, close contact with the king. Writing less than two years after Seymour's death, Ferrers shapes "Wudstocke" to force Seymour's former followers to recollect, no matter how reluctantly, what Crowley would later suggest and what Ferrers himself appears to have observed firsthand, namely, King Edward's antipathy toward his uncle in the last years of Seymour's life. As several historians have noted, it is questionable whether the young king ever felt much affection at any time for his domineering uncle. Certainly, however, any love Edward might have held for his governor was lost during the October 1549 coup, when Seymour used the king as a sort of hostage against his political enemies, frightening Edward with tales of desperate conspirators seeking his murder and, later, carrying his ailing young nephew off in the middle of the night to Windsor Castle "more like a piece of infinitely valuable baggage than the fledgling Tudor monarch he was."[24] After the coup Edward was noticeably cool toward the disgraced former Protector. Indeed, as Ferrers's poem obliquely suggests, Edward's antipathy may well have grown into outright hostility in reaction to Seymour's intemperate verbal attacks on John Dudley and his allies at this time—men the young king strongly supported.[25]

23. See Lucas, "Conspiracy and Court Revels." While Dudley did not appoint Ferrers to his place as Master of the King's Pastimes or use him to distract the allegedly heavy-hearted king, he did order Ferrers to perform as Lord of Misrule in London in a bid to mollify restless Londoners. See ibid., 31–39.

24. Jordan, *Edward VI: The Young King*, 510. For evidence that Edward had chafed under Seymour's governance even during the earliest months of the Protectorate, see ibid., 374–77.

25. Jordan, *Edward VI: The Threshold of Power*, 82. Ferrers evokes thoughts of Seymour's specific political complaints against the Dudley regime in the last months of his life through his mention of Wudstocke's asking for a reckoning of the realm's revenue and Wudstocke's assistance to the soldiers who remained unpaid after the English-held French town of Brest was "solde" back to the Duke of Brittany. These two anecdotes attesting to Wudstocke's concern for the commonwealth suggest Seymour's strong criticism of the Dudley regime's "sale" of English-held Boulogne to the French in 1550 and his charges of corruption against Dudley and his allies. Furthermore, they recall in particular the chief political scandal of April 1551, the time of Seymour's alleged aborted rising against Dudley. In that month one of John Dudley's closest allies, Sir John Yorke, improperly diverted funds received by the treasury after the return of Boulogne and quickly lost them speculating on the monetary exchange in Antwerp. In considering action against Dudley in 1551, the Earl of Arundel advised Seymour to seize Yorke even before he seized Dudley, in order to use Yorke to implicate Dudley in his ally's crimes. For the controversy surrounding the "sale" of Boulogne, see chapter 4. For Yorke's actions and the widespread outrage they provoked, see Jordan, *Edward VI: The Threshold of Power*, 458–59; Brigden, *London and the Reformation*, 504–5, 513.

Certainly all evidence suggests that Edward fully believed the reports he received of Seymour's plots and aborted risings. Furthermore, in the wake of his uncle's arrest the king showed no discernible sympathy for Seymour's plight. Rather, while continuing to monitor the events leading up to Seymour's trial, Edward happily turned his attention largely to other matters, including the festivities surrounding Mary of Guise's visit to England, news of foreign conflicts, and, in November and December, the evolving plans for his yuletide celebrations.[26] In reading of Richard's hatred for his presumptuous uncle, readers are meant to recollect Edward VI's own behavior in 1551 and to construe it as they do King Richard's in the poem, not as mere indifference to Seymour's fate but as evidence of a carefully controlled hatred, a hatred that spurred the young king to thoughts of vicious retribution against his reckless but (in Ferrers's mind) legally innocent kinsman.

Through his description of Richard's role in Wudstocke's capture and "execucion," Ferrers then suggests that this hatred led Edward to ensure first his uncle's arrest and then his violent death. Ferrers describes how an angry King Richard came to visit Duke Thomas when Wudstocke was confined to his residence by illness. Dissembling his hatred, Richard greeted his uncle with "friendly vysage," lulling Wudstocke into a false sense of security before suddenly setting his "bande" of royal officers upon him (98). It was Richard's duplicity, Wudstocke insists, that led directly to the duke's capture, and it was on the king's orders that Richard's servants brought Wudstocke to his demise.

By this account of Richard's betrayal of his unsuspecting kinsman, Ferrers leads evangelical readers once more to confront and accept painful memories of Edward VI's key role in the arrest and execution of his own uncle, Edward Seymour. Wudstocke's confinement to his residence for illness in the poem recalls Seymour's similar confinement in September and early October 1551, when the death of a servant from sweating sickness forced Seymour's household into self-imposed quarantine. King Edward learned of Sir Thomas Palmer's accusations on October 8, four days after Seymour's return to court; Edward, however, successfully hid his knowledge of Seymour's scheming until such a time as Seymour might be captured. On October 16, 1551, Edward issued an invitation to Seymour to join him for dinner. Seymour, unaware of Palmer's confession, seems to have entertained no suspicions about Edward's intentions in arranging this meal, and as "Wudstocke" suggests, the young king appears artfully to have dissembled his emotions during their dinner together under a false "coulour of kyndenes." It was in this way, Ferrers's poem

26. *CSP, Span.*, 10:390; Jordan, *Chronicle*, 86–97; Lucas, "Conspiracy and Court Revels," 26–30.

reminds, that Seymour was lulled into the false sense of safety that allowed royal officers to seize him as he left Edward’s table.[27] In a similar manner, by making Wudstocke’s capture just one part of Richard’s preconceived plan to bring his uncle to his death, the poem further suggests Edward’s continuing role in bringing about Seymour’s demise. Although many would later choose to believe that Edward was distracted from Seymour’s fate in the wake of his uncle’s conviction, it was in fact Edward himself who, in a note written in his own hand on January 19, 1552, commanded the Privy Council to execute Seymour with all due speed.[28] Though it may have been John Dudley who arranged Seymour’s conviction, it was Edward himself, Ferrers’s poem urges readers to acknowledge, who assisted Dudley in Seymour’s capture and who personally ensured his uncle’s untimely death.

Finally, Ferrers moves his readers to construe King Edward’s roles in capturing and executing his uncle not as mere acts of political expediency but as deep and terrible sins. In the poem Wudstocke bitterly inveighs against Richard’s entrapment of him, execrating his nephew’s cold-blooded betrayal of his own kinsman as nothing less than an act of “treason” (93). Worse, Wudstocke declares, was the king’s arrangement of his uncle’s illicit “execucion,” an outrageous, even unnatural deed “odious to God and to man” (98–99). Such an act of wickedness, the poem declares, could not help but bring down God’s wrath upon its perpetrator:

> Thus hate harboured in depth of mynde,
> By sought occasyon burst out of newe,
> And cruelty abused the lawe of kynde,
> whan that the Nephewe the Vncle slewe,
> Alas king Rycharde sore mayst thou rewe:
> whiche by this facte preparedst the waye,
> Of thy harde destynie to hasten the daye.
>
> For blood axeth blood as guerdon dewe,
> And vengeaunce for vengeaunce is iust rewarde,
> O ryghteous God thy iudgementes are true,
> For looke what measure we other awarde,
> The same for vs agayne is prepared:
> Take heed ye princes by examples past,
> Blood wyll haue blood, eyther fyrst or last. (99)

In maliciously arranging his innocent kinsman’s death, Richard II perverted the “lawe of kynde” (98). Such a shockingly cruel and immoral action out-

27. Jordan, *Edward VI: The Threshold of Power*, 83–85.

28. Ibid., 100; Tytler, *England under the Reigns of Edward VI and Mary*, 2:68–70.

raged even God himself, who could never let such a monstrous deed go unpunished.

Ferrers crafts Wudstocke's impassioned outburst against his nephew to lead readers to view Edward's moves against Seymour as they do Richard's betrayal and "execucion" of Wudstocke in the poem—as malicious and even unnatural sins. So outraged is Ferrers at Edward's hand in Seymour's destruction that he urges readers to accept that which for many in later years would become all but unthinkable: that the death of the young king less than two years after Seymour's was providential retribution for his uncle's violent end. Ferrers's oblique assertion of Edward's role in Seymour's execution is nearly unique in the printed accounts of the Tudor period, which tended to place the blame for Seymour's death solely on Seymour himself, or (in the manner of Ferrers's own "Somerset") on John Dudley and his allies. Writing just over two years after Seymour's death, however, Ferrers could hope to find acceptance for his bold charges precisely because he builds them upon the earliest reactions of many of Seymour's admirers to the former Protector's controversial demise. In the immediate aftermath of Seymour's death, many of his partisans indeed quietly blamed King Edward for Seymour's execution, despite vigorous attempts by the Dudley-led government to suppress such views. One Elizabeth Huggins, for instance, was imprisoned in 1552 after declaring Edward to be an "unnatural nephew" for his part in his uncle's destruction. Just as Ferrers himself would later suggest in "Wudstocke," Huggins asserted that those responsible for Seymour's slaughter would have to answer for his blood. In a similar vein, the chronicler Thomas Cooper remembered that in the wake of Seymour's beheading "manye that bore affection to [Edward Seymour] talked that the younge kynge was nowe to be feared, seynge bothe his uncles were dispatched oute of the waye."[29] This image among Seymour's supporters in 1552 of Edward as a cold and vengeful monarch who would allow his own uncle to be "dispatched out of the waye" is precisely the characterization Ferrers angrily seeks to revive as the true portrait of King Edward at the time of Seymour's death. By 1551, Ferrers's poem insists, Edward was no longer the helpless child he had been during Seymour's Protectorate but rather a self-possessed, headstrong, and dangerous prince, much like a "curst" cat or a wild lion in his ability to exercise fearsome cruelty when challenged or crossed (95). Far from the idealized "godly imp" of hagiographic memory, England's rapidly maturing king was by this time nothing less than a budding Henry VIII, a proud and willful monarch quick to act on personal

29. Jordan, *Edward VI: The Threshold of Power*, 432–33; Thomas Cooper, *Coopers Chronicle*, fol. 353v.

jealousies, even when such impulses led him far beyond the accepted boundaries of justice or morality.[30]

Ferrers’s account of Wudstocke’s murder and the providential justice meted out in response to it thus urges Marian readers to turn the dominant and deeply troubling view of Seymour’s demise completely on its head. As we have seen, many in Edward’s and Mary’s reigns interpreted Seymour’s death as providential vengeance against the former Protector for the unjust execution of his brother Thomas. By contrast, Ferrers leads readers of “Wudstocke” to see Seymour as an innocent unjustly afflicted by the malice of other men. Far from an act of divine will, Seymour’s destruction was nothing less than an affront to the Lord. It was not Seymour whom God struck down in a fit of providential anger, Ferrers’s exemplum suggests, but the man most instrumental in ensuring his “vniust” death, England’s revered young monarch.

Fortune, Providence, and the “Tragical” Career of Edward Seymour

Even if Ferrers’s poem leads them to dismiss the haunting fear that Seymour’s death was an instance of divine vengeance, Seymour’s followers would be left at the end of “Wudstocke” with one final and persistent question still unanswered: why God did not act to protect Edward Seymour from the disasters that destroyed first his Protectorate and then the Protector himself. If Seymour had been a man of duty and rectitude during his time in power, as “Somerset” and “Gloucester” urge readers to believe, why did the Lord allow this good man to be driven from office? If Seymour did not incur guilt in the matter of his brother’s death, as “Somerset” suggests, and if in fact God was outraged by Edward Seymour’s execution, as “Wudstocke” implies, why did he allow Seymour to die in such a humiliating, violent, and untimely manner? By the logic of the manifest providentialism adopted by so many evangelical supporters in response to Seymour’s successes, God should have rewarded his appointed “sword bearer” for his virtuous rule, not plagued him. Yet Seymour’s godly Protectorate was ended within three years of its creation, and Edward Seymour himself died a beheaded felon.

No matter how seemingly illogical Seymour’s tragedies were in the terms of his followers’ worldview, they did occur. To attempt to reconcile these

30. Ferrers evokes such thoughts as well in the last stanza of “Humfrey Duke of Gloucester,” in which he warns that “kinges most parte, be Ielous of their kynne” (459). This assertion (and his further warning against high nobles courting popular support) makes little sense in the context of the poem itself. Coming after the account of Gloucester’s murder, however, it offers a suggestion similar to that in “Wudstocke” of Edward’s willful hatred of his popular uncle, a man who by 1551 he had come to consider a threat to his own royal power.

events to the providentialist beliefs through which Seymour's admirers had interpreted his early successes as evidence of divine favor would run counter to the very project of exoneration that Ferrers pursues in his retrospectively topical exempla. It is in response to this dilemma that Ferrers crafts the opening and closing stanzas of the last of his poems written on the subject of Edward Seymour's travails, "Edmund Duke of Somerset." In these lines in particular, and in the openings of "Gloucester" and "Wudstocke" as well, Ferrers urges readers to adopt an explanation of worldly events different from that offered by the all-encompassing manifest providentialism that so many had embraced in the early days of the Protectorate. By insisting in each of these poems on the overwhelming power of fortune in human affairs, Ferrers offers his troubled readers a means by which they might acknowledge the reality of Seymour's disasters without having to deny the rectitude of the Protector or those ideals they had shared with him.

In "Edmund Duke of Somerset" Ferrers portrays Edmund as an afflicted sufferer seeking to comprehend the reasons for his unmerited troubles. Ferrers's Somerset appears as an emotionally devastated victim, one with whom anguished readers could empathize in his quest to understand how a good man could fall victim to earthly tragedy. Ferrers imbues his Somerset with classic signs of psychological trauma. First, he is haunted by intrusive memories that force him repeatedly to return to the most psychologically painful moments of his life. Throughout the poem, Humfrey of Gloucester's death and Somerset's mistaken consent to it, the Duke of York's machinations, and Henry VI's suffering at York's hands come back to Somerset, seemingly with the emotional force of their first occurrence. One of the most striking instances takes place in the middle of an account of the Duke of York's triumphs over Henry VI after the battle of St. Albans. While narrating these events, which occurred after his death, Somerset suddenly breaks off from his chronological narrative to exclaim:

> Thou lookest Baldwyn I should my selfe accuse,
> Of some subtyle dryft or other lyke thyng,
> Wherein I should my prynces eares abuse,
> To the Dukes foes overmuch adhering,
> Though some mens practise did me therto bryng,
> My fault only consisted in consent,
> Forgeve it me, for sore I dyd repent. (400)

It is only by reading the next stanza that readers understand that Somerset has turned here from later events to dwell once again on Duke Humfrey's loss. Memories of Gloucester's death have intruded upon him, disrupting Somerset's narrative and casting him back to the moment of his greatest anguish. So powerful are these and other memories that Somerset finds no relief from them even in the afterlife.

Second, Ferrers portrays Somerset as afflicted by what we would today call survivor guilt, the experience of irrational feelings of responsibility and guilt over events for which a sufferer was neither responsible nor guilty. In the poem Somerset dwells almost solely on the failures of Henry VI's reign, including Gloucester's death, York's triumphs, and the Yorkists' persecution of the king. Somerset holds himself culpable for all these disasters, even as he insists that he had only worked to prevent them. Despite demonstrating his innocence of Gloucester's death, Somerset nevertheless castigates himself for "want of foresight" and "overlight credence" in not having seen through lies that he and "other moe" could not have known were untrue. In his disturbed state, he blames his own "folly" for his inability to perceive Suffolk's plots and even goes so far as to construe his opposition to the Duke of York as the chief cause of York's victories (390, 389, 400). So low has his self-esteem fallen and so guilt-stricken does he feel that he "repent[s]" a crime of which he was innocent and even begs a commoner, *Memorial* compiler William Baldwin, personally to forgive him for his unwitting act.[31]

Most troubling for Somerset is the incongruence between his expectations of worldly justice (earthly reward for doing good) and the undeniable fact of the tragic occurrences that shaped his career. Somerset expected his good intentions to meet with success; nevertheless, despite his uniformly virtuous intent, Somerset found only failure and tragedy: he fell victim to plots by the evil nobles Suffolk and York, lost English Normandy to the French, allowed his innocent cousin Gloucester to die, left his prince at the mercy of his most cruel enemy, and forfeited first his high position and then his own life. No supernatural agent prevented these disasters or came to his aid. Rather, despite Somerset's best efforts, "traytours dyd triumphe, true men lay in the dust," including all of those whom he had sought to protect (399).

In dramatizing Somerset's struggle to comprehend these seeming contradictions, Ferrers presents a blueprint for readers to use in answering their own questions about why a good man such as Edmund Beauford or Edward Seymour might fall. Ferrers begins his poem by having Somerset haltingly examine several different explanations for the numerous tragedies of his life:

31. On survivor guilt, see McCann and Pearlman, *Psychological Trauma*, 165–66. Somerset's "survivor guilt" may be a displaced manifestation of Ferrers's own, since Ferrers was a member of the Parliament that attainted Thomas Seymour. Although there is no record of how Ferrers voted in this matter, it may well be that he too "consented" to Thomas's death and thus experienced the same guilt feelings and the same desire to blame lack of true knowledge, not "vice," for his decision that Somerset shows in the poem.

Some I suppose are borne vnfortunate,
Els good endeauours could not yll succede,
What shal I call it? yll Fortune or fate,
That some mens attemptes have never good speede,
Theyr trauayle thankeles, all bootles theyr hede:
Where other vnlyke in workyng or skyll,
Outwrestle the world, and wyeld it at wyll,

. . . .

For I of Somerset which duke Edmund hight,
Extract by discent from Lancaster line,
Were it by folly or Fortunes fell desptye,
Or by yll aspecte of some crooked sygne,
Of my workes never could see a good fine:
What so I began dyd seldome wel ende:
God from such Fortune all good men defend.

After considering various causes for the tragedies of his life, Somerset can reach only one conclusion: that he was born unlucky and "to all mishap . . . predestinate." God did not directly intervene in worldly affairs to cause his suffering; Somerset was "borne vnfortunate" and tragically fated to live in a time when evil men preyed on the virtuous for their own political gain (388–89).

Such assertions lead Seymour's former followers to view the Protector's suffering not through providentialist interpretive strategies but instead through the older but still vital system of Christian causal belief which held fortune rather than providence to be the chief cosmic agent in worldly affairs. In presenting Somerset's tragedies as the effects of unavoidable misfortune, Ferrers draws upon the pattern of his literary model, John Lydgate's *Fall of Princes* (ca. 1431–1439), the work to which the *Memorial of suche Princes* was originally appended. Lydgate's poem displays in voluminous examples the dangerous unpredictability of human life and warns of the sudden, inexplicable reversals of fortune to which even the best of men and women are subject. It teaches that fortune and worldly mutability often exert a malign influence on human endeavors, and since God only selectively intervenes in worldly affairs, no man, not even the most pious, should count on receiving justice in this transitory life. Instead the virtuous should look for reward not in this world but in heaven.

In each of his three tragedies meant to move readers to rewrite the legacy of Edward Seymour, Ferrers asks them to embrace just such a concept of fortune as the ultimate cause of Seymour's suffering. While never denying God's ability to intervene directly in mundane affairs, each of Ferrers's exempla warns that fortune and its seeming gifts of worldly success often exert a malign influence on even the best-intentioned men and women, and that the Lord does not always protect the virtuous from misfortune or human malice. Good men often do fall, and wickedness often succeeds, Ferrers's poems teach, no matter how unjust such an outcome might seem. Seymour may have succumbed to folly in believing his enemies' lies about his brother and by recklessly plotting to regain his former powers in the wake of his deposition. He may, too, have been cruelly afflicted throughout the last years of his life by his political rivals and even by the prince he had once worked so hard to protect. Yet all of these tragedies, the opening of "Somerset" suggests, are at bottom the products of ill fortune. By urging readers to ascribe Seymour's suffering to misfortune, of course, Ferrers requires from them no moral condemnation of the fallen Lord Protector to explain his travails; all they must do is acknowledge the pervasiveness of fortune's power and the radical amorality of its tragic effects.

In short, Ferrers calls upon his readers to interpret Seymour's troubles in the same way they do Somerset's, Gloucester's, and Wudstocke's: not as divine punishment for any alleged "spot of vice" in their fallen hero but solely as the lamentable effects of bad luck and the "noughty time" into which Seymour was thrust, a period of ruthless ambition that turned his simple innocence, his achievement of worldly success, and his rise to high office into terrible liabilities (402).[32] Like all three of Ferrers's protagonists in these

32. Ferrers was not the first Protestant observer to suggest that Seymour's miseries had arisen from ill fortune and fate. In a letter from England the Oxford reformer John ab Ulmis informed the Swiss theologian Heinrich Bullinger that in Seymour's miseries "you may hence perceive how various and changing is the condition of human life, how fickle and inconstant is fortune, . . . how wretched and miserable is the life of courtiers!" (Robinson, *Original Letters*, 2:444). Scholars who approach the *Mirror* as a work of philosophical instruction often condemn the collection as incoherent for presenting tragedies of both fortune and direct providential judgment. Following Lily B. Campbell, many critics assume the *Mirror* to have been designed to exemplify God's manifest ordering of human affairs, and thus they suggest that the *Mirror* authors' decision to include tragedies of fortune in their work must have arisen from their inability to comprehend fully the very doctrine of providence they had supposedly set out to teach. Frederick Kiefer suggests, for instance, that "the soundest generalizations about the narratives [in the *Mirror*] acknowledge that the relationship of providence and Fortune varies from poem to poem, reflecting the author's attitude. When the poet is most confident that he understands the justice of God's ways, he denies the phenomenon of chance and implicitly rejects Fortune by restricting her role or excluding her from the narrative. However, when injustice seems to prevail and when a character's death lends itself to no easy explanation, the poet forgoes a too strident assertion of providential design and allows Fortune to become the presiding deity of the narrative" (Kiefer, "*A Mirror for Magistrates*," 121). While Kiefer argues that the authors' practice of ascribing causal events variously to providence and fortune arises from their intellectual difficulties in analyzing historical subjects, I suggest, by contrast, that it most often arises from the authors' need for psychological comfort. When "mirroring" the troubles of mid-Tudor figures whom the authors held to be good men or women, the poets make their exempla tragedies of fickle fortune. When depicting contemporary persons or actions they oppose, the authors moralize their protagonists' miserable ends as instances of divine justice.

poems, Edward Seymour is to be recalled as a figure not of scorn but of pity, as a virtuous but unlucky and unfairly maligned man for whom, save for his undeserved affliction by "yll Fortune," his "glory might have growen where as ensewed gryefe" (388, 401).

Such an understanding offers readers not just the comfort of rejecting accounts that cast Seymour's fall as proof of his sinfulness but even, in the manner of the "Salisbury" poet's opening lines on John Lord Montague, the means to celebrate the Protector in the midst of his failures. By emphasizing the effects of chance and worldly influences on human endeavors, Ferrers urges readers to look away from Seymour's disappointing efforts—whose success or failure was ever in the hands of wayward fortune—and toward the ever laudable intentions for king and country with which, they believed, he had established his godly Protectorate. Such a focus on intent ultimately moves readers' thoughts from the events of this world to the absolute moral calculus of heaven, which judges by the heart and not by the act. The reward for the good—whether for Edward Seymour or for his evangelical followers, who suffered in Mary's reign from his loss and the loss of Reformation England—need not be on earth but in heaven. Divine justice for the virtuous exists, even if it comes only in the afterlife. One should thus strive in life for right and justice, Ferrers suggests, but also look for a "good fine" not in this life but in the next (389). The world is not always a just place, but one must trust that there is always a just cosmos.

By leading readers to revalidate their faith in the rectitude of Edward Seymour and to quell their fears that God had judged against the Protector and all for which he stood, Ferrers seeks to restore their shaken confidence. The rehabilitation of Seymour's memory, coupled with the general support all the *Memorial-Mirror* poems give to ideals popularly associated with his government policies—including protection of the poor, strong English nationalism, commitment to social and economic justice, and the duty of English governors (including the monarch) to all those under them—further reestablishes these principles as firm bases for political intervention. Freed from their doubts about the Protector, Seymour's scattered former followers might once again rebuild themselves into a like-minded, principled community and confidently employ the ideals they associated with Seymour as standards by which to weigh current government policies and as firm foundations on which to protest any government actions that might deviate from them. Restoring confidence in their own rectitude and in the principles to which so many had devoted their lives could work to reconstitute and reinvigorate the shattered English evangelical community and make it once again a confident voice of admonition and even protest in the face of the unfolding worrisome events of Mary’s reign. Such renewed confidence could offer comfort, consolation, and a new sense of purpose to the suffering “Englysh flocke” living under the Catholic queen. It was toward this vital end that George Ferrers crafted his poems on the “tragical history” of Edward Seymour and risked censorship, suppression, and even punishment by Marian authorities in the hopes of leading to it those who, like himself, had once revered the “good Duke” and the ideals for which he stood.

CHAPTER FOUR

A Memorial of suche Princes and the Loss of Imperial England

George Ferrers was not alone in pursuing a retrospectively topical project in *A Memorial of suche Princes*. Three other *Memorial* authors, each anonymous, also craft exemplary narratives designed to return readers to what they saw as the chief political disasters of the Edwardian period. Their poems handle subjects different from the domestic political tragedies of Ferrers's works. Instead these works strive to guide readers in their response to the haunting failure of the English imperialist ideal, that proud, nationalistic ethos of "glorious" expansionism abroad and patriotic independence at home which many saw as the very wellspring of national pride and strength. Through three poems ostensibly portraying some of the worst foreign policy disasters of Henry VI's rule, these authors seek to explain how the great promise of English imperialism could have gone unfulfilled, to console those suffering from the abandonment of the imperial ideal in the wake of Edward Seymour's fall from power, and to warn current governors not to allow what the authors feared would be the complete destruction of English pride and sovereignty in the reign of Queen Mary. Two of these poems, "How Thomas Montague the earle of Salysbury in the middes of his glory, was chaunceably slayne with a piece of ordinaunce," and "How king Iames the first for breaking his othes and bondes, was by gods suffrauns miserably murdred of his owne subiectes," offer consolatory models for understanding and coming to terms with the failure of England's expansionist dreams. The third, "How Lorde William Delapole Duke of Suffolke was worthily punyshed for abusing his Kyng and causing the destruction of good Duke Humfrey," pursues two distinct projects. It first moves readers to indict the dominant political figure of Edward VI's last years, John Dudley, Duke of Northumberland, for the destruction of the proud imperial ideal and for the concomitant introduction of sin and murder into the highest levels of the English state. It then issues an admonitory plea to the officers of the current, Marian regime, urging them to protect the nation from the widely feared threat of foreign dominance posed by England's new Habsburg monarch, Philip of Spain.

The Rise and Fall of Mid-Tudor Imperialism

Since at least the time of King Henry V, England's rulers understood themselves to be imperial monarchs whose status and rank derived in direct succession from Charlemagne and the Roman emperor Constantine.[1] It was Henry VIII, however, who gave the rhetoric of English imperialism new meaning and vigor, particularly in the last two decades of his reign. Throughout his time in power, Henry had presented himself to the world as a proud, bellicose ruler. He actively cultivated the values of late-medieval chivalry at his court, and both he and his nobles eagerly sought out opportunities to display their martial prowess, either through military excursions abroad or through elaborate chivalric displays at home.[2] Henry considered England not just a kingdom but an empire, and he vigorously sought to bring nearby lands into subjection to the English crown. By the 1530s his zeal for foreign conquest had become linked with an increasing sense of pride in "Englishness" and English self-determination. The king's consolidation of secular and religious power after the break from Rome helped to create a new sense of national self-consciousness, "an enhanced feeling," in Alan Smith's words, "that England was both very different from and much superior to other European states." In the iconography and official language that identified Henry's England as an "imperial" realm, two notions of imperialism soon became intertwined: imperialism as the subjugation of an aggregation of territories to one (English) monarch, and imperialism as the claim by the English monarch to absolute sovereignty in his own lands.[3]

1. For a survey of early modern English assertions of imperial status, see Hoak, "Iconography," 54–103.

2. Gunn, "French Wars of Henry VIII," 34–37; Mayer, "On the Road to 1534," 29; Helen Miller, *Henry VIII and the English Nobility*, 158, 160–61; Hoak, "Iconography," 89. Henry spent almost a quarter of his reign at war with France, and he mounted substantial attacks on the Scots in 1513, 1542, 1544, and 1545. These Scottish expeditions were in addition to the almost constant smaller-scale border skirmishes between England and Scotland that occurred throughout Henry's reign.

3. Alan Smith, *Emergence of a Nation State*, 88; Levack, *Formation of the British State*, 2; Hoak, "Iconography," 54–103. As we saw in chapter 1, William Baldwin expresses his own continuing support for this lost concept of "imperial" England through the iconography of the title page of *Memorial of suche Princes*.

The ideals of Henrician imperialism guided English foreign policy well into Edward VI's reign. The young King Edward's Protector of the Realm, Edward Seymour, Duke of Somerset, pursued the same sort of "glorious" expansionist schemes that had characterized "the triumphant reign" of Henry VIII. The rhetoric of honor that surrounded Seymour's foreign policy, however, was noticeably less personal than that employed by King Henry. The Protector's supporters understood Seymour to engage in foreign conflicts not so much to augment his own glory (or that of his young king, who did no fighting), but to achieve idealistic ends and to augment the honor of the nation as a whole.[4] As had Henry before him, Seymour won fervent popular support for his imperialist schemes, despite the severe financial burden they placed on the people. Modern historians tend to dismiss Henry's and Seymour's expansionist designs as wasteful, foolhardy missteps.[5] Most men and women of the time, however, saw them as glorious endeavors, wellsprings of English pride and the very means by which England could come to assume its rightful place as one of Europe's chief political powers.

It is to the initial, seemingly limitless promise of English imperialism and to its sudden, shocking failure that the poems "Salisbury," "James I," and "Suffolk" respond. In particular, these works seek to confront, to explain, and to offer consolation for the humiliating end of mid-Tudor England's two chief expansionist obsessions: the attempt to force Scotland to accede to union with England and the drive to enlarge and maintain an English presence in France.

In the 1530s and early 1540s Henry VIII moved to extend English hegemony over all of the British Isles. In 1536 he incorporated Wales into the English state, imposing both English law and English religion upon the Welsh. Five years later he declared Ireland a monarchy and proclaimed himself its king. Only Scotland remained outside English control. Henry understood the king of England to be the rightful ruler of Scotland and strove in the 1540s to join the two kingdoms under English sovereignty. His government's policy toward the Scots during this time has been aptly described as "a mix-

4. See, for instance, the rhetoric of English glory won in Seymour's victory over the Scots at Pinkie in William Patten's *Expedition into Scotland of . . . Edward, Duke of Somerset*, the best-known account of the 1547 Scottish invasion. While Patten gives fervent praise to Seymour, he ultimately awards the victory not just to Seymour and his troops but to every Englishman. Even though the majority of English citizens remained at home, "far from any danger of the loss," they too, he insists, cannot "be but full partners of the winning," for the English victory over the Scots is merely an expression of a general English national greatness (Patten, *Expedition*, 156). See also Hooper, *Declaracion of Christe*, sigs. A2r–A4v.

5. See, for instance, Elton, *Reform and Reformation*, 308, 341; Guy, *Tudor England*, 190–93, 203.

ture of blandishments and violence": it was composed of rapid shifts between diplomatic overtures and vicious martial invasions. At the beginning of the decade Henry attempted to influence Scottish affairs by playing the role of the wise uncle to his nephew James V, sending James unsolicited letters of guidance on religion and government. When James refused to attend a requested meeting at York in 1541, however, his uncle's policy quickly turned to violence. The following year the English invaded Scotland, delivering to the Scots a devastating blow at the battle of Solway Moss. Although few were actually killed in the battle, the Scottish forces were routed, and a great number of the Scottish nobility fell into English hands. When King James V died just a few weeks later, his death was commonly said to have resulted from his anguish over Scotland's defeat.[6]

In the wake of Solway Moss, Henry abandoned violent methods and turned to diplomatic ones. In the hopes of setting up an anglophile faction in Scotland, Henry compelled the Scottish nobles captured at Solway Moss to pledge to support English interests in their own country. This period of peaceful overtures culminated in the Treaty of Greenwich (1543), which betrothed England's Prince Edward to the infant Mary, Queen of Scots. The goal of the English-dictated treaty was to unite the two countries by uniting their present and future rulers, with England as the dominant partner in the proposed new "British" kingdom. Nevertheless, painful memories of English aggression, a strong diplomatic campaign by France, and the presence of a powerful anti-English faction in the Scottish Parliament turned Scottish sentiment decisively against the proposed union. To Henry's great anger, in December 1543 the Scottish Parliament—whose members included the allegedly "assured" pro-English Scots recruited after Solway Moss—refused to ratify the sealed Greenwich Treaty. After the accord was rejected, violent invasion once again became the English policy. Henry ordered Edward Seymour, Earl of Hertford (the future Duke of Somerset), to lay waste to Leith and Edinburgh as a punitive lesson. Rather than reducing the Scots to submission, however, Seymour's bloody excursions produced only more intransigent Scottish resistance to England's political overtures. Until his death Henry's Scottish policy continued to mix inconclusive border raids and martial incursions with ineffectual overtures to Scottish leaders. The battle for Scotland was fated to continue well into Edward's reign.[7]

6. Hechter, *Internal Colonialism*, 74; Scarisbrick, *Henry VIII*, 425 (for quote), 436; Ridley, *Henry VIII*, 368. For Henry VIII's claim to sovereignty over Scotland, see his *Declaration, Conteynyng the Iust Cavses and Consyderations, of this Present Warre with the Scottis.*

7. Elton, *Reform*, 306–7; Jordan, *Edward VI: The Young King*, 241–43; Scarisbrick, *Henry VIII*, 444, 452. *Memorial* author Sir Thomas Chaloner served Seymour during the 1544 Scottish expedition as the courier of funds for Seymour's troops (Millar, *Tudor Mercenaries*, 148).

While Henry VIII's interest in Scotland was strong, his chief martial dream was to renew war with England's longtime enemy France. Throughout his reign Henry had claimed the French crown as his own and had maintained a strong desire to regain English lands in France lost under Henry VI.[8] In 1544 Henry, along with the chief military men of his day, traveled with an army of forty thousand men to Calais. Led in part by John Dudley, Viscount Lisle (the future Duke of Northumberland), an English force besieged and captured the fortified town of Boulogne. Henry saw the taking of Boulogne as one of the great victories of his reign. He entered the captured city in the manner of a triumph, with a sword borne naked before him "like a noble and valyaunt conqueror."[9]

After the first flush of victory, however, the French war and the occupation of Boulogne proved to be tremendous financial drains. William Paget, Stephen Gardiner, and other Englishmen involved in diplomacy urged Henry to make peace and return Boulogne; Henry, however, saw Boulogne as a proud symbol of English (and his own personal) imperial power and strove to hold on to it at all costs. Over the next two years the war dragged on as the French laid siege to Boulogne and sent pirating expeditions against English merchant vessels. Henry reluctantly came to realize that he would have to make peace with France. Although he originally refused to consider giving up Boulogne, he finally agreed in 1546 to the Treaty of Campe, negotiated by William Paget and John Dudley, which specified that the English would occupy Boulogne until 1554, at which time it would be returned to the French. Even though he ultimately agreed to the treaty, Henry was full of misgivings and to the end clung to the hope (suggested to him by Paget) that in the eight years before Boulogne was due to be returned, new victories might allow the town to remain English.[10]

Henry died soon after approving the Treaty of Campe. After his death, Edward Seymour, now Duke of Somerset, took charge of the English government. Seymour was obsessed with bringing to fruition Henry's scheme for uniting England and Scotland. Shortly after his assumption of the protectorship, Seymour led an expedition into Scotland designed to compel the Scots to honor the marriage provisions of the Treaty of Greenwich. After issuing a proclamation which insisted that he sought only peace with the Scots, Seymour entered Scotland, capturing towns and castles, and finally defeating

8. Potter, "Foreign Policy," 108; Gunn, "French Wars of Henry VIII," 38.

9. Hall, "Henry VIII," in *Union*, fol. 259r. Hall suggests that Henry sought to conquer no further French lands only because Henry's ally Charles V treacherously made a separate peace with the French king.

10. Scarisbrick, *Henry VIII*, 450, 464; Gammon, *Statesman and Schemer*, 105–6.

the assembled Scottish forces at Pinkie Clough. The English lost about 250 men at Pinkie, the Scottish at least ten thousand. It was (to English minds) a glorious victory, one in which *Memorial* authors George Ferrers and Thomas Chaloner took part as gentlemen servants of the Lord Protector.[11]

Seymour followed his victory with a new round of attempts at reconciliation and friendship with the Scots. Rather than lay waste to the country, Seymour established numerous English garrisons designed to lend support to friendly Scottish nobles, who, Seymour hoped, would persuade their countrymen to accept the Greenwich accord. Furthermore, he began a print campaign of peace overtures that attempted to woo the Scottish people as a whole to the idea of a single Anglo-Scottish "empire" called Britain.[12]

The Scottish nobles who had agreed to further English interests in Scotland quickly turned against England, however, when they perceived it was safe to do so. The Scots appealed to the French for aid soon after the massacre at Pinkie, and in July 1548 the Scottish Parliament unanimously approved a Franco-Scottish alliance that signaled the end of Seymour's Scottish policy. Most galling for Seymour was the new Franco-Scottish marriage agreement that betrothed Mary, Queen of Scots, to the Dauphin in terms that seemed almost to parody those of the Treaty of Greenwich. Soon after ratification of the agreement, the young Queen Mary was sent to France to live with, and to marry (when she came of age), the French prince. In return, the French sent ten thousand troops to Scotland to help fight the English in the ongoing skirmishes between the two countries. Protecting the border and supporting the new garrisons quickly became crippling burdens on the English treasury.[13]

In the wake of these developments, Seymour once again turned his thoughts to invasion; he was in the process of building up a new expeditionary force when he was deposed in 1549. His focus on Scotland helped lead him to mishandle the early stages of the 1549 rebellions in his own country. Seymour offered the rebels mainly conciliatory rhetoric, attempting to appease them in part so that his gathered forces could be sent to Scotland rather than be diverted to put down their uprisings.[14] Seymour's leniency only emboldened the rebels, and the violence in the countryside soon raged out of control. In August the most powerful men on the Privy Council took matters into their own hands, gathering forces to suppress the rebellions

11. Elton, *Reform*, 340; Jordan, *Edward VI: The Young King*, 247, 252–63; Bush, *Government Policy*, 1.

12. Bush, *Government Policy*, 2, 7–40; Jordan, *Edward VI: The Young King*, 268–80.

13. Jordan, *Edward VI: The Young King*, 283–91; Elton, *Reform*, 341.

14. Bush, *Government Policy*, 160–61.

themselves and ultimately charging Seymour with misgovernment and deposing him from office in October 1549.[15]

Meanwhile, English-held Boulogne remained a serious drain on England's money and manpower. The new French king, Henri II, wanted Boulogne returned to France years before the date specified by the Treaty of Campe. Henri seized the initiative in 1549, declaring war on England and attacking Boulogne while the English government was preoccupied by its domestic conflicts. The politically unstable Dudley regime came to the conclusion that Boulogne was not worth defending for the full term of the Campe treaty. Dudley sought to end hostilities with France by offering to return Boulogne before the negotiated date. William Paget, who with Dudley had negotiated the Treaty of Campe, now concluded an inauspicious peace with France in the Treaty of Boulogne (1550), which entailed returning Boulogne four years early and for only half the compensation that the Treaty of Campe had specified.[16] While the English still held Calais and were able to defend their border with Scotland during Dudley's ascendancy, the grand expansionist policy of the preceding years was abandoned in favor of what seemed to many an almost desperate pursuit of amity with the French. The new Dudley-led regime also gave up on Seymour's plan to unite England and Scotland. Most of Seymour's important garrisons fell within months of his deposition, and in 1551 England ratified the Treaty of Angers, whose terms ended for good the "rough wooing" of the Scots that had guided Anglo-Scottish relations for almost a decade.[17]

By the time the poems of *A Memorial of suche Princes* were being composed (1554), the English imperialist policy of the 1540s had been completely overturned. Not only did the current monarch, Queen Mary, decline to challenge Scotland or France, but also to the horror of many she announced that she intended to marry the powerful foreign prince Philip of Spain, a move that even numerous of her well-wishers saw as a potentially mortal blow to English sovereignty. In contemplating the Spanish match, many feared that England would be condemned to permanent status as a second-rate power: the "Common humour" of Englishmen and women at the time was said to be one of fear that their nation would become nothing more than an inglorious, submissive client state of the mighty Habsburg Empire.[18] Worse, such fears were accompanied by the bitter knowledge that the dream of a powerful and independent English empire had been lost not through honorable defeat

15. See chapter 1.
16. Elton, *Reform*, 359.
17. Jordan, *Edward VI: The Young King*, 299–300; Elton, *Reform*, 341, 359–60.
18. Ham, "Auto-biography of Sir James Croft," 53.

on the battlefield but through the foreign policies of the very monarch and her officers supposedly charged with protecting English lands and English glory.

"Thomas Montague, Earl of Salysbury," and the Failure of English Expansionism

The first of the *Memorial* poems born from the loss of the imperialist ideal is "How Thomas Montague the earle of Salysbury in the middes of his glory, was chaunceably slayne with a piece of ordinaunce." In the poem, Thomas of Salisbury returns from his grave to rehearse his glorious life and sudden, unfortunate death. After a short section handling his father's rebellion against King Henry IV, Salisbury turns to his own life narrative, a bravura recollection of his military and political triumphs in the early fifteenth century.[19] Salisbury's ghost recalls how during his life he won success in all his endeavors. Under Henry V, Salisbury quickly rose to prominence through his skill in foreign dealings, both through military campaigns and through his participation in diplomatic negotiations (146). When Henry V's "pore litle babe" Henry VI received the crown, Salisbury continued to serve his country both at home and abroad. According to the poem, he often bore "rule at home" in the place of England's Protector of the Realm, Humfrey, Duke of Gloucester. The English people loved Salisbury, whom they called the "good earle," for his uniquely gentle, caring periods of domestic rule (147).

Salisbury, a man both "in peace and war wel skilled," won his greatest success campaigning on foreign soil. In France, Salisbury's peaceful disposition led him always first to negotiate with besieged towns, promising their citizens that they would be "frendly vsed" if they surrendered to him (147–48). To those who came armed against him in the field, however, he offered fierce battle. Through his mixed methods of "mild" negotiation and brutal violence, Salisbury earned numerous victories in France, capturing towns, defeating French armies, and destroying over three dozen forts. His long string of conquests came to an end only when, on the verge of his greatest victory (the capture of the town of Orlyaunce [Orléans]), a French artillery shell chanced to hit a wall near him, driving a sharp piece of iron grating into his cheek. He died less than a week later from this freak accident, still in "the middes of his glory" (152, 154).

In constructing his narrative, the "Salisbury" poet departs markedly from his two historical sources, Edward Hall's *Union* and Robert Fabyan's *Chron-*

19. For a reading of Salisbury's opening defense of his father, see chapter 2.

icle. In their works Hall and Fabyan both present Salisbury solely as a fierce and relentless warrior. Neither chronicler ascribes to Salisbury the naturally gentle disposition bestowed on him by the poem, nor does either mention Salisbury's employing any uniquely "frendly" style of negotiation with towns held under siege.[20] Finally, nowhere in the poet's sources is there any suggestion that Salisbury carried out "rule at home" in the place of England's Lord Protector. On the contrary, Hall and Fabyan both portray Salisbury as spending his entire career under Henry VI fighting on French soil.

Although the name of the protagonist of "Salisbury" and the list of his French victories may be those of the fifteenth-century Lancastrian hero Thomas Montague, Earl of Salisbury, the character and methods of the poem's Salisbury are without precedent in the poet's sources. The poet endows his chief character with such attributes precisely to conjure up in readers' minds memories not of the historical earl but of the recently deceased Edward Seymour, Duke of Somerset. The poet's description of Salisbury's rise to prominence through martial and diplomatic skill is meant to recall Seymour's own similar rise under Henry VIII; his assertion that his protagonist ruled England in place of the Lord Protector recalls Seymour's own tenure in that office; and his several identifications of Salisbury as the "good earle" evoke memories of Edward Seymour's well-known title "the good Duke," bestowed on him by his supporters among the common people.[21] More pointedly, the description of Salisbury's "vertuous life, fre hart, and lowly mind," as well as his reputation for mild domestic governance, stirs up strong memories of the idealized public image that Edward Seymour had enjoyed in the heady days of his Protectorate. As we have seen, Seymour's admirers understood Edward VI's Lord Protector to have been an ever gentle, virtuous, and loving leader, a man whose innocent and kindly disposition guided him in his benevolent rule of the nation.[22] John Foxe's assessment of Seymour's character may stand as but one example of many similar tributes to Seymour's supposed traits of humility and purity. For Foxe,

> there was alwayes in [Edward Seymour] great humanitie, and such meekenes and gentlenes, as is rare to be found in so high estate. He was prone and ready to geue eare vnto the complaints and supplications of the poore, and no lesse attentiue to the affayres of the co[m]mon wealth. Which, if he had lyued

20. Hall presents Salisbury as a man of unrelieved ferocity, one so far from promising "gentle" treatment of resistant French towns that the mention of his name alone was enough to throw their townspeople into terrified panic. See Hall, "Henry VI," fols. 2r, 4r, 9v, 11v, 22r. Fabyan offers no description in his chronicle either of Salisbury's character or of his methods.

21. *Mirror*, 142, 147, 152. For Edward Seymour's reputation as "the good Duke of Somerset," see chapters 1 and 2.

22. See chapter 1.

> together with king Edward, was like to do much good in reformyng many misorders within this realme. He was vtterly ignorant of al craft and deceit and as farre voyd of all pride and ambicion, as he was from doing of iniury, being in deede vtterly voyd of both.[23]

The "Salisbury" poet's unhistorical praise of his protagonist's "lowly mind" evokes memories of Seymour's reputation for "meekness"; his description of Salisbury's "vertuous life" suggests Seymour's alleged inability to do injury as well as his concern for the commonwealth, and his declaration of Salisbury's "fre hart" parallels the belief of Seymour's admirers in their hero's "great humanity."

In a similar manner, Salisbury's insistence that "in assaultes due mildnes passeth farre / Al rigour, force, and sturdy violence" echoes the celebrated rhetoric of mildness and friendship that Seymour adopted in his attempts to bring Scotland under English hegemonic control (147). Seymour first employed such language in a widely disseminated proclamation issued shortly before his invasion of Scotland on September 4, 1547. In this work, which was addressed to the Scots but released in both Scotland and England, Seymour insisted that he and his English forces came to Scotland only as men bent on altruistic ends, as concerned well-wishers who "are come in this maner, whiche pretendeth a force in apparence (but not in deede) onely to defende and maintein the honor of bothe the Princes and realmes" of England and Scotland equally. The English expedition, Seymour insisted, would "come into this realme not as an enemie . . . but as a frend," a friend whose goal was not to conquer but to join the two kingdoms as peacefully as possible so that both their peoples could exist in "a frendly kynde of liuying" as "Britons." Unlike the openly bellicose Henry VIII, Seymour asserted no claims of English overlordship over Scotland, nor did he threaten any act of revenge on the Scots as a whole for reneging on the Greenwich treaty. Instead Seymour promised safety and "free libertie" to any Scot who would pledge himself to the English cause and promised that the English would do "the least hurte or domage that we can" to Scottish lands.[24] Of course to the Scots, such rhetoric rang bitterly hollow in the wake of the slaughter at Pinkie Clough; in England, however, the Protector's admirers treated this proclamation as a window onto Seymour's soul, as a true revelation of his intentions in

23. Foxe, *Actes and Monuments*, 132[2] (page 1322 is misprinted as 1323 in the copy owned by the Huntington Library).

24. Edward Seymour, Duke of Somerset, *Edward, Duke of Somerset . . . : To all . . . of the Realme of Scotlande*. This proclamation was disseminated in Scotland and printed for English readers in London. Seymour indicated in the opening of his proclamation that it was made in his name alone, and not in the king's or that of the Privy Council, emphasizing that this profession of reluctance to invade and promise of good treatment was his personal pledge to the Scots.

Scotland, and as clear evidence of his underlying virtuous nature.[25] It is this image of Seymour as the loving, reluctant military leader that the poet urges readers to revive through the Salisbury of his poem.

The poet evokes such memories both to explain and to offer consolation for the painful, unforeseen collapse of Seymour's "glorious" imperialist designs. Despite their fervent support for the Protector and his goal of uniting England and Scotland, Seymour's former admirers could not help but admit that his almost obsessive dream of a new "British" empire under English hegemonic control never came to pass. The humiliating, desultory end of Seymour's long-cherished designs on Scotland left his supporters in a psychological bind, torn between their desire to believe in the rectitude of their former hero and his foreign policies and their painful knowledge that both Seymour and his chief foreign policy undertaking had ended only in failure.

"Salisbury" takes readers back to this time and urges them to interpret Seymour's failure to achieve his imperialist ends in terms not of ignominious defeat but of glorious promise unfulfilled. The details of the poem direct readers' thoughts away from the controversial end of Seymour's expansionist schemes and toward memories of the celebrated military and diplomatic successes Seymour had once enjoyed. By evoking thoughts of his numerous decisive victories over foreign forces throughout his lifetime, the poet seeks to have readers embrace the idea that Seymour could easily have achieved similar success had he only been allowed to remain in power long enough to pursue his imperialist designs to ultimate fruition.

To stir such thoughts, the "Salisbury" poet devotes the great majority of his narrative not to the tragic nature of Salisbury's demise but to a celebration of his victorious life. Through his long, detailed lists of the numerous victories Salisbury achieved by employing his mix of mild rhetoric and fierce martial skill, the poet urges readers to recollect and to celebrate the similarly long list of successes Edward Seymour had achieved through his own use of "friendly" rhetoric and martial prowess in the years before his deposition. Reflecting the fact that the French were England's main opponents in Scotland after 1547, the poet's description of the ease with which Salisbury defeated all his French foes suggests the similar success Edward Seymour might have achieved had he only been allowed to invade Scotland once more. In the poem, the ghostly Salisbury describes how his engagements with French and Scottish forces always resulted in English victories. In France, Salisbury and

25. For contemporary testaments to the belief that Seymour was a reluctant, peaceable warrior, see Patten, *Expedition*, 62, 68; Foxe, *Actes and Monuments*, 1323; Grafton, *Grafton's Chronicle*, 2:501, 508.

his soldiers easily moved from one triumph to another; in fact, many of his foes simply fled at the mere sight of the mighty English leader and his men.[26] The poet, tellingly, uses the term "frenchly" to describe the manner in which French troops "tooke them selves to flight" before Salisbury's forces, implying that running away is a characteristic trait of the French when faced with the superior soldiers of England (151).

The poet, in fact, works formally as well as thematically to suggest how rapidly Seymour's English troops might have won victories over their French foes. While the stanzas on the domestic troubles of Salisbury's father which begin the poem contain many end-stopped lines, most of the seven-line stanzas recounting Salisbury's victories contain only one or two full stops. This sudden breathless quickening of the reading experience impresses upon readers a sense of swiftness as Salisbury races from victory to victory. The poet also takes the large number of town, fortress, and battle names that he finds in Hall's narrative and compresses them into a small, tightly packed space of only one hundred lines, filling whole stanzas with the names of Salisbury's victories. The effect is to all but overwhelm readers with the rapid catalogue of triumph:

> But to returne, in Mayne wan I at length,
> Such towns & fortes as might either helpe or hurt,
> I manned Mayon & Suzans townes of strength,
> Fort Barnarde, Thanceaux, & S. Cales the curt,
> With Lile sues Bolton, standing in the durt:
> Eke Gwerland, Susze, Loupeland and Mountsure,
> With Malicorne, these wan I and kept full sure. (150)

With this evocation of the easy French victories rung up by his mild yet warlike fifteenth-century protagonist, the poet encourages readers to believe that the sixteenth-century leader whom Salisbury resembles, Edward Seymour, could have achieved similarly quick and decisive success had he ever been allowed to take the field against the new French forces in Scotland.[27]

The poem also insists on the success of Salisbury's morally laudable peace overtures in order to imply the similar success Seymour would have found by employing the same means in a new Scottish invasion. Salisbury's offers

26. When the poem does show a valiant foreign warrior (such as Baldwin of Toyser), the inevitable defeat of such a foe only adds that much more glory to the victorious English soldiers (*Mirror*, 149–50). Like many of his mid-Tudor contemporaries, the "Salisbury" poet celebrates the "Englishness" of the troops and ignores the contributions of foreign mercenaries who often fought in English campaigns.

27. Seymour had already successfully fought and defeated French troops abroad. His expulsion of a much larger French army from the lands surrounding Boulogne (1545) was seen by contemporaries as one of his greatest victories (Patten, *Expedition*, 60–61).

of "frendly" use, the poem declares, "neuer were refused / Of any towne, or surely very seelde." In fact, after hearing of the "fauour" he had shown to inhabitants of other cities, two towns (Mewne and Jargeman) even sent representatives to Salisbury to bestow their keys on him before he was within two days' march of their walls, an image designed to put readers in mind of the numerous Scots whom Seymour's "friendly" 1547 invasion had attracted to the English side both before and after Pinkie. Readers could recall how the pale formed by Seymour's protective garrisons brought numerous "townships in the hither parts of [Scotland] into an honest obedience unto the King's Majesty," just as Salisbury had led French towns to allegiance to Henry VI in the fifteenth century (148, 151).[28] In this way the poem urges readers to conclude that a new expedition led by Seymour himself (one that Seymour had often spoken of during the Protectorate) could have finally brought Scotland under English control, achieving this end as much through the influence of Seymour's much-lauded "sweet and peaceable" overtures as by his military might.[29]

Finally, through its account of Salisbury's "unfortunate" end, the poet moves readers to dismiss the troubling implications of Seymour's failure to unite the kingdoms and to accept that failure as simply the unmerited result of blind fortune. "Salisbury" is the only poem of the *Memorial* that presents its protagonist's fall solely as the result of unmotivated accident. In this poem, unlike others of the collection, there is no attempt to find either a providential cause for Salisbury's sudden demise or one rooted in the faults of its protagonist or his political rivals. Rather, Salisbury's loss on the cusp of capturing Orlyaunce is portrayed as an instance of tragic bad luck, a freak accident rather than a divinely ordered event. Salisbury's failure to achieve ultimate victory in France thus provides a comforting model by which readers could interpret Seymour's failure to unite the kingdoms of Scotland and England as similarly the product of random, undeserved misfortune. As we have seen, in the wake of Seymour's deposition the Protector's enemies proclaimed Seymour himself to be the chief cause of England's foreign policy disasters.[30] "Salisbury," by contrast, excludes any suggestion of fault either in its protagonist or in his grand imperialist vision of foreign conquest. Instead of explaining Salisbury's demise in terms of personal or political failings, the

28. Bush, *Government Policy*, 32; Patten, *Expedition*, 59.

29. Until the end of his rule, Seymour's rhetoric was that of complete confidence that Scotland would be his (whether by peaceful overtures or through war) after a planned final invasion of the nation. See, for instance, Nicholas Pocock, *Troubles*, ix, 148–49; and Pollard, *England under Protector Somerset*, 139.

30. For such charges, see, for example, Nicholas Pocock, *Troubles*, 96, 115–16; Stow, *Annales* (1592), 1016; Cavendish, *Metrical Visions*, 106. See also chapter 1.

poem's moral simply asks readers to accept that even the greatest of men cannot know the outcome of their plans. Recalling how he had renewed his campaigns in France and seemed poised to take Orlyaunce, Salisbury exclaims:

> See Baldwin the vncertaynty of glory,
> How sodayne mischief dasheth all to dust.
> And warne all princes by my broken story,
> The happiest Fortune chiefly to mistrust.
> Was neuer man that alway had his lust.
> Than such be fooles, in fancy more then mad,
> Which hope to haue that neuer any had. (153)

That Salisbury did not win Orylaunce and that Seymour did not win Scotland, despite the promise awakened by both men's glorious and morally laudable careers, must be seen as tragic freaks of fortune. Both had experienced only success in the past and expected only more success in the future. No matter what the ultimate outcome of their dreams of conquest, the poem suggests, both should be remembered by their admirers as men who ended their lives on the very cusp of new victory and who were lost while still "in the middes of [their] glory."

Tragedy as Therapy: "James I" and the Failure of Union

As we have seen, up to the time of Seymour's deposition the Protector's supporters had continued to have high hopes for Seymour's dream of an Anglo-Scottish unity created under English hegemony. After Pinkie, Seymour had made advances to the most powerful Scottish nobles and almost all had accepted England's terms.[31] The Scottish problem appeared on its way to being solved. But just as the anglophile party that Henry VIII had created out of the Scottish nobles captured at Solway Moss turned against England after 1542, so Seymour's most powerful Scottish allies began to slip away after 1547 to support a French alliance. To his admirers' chagrin, Seymour was never able to bring Scotland under English control or even to build up through negotiation a dominant anglophile party in Scotland.

31. Bush, *Government Policy*, 20–21. For a detailed view of the remarkable side switching of the Scottish magnates during Henry's and Edward's reigns, see the articles on the Earl of Arran (Regent of Scotland during Edward VI's reign), the Earl of Angus (Henry VIII's brother-in-law and stepfather of James V), and Lord Huntly (the former Chancellor of Scotland) in Matthew and Harrison, *Oxford Dictionary of National Biography*. The latter two Scottish nobles had actually spent time in England (as a refugee and a prisoner, respectively), with Angus residing there for a decade.

It is the sorrow over Seymour's failed hopes and untimely end that colors the remarkable prose passage following the Salisbury poem. There Baldwin represents the *Memorial* authors as driven into "dumpne[s]" over the early, sudden end of Salisbury's glorious career. Although the author of "Salisbury" worked to evoke only the highlights of Seymour's career as a foreign policy leader, his fellows nevertheless cannot help but dwell on Salisbury's "wofull destynye" to die young and the misery for England that resulted from the loss of such a hero. Baldwin seems to recognize that he and the other authors cannot limit the emotional resonances of their narratives: against all intent, they themselves are driven into "dumpne[s]" by a poem chiefly designed to mitigate such woe by recalling Seymour's glory and promise (154).

In response to the authors' melancholy, a new, unnamed poet speaks up, declaring that he has a poem to "quicken vp [their] spirites." This poem is "How king Iames the first for breaking his othes and bondes, was by gods suffrauns miserably murdred of his owne subiectes." On its face, the dismal subject matter of this tragedy would seem to offer little to "quicken vp" anyone. In the poem the ghost of James I appears before the authors to relate the sins and mistakes of his tragic life. During James's early childhood, his weak father, Robert III, had turned over rule of Scotland to James's uncle, Walter of Albany.[32] The new Regent, however, soon began to "fetch a fetch" to get the crown for himself (155). Walter took James's elder brother, Davy of Rothsay, under his supervision and arranged that the vice-ridden prince would slowly be starved to death. Davy's murder prompted the fearful King Robert to send young James to France to keep him out of Walter's hands. En route to France, James's ship blew off course to England, where the prince was captured by Henry IV.[33] James remained a prisoner in England for eighteen years, during which time he was well educated and treated kindly by the English. Eventually, in Henry VI's reign, James was released. He married

32. The "James I" poet follows Hall's *Union* for the basic historical circumstances of his narrative. As a consequence, he repeats Hall's confusion about the identity of the Regent of Scotland during King Robert III's last years. While in his chronicle he initially identifies the Scottish Regent correctly as Robert, Duke of Albany, Hall later mistakes Robert for Walter, Earl of Atholl (Hall, "Henry IV," in *Union*, fols. 17r, 26v). Robert of Albany and Robert III were sons of Robert II by his first wife (Robert III's original given name had been John); Walter was a son of Robert II by his second wife. Although Hall correctly distinguishes Robert of Albany from Walter of Atholl during his later discussion of the death of Duke Murdo, the author of "James I" continues to conflate the two men (Hall, "Henry VI," fol. 53v). Since the poet later shows that he is aware that Duke Murdo is the son of Walter's elder brother, Robert of Albany, it appears that the conflation of Robert and Walter is intentional. The "James I" poet combines the two men, it seems, in order to create for the sake of simplicity a single character suggesting the various anti-English figures in sixteenth-century Scotland who helped lead formerly anglophile Scots away from English control. For the historical James I and the events of his reign, see Brown, *James I*.

33. James was twelve years old at the time of his capture (Brown, *James I*, 17).

the Duke of Somerset's daughter (a cousin to Henry) and was allowed to return to Scotland to assume his deceased father's crown. Before he left, James pledged eternal amity toward England.

Despite an initial, brief period of good rule in Scotland, James soon succumbed to the savagely amoral culture of Scottish politics. The dissembling Walter convinced James that Duke Murdo, an innocent man, was the one responsible for Davy's death.[34] James fell victim to his uncle's deception and quickly had Murdo executed. Walter then counseled James to forsake England for a French alliance. James, by that point himself steeped in vices, agreed, for no other reason than a belief that it is "madnes for a king to kepe his troth" (159). After breaking from his former friends in England, however, he was eventually set upon by his scheming uncle, who spurred several men to kill King James in his own Privy Chamber.

The events of James's tragic career would seem best suited to a moral exemplum warning against the treachery of near kin (Walter) or to an admonition against the sin of regicide. Yet surprisingly, the primary moral the poet draws from James's death is that God hates princes who do not hold to their oaths. Certainly the poet denounces the murder of Duke Murdo, James's own flesh and blood. Nevertheless, he presents this crime as minor compared to James's more heinous sin of not keeping his word: "See Baldwin Baldwin, the vnhappy endes, / Of suche as passe not for theyr lawfull oth: / Of those that causeles leaue theyr fayth or frendes" (160).

In its narrative and moral, then, "James I" presents modern readers with at least two interpretive difficulties: first, why does the "James I" poet insist that this gloomy tale of murder will "quicken vp" the spirits of the *Memorial* authors, and second, why does he emphasize above all the "sin" of oath breaking in a narrative filled with seemingly more heinous crimes such as rebellion and regicide? To answer these questions and to understand the significance of "James I" as a whole, one must approach the poem in the same manner as "Salisbury," in the context of the decade-long "rough wooing" of Scotland.

"James I," like "Salisbury," is directed foremost to the men and women who had supported the former Lord Protector's policies and still revered their legacy. Rather than focus on England's leaders, however, the "James I" poet shapes his narrative of fifteenth-century affairs to reflect the Scots' role in the collapse of the later, sixteenth-century plan for Anglo-Scottish union. The portrayed similarities between events of the two eras are designed to encourage readers to respond to James I's "treachery" against England with the

34. Duke Murdo is the historical Murdac Stewart, Duke of Albany (d. 1425), son of Robert of Albany.

emotions provoked by the similar Scottish "treachery" of the mid-sixteenth century. When James suddenly falls victim to murder for his crimes, readers are meant to experience his providential downfall as a vicarious literary substitute for the longed-for vengeance against the hated sixteenth-century Scottish leaders whose "crimes" he shares. Though couched as a warning to the Scots to avoid oath breaking and murder, "James I" is not so much an admonition as a displaced revenge fantasy, a therapeutic narrative for readers still pained by the failure of Henry VIII's and Seymour's Scottish policies.

"James I" is at once informed by and works as a confirmation of deeply held English beliefs about the moral and political failings of the Scots and the cultural superiority of the English.[35] The Scottish figures in the poem all typify the worst aspects of sixteenth-century Scottish political behavior (as understood by the English). The members of the Stewart royal family are gullible, wavering, and depraved. King Robert is timorous and weak: he is able neither to avenge his eldest son's death nor to protect his younger son from intrigue in his own court. Davy Rothsay is a corrupt adulterer who easily falls prey to his scheming uncle. Despite a promising start, James is himself by the end of his life vicious and bereft of moral conscience. In Scotland's vacuum of assertive leadership, Walter, the scheming machiavellian figure, is the only true ruler of Scotland, and he controls all through manipulation and murder. The Scottish political leaders of the poem are clearly unable to rule their own country in any stable or orderly fashion, and Scottish political culture is characterized as one of violence and conspiracy, in which kinsmen murder kinsmen and plot constantly against one another. The poem portrays Scotland as a country desperately in need of the sort of civilized political guidance it is unable to provide for itself.

By contrast, the guiding model of good rule in the poem is Lancastrian England. Ignoring the numerous images of English internal discord that occupied previous poems in the *Memorial*, the "James I" poet figures England and its rulers as models of civility and order. In "James I" the leaders of England (Henry IV, Henry V, and the nobles who rule during the minority of Henry VI) are moral, kind, and wise. After capturing James when his

35. Xenophobic views of the Scots were shared by virtually all Englishmen who dealt with them during this period. Even Henry VIII's ambassador to Scotland, Sir Ralph Sadler, complained that "never man had to do with so rude, so inconstant and beastly a nation as this is," while Thomas Wharton, one of England's chief military leaders in the North, denounced the Scots' "natural inclination" to "falsehood and cruelty" in dealing with the English (Ridley, *Henry VIII*, 379; Bush, *Government Policy*, 31). In his chronicle, Edward Hall portrays Scottish rulers, both past and present, as "falce fraudulent" men and the Scottish people as a whole as "braggyng and bostyng," "barbarous, sauage, rude, and without all good nurtur" (Hall, "Henry VI," fol. 4v, "Henry IV," 28v). See also Hall, "Henry IV," fols. 17r–18r, 26v–28v; "Henry VI," fols. 4v–5r; 52v–53v.

ship is blown off course to England, Henry IV does not exact revenge on the young Scot for his country's past invasions of England but instead laudably attends to James's education in a manner commensurate with both chivalric and humanistic ideals:

> But good king Henry seing I was a child,
> And heyre by ryght vnto a realme and crowne,
> Dyd bring me vp, not lyke my brother, wylde
> But vertuously in feates of high renowne:
> In liberal artes in instrumentall sowne:
> By meane wherof whan I was after king,
> I did my realme to ciuil order bring. (157)

Henry IV is figured as a surrogate father for James, one who protects, guides, and educates the young prince in a manner foreign to the culture of the Scottish court.

In Henry IV's paternal nurturing of James, the poet presents an exemplary image of the beneficial relations between England and Scotland that had been promised by the English propaganda works urging union of the kingdoms. These works had portrayed the English bids for dominance in Scotland as offers of paternal oversight and friendship: the English desire to place Scotland under the rule of Edward VI, they claimed, was an altruistic one born of concern for the Scots' own welfare.[36] England's past and present meddling in Scottish affairs was presented as an expression of concern for Scottish well-being, an attempt to save the Scots from themselves.[37] Thus Henry VIII desired to be understood as the Scottish leaders' best protector, asserting—even as he declared war on Scotland—a past relation with James V similar to that portrayed between Henry IV and James I in the poem.[38] In negotiations, further, Henry had demanded that Scotland send the young Mary, Queen of Scots, to England to receive the proper education he felt she

36. Although English writers asserted various types of actual and/or metaphorical familial relations in speaking of English leaders and the Scots, all their writings shared ultimately a common paternalistic tone. Thus Seymour himself told the Scots that his "loving" appeal to them to join the kingdoms was made "euen as the father to the sonne, or [as] thelder brother would do to the yonger brother" (Edward Seymour, *Epistle or Exhortacion*, 238–39). See also Brodugan [Sir Thomas Smith?], *Epitome of the Title*, 250; and Harryson (or Henrisoun), *Exhortacion*, 235.

37. See, for instance, Harryson, *Exhortacion*, 208–9; Edward Seymour, *Epistle or Exhortacion*, 238–39, 242–43; Brodugan, *Epitome*, 254–56. That English aggression was ultimately responsible for many of the Scottish miseries these works deplore does not trouble their authors.

38. Henry VIII insisted that "we in his youth & tender age preserued and maynteined [King James V] from the great danger of other, and by our authoritie and power conduced hym sauely to the reall possession of his estate" (Henry VIII, *Declaration*, 192). James V was Henry's nephew, and much of the *Declaration* is couched in a tone of anger and disappointment over James's "unnatural" disobedience to his older, wiser kinsman.

could not receive from her countrymen. Seymour's propagandists had argued for union between Scotland and England on the basis that only union could raise the Scots to English levels of civility, godliness, and good order.[39] The relationship between Henry IV and James I in the poem appears to offer readers a historical confirmation of the relationship that Scotland could have enjoyed (according to the English) had it not resisted these overtures. When James returns to his country and brings it to "ciuil order" through the application of the cultural values learned in England, the poem asserts with the cachet of seemingly proven historical example that English cultural influence has already produced just the sort of ameliorating result the propaganda of the 1540s promised it could bring to the "savage" sixteenth-century Scots (157).

The poet, however, does not present solely the value of teaching English cultural principles to the Scots. He shows as well the necessity for English political oversight of Scotland. It is only when James leaves the sphere of English influence that he falls into sin and vice. In Scotland, and thus away from direct English control, James reverts to the Scottish national "type," as portrayed by the other Scottish characters in the poem—to the "naturally" vacillating, treacherous disposition of his countrymen.[40] James's moral collapse results from a combination of the "nature" of his gullibility and lack of firm character (traits shared with his father and brother) and the "nurture" of his manipulation into vice and political blunders by his corrupt uncle Walter. Without the direct influence of the Lancastrian kings, James loses all ability to reason: as he admits, he breaks faith with England simply because "I did iudge / It madnes for a king to kepe his troth" (159). In portraying James's moral breakdown, the poet attributes to James the most despised actions of the sixteenth-century Scottish leaders, including breaking his oath to England, allying himself with the French, and even invading England. Through this irrational, ungrateful rejection of English kindness, the "James I" poet seeks to awaken in readers the same hurt, stunned response provoked by similar Scottish "perfidy" after Solway Moss and, later, Pinkie Clough (158).[41]

39. Franklin, *Scottish Regency*, 58. For Edwardian offers of beneficial guidance to the Scots (religious and secular), see Harryson, *Exhortacion*, 210, 221, 231; Edward Seymour, *Epistle or Exhortacion*, 242; Brodugan, *Epitome*, 255; Patten, *Expedition*, 68–75.

40. Compare Hall: "After [James] had once taken the ayre and smelled the sent of the Scottishe soyle [he] became like hys falce fraudulent forfathers, an vntrue prince, and like his proude pratynge progenitors toke the ymage of a braggyng and bostyng Scot" ("Henry VI," fol. 4v).

41. The sense of hurt and bafflement is registered by Patten when he asks the Scots, "O, how may it be thought to be possible that ye should ever forget, or else not ever remember the great munificence of our most magnificent Prince, our late King [Henry VIII]!" (*Expedition*, 67).

To modern eyes, the Scots' abandonment of English-dictated pacts imposed on them under duress is quite understandable. It nevertheless shocked the English supporters of union, who were convinced that England was offering only unprecedented kindness to the Scots. Henry had publicly offered to give up claims of lordship over Scotland and to marry his only son to the Queen of the Scots. Seymour, in turn, had offered to dissolve the English nation and make it a partner with Scotland in a new "British" nation. The supporters of the English policy toward Scotland of the 1540s could not understand the continued hostility to such magnanimous English designs. The Scots' rejection of all these "gifts" stung as only the brusque rejection of an act of kindness could.

The poet's narrative attempts to soften the hurt still felt by English readers. It suggests that the failure of Anglo-Scottish union was due not to English mistakes or flaws in Seymour's vision for a new united Britain, as those who deposed him charged, but only to defects in the Scottish culture and character, the reasons Seymour's own propagandists offered for Scottish intransigence.[42] James's irrational actions confirm that "madnes" in relations with England is simply an essential characteristic of Scottish leaders past and present, and thus the only reason that need be sought for the failure of Anglo-Scottish accord in modern times.

In its narrative of kindness recompensed by treachery, the poem has thus far offered little to "quicken vp" English spirits. Yet all that occurs in the first hundred lines of the poem is presented chiefly to position readers for the poem's conclusion, to heighten the pleasure of seeing a turncoat Scottish leader come crashing down from the highest of estates. In his chronicle Hall narrates James's murder as a purely political act, one more outrageous event in the bloody history of Scottish politics.[43] In the final stanzas of "James I," however, the poet departs from his source to give his poem a new, distinctly spiritual cast. In Scotland, James indulges in so many vices (including perfidy) that he becomes forsaken by God. James immediately follows his lament for the lost state of his soul with the report of the action his graceless condition produced, his decision to break faith with England:

> Whan I had learned to set my othe at nought,
> And through much vse the sence of sinne exyled,
> Agaynst King Henry, what I could I wrought,
> My fayth, my othe, vniustly foul defiled.

42. See, for instance, Brodugan, *Epitome*, 253; Patten, *Expedition*, 66; Edward Seymour, *Epistle or Exhortacion*, 238, 241.

43. Hall, "Henry VI," fol. 53v.

> And while sly Fortune at my doinges smiled,
> The wrath of God which I had wel deserued,
> Fell on my necke, for thus loe was I serued. (159)

James admits to the world that his decision to renege on his oath to England was not so much a political mistake as the sin of a reprobate.

The sudden change in tone in the later stanzas from the straightforwardly narratorial to the religio-moral serves to place the account of James's fall and death explicitly within the logic of the Seymour regime's propaganda works on Scotland. These works, highly colored by the rhetoric of divine providence, insisted that God fully supported England's designs on Scotland and had mandated that the two nations unite.[44] Scottish resistance to the union of the crowns, these works warned, was resistance to God's command. Divine vengeance must follow continued Scottish intransigence, for God was as outraged as England's leaders had been at the "treachery" and oath breaking of the Scots.[45]

Such rhetoric, in fact, had been Seymour's own. In his *Epistle or Exhortacion* to the Scots, Seymour had promised dire providential consequences for sixteenth-century Scots who broke faith with England, and had even cited Scottish history for edifying examples. Seymour pointed to the death of James V—widely believed to have been brought about by anguish over the loss at Solway Moss—as God's judgment upon an oath breaker. "Your last Kyng," Seymour writes, "after a promise broken contrary to his honour: and a misfortune [the English victory at Solway Moss] by iust iudgement of GOD folowyng vpon it, GOD either by sorowe, or by some other wise at his inscrutable pleasure, did take away from you." In moralizing the past in this manner, Seymour issued a warning to present Scottish leaders. He identified the current Regent, the Earl of Arran, as one more of the many Scottish leaders "who so often hath falsefied their faithe & promise" to the misery of their country. The implication was that Arran must suffer a fate similar to James V's if the provisions of the Greenwich treaty were not upheld.[46]

44. Seymour asked the Scots, "What can any wise or any Christian manne, that thynketh the worlde to be gouerned by Gods prouidence, and not by fortune, thinke otherwise, but that it was Gods pleasure it should bee so, that these twoo realmes should ioyne in mariage, and by a godly Sacrament, make a Godly, perpetuall, and moste frendly vnitie and concord" (*Epistle or Exhortacion*, 240). See also Harryson, *Exhortacion*, 209–10, 235. The assertion of the divine directive for union was not just propaganda for the moment. As Brian Levack notes, the idea that union was a mandate from God continued to inform writers on the subject well into the seventeenth century (*Formation of the British State*, 7–8)

45. See, for instance, Edward Seymour, *Epistle or Exhortacion*, 241, 245; Harryson, *Exhortacion*, 235; Patten, *Expedition*, 73–75.

46. Edward Seymour, *Epistle or Exhortacion*, 239–40, 245.

Yet as Seymour's supporters were painfully aware, the Greenwich treaty was never honored, but no divine punishment of the Scottish leaders had come to pass. The English never had the satisfaction of seeing revenge visited upon Arran or any of the other side-switching Scottish nobles for their "crime" of breaking faith with England. "James I" supplies a literary substitute for that missing satisfaction, conjuring up painful memories of Scottish perfidy in order to assuage them. The conclusion of "James I" operates on Seymour's providential logic: it moralizes the death of an earlier forsworn Scottish ruler, making it a "mirror" of God's hatred of the "sins" of current Scottish leaders. Furthermore, it *enacts* this death, delivering a displaced experience of revenge on a figure epitomizing all the most hated acts of the sixteenth-century Scottish nobles. James I's demise occurs for the very reasons that Seymour's former supporters expected the Scots to be struck down: for spurning their "binding" contracts and pledges of amity to England. In the poem James meets a satisfyingly horrible end: he is murdered in his Privy Chamber by his own "seruaunts," on the orders of his most trusted counselor (154). The poet registers the horror of regicide shown by Hall, but this horror is evoked only to heighten the excitement of seeing God deliver such a mighty blow to the unrighteous. Adding to the sense of the justness of James's downfall, the poet has James himself decline to condemn his two assassins for their actions. Instead James condemns only his own political choices, most strongly his breach of faith with England. The last line of the poem is a confirmation of the English warnings to the Scots in the propaganda writings on Scotland: "God hates hyghly suche as are foresworne" (160). Reveling in James's destruction for the crimes of the sixteenth-century Scottish leaders may not have ameliorated all the pain of those who expected God to lead them to a hegemonic incorporation of Scotland into a new British state, but the poem does offer in its vicarious experience of revenge enough to "quicken vp" temporarily the spirits of those still saddened by the dismal and unexpected failure of Henry VIII's and Seymour's "godly" Scottish policy.[47]

The poet's narrative also offers, more obliquely, a hopeful suggestion that revenge on the sixteenth-century Scots may yet come to pass. In the last stanza the ghost of James I invites readers to apply the lessons of his fall to Scotland's current rulers: "Warne, warne all princes," James implores Baldwin, "all lyke sinnes to loth, / And chiefely suche as in my Realme be borne, / For God hates hyghly suche as are forsworne" (160). While this appears to be a warning to Scots who may in the *future* consider breaking their oaths, it also

47. Thus in the prose passage following "James I" the authors evince none of their previous melancholy brought on by the end of "Salisbury" (*Mirror*, 161).

emphasizes God's anger with those who have *already* become forsworn. The Scottish leaders who rejected the Treaty of Greenwich have already "sinfully" indulged in the practices for which God struck down James. Thus for these Scots, James suggests, there is no avoiding the providential punishment that felled him a century earlier. That this punishment has not yet arrived is of no concern. Fortune seemed to smile, too, on James right up to his sudden fall: God allowed him to reign for fifteen years before smiting him. The poem thus offers the comforting suggestion that God's plan for the current Scottish leaders is not yet fully revealed. At the time the *Memorial* was printed, only five years had passed since the collapse of Protector Somerset's Scottish policy and only about two years since his execution, the event that finally dashed all hopes for pursuit of Seymour's Anglo-Scottish union. According to the "history" recounted in "James I," readers could still hope for a real-life revenge on the Earl of Arran and his fellow Scottish nobles. The fact that Arran was forced to surrender his office of Regent to Mary of Guise in the year in which the *Memorial* was compiled (1554) may well have given hope to the poet's audience that God's vengeance on Arran and all the other forsworn Scottish nobles might soon be at hand.[48]

The Consequences of Weakness: "Suffolk"

The last and most allusively complex of the three *Memorial* poems on foreign affairs is "How Lorde William Delapole Duke of Suffolke was worthily punyshed for abusing his Kyng and causing the destruction of good Duke Humfrey." The "Suffolk" poet asks readers to understand recent foreign policy decisions in terms of Delapole's notoriously disastrous fifteenth-century foreign dealings, thereby mapping the recent antiexpansionist and antinationalist policies of John Dudley and Mary I onto a narrative "proving" that just these policies (particularly the marriage plans) would, if not checked, lead England into a period of shameful weakness abroad and civil war at home matching that of Henry VI's tragic reign.

The "Suffolk" narrative begins during the glory days of English victories in France and ends on the cusp of the Wars of the Roses. In the poem Suffolk presents himself as a former English military leader whose early career was made "at warre in Fraunce." His single most important conquest, he claims, was the taking of Awmarle (Aumale), "a strong built towne, with cast[l]es, walles, & vaultes." He values this victory above all others, even above his capture of Joan of Arc (163–64).

48. By the time of his resignation, it was said that all the lords of Scotland were opposed to Arran and his rule (Franklin, *Scottish Regency*, 178).

Despite early success against the French, England was eventually forced to seek a peace with the king of France. Suffolk took the chief role in the negotiations. Although France had long been England's bitter enemy, Suffolk nevertheless quickly became close with his French counterparts. During the long negotiations he decided to seek a "perfite peace" with his new friends through a treaty betrothing the French king's niece, Margaret of Anjou, to the young English monarch, Henry VI (165). Obsessed with winning peace with France and with finding Henry a wife, Suffolk agreed to even the most disadvantageous demands the French put before him. He demanded no dowry for Margaret and cheerfully surrendered numerous English possessions in France, including the last defenses of English-held Normandy.

Upon announcing the marriage treaty to England, Suffolk received a horrified response from the virtuous "good Duke" Humfrey of Gloucester, the king's uncle and former Protector of the Realm:

> But whan this mariage throwly was agreed
> Although my king were glad of such a make,
> His vncle Humfrey abhorred it in deed,
> Because therby his precontract he brake,
> Made with the heire of the erle of Arminake,
> A noble maide with store of goodes endowed,
> Which more than this with losse, the duke allowed. (165)

Duke Humfrey pronounced the new marriage "aduowtry" because it broke Henry's previous marriage covenant to the Earl of Armagnac's daughter (165–66).[49] Suffolk, thinking only of his own political advancement, murdered Humfrey to silence his outraged opposition to the marriage Suffolk had arranged for his youthful king.

Unfortunately for Suffolk and England, the marriage quickly proved disastrous. After England handed over the formerly English lands to the French, the truce collapsed, and the French King Charles began seizing additional English possessions. The losses in France made the English people "curse the mariage / Esteming it the cause of every loss" (167). Henry's outraged subjects flooded Parliament with bills, and the English people continued to express their hostility toward Suffolk and Queen Margaret even after Henry moved Parliament "fro place to place" to escape their protests. Following an aborted popular uprising, Henry and Margaret found themselves unable to protect Suffolk against the hatred of the people. Suffolk was exiled and, while sailing to France, was taken by a ship belonging to the Earl of Devonshire. Its captain, charging that Suffolk had murdered Humfrey and caused "the King

49. Hall evinces a similar horror of Suffolk's breaking of a precontract.

vnlawfully to wed," took justice into his own hands and beheaded Suffolk on his boat. "A piteous ende," Suffolk's ghost laments, but one he fully deserved for his crimes (167–69).

"Suffolk" and the Policies of John Dudley

By all evidence, "Suffolk" followed George Ferrers's "Humfrey Duke of Gloucester" in *A Memorial of suche Princes*. As we have seen, Ferrers shaped his character of the "good Duke" of Gloucester to elicit memories of the recently deceased "good Duke" of Somerset, Edward Seymour. Thus, when the "Suffolk" poet identifies his protagonist as "one of the chiefest of duke Humfreyes destroyers" and, soon after, as "the prince duke William de la Poole . . . / That found the meane Duke Humfreyes blud to coole," readers are prompted to think of the Tudor noble universally credited with Edward Seymour's destruction, John Dudley, Duke of Northumberland (161, 163).[50] Dudley, readers would remember, had been a celebrated military leader whose rise to prominence, like Suffolk's, came "at warre in Fraunce": Dudley earned his knighthood while fighting in the 1523 French campaigns, and he served extensively in the field in that country, as well as in Scotland, over the next two decades (163). More tellingly, the poet has Suffolk identify as his most memorable victory the taking of a single town, Awmarle. The value the "Suffolk" poet accords to the capture of Awmarle is unprecedented in his historical source, Hall's *Union*.[51] The poet dwells upon Awmarle's strong fortifications and the glory that came from its capture to conjure up for mid-Tudor readers memories not of the historical Suffolk's conquest of a relatively inconsequential French town but of John Dudley's important part in the widely celebrated capture of Boulogne, the fortified French city whose surrender to English forces in 1544 was celebrated as the greatest military victory of Henry VIII's last years.[52]

The poet stirs memories of Boulogne's capture in order to recall to readers Dudley's early, vital support for the imperialistic schemes of Henry VIII and Protector Somerset. He does so, however, not to celebrate Dudley's past victories on behalf of English expansionism but to heighten the sense of pathos raised by his poem's ensuing narrative of English capitulation and loss. In the poem, Suffolk recalls his conquest of Awmarle only to lament the subsequent

50. For evidence that "Suffolk" originally followed "Gloucester" in the *Memorial*, see the table of contents of the 1559 *Mirror* (523). For "Humfrey Duke of Gloucester," see chapter 2.

51. Hall, "Henry VI," fol. 30v.

52. Dudley was one of the military leaders of King Henry's assault on Boulogne; upon the city's capture, Henry VIII made Dudley its first English governor. As Captain and Seneschal of Boulogne, and later, on the seas, as Lord High Admiral, Dudley remained instrumental in defending the town until the signing of the Treaty of Campe. See Loades, *John Dudley*, 64–80.

surrender of that city and numerous other hard-won French towns. "But what prevayled it these townes to winne," Suffolk's ghost exclaims,

> Which shortly after must be lost againe,
> Wherby I see there is more glory in
> The keping thinges than is in their attayne:
> To get and kepe not is but losse of payne.
> Therfore ought men prouide to saue their winnings
> In al attemptes, els lose they their beginninges.
>
> Because we could not kepe the townes we wunne
> (For they were more than we might easely wyelde)
> One yere vndyd what we in ten had doen:
> For envy at home, and treason abrode, dyd yelde
> Kyng Charles his Realme of Fraunce, made barain fielde,
> For bluddy warres had wasted al encrease,
> Which causde the Pope helpe pouerty sue for peace. (164)

Suffolk insists that it was "envy at home, and treason abrode," as well as the fact that the towns the English forces had won "were more than we might easely wyelde," that led England to sue France for peace. The causes Suffolk lists are not those that compelled truce negotiations between England and France in 1444; they are, however, the very ones that compelled the English government to seek peace with France in 1550.[53] The poet's execration of "envy" as a key to the failure of England's foreign designs recalls to readers the 1549 rural rebellions—risings whose ferocity was widely ascribed to their participants' envy of the upper classes—that diverted needed troops from the defense of English-held French lands. His description of "treason abrode," furthermore, precisely recalls the notorious cause of England's sudden loss of its defenses around Boulogne in the first days of the 1549 French war.[54] Finally, the burdensome debts England accrued in defending Boulogne simply became too great for the depleted royal treasury to bear: by 1550 the "pouerty" brought on by the costly foreign adventures of Henry VIII and Edward Seymour indeed made Boulogne and its surrounding forts "more than [England] might easely wyelde."[55]

53. Compare Hall, "Henry VI," fol. 65r.

54. The French gained control of the English forts surrounding Boulogne in August 1549 by bribing the camp commanders charged with protecting them. As a result, the English were forced to abandon all their Boulonnais possessions save for the town of Boulogne itself (Jordan, *Edward VI: The Young King*, 303; Jordan, *Edward VI: The Threshold of Power*, 117).

55. Although the "Suffolk" poet suggests that the pope helped in bringing France and England to peace negotiations, there is no mention of the pope or his representatives in Hall's list of the peace mediators ("Henry VI," 65r). The poet's inclusion of the pope may be an oblique attack on Dudley's perceived crypto-Catholicism, which many Protestants believed to have been the secret guide of his policies during his ascendancy. See chapter 2 and Jordan and Gleason, "Saying of John Late Duke of Northumberland."

When Suffolk, now wiser in death, declares, "To get and kepe not is but losse of payne," and "Therfore ought men prouide to saue their winnings / In al attemptes, els lose they their beginnings," his pathetic words are those of a military hero who has found his hard-won victories betrayed by the political blunders of his nation's government. Of course the bitter truth on which the poet urges readers to dwell is that both the Suffolk of the poem and the man he resembles, John Dudley, were at once the betrayed and the betrayers. As a military leader, Dudley had played key roles in winning Boulogne and its surrounding territories and in defending them from subsequent French attacks. Yet as a leading member of Edward's Privy Council, he saw no means to "prouide to saue" the very city he had once so famously commanded. When Suffolk morosely concludes that "there is more glory in / The keping thinges than is in their attayne," he expresses the melancholy verdict of all those who suffered from the loss of Henry VIII's grand symbol of English imperial might.

If "Suffolk" initially invites readers to pity Dudley for the forced return of lands he himself had conquered, its narrative soon guides them to indict him for so exceeding the demands of necessity as to destroy the English imperialist project altogether. The poet shapes his narrative of Suffolk's disastrous pursuit of a "perfite peace" with France to evoke memories of Dudley's own francophile foreign policy during his years of ascendancy (1550–1553), and he presents that foreign policy as the true reason for the failure of English expansionism abroad and as a chief catalyst of the sin and murder at home that afflicted the highest men of King Edward's last years.

The poet details Suffolk's excessive surrender of English-held lands during his peace negotiations as a means to condemn what many saw as a similar excessive sacrifice of English foreign holdings in Dudley's own French peace compact, the Treaty of Boulogne (1550). Through this treaty England ended its war with France by returning to the French the costly embattled city of Boulogne. In sealing this treaty, however, Dudley's government went far beyond merely returning a single French holding; rather it acceded to the French demand that it abandon every one of its Scottish possessions as well.[56] In agreeing to the Boulogne compact, English negotiators in essence ceded control of Scotland to the French, thereby wiping out at once all of the celebrated gains that Edward Seymour—and at least two of the authors of *A Memorial of suche Princes*—had scant years before so proudly fought to achieve. In order to heighten readers' outrage at the "surrender" of the Scot-

56. Jordan, *Edward VI: The Threshold of Power*, 148. Although he remained in London during the negotiations, Dudley was the guiding spirit behind the Boulogne treaty (Loades, *John Dudley*, 155).

tish forts and garrisons England had established under Seymour, the poet portrays Suffolk as twice lamenting that his peace treaty allowed Mauntes and Mayne in particular to fall into French hands (165, 167). Suffolk recounts:

> But ere I could the graunt of her attayne,
> All that our king had of her fathers landes,
> As Mauntes the citee, the county whole of Mayne,
> And most of Aniow duchy in our handes,
> I did release him by assured bandes.
> And as for dowry with her none I sought,
> I thought no peace could be to derely bought. (165)

Mauntes (Le Mans) and Mayne (Maine), *Memorial* readers would know, were two of the conquests particularly celebrated in "Salisbury," the poem that evoked stirring memories of Edward Seymour's earlier expansionist foreign policy and his glorious victories in Scotland (149).[57] If events forced England to return Boulogne in 1550, it was John Dudley's foolishness alone, the poem urges readers to believe, that led England to negate its years of expansionist glory and martial victory through a self-imposed, humiliating abandonment of all of its recently won imperial possessions.[58]

By conflating the ignominious surrender of English possessions to France with its next allusive episode, the marriage pact Suffolk concludes between his young king and Margaret of Anjou, the poem seeks to evoke memories of Dudley's own Anglo-French marriage scheme, concocted in the wake of the Treaty of Boulogne, and to lead readers to impugn that treaty by linking it to the "surrender" brought about by the Boulogne pact. In May 1551 the Dudley-led Council sent an embassy to France to seek the hand of Henri II's six-year-old daughter, Elizabeth of Valois, for its king. As in "Suffolk," negotiators sent to treat of the marriage met "as frendes" and in great conviviality. Furthermore, like Suffolk's treaty, the marriage pact (the Treaty of Angers) finally agreed upon was dictated almost solely by the French. Suffolk's ignominious acceptance of Margaret without a dowry is starkly reminiscent of the Dudley-led government's own capitulation in its marriage negotiations, in particular its humiliating acceptance of a dowry from France that was over a million crowns less than it had sought.[59] More important, by identifying Suffolk's French marriage plan as the "cause of every losse" England suffered

57. In the poem, the capture of Le Mans ("Mawns") is portrayed as one of Salisbury's most difficult sieges (149).

58. For popular discontent over the Treaty of Boulogne, see *CSP, Span.*, 10:47, 54; Jordan, *Edward VI: The Threshold of Power*, 122; Brigden, *London and the Reformation*, 503.

59. Jordan, *Edward VI: The Threshold of Power*, 127–31.

in its wake, the poet urges readers to view the Treaty of Angers in a similar light, and to judge it as the final blow to England's long-cherished self-conception as a proud and strong nation. Dudley's marriage treaty sounded the death knell for Edwardian England's greatest expansionist project, union with Scotland. By creating a new marriage pact for his monarch, Dudley abandoned the terms of the Treaty of Greenwich, which had betrothed Edward to Mary, Queen of Scots, as part of Henry VIII's scheme to bring the Scottish crown to England. The Greenwich treaty was the document on which Henry and Edward Seymour had built their Scottish policy over the previous years, and on its fulfillment rested Seymour's grand vision for a new British empire ruled under English hegemony. By creating a new marriage compact for his monarch, Dudley swept away the very logic on which Seymour's imperialist foreign policy had been constructed, granting France what appeared to be permanent control over Scotland, allowing the marriage of Edward VI's intended bride to the Dauphin (the heir to the same French crown England's monarchs had for so long claimed as their own), and, finally, destroying decades of long-cherished dreams of bringing the British isle under English control. Readers are meant to view Dudley's pursuit of French amity in precisely the same light as Suffolk's disastrous attempt to secure lasting peace with France: as a foolish, humiliating capitulation to England's longtime enemies and, in terms of its blow to national pride and strength, a peace "to[o] derely bought" (165).

Not only does the "Suffolk" poet blame John Dudley for England's humiliating loss of power and prestige abroad but also he indicts Dudley for introducing sin and murder into the highest political circles at home. As we have seen, the poet evokes the chief Edwardian champion of English expansionism, Edward Seymour, through his figure of the virtuous "good Duke" Humfrey. He does so in order to provide a model for construing Seymour's opposition to the French marriage as above all moral, not political, in motivation, and for coming to believe that it was Seymour's virtue rather than his widely alleged jealousy or ambition that was the "true" cause of his execution in the wake of the Angers treaty.

Seymour, as we have seen, understood the Treaty of Greenwich to be a binding covenant for marriage; he had spent most of his Protectorate, in fact, attempting to find ways to effect its provisions. In the wake of the Angers negotiations, Seymour spoke openly and forcefully against the new French marriage plan that would replace the one created by the Greenwich treaty.[60] The poet's account of Humfrey's opposition to Suffolk's marriage

60. *CSP, Span.*, 10:227; Jordan, *Edward VI: The Young King*, 268.

scheme is meant to suggest to readers Seymour's own opposition to Dudley's similar plan and to lead them to understand that opposition just as they do Humfrey's, as an act not of political jealousy but of high moral principle. Just as Duke Humfrey opposed Suffolk out of a desire to prevent Suffolk from leading his naïve monarch into sin, so too did Edward Seymour oppose Dudley's French marriage plans out of a pious fear that forsaking the terms of the Greenwich treaty would lead young Edward VI into damnable acts of perfidy (by breaking his sealed bond to Mary, Queen of Scots) and adultery (by cohabiting with a woman other than his contracted "bride"). The poet leads readers to understand Seymour's death in 1552, then, as a result of precisely this moral stance against Dudley's "sinful" marriage treaty. The poet breaks with his historical source, portraying Suffolk's murder of Humfrey as arising not from his and Margaret's jealousy of Humfrey's power over Henry VI, as Hall declares, but from Humfrey's pious opposition to Suffolk's French marriage pact. He further implies that Humfrey's death came quickly after Suffolk sealed the marriage treaty and not, as Hall relates, three years after that pact was concluded.[61] The suggestion that Humfrey died soon after Suffolk's marriage negotiations recalls to readers Edward Seymour's own execution, which followed quickly after the Angers treaty was ratified. By evoking the coincidence of the treaty's ratification and Seymour's execution, the poem moves readers to draw a causal link between Seymour's opposition to the Angers pact and his death soon after. To reinforce the sense that it was Seymour's principled opposition to Dudley that brought about his execution and not the jealous ambition with which he was charged, the poet has Suffolk himself, Humfrey's murderer, declare virtue to be the true cause of Humfrey's death: "Thus righteousnes brought Humfrey to rebuke / Because he would no wickednes allowe, / But for my doinges I was made a duke" (166).[62]

Thus, while he manifestly displays in his poem the tragic political consequences of weakening English strength abroad, the poet nevertheless makes his final point about Dudley's reversal of Henry's and Seymour's foreign policies an ethical one, reflecting the providential perspective of so many of Seymour's supporters. Although the ship's captain executes Suffolk for a variety of crimes, including murder, Suffolk's chastened spirit sees his "breach of lawful bond or oth" as the sole cause of his fall,

61. Hall, "Henry VI," 68v.

62. Seymour was executed less than two months after the Treaty of Angers was ratified, and in fact received his death sentence on the day before its ratification (December 2, 1551). Suffolk's last line recalls to readers the fact that Edward created Dudley Duke of Northumberland five days before Seymour's arrest in 1551 and but a few months before Seymour's execution in January 1552.

A piteous ende, and therfore Baldwin warne,
All pyers and princes to abhorre vntroth,
For vicious grayne must cum to fowl endes barne:
Who brueth breach of lawful bond or oth,
God wil ere long, cause all the world to loth. (169)

In forsaking the king's first marriage contract, Suffolk led his monarch to commit the same deadly sin of oath breaking that the sixteenth-century Scottish leaders had committed in their rejection of the Greenwich pact. We have seen how strongly the *Memorial* authors condemn "such as are forsworn" in the context of the "James I" poem. Suffolk's chief crime (and thus Dudley's), according to "Suffolk," was "causing the King vnlawfully to wed." He "abused" his king in pursuit of his own foolhardy schemes and his personal desire for advancement. It was precisely his leading Edward into perfidy that caused "all the world to loth" Dudley, eventually bringing about his ignominious execution. Ultimately Dudley died, according to "Suffolk," not for supporting Queen Jane or for taking up arms against Mary Tudor but for sinning against God himself.

"Suffolk" and the Policies of Mary I

There is more to "Suffolk," however, than an exemplary evocation of Edwardian history, for the same concerns about English weakness and the danger of a foreign marriage raised during Dudley's regime were raised with even greater urgency in Mary's reign. Edward VI had died before his "adulterous" marriage was ever consummated. Mary, by contrast, had recently joined herself in marriage to a powerful foreign spouse at the time "Suffolk" was composed. Her husband's reputation for repression during his residency in the Netherlands (1549–1551) was well known in England. The imperial ambassador Jehan Scheyfve admitted that the English "dreaded the rule of Spaniards," and numerous English writers predicted the loss of native rule and even the destruction of the English nobility under Habsburg dominance.[63] Mary, notoriously, was the "Spanish Tudor," who maintained a staunch opposition to the religious policies (particularly the declaration of royal supremacy) of her father's and brother's reigns. She evinced little nationalist feeling, expressing publicly a pro-English sentiment in defending her marriage plans only when pressed by the Wyatt rebels.[64]

For the supporters of English imperialist nationalism, Mary's policies could hardly have been worse than they were. The queen's marriage plans

63. *CSP, Span.*, 11:227–28; Loach, *Parliament and the Crown*, 184–91.

64. In her Guildhall speech of February 1, 1554, cited by many historians as the decisive act that rallied wavering Londoners to her side during Wyatt's revolt.

were virtually an inversion of Seymour's policies. Seymour had wanted to wed the Scottish queen to the male ruler of the more powerful England, thus making Scotland part of an empire dominated politically and culturally by the English. Mary, by contrast, sought to wed Philip, the male regent of the more powerful Spain (and heir to the Holy Roman Emperor), thus making England part of a foreign empire dominated politically and culturally by the Spanish. The irony was bitterly apparent. In the 1540s a Scot had responded to Henry VIII's insistence that Mary Stewart wed Prince Edward by protesting, "If your lad were a lass and our lass were a lad . . . could you be content that our lad should marry your lass and so be King of England?"[65] The English were now faced with the same fear of loss of independence, national sovereignty, and even national self-definition that had so troubled the Scots when England was ascendant. How long could a Spanish king consort remain just a husband to the English queen before his gender and political power made him a king regnant? Mary was well known to have been led in her policy decisions by the Spanish ambassador, Simon Renard. How much more would her husband control her every decision, and thus control the country itself? What would be the status of the English nation under a monarch who owed his first allegiance to Spain and who saw England not as his homeland but as but one more imperial possession?[66]

In addition to its commentary on Dudley's rule, "Suffolk" serves as a warning for Marian magistrates on the question of the extent of Philip's power in England. The poem offers a topically applicable historical narrative which suggests the tragic consequences that would result if English magistrates allowed Mary to rule by her own inclinations or to be dominated by her new spouse. "Suffolk" presents readers with parallels between its Queen Margaret and the Spanish Prince Philip and between its Henry VI and the current queen, Mary. First, the poet emphasizes Henry's attraction to Margaret's personal qualities. Margaret in the poem is portrayed as well educated, beautiful, "fayre spoken, pleasaunt, a very princely piece, / In wit and learning matcheles hence to Grece"(165). Her "princely" qualities and the invocation of Greece suggest the similar reputation of Philip among his supporters as a highly cultured, humanist-educated prince, the image that had attracted Mary to Philip long before she met him.[67] More tellingly, "Suffolk" describes Margaret as "Duke Rayners daughter of Aniow, king by stile, / Of Naples, Iersualem, and of Scicil yle" (165). According to Hall, these were indeed Rayner's titles, but Hall makes it clear that Anjou was Rayner's only

65. Quoted in Wernham, *Before the Armada*, 211.
66. For some expressions of these concerns, see Richards, "Mary Tudor," 915–24.
67. *CSP, Span.*, 11:288–93, 296, 357.

important domain.[68] By invoking all these titles in his poem, the "Suffolk" poet recalls to readers the similarly titled Philip of Spain, who was styled "King Philip" not as the ruler of Spain (he was only the Prince of Spain at that time), but through his claims to the kingship of Naples and Jerusalem, titles that his father the emperor bestowed on him shortly before his wedding.[69] Mary's Chancellor, Stephen Gardiner, had in fact first declared these new kingly titles to England at the wedding ceremony itself in order that "it might well appeare to all men that the Quenes highnes was the[n] maried, not only to a Pri[n]ce, but also unto a king."[70] On August 1, 1554, Philip and Mary issued a proclamation listing their new titles that should be used in all writings: "Philip and Mary, by the grace of God, king and queen of England, France, Naples, Jerusalem, and Ireland: defenders of the faith; princes of Spain and Sicily; archdukes of Austria; dukes of Milan, Burgundy, and Brabant; counts of Hapsburg, Flanders, and Tyrol." Notably, Naples and Sicily were lands where Spanish mistreatment of the native peoples was notorious.[71]

Second, the poet shapes his Henry VI to bring to mind Mary I and to emphasize the unreasoning, personal nature of her desire for a Spanish match. Although Hall claims that Suffolk far exceeded his commission for peace in arranging the marriage, the *Memorial* implies that Henry VI asked Suffolk to find him a mate, a reflection of Mary's role as the chief pursuer of the Spanish match (165).[72] Furthermore, when Suffolk seals a treaty that is inimical politically and morally to England, Henry nevertheless approves it wholeheartedly, for "love and beauty in the king so wrought / That neither profite or promise he regarded, / But set his vncles counsayle still at nought: . . . / Thus vertue starves, but lustfoode must be larded" (166). Henry's actions figure Mary's own zeal for a Spanish marriage, which was believed by many to be purely the product of irrational willfulness and private affection. Mary, like the Henry VI of the poem, was attracted to Philip without ever having met him: after seeing his portrait, she declared herself "half in love" with him by dint of his physical beauty alone.[73] When a delegation came to her from both houses of Parliament to speak against a foreign marriage, her response was notoriously one of emotion and stubborn defense of her private desire to marry Philip. After hearing the arguments of the Speaker of the House of Commons against the rumored Spanish match, Mary rebuked him for his

68. Hall, "Henry VI," fol. 65v.
69. Philip also held the title prince of Sicily.
70. Elder, *The Copie of a letter*, sig. A6v.
71. Loach, *Parliament and the Crown*, 184–86.
72. Hall, "Henry VI," fol. 65r.
73. Loades, *Mary Tudor: A Life*, 203.

effrontery and then declared in response to his carefully composed discourse that "to force her to take a husband who would not be to her liking would be to cause her death, for if she were married against her will she would not live three months, and would have no children, wherefore the Speaker would be defeating his own ends [to settle the succession]." Mary complained further that those opposed to the marriage were not properly taking her "personal inclination" into account.[74] Henry VI's selfish insistence on marrying the powerful royal bride for whom he had conceived a strong personal desire is a forceful evocation of Mary's similar insistence on the powerful foreign husband against whom she would hear no argument. The disastrous consequences of Henry's marriage urge readers, through the rhetoric of historical example, to fear similar disastrous outcomes for another royal marriage based on personal inclinations rather than national concerns.[75]

Furthermore, the poem's horror at the "adulterous" nature of Henry and Margaret's marriage would serve as an even greater warning of the consequences of Philip and Mary's marriage than it would of the dangers of Edward VI's impending French match. The widespread opinion in Europe in 1553 was that Philip had contracted to marry (or had already married) the Infanta Maria of Portugal. Even Philip's own father was concerned that the negotiations for Maria's hand had gone too far by the time he asked Philip to end the Portuguese negotiations for him to woo the English queen.[76] According to Renard, it was "generally believed over here [in England] that my lord, our Prince [Philip], is married to the Portuguese princess." Even Mary

74. *CSP, Span.*, 11:363–64. The discourse presented by the Speaker (Sir John Pollard) was "illustrated by historic examples"; unfortunately, it is unknown whether the examples of Henry VI and Margaret of Anjou were among those he offered the queen. See also Loach, *Parliament and the Crown*, 78–79.

75. The "Suffolk" poet employs the term "lustfoode" in this passage to suggest Henry's physical desire for Margaret (though the poet stresses that Henry has neither met nor even seen his intended queen) but also to condemn the irrational and dangerously selfish determination of the king to have his personal desire for a spouse fulfilled, even to the point of willingly entering into "aduowtry" (166). The author's use of the term "lust" echoes its use in early modern writings on the subject of royal tyranny in general (denouncing the "lust of the prince" as the basis for tyrannical government), and in works opposing Mary's rule in particular. See, for example, the anti-Marian pamphlets *A Warnyng for Englande Conteynyng the Horrible Practises of the Kyng of Spayne*, sig. A2v; Luther, *A Faythful Admonycion of a Certen Trewe Pastor and Prophete*, sig. C2r; and Ponet, *Shorte Treatise*, sigs. A6v, C6r, F5r. While several poems of the *Memorial* offer denunciations of lechery in princes, the chief use of the term "lust" in these works is in the sense of irrational, immoderate, and harmful personal desire, and it is used in this sense most often in those poems specifically designed to dissuade Marian magistrates from allowing their queen to rule England in accordance with her personal wishes rather than with the principles of justice and law. For its use in this fashion in *A Memorial of suche Princes*, see chapter 5 and, among other examples, *Mirror*, 77, 103, 113.

76. Loades, *Reign of Mary Tudor*, 58.

herself had declared "that she was very sorry to hear that his Highness had married his near relative, the Princess of Portugal."[77]

If the doubt about a precontract was finally dismissed by Mary, it remained a real issue to those who opposed the match. Renard reported in January 1554 that "slanderous placards" had been posted denouncing Mary's desire to marry a man "who is already promised and married to the Infanta of Portugal."[78] The charge remained current in oppositional pamphlets and broadsides both before and after the marriage. The anonymous author of the pamphlet *Certayne Questions Demaunded and Asked by the Noble Realme of Englande*, for instance, raises the precontract question, declaring that Philip was betrothed to another and thus his marriage to Mary was adulterous and any child they produced would be a bastard.[79] The issue of a precontract was an important one in current debate over the Spanish marriage. Its central place in a historical narrative of an earlier, disastrous foreign marriage could not help but invite readers to apply the poem's portrayed results of such "adultery" to the probable consequences of their own monarch's match.

Thus in pointing to the Spanish marriage in its details, the poem at once ties Mary's marriage to the political blunders of the Dudley regime and plays out, in the rest of its narrative, what it presents as the political and providential consequences of joining a weak English monarch to a powerful foreigner in an immoral marriage. Margaret's first act as queen is to order (with Suffolk's assistance) the murder of Humfrey of Gloucester, the virtuous defender of the commonwealth.[80] Later, neither Margaret nor Henry prevents Margaret's uncle, the French king, from reconquering English-held Normandy, despite the evident anger of the English people. Henry's and Margaret's rule produces a popular rebellion and hostile Parliaments, both of which single out Suffolk, the chief magistrate who brought Margaret to power, as the target of the people's rage. The warning to Marian magistrates is that, in pleasing his love-besotted monarch by supporting and arranging his marriage, Suffolk has in fact "abused" him, for he has alienated the English king

77. *CSP, Span.*, 10:154, 193, 212–13; see also 10:295. The fear of the moral consequences of breaking a precontract was not confined to opponents of the marriage: Mary herself had asked Renard to tell her the truth about Philip's marriage plans with the Infanta, for, she told him, a binding precontract would be the only thing that could dissuade her from marrying Philip (10:330). Renard forwarded Mary's note to the emperor, asking Charles himself to assure her that there was no contract between Philip and the Infanta (10:331).

78. Ibid., 12:17.

79. *Certayne Questions*, sig. A3v. Internal evidence dates this work to 1555. See also *A Warnyng for Englande*, sig. A7r.

80. Cf. *Certayne Questions*, sig. A5r, which suggests that Philip will murder the English nobility to "sauegarde" his rule just as William the Conqueror had done before him.

from his own people. Echoing Ferrers in "Robert Tresilian" and Baldwin in "Lord Mowbray," the "Suffolk" poet warns that when a magistrate serves his monarch's wishes to the detriment of the "profite" of the realm, he will only cause his monarch's rule (and his own life as well) "the shorter tyme to dure" (166, 77).[81] As the succeeding poems in the *Memorial* will display, the hatred Henry VI produces through his ill-conceived marriage to a dominating spouse and his refusal to maintain English strength abroad leads directly to the success of Cade's rebellion, to York's violent attempt at the crown, and, ultimately, to the destruction of what the *Memorial-Mirror* authors describe as "millions of the commons" and "all the nobility" of England in subsequent years.[82]

The political consequences of Henry VI's foreign marriage thus displayed would present themselves as gravely admonitory to Marian readers reflecting on their own monarch's policies in 1554. Mary already had suffered a revolt (Wyatt's rebellion) over her foreign marriage and had actually summoned the April 1554 Parliament to Oxford rather than to London to avoid further instances of unrest. The political consequences of the Spanish match and its attendant unpopularity could seem to be proceeding along the same trajectory as the earlier consequences of Henry VI's foreign match.[83]

"Suffolk" offers Mary's magistrates a lesson that is not only political but moral as well. In portraying Suffolk's divinely sanctioned murder at the hands of an enraged Englishman, the poem warns that even if the monarch commands a magistrate to carry out an immoral act, the fault in performing that deed is at least as much the magistrate's as it is the monarch's. No matter what the king commanded in the matter, Suffolk bore the responsibility for "causing the King vnlawfully to wed" because he did not oppose his king when Henry based a politically vital decision on his personal desires (168). In the eyes of man and God alike, the poem warns, the magistrate who fulfills a monarch's pernicious commands is as culpable as the monarch for any of

81. See chapter 5.

82. See *Mirror*, 174, 188, 196.

83. Loach, *Parliament and the Crown*, 91. Of course this poem and its tale of the loss of English possessions in France would only gain greater significance upon its publication in 1559, after Mary's government had lost the last of the English holdings in France in the previous year. Early in Elizabeth's reign, Sir Thomas Smith noted angrily that no French king or any of the "pernicious dissensions" of the time of the Wars of the Roses had been able to dislodge the English from France. "I do assure you," he continued, "for my part . . . I question, if I should have lived through five hundred years heretofore past, I should have seen England at any time weaker in strength, men, money, and riches, than it was in the time when we wrote *King Philip and Queen Mary*, King and Queen of so many kingdoms, dukedoms, marchionates. For all those wily titles, our hearts, our joy, our comfort was gone" (quoted in Strype, *Life of the Learned Sir Thomas Smith*, 52).

the ruler's sins.[84] Thus, in the wake of Wyatt's rebellion, when Parliament and Mary's officers were eager to please and to prove their loyalty to their monarch, "Suffolk" warns English magistrates against allowing their queen too free a hand in letting personal desires guide her political actions. Magistrates "oppresse" and even abuse their queen by permitting her to persist in political and moral errors, and the consequences will redound tragically for those who countenance her misdeeds: "Was never prince [i.e., high noble] that other did oppresse / Unrighteously, but died in distresse" (169).

Although the "Suffolk" poet directs his admonitory exemplum to all English officers, one Marian magistrate in particular could find the poem's lessons highly applicable to his own career. William Paget was the chief architect of the Treaty of Boulogne as well as of the Spanish marriage.[85] He was a *politique*, an adaptable man who could further the policies of both John Dudley and Queen Mary with little ideological compunction. In a poem that conjures up memories of so many of the events of Edward's and Mary's reigns, the "Suffolk" poet may well have sought to give pause to Paget, as well as those who worked with him, by suggesting that any further attempts to increase Spanish power over England through indiscriminate service to Philip would only hasten their downfall. If the Spanish marriage was a fait accompli after the collapse of Wyatt's rebellion, the extent of King Philip's powers was still unsettled. Would he be crowned or remain only a consort? Would he rule England if Mary were to die? Would any marriage treaty limiting his powers be binding once he held sway? To Paget and other Edwardian holdovers who supported Philip, "Suffolk" offered strong persuasion not to allow the Spanish prince full power over England and its queen. In "Suffolk" and the subsequent *Memorial* poems detailing the miseries that Henry VI's foreign marriage brought to England, magistrates could see "as in a loking glas" the consequences of pursuing English foreign dealings along the current track: shameful impotence abroad and chaos and civil conflict at home (65).

84. This is also the point of "The infamous ende of Lord Iohn Tiptoft Earle of Wurcester, for cruelly executing his princes butcherly commaundments" (*Mirror*, 197–202).

85. Loades, *Reign of Mary Tudor*, 66; Gammon, *Statesman and Schemer*, 166–68.

CHAPTER FIVE

Royal Power and the Abuse of the Law in *A Memorial of suche Princes*

In the preceding three chapters I have examined chiefly *Memorial-Mirror* tragedies created to confront and to interpret the disasters of England's Edwardian past. Here, by contrast, I turn my attention to the other great topically engaged project of *A Memorial of suche Princes*, the presentation of admonitory exempla designed to lead Marian magistrates to eschew ongoing or anticipated political practices to which the *Memorial* authors were opposed.

The politically admonitory exempla are the best known of all the tragedies of the 1559 *Mirror for Magistrates*, for it was these poems that William Baldwin chose to emphasize above all others in his lengthy dedicatory epistle to the volume. In this dedication, Baldwin mentions neither his work's origin as a continuation of Lydgate's *Fall of Princes* nor the presence of several retrospectively topical tragedies among its narratives. Instead he presents his newly titled *Mirror for Magistrates* as a work of engaged political counsel, one whose overriding purpose is the guidance of England's governors in their day-to-day political behavior. Addressing "the nobilitye and all other in office," Baldwin urges magisterial readers to use his collection in the manner of a "myrrour," in which, "as in a loking glas, you shall see (if any vice be in you) howe the like hath bene punished in other heretofore, whereby admonished, I trust it will be a good occasion to move you to the soner amendment" (65–66).

Though written several years after the compilation of *A Memorial of suche Princes*, Baldwin's dedication conveys many of the principles that guided him and his fellow *Memorial* poets in creating their Marian admonitory exempla. This epistle begins with a pessimistic meditation on the difficulty of persuading dutiful men to assume rule in a commonwealth. Because the life of an upright officer is one chiefly composed of "payneful toyles," it follows that "in whatsoever realme such provision is made, that officers be forced to do their duties, there is it as harde a matter to get an officer, as it is in other places to shift of[f], and put by those, that with flattery, bribes and other shiftes, sue and preace for offices" (63). Too often only the ambitious seek political station, viewing such positions as springboards to greater power or riches. Such men strive for high place solely for personal gain; they do not "seeke . . . to helpe other, for whiche cause offices are ordayned" (64). It is difficult to find men who will fulfill the magistrate's chief task of working "to helpe other," Baldwin complains, for any man conscientious enough to undertake such a charge will necessarily hesitate before assuming the heavy responsibilities that political office demands.

Although it is hard to attract such men, much depends on finding them, for Baldwin ascribes enormous power to a nation's officers. His discussion of the influence of magistrates on all those under them must be quoted in full, for it is central to understanding the logic behind many of the poems of *A Memorial of suche Princes* and the 1559 *Mirror for Magistrates*:

> Where the ambicious seeke no office, there no doubt, offices are duly ministred: and where offices are duly ministred, it can not be chosen, but the people are good, whereof must nedes folow a good common weale. For if the officers be good, the people can not be yll. Thus the goodnes or badnes of any realme lyeth in the goodnes or badnes of the rulers. And therfore not without great cause do the holy Apostels so earnestly charge vs to pray for the magistrates: For in dede the welth and quiet of everye common weale, the disorder also and miseries of the same, cum specially through them. I nede not go eyther to the Romans or Grekes for proofe hereof, neyther yet to the Iewes, or other nacions: whose common weales have alway florished while their officers were good, and decayed and ranne to ruyne, whan noughty men had the regiment, Our own countrey stories (if we reade & marke them) will shewe vs examples ynow, would God we had not seen moe then ynowe. I purpose not to stand here vppon the particulers, because they be in part set furth in the tragedyes. Yet by the waye I note (wishing all other to do the like) namely, that as good governers have never lacked their deserved renowme, so have not the bad escaped infamy, besides such plages as are horrible to hear of. (64–65)

Baldwin understands the moral health of any populace to be absolutely dependent on the moral health of its governors. In Baldwin's formulation, the political actions of each and every officer have consequences that reach far beyond any local, immediate impact they may have, for taken together they shape the civic behavior of all those under the magistrates' rule. Good governors bring "welth and quiet" to the land; bad governors bring only "disorder . . . and miseries [to] the same." Tragically, England's long history of corrupt rulers and the misery they have brought to the nation, Baldwin notes ruefully, provides strong evidence for his claim.

To prevent "disorder . . . and miseries" in the realm, magistrates must dedicate their chief energy to a single task: ensuring justice for every member of the commonwealth. According to Baldwin, this duty is not merely the highest calling of a magistrate; it is also a divine commandment. "For as Iustice is the chief vertue," he explains,

> so is the ministracion therof, the chiefest office: & therfore hath God established it with the chiefest name, honoring & calling Kinges, & all officers vnder them by his owne name, Gods. Ye be all Gods, as many as have in your charge any ministracion of Iustice. What a fowle shame wer it for any now to take vpon them the name and office of God, and in their doinges to shew them selves divyls? God cannot of Iustice, but plage such shameles presumption and hipocrisy, and that with shamefull deth, diseases, or infamy. (65)

Here and elsewhere in this dedication Baldwin excludes any perception of magistrates as primarily crown servants or royal officers. It is not to the monarch that magistrates owe their first duty, Baldwin suggests, but to their sacred charge to ensure justice for all in their care.[1] Indeed, in his formulation, "Kinges" themselves are but one more type of magistrate, men enjoined to "helpe other" and to labor for the equitable distribution of justice in the realm just as much as any other officer. The consequences of neglecting these duties are immense. Any magistrate who refuses to secure justice for all insults the Lord by taking up God's "chiefe office" without serving his will (65). Such men are "divyls"; they can and will fall.[2]

The politically admonitory tragedies of *A Memorial of suche Princes* and the 1559 *Mirror for Magistrates* work within the logic Baldwin displays in his dedication. They insist that an officer's chief duty is the protection of justice for all in the realm. They suggest that even local acts of malfeasance have far-reaching and devastating consequences, and they warn that magisterial corruption will eventually redound tragically upon the heads of those who engage in it. While the numerous admonitory poems of the collection warn officers against a host of specific political crimes and faults, it is those warning them not to place the will of the monarch above the interests of justice in the nation that achieve greatest prominence in the *Memorial* and the 1559 *Mirror*. The authors not only invest these tragedies with some of the most fervent rhetoric and vivid imagery of the collection but also give them pride

1. Baldwin's arguments here parallel those of John Ponet in *A Shorte Treatise of Politike Power*; see sigs. B3v, C4v.

2. Baldwin draws in this passage on the admonitory language of Psalm 82, which threatens great punishments for those in power who "geve wro[n]g judgement" and neglect their duties. "Ye are Goddes," the Psalmist warns the "mighty" of Israel, "and ye are chyldren of the moost hyest. But ye shall dye lyke men, and fall lyke one of ye princes" (quoted from *The Byble in Englyshe*).

of place in their work, devoting four out of the first five poems in the *Memorial-Mirror* volume to precisely this theme.

The emphasis that the authors place on these tragedies arises from the urgent political purpose for which they were composed. Far from being abstract musings on enduring problems of governance, as *Mirror* scholars traditionally have characterized them, these works are in fact engaged acts of political intervention. They seek to do nothing less than alter the political behavior of Marian England's highest officers, moving them to eschew courses of action that the authors feared would lead the country into injustice, tyranny, and even civil war.

Here I examine three such works: George Ferrers's tragedy "The fall of Robert Tresilian chiefe Iustice of Englande, and other his felowes, for misconstruyng the lawes, and expounding them to serue the Princes affections"; William Baldwin's "Howe the Lorde Mowbray promoted by Kyng Richarde the seconde, was by hym banyshed the Realme, and dyed miserably in exyle"; and Sir Thomas Chaloner's "Howe kyng Richarde the seconde was for his euyll gouernaunce deposed from his seat, and miserably murdred in prison." Each was composed in the first year of Mary's reign (July 1553–July 1554), and each takes as its theme the dangers that must inevitably result whenever English officers place service to the monarch's will above the interests of justice, right, and law in the realm. Through "Robert Tresilian," Ferrers urges his fellow members of the Marian legal community to abhor recent misconduct by several of the queen's chief judicial officers and to resist the ever-present temptation to subvert justice and legal principle in order to serve the monarch's desires. In "Lord Mowbray," Baldwin extends Ferrers's warning to all English officers, admonishing governors against leaving "the lawe, to serve the princes lust," and urging them to challenge, to oppose, and, if necessary, even actively to resist a monarch who acts unjustly (105). Finally, Chaloner uses "Kyng Richarde the seconde" to issue a warning to Mary herself, displaying what his exemplum suggests is the tragic end that will come to any English monarch who seeks to rule without regard for justice and the traditional political and legal limits constraining royal power. Each of these poems seeks to persuade the queen and her men that attempts to increase the monarch's power at the expense of law and justice will result only in the sort of tyranny, corruption, and even rebellion that marked the terrible last years of Richard II's reign. Just as forcefully, they insist that those who will suffer most from such acts of misrule are the erring monarch him- or herself and those very magistrates who sought to benefit from fulfilling their sovereign's illicit commands.

Royal Will and the Abuse of the Law in Mary's Early Reign

Perhaps no other secular concern caused as much apprehension among English evangelicals in the opening months of Mary's reign as the perceived willingness of the queen's chief officers to hold their devotion to the new monarch's wishes above their adherence to English law. Such concerns arose quickly in the wake of Mary's accession, as England's new, religiously conservative queen and her supporters sought to undo six years of Edwardian religious innovations. Despite their monarch's well-known hostility to evangelical practices, evangelicals continued to celebrate their faith openly in the months following Mary's rise to power, taking refuge in the fact that the religious laws of the land remained those established by the Edwardian Act of Uniformity (1552). In their zeal to rid England of Edwardian religious practices, however, many of Mary's officers simply ignored the existence of this act, permitting and even encouraging traditional rites to replace the legally sanctioned evangelical ones and arresting or otherwise persecuting many of those who refused to conform to the queen's religious preferences.[3] The suffering of such men became notorious among evangelicals through word of mouth and through angry surreptitious pamphlets.[4] One episode that caused particular outrage among English evangelicals was that of Sir James Hales, a respected judge of the Common Pleas. In July 1553 Hales had been the only high justice to refuse to sign the document that excluded Lady Mary from the throne. He based his objection not on matters of religion (Hales was in fact an evangelical) but on his strict adherence to legal principle: the 1544 Act of Succession had named Mary as Edward's heir should Edward die without issue, and Hales would not countenance any attempt to subvert statute law. Despite his support for Mary's right to the crown, Hales was nevertheless confronted by Chancellor Gardiner in October 1553 when he attempted to take his oath as one of Mary's chief judges. Upon hearing Gardiner take him to task for a recent judgment against a group of priests who had illegally celebrated the Mass, Hales insisted that he had ruled against those clerics solely because their actions violated the Edwardian religious statutes still in force under Mary. According to the 1553 pamphlet that recounted Hales's troubles, Gardiner admitted in response that the statutes

3. Loades, *Oxford Martyrs*, 112 15. John Foxe records the names of numerous men illegally arrested in 1553 for evangelical activities still sanctioned by statute law. See, for instance, Foxe, *Actes and Monuments*, 1395–96, 1586. The repeal of the Edwardian religious statutes did not come into force until December 20, 1553 (Foxe, *Actes and Monuments*, 1396).

4. See, for instance, the preacher Robert Horne's lengthy denunciation of his unjust handling by Chancellor Gardiner in Calvin, *Certaine Homilies*.

of the realm indeed forbade celebration of the Mass; nevertheless, he bluntly told Hales that when ruling from the bench, Hales should have had more respect for the queen's will in such matters than for the "rigour of the law." Hales was denied the opportunity to swear his oath and shortly thereafter was deprived of office and imprisoned. He remained incarcerated for his "crime" of enforcing statute law even as the poems of *A Memorial of suche Princes* were being composed.[5]

Fears that Mary's chief officers placed service to royal will above devotion to the interests of equitable justice became particularly acute in the wake of Wyatt's rebellion, when the possibility of organized evangelical opposition to the queen's policies collapsed, the arrival of Philip of Spain loomed, and Mary and her religious conservative supporters in office exercised newfound strength. By spring 1554 there was an almost paranoid dread among evangelicals that Mary and her powerful, foreign-born intended spouse would simply ignore the liberties and protections of their subjects altogether, abrogating English laws and reducing the kingdom to an absolute monarchy. Such concerns were trumpeted regularly by oppositional pamphleteers and expressed privately by evangelical members of Parliament, men whose law-making powers would, of course, be completely destroyed by any move to absolute rule.[6] The fears of some Parliamentarians for the future of English law under Philip and Mary are perhaps best exemplified by the remarkable reaction that greeted a bill introduced into Parliament in the spring of 1554. This bill sought simply to confirm that an English queen regnant enjoyed the same power as an English king regnant. Nevertheless, one evangelical member of the House of Commons, Ralph Skinner, dared to express what seems to have been a widespread fear that this bill—which suspiciously sought to deal with a doubt about royal authority that had never previously been raised—had a more sinister, secret purpose. It may well be a blind,

5. "The Communication betwene the Lorde Chauncelour and Iudge Hales," printed in Foxe, *Actes and Monuments*, 1458. The "Communication" was originally printed in pamphlet form by Baldwin's friend John Day (under the pseudonym Michael Wood) in October 1553 and disseminated surreptitiously among evangelicals (*STC* 11583).

6. For a survey of the surreptitious literature warning that the Spanish would destroy English laws and institutions, see Loach, *Parliament and the Crown*, 184–90. Although they felt such fears most strongly, it was not merely the evangelicals in Parliament who voiced concerns about Mary's intended Spanish match. At his April 1554 trial Sir Nicholas Throckmorton recalled that the horrified reaction of numerous parliamentarians, including some of Mary's strongest religious conservative supporters, to the idea of a Spanish marriage for the queen. From his observation of the widespread fears of Spanish rule among the Parliament men, Throckmorton declared in court that in late 1553 "the whole consent of the realm" stood against the marriage and the consequences it seemed to promise for the nation (Patterson, *Trial of Nicholas Throckmorton*, 37–38).

Skinner told his fellows, "whereby Mary was released from the provisions of Magna Carta and the Charter of the Forest, the 'sacred Charters' that God had provided for his people of England." Skinner further voiced his concern that the queen planned to follow the practice of William the Conqueror, "who seised the Landes of the Englishe people" and redistributed them as he desired. William Fleetwood, the Recorder of London who reported Skinner's speech, himself suspected a different purpose for the bill: Fleetwood was of the opinion that the bill had been introduced to forestall certain royal counselors from attempting to persuade Mary that, since English statutes mentioned only English *kings* and not English queens, she did not need to consider herself bound by statute law.[7] These divergent yet equally suspicious interpretations of the bill indicate the depth of Protestant Parliamentarians' fears that their queen, with the aid of certain of her high officers, might seek to extend her royal power beyond its heretofore legal limits. After Philip's arrival in England, such doubts persisted among English evangelicals, and in fact may only have increased. Although Mary and Philip had agreed to a contract limiting Philip's power in England, many suspected that the king and queen would soon refuse to respect its provisions. Numerous oppositional writers insisted that, after rejecting the provisions of the contract (which had been made statute law), Mary and Philip would simply ignore the existing English statutes defining the royal prerogative and re-create the powers of the monarchy to assume absolute power in the realm.[8]

The Trial of Sir Nicholas Throckmorton

For many, the April 1554 treason trial of the evangelical courtier and Parliamentarian Sir Nicholas Throckmorton stood as the most disturbing attempt yet by Marian officers to bend English law to serve illicit royal desires. In the wake of Wyatt's failure (January 1554), Mary and her chief officers had struck against several prominent English men and women who had not actually risen with Wyatt but who had sparked the queen's suspicion or anger. The first to suffer were Lady Jane Grey and her husband, Guilford Dudley, executed on February 12, 1554—to the outrage of evangelicals—not for any recent acts but simply to prevent them from becoming rallying points for future rebels.

7. Loach, *Parliament and the Crown*, 96–97; Bindoff, *History of Parliament*, 3:324. The text of Fleetwood's discussion of this bill is printed in Alsop, "Act for the Queen's Royal Power."

8. Harbison, *Rival Ambassadors*, 103; Loach, *Parliament and the Crown*, 184–91; Samson, "Changing Places."

At nearly the same time, the Earl of Devonshire, the Marquess of Northampton, and even Mary's own sister, Princess Elizabeth, were taken into custody. Furthermore, Mary ordered the arrest of several evangelical gentlemen who, like Devonshire, Northampton, and Elizabeth, had not risen with Wyatt but whom she nevertheless felt should be condemned for complicity in Wyatt's acts of treason.[9]

Sir Nicholas Throckmorton was the first of these prisoners to stand trial, and it was in direct response to the malfeasant actions of Throckmorton's judges on behalf of the queen that George Ferrers composed his tragedy "The fall of Robert Tresilian chiefe Iustice of Englande, and other his felowes, for misconstruyng the lawes, and expounding them to serue the Princes affections." In late 1553 Throckmorton had expressed misgivings about Mary's Spanish marriage, and he had had conversations with several of the men who would later become leaders of Wyatt's revolt. Thus, while Throckmorton did not participate in Wyatt's rising, the queen still held him to be a dangerous enemy and strongly desired his condemnation for treason. In April 1554 a juridical commission of oyer and terminer was set up, composed mostly of prominent supporters of the queen and of legal men eager for advancement. All were persons of substance who had much to gain by currying Mary's favor and much to lose by incurring her dislike. Each knew that Mary wished Throckmorton's successful conviction to stand as a precedent to justify further such convictions of nonparticipants in Wyatt's rising, including, perhaps, her sister, Elizabeth.[10]

The judges, led by Mary's Lord Chief Justice, Sir Thomas Bromley, strove to assist the queen's attorney in securing a guilty verdict against Throckmorton. They did not allow Throckmorton to know the specific laws by which he was to be judged, they sent away the witnesses who were present to testify on Throckmorton's behalf, and they allowed illegal testimony by untrustworthy witnesses to be presented against him. The commissioners, however, were faced with one difficult problem: Throckmorton had done nothing

9. For some of these, see Foxe, *Actes and Monuments*, 1396–98.

10. Loach, *Parliament and the Crown*, 92; Patterson, *Trial of Nicholas Throckmorton*, 8. In the wake of Throckmorton's trial, evangelicals produced a remarkably complete transcript of the courtroom proceedings and disseminated it among their coreligionists. Holinshed's account of the trial is almost certainly a reprint of this original, no longer extant version. See "The Order of the Araignemente of Sir Nicholas Throckemorton Knight," in Holinshed, Harrison, and Stanyhurst, *Laste Volume of the Chronicles*, 1737–55. Patterson, *Trial of Nicholas Throckmorton*, provides a modern critical edition of the "Order of the Araignemente"; all further references to the "Order of the Araignemente" are to Patterson's edition. Patterson also offers an important study of Throckmorton's trial in *Reading Holinshed's Chronicles*, 154–83. See as well Brigden, *London and the Reformation*, 551–54.

punishable by statute law. Mary's first Parliament, of which Throckmorton had been a member, had returned the definition of treason to that of the 1352 Treason Act of Edward III. This act pronounced it treason to attempt the murder of the king, queen, or heir to the throne by an overt act, but it did not consider words alone to be treason. Throckmorton had certainly spoken against the Spanish marriage and had had extensive contact with the chief rebels in the months before the uprisings, but his misgivings about the Spanish marriage and his speculation about the possibility of a rebellion had remained only talk. He had not taken arms against his queen, and so could not be prosecuted for treason under the current law.[11]

The court's response was to subject the treason statute to unprecedented and obviously prejudiced interpretations in order to aid the crown's case—what Throckmorton called "wresting and exceeding" the law.[12] Through specious reasoning, the judges allowed the argument of the queen's attorney that "compassing" (i.e., contriving) to depose the monarch was the equivalent both of actively attempting to kill her and of levying war against her, offenses that were defined as treason under the Marian statute. To get around the fact that the current statute was clear in its exemption of speech from the definition of treason, the commissioners alleged the existence of "divers other treasons at this day in the common law." These were "as the judges can declare"; that is, they were to be deduced from an allegedly relevant set of cases and declared applicable solely on the judges' discretion, a set of precedents that the judges, against established legal practice, insisted were to be given greater weight than the Marian Treason Act which Parliament had so recently declared to be the law of the land.[13]

Throckmorton forcefully challenged this "wresting and exceeding" of statute law. He defended the supremacy of the statute and demanded that the commissioners apply their legal reasoning as it had been applied in other cases. He reminded the court that even Stanford, the queen's attorney charged with prosecuting him, had declared in Parliament that statute law should be read "by the letter," without unprecedented judicial interpretations, "considering the private affections many times both of princes and ministers within this realm, for that they were men and coulde and woulde err, it should be no security, but very dangerous to the subject, to refer the construction and extending of penal statutes, to any judge's equity (as you termed it), which might either by fear of the higher powers be seduced, or by ignorance and

11. Patterson, *Trial of Nicholas Throckmorton*, 16–20; Loach, *Parliament and the Crown*, 76–77. For this repeal statute, see Elton, *Tudor Constitution*, 69.

12. Patterson, *Trial of Nicholas Throckmorton*, 33.

13. Ibid., 62.

folly abused."[14] Throckmorton made it plain that he realized it was only to please "the queen's highness, my adversary," that the judges at his trial had advanced the legal interpretations they did, and he openly lamented how easily judges could tailor their decisions to their monarch's desires, for "when it pleaseth the higher powers to call any man's life and sayings in question, then there be constructions, interpretations, and extensions reserved to the justices and the judges' equity." In a pointed jab at his own commissioners, Throckmorton warned the jury that in a case such as his, "judges be rather agreeable to the time than to the truth."[15]

Throckmorton argued with the court from seven in the morning until five in the evening, quoting the Marian treason statute to the jury from memory and boldly repeating his demand that statutes be interpreted by the letter, not by "construction." Against all expectations, the jury of twelve citizens found him innocent. The response was quick and remarkable. When the guards carried Throckmorton back to the Tower after acquittal, "the people showed their joy by shouting and throwing their caps in the air." The rebel Wyatt's head, which had sat upon a gibbet since his execution, was stolen away in the middle of the night.[16] Queen Mary was so upset by her defeat that she fell ill for three days. The Spanish ambassador reported that "attempts are being made to punish the judges" for their failure to secure a victory for the crown.[17] Many celebrated Throckmorton's escape from the obviously vindictive attack by the queen. Although Throckmorton did escape with his life, he did not escape with his liberty. The court returned him to the Tower to await unspecified new charges. Worse, it imprisoned the whole twelve-man jury as well for daring to acquit a man who had provoked the queen's dislike. Throckmorton and the unfortunate jurors were all languishing in prison as Ferrers's poem on Tresilian was being composed in 1554.[18]

"Robert Tresilian": Royal Will and Judicial Injustice

George Ferrers constructs his tragedy "The Fall of Robert Tresilian" both as an indictment of the Throckmorton commissioners and as an attempt to dissuade other Marian legal professionals from following the lead of the

14. Ibid., 65. See also Patterson, *Reading Holinshed's Chronicles*, 170–75.
15. Patterson, *Trial of Nicholas Throckmorton*, 47, 76–77.
16. Brigden, *London and the Reformation*, 522.
17. *CSP, Span.*, 12:221.
18. The jurors remained in prison until December 1554. Throckmorton was not released until January 1555 (Brigden, *London and the Reformation*, 554; Bindoff, *History of Parliament*, 3:460).

Throckmorton judges.[19] In the poem, King Richard II's Chief Justice, Robert Tresilian (d. 1388), returns from the dead with "other his felowes" to lament their crime of "misconstruyng the lawes, and expounding them to serue the Princes affections" (73). In an impassioned confession Tresilian recalls how he and his fellow corrupt jurists began their careers as men of skill and probity in legal affairs. Soon, however, they allowed their devotion to justice to become undermined by a lust for wealth and advancement. Both for their own benefit and for that of their monarch, the judges began willfully to subvert the legal process in their law courts, rigging each trial in favor of whichever side might bring them the most in wealth or political advancement. Their chief method, Tresilian reveals, was the intentional misconstruction of English statute law. "The lawes we interpreted and statutes of the lande," he recalls,

> Not trulye by the texte, but nuly by a glose:
> And wurds that wer most plaine whan thei by vs wer skande
> We turned by construction like a welchman's hose,
> Wherby many one both lyfe and lande dyd lose:
> Yet this we made a mean to mount aloft on mules.
> To serue kings in al pointes men must sumwhile breke rules. (77)

In both the interpretation of the law and the control of court procedure, their personal authority over those before them was absolute, "so that to whether syde so euer we did wey, / Were it right or wrong it past without repriefe" (75–76).[20]

Their most damaging deeds as jurists were those they undertook on behalf of their monarch. Through the ability of his judges to make even the most unjust of his actions appear to be legal, King Richard soon found himself free to act on his every whim, no matter how illicit. The result, Tresilian declares,

19. Ferrers and Throckmorton were well known to each other by the time "Tresilian" was composed. Under Henry VIII, Ferrers served as a page in the King's Chamber at the time Throckmorton was employed in the service of Queen Catherine Parr; both men also appear to have enjoyed the patronage of Catherine's second husband, Sir Thomas Seymour. Later both were Edwardian court figures, both were important landowners in Hertfordshire, both participated in Edward Seymour's 1547 invasion of Scotland, and both served in King Edward's two Parliaments. Throckmorton's interest in evangelicalism may have acquainted him with the strongly Protestant Baldwin as well. Interestingly, in the 1563 edition of the *Mirror for Magistrates,* Baldwin remarks that Throckmorton's uncle Thomas, Lord Vaux, had promised to write the tragedy of Edward V and his brother for the post-suppression "Second Parte" of *A Memorial of suche Princes* (*Mirror,* 297). Furthermore, when one of Throckmorton's nephews wrote in Elizabeth's reign a biography of his uncle Sir Nicholas, he chose to compose his narrative in precisely the form of Ferrers's "Robert Tresilian," as an admonitory verse *de casibus* tragedy narrated by the ghost of his poem's protagonist. See Nichols, *Legend of Sir Nicholas Throckmorton.*

20. On the extensive power of early modern judges in court proceedings, see Harding, *Social History of English Law,* 119–39.

was tyranny, as Richard "set his lusts for lawe" and gained "power absolute both to saue and spyll" (77). It was just such abuse of the law that led directly to Tresilian's and his fellows' downfall. With no independent system of justice to oppose the king's assaults on his own subjects, the afflicted "Baronye of Englande," supported by the equally suffering commons, initiated a rising against King Richard (the Lords Appellant's rising of 1387). The Lords wrested control of the realm from their king and called a Parliament, which established new restraints on the monarch's power and exiled or executed the pernicious magistrates who had led King Richard into his criminal acts. Among those put to death was Robert Tresilian, "dampned to the gallowes most vyly as a thiefe" (79). Tresilian's spirit ends his oration by warning all "Iudges and Iusticers" in England to avoid his and his fellows' corrupt practices or risk an end as violent and as miserable as his own (73).

Annabel Patterson was the first to suggest that George Ferrers composed "Robert Tresilian" as a response to the malfeasant practices of the Throckmorton commissioners. It was precisely Chief Justice Bromley and his associates whom Ferrers urged readers to indict, Patterson proposed, when he had his Tresilian denounce "sum in latter dayes" who had emulated Tresilian's corrupt practices but who had as yet escaped due punishment for their crimes (80).[21] An examination of Ferrers's changes to his source material for this tragedy supports Patterson's suggestion. In the charges lodged against King Richard's chief legal men in Ferrers's source, the rolls of Parliament, Chief Justice Tresilian and his fellow justices indeed are accused of abusive actions in office, but the method of "mysconstruying" or "wresting" statute law that Ferrers ascribes to them in "Robert Tresilian" is never mentioned (71). In addition, Ferrers's assertion that Richard's judges committed their acts of malfeasance on behalf of their king is similarly without precedent in Ferrers's source. In fact, far from assisting King Richard in his misrule of the realm, as Ferrers's poem suggests, Tresilian and his fellows are actually accused by Parliament of working *against* the king, as befitted the convenient fiction adopted by the Appellant Lords that their rising was meant merely to expose to the innocent Richard II the existence of highly placed traitors around him.[22]

Although Tresilian's style of judicial malfeasance and his corrupt actions on behalf of his monarch are both without foundation in Ferrers's source, they are precisely the practices that Throckmorton's commissioners pursued during Throckmorton's trial. In the face of such brazen acts of corruption

21. See the introduction to this book and Patterson, *Reading Holinshed's Chronicles*, 160–61.

22. For the historical charges against Tresilian and his fellow judges, see Strachey, *Rotuli Parliamentorum*, 3:229–33.

committed by Mary's chief judges to satisfy royal will, the lawyer Ferrers crafts "Robert Tresilian" to persuade all of England's "Iudges and Iusticers" that no justification, even that of royal command, can excuse the pernicious practice of judicial abuse of English laws and English legal procedure. He warns further that if such actions are allowed to persist unchecked, they will produce terrible consequences for the realm, including the affliction of the people, civil unrest, and finally the deaths and even the damnation of the very men who thought to gain most from freeing their monarch from the rule of law.

In their own minds, Throckmorton's judges may have justified their manipulation of the law as an irregular but necessary means to accomplish a higher good—the conviction and execution of a man whom their queen held to be an enemy. Ferrers, by contrast, urges his fellow legal men to believe that such behavior is evil in and of itself, no matter for whom or for what purpose it is undertaken. Tresilian's ghost flatly declares any judge's intentional misinterpretation of statute law to be a pernicious "wrestyng of the right." No excuse could ever justify such an act, the poem would have its readers believe, for a judge's willful misconstruction of English law is a deed of "falshode" that is wrong by its very nature (80, 79).

Not only is such behavior criminal, but it is deeply sinful as well. In the midst of a bitter outburst against the "endles thyrst of golde" that helped to lead him and his fellows into King Richard's corrupt service, Ferrers's Tresilian exclaims:

> Thou madest vs forget the fayth of our profession,
> When sergeantes we were sworne to serue the common lawe.
> Whiche was that in no poynte we should make digression
> From approued principles in sentens nor in sawe:
> But we vnhappy wretches without all drede and awe
> Of the Iudge eternall, for worldes vayne promocion,
> More to man than God dyd beare our hole deuocion. (76–77)[23]

Ferrers presents a judge's duty to the "approued principles" of the English legal community in explicitly religious terms, identifying it as the very "fayth" of the legal profession. By the logic of Ferrers's poem, to abandon this "fayth" through the willful misconstruction of the law must be understood as an act akin to apostasy, for by departing from the "approued principles" of the legal community, an English judge consciously rejects the virtuous example of the "Iudge eternall" and thus reveals himself to be a sinner in defiance of God's

23. Ferrers echoes in this stanza Throckmorton's own words during his trial, in which he expressed to the judges his desire to "be tried by faithful just men, which more fear God than the world" (Patterson, *Trial of Nicholas Throckmorton*, 30).

will. Such behavior, Ferrers's poem warns, cannot but be reckoned against the erring jurist when he comes before the "iust iudge supreme" on the day of judgment (80).[24]

Of course, unrestrained judicial malfeasance not only endangers the soul of the judge who engages in it but also inflicts terrible injury on the innocent men and women who come before malfeasant officers in courts of law. Ferrers's Tresilian recalls the ease with which he and his fellow corrupt jurists inflicted injury on any in their courts whom they chose to make suffer. "At sessions and at syses we bare the stroke and swey," Tresilian declares,

> In patentes and commissions of *Quorum*, alway chiefe:
> So that to whether syde so euer we did wey,
> Were it right or wrong it past without repriefe,
> We let hang the true man sumwhiles to saue a thiefe
> Of golde and of syluer our handes were neuer emptye,
> Offices, fermes, and fees, fell to vs in great plentye. (75-76)

Their authority to manipulate verdicts through their control over the interpretation of law allows malfeasant jurists to engage in acts of legally sanctioned robbery and even murder. Worse, when judges ally themselves in corruption with their monarch, they exercise such unjust power with impunity, for it is the prince alone who has the authority to remove an erring justice. When he has Tresilian blandly admit that he and his fellows "let hang the true man sumwhiles to saue a thiefe," Ferrers offers a grim reminder of the grievous human consequences that legal abuse holds for those who deserve injury least: the innocents who come to England's legal officers seeking impartial justice.

Worst of all, when a judge turns his willful misconstruction of English statutes to the service of the prince, he endangers the rights and legal protections of every subject in the realm. If high English judges are willing to shape their legal interpretations from the bench to the dictates of royal will, they run the risk of granting the monarch all but absolute power in the realm. Treslian recalls how Richard's chief judges turned their ability to create binding interpretations of parliamentary statutes to the fulfillment of King Richard's every desire, arguing away in the process all legal impediments to the monarch's authority. The result was tyranny:

> So wurkyng lawe lyke waxe, the subiecte was not sure
> Of lyfe, lande, nor goods, but at the princes wyll:
> Which caused his kingdome the shorter tyme to dure,
> For clayming power absolute both to saue or spyll,

24. Compare Throckmorton's own repeated warnings to his commissioners of the divine punishment awaiting malfeasant judges (ibid., 32, 64).

The prince thereby presumed his people for to pyll:
And set his lustes for lawe, and will had reasons place,
No more but hang and drawe, there was no better grace. (77)

With the monarch allowed unjustly to transcend "the lymittes of his law," and with the people stripped of every legal protection against monarchical injustice, tyranny reigned, and all in England went "to wracke, vnlyke of remedie" (78).

Ferrers crafts his disturbing portrait of England's miseries under a monarch allowed to control judicial behavior as an admonitory "mirror" for contemporary readers, one that urges them to study the supposedly historically proven consequences that will result if the actions so recently undertaken by Queen Mary's chief legal officers are not opposed and abandoned. In reading of the behavior of England's "raging" King Richard, readers are to ponder what their own queen might do if she were placed by her judges in similar circumstances. As we have seen, many English evangelicals held Queen Mary to be, like Ferrers's King Richard, a willful and "affectionate" ruler, one who many feared would be willing to subject the nation to brutal oppression (through the "bringing in of the Spaniards") solely to satisfy her own "lustes."[25] Ferrers constructs his tragic tale of Ricardian England's descent into tyranny to move England's judges to fear a similar fate for Marian England should they adopt the practice of tailoring their interpretation of the laws to suit their monarch's wishes.

Only by resisting monarchical pressure to serve the queen's desires rather than the interests of justice, Ferrers's poem suggests, can "Iudges and Iusticers" prevent the unjust encroachment of royal power upon the legal protections of English subjects (73). Furthermore, Ferrers insists, such resistance is the only means by which the nation can avoid the oppression and resultant rebellion and civil disorder that will necessarily follow (so his poem claims) the introduction of de facto royal absolutism into England. Ferrers attempts to persuade Marian officers that the people of England will never quietly endure sustained unjust persecution by a monarch and his or her magistrates but will eventually repay such persecution with resistance and even with violence. According to the poem, after Richard's subjects discovered that there

25. For the view that Mary was a willful monarch led chiefly by her "lustes," see chapter 4, n. 75. See also John Knox's 1554 pamphlet *A Faythfull Admonition*, in which Knox, employing the same language of "rage" supplanting reason as Ferrers does in "Robert Tresilian," insists that Mary's rule had confirmed the old saying that "the usurped government of an affectionate woman is a rage without reason" (Knox, *Faythfull Admonition*, 3:296). At his trial, Throckmorton boldly admitted his fear (shared, he noted, by many others) that tyranny would be the inevitable result of Queen Mary's decision to wed the Spanish prince (Patterson, *Trial of Nicholas Throckmorton*, 37–38, 49–50).

was no orderly means for redress from the suffering imposed on them by the king and his justices, they simply withdrew their obedience from both their monarch and the traditional "rules" of proper interaction between rulers and ruled (77). Nobles and commoners alike turned to the only effective tool left to them for ending their unwarranted affliction, an armed uprising:

> The Baronye of Englande not bearing this abuse,
> Conspyring with the commons assembled by assent,
> And seynge neyther reason, nor treaty, coulde induce
> The king in any thing his Rygor to relent,
> Mawgree all his might they called a parlyament
> Francke and free for all men without checke to debate
> As well for the weale publyke, as for the princes state.
>
> In whiche parlyament muche thinges was proponed
> Concerning the regaly and ryghtes of the crowne,
> By reason kynge Richarde, whiche was to be moned,
> Full lytell regardynge his honour and renowne,
> By synister aduyse, had tourned all vpsodowne.
> For surety of whose state, them thought it dyd behooue
> His corrupt counsaylours, from him to remooue. (78)[26]

Ferrers paints this joint rising by the nobles and commons as the inevitable response of a suffering people to the debilitation of all orderly systems of justice in the realm. Exemplifying William Baldwin's belief that the civic behavior of a people lies in direct relationship to the morality of its officers, Ferrers's narrative suggests that rebellion will invariably occur whenever corrupt judges misconstrue the law in order to give free rein to their monarch's illicit desires. If officers want an orderly, virtuous people who will stay within legal bounds in their behavior toward them, they too must be orderly, virtuous, and bound by the traditional "rules" of English law. If these officers refuse to distribute justice equitably through the means of the established legal system, the men and women of England will not abandon their desire for just handling and meekly suffer the depredations of those above them; rather

26. Tresilian and the others had been made the king's counselors after his "wyse and wurthy" counselors were driven away. As noted in chapter 3, the Lords Appellant's rising was led by five chief nobles, the Duke of Gloucester and the Earls of Arundel, Warwick, Derby, and Nottingham. In "Tresilian," by constrast, Ferrers makes this revolt the corporate decision of the entire "Baronye of Englande," in league with the "commons assembled by assent." His purpose, of course, is to suggest to readers that abuse of the law in the service of the prince is an act that will provoke the fury not merely of a handful of powerful magnates but of each and every member of the English nation. Furthermore, in creating this highly unhistorical portrait of the Lords Appellant's rising, Ferrers seeks to evoke memories in readers' minds not of the 1387 rising against King Richard but of an earlier baronial revolt, the rising against King John that brought to England its most celebrated document limiting royal authority, Magna Carta. See Lucas, "Let none such office take."

they will turn to any means necessary to win freedom from their oppression and to restore the rights, the liberties, and the restraints on royal power lost through pernicious judicial malfeasance.

In recounting the reestablishment of justice in Ricardian England, Ferrers leads readers to dwell not on the actions of the "Baronye" who led the rising against King Richard but on those of the Parliament called by the nobles, which reestablished the "rules" of just interaction between sovereign and subjects that King Richard's officers had destroyed (77). Ferrers casts the actions of the Appellant Lords' Parliament in this poem in a celebratory light, emphasizing its permitting of "francke and free" debate and its members' concern for the "weale publyke, as [well as] for the princes state" (78).[27] In sharp contrast to his portrait of Richard's pernicious "corrupt counsaylours," Ferrers portrays the men of Parliament (a group of which he himself had long been a member) as those most qualified to establish the just limits on the "ryghtes of the crowne" (78). It is Parliament's statutes and their proper application, Ferrers's poem insists, that will best secure the "surety of [Richard's] state" by setting proper limits on monarchical power (79). Any judge who seeks to undo those limits by wrongfully augmenting his monarch's authority will ultimately only weaken his ruler's hold on power. Permitting the ruler to transcend "the lymittes of his lawe," the poem vigorously warns, will result in the brutal exposure of the unspoken power the ruler's subjects have over their prince—a bold point to dramatize in the months following Wyatt's nearly successful rising.

To ensure that the new parliamentary limits on the king's power would be properly enforced, Parliament punished Richard's corrupt officers, including Tresilian and the other malfeasant judges. Tresilian, formerly England's highest legal officer, ended his life "dampned to the gallowes most vyly as a thiefe," a "most iust punycion," Tresilian confesses, and one that he knows will be followed by God's even more terrible condemnation of him on the day of judgment (79). Although, as the last stanza of Ferrers's poem acknowledges, the Throckmorton commissioners had not received any sort of punishment by the time "Tresilian" was written, Ferrers nevertheless insists that they will not be able to escape their ultimate punishment before the "iust iudge supreme," a fact that only adds urgency to Tresilian's admonitions against further abuse of the law "to serue the Princes affections" (80, 73).

Only judges "vncorrupt and vpryght in doome," the poem suggests, can protect sixteenth-century England from the culture of violence and revolt

27. Parliament's irregular act of self-convocation in this poem is Ferrers's invention. Historically it was Richard II who called this Parliament. See Tuck, *Richard II and the English Nobility*, 112–13.

that brought such misery to the realm, and ultimately to King Richard and his officers, in the late 1380s (73). Similarly, only by adhering to "approued principles" can the judges themselves hope to have long, healthy, and satisfying careers, careers admired by the people who depend on such men for justice and approved by God himself. Through "Robert Tresilian," the lawyer and Parliamentarian George Ferrers urges all future judges who might contemplate following their monarch's wishes rather than adhering to the accepted principles of legal interpretation—whether their monarch be Queen Mary, under whom the poem was written, or the new queen, Elizabeth I, under whom the work was first published—to recall Tresilian's tragic fate and forever eschew such practices.

"Mowbray": Absolutism and the Destruction of Justice in England

William Baldwin's "Howe the Lorde Mowbray promoted by Kyng Richarde the seconde, was by hym banyshed the Realme, and dyed miserably in exyle" expands on the admonitory message of Ferrers's "Robert Tresilian." Baldwin's poem warns not just legal men but all high officers that devotion to the monarch's will rather than to the interests of justice will cause harm to subjects, to the prince, and to England's unjust officers alike.

In "Lord Mowbray," the ghostly Thomas Mowbray, Duke of Norfolk, appears in "sorowe and shame" to recall his fall from probity and high place into corruption and a tragic demise. Baldwin's Mowbray relates how in the early years of Richard II's reign he rose to preeminence as Earl Marshal of the Realm. It was in this role that "the Piers and people ioyntly to me came," Mowbray recalls, with complaints against King Richard's counselors, who had brought misery to the nation through their "sale of Iustice, right and lawe" (101–2). On the people's behalf, Mowbray raised an army and led the Appellant Lords' forces against Richard's pernicious officers. Using the strength of his gathered army, Mowbray compelled the king to purge his corrupt favorites and to replace them with new, upright men of the Lords' own choosing. In the wake of his rising, Mowbray himself became Richard's chief counselor, in which position, Mowbray sadly confesses, "selfe loue bred." The newly advanced Mowbray soon strove not to protect justice but to protect his high place as Richard's chief counselor through currying royal favor. To win "the kinges good wyll," Mowbray did not merely offer support for all of Richard's desires but even made the king's every "lust [his] lawe," zealously seeking to satisfy his monarch's whims, no matter how immoral or unjust (103). Mowbray's willingness to execute Richard's every command allowed the king to give free rein to his desires, resulting in acts of tyrannous misgovernment that outraged the realm's highest nobles. In the face of Richard's depredations, those who had earlier joined with Mowbray to lead the Lords Appellant's rising came once more to their former ally (who had dissembled to them the extent of his devotion to the king) for assistance in ending Richard's "ruyne" of the commonwealth. This time, however, Mowbray betrayed his former allies to his vicious monarch, who had these unfortunate nobles "gyltles made awaye" (104). Later, after the virtuous Henry Bolenbroke, Earl of Hereford, revealed to Mowbray his own misgivings about Richard's rule, Mowbray maliciously reported Bolenbroke's words to Richard as treasonous.[28] Rather than reward Mowbray, however, Richard turned upon his chief henchman, banishing from the realm both Mowbray and Bolenbroke alike. Exiled, penniless, and falsely accused of robbing the king, Mowbray moved from country to country, burdened with the reputation of a "traytour" for his act of misrepresenting Bolenbroke's laudable concerns to Richard as expressions of treason. The once proud Mowbray finally died of grief in Venice, poverty stricken, branded with "defame," and miserable in the knowledge of his rival Bolenbroke's later success and of his own unexpected betrayal by the very monarch whom he had once gone to any lengths to serve (108).

In his account of Mowbray's career, Baldwin takes great liberties with his chief historical source, Robert Fabyan's chronicle. Fabyan offers only a brief mention of Thomas Mowbray in connection with the Lords Appellant's rising, listing him merely as the last and least important of all its named participants. Baldwin, by contrast, casts Mowbray as the key figure in this revolt, naming him as the captain of the Appellants' army and as the man who assumes the role of King Richard's chief counselor in the wake of the Lords' victory. Similarly, while Fabyan delcares that the Appellant Lords rose against Richard solely to oppose the influence of pernicious royal favorites, Baldwin makes the rising one against not favorites but crown "offycers" and claims that Mowbray and the other Lords opposed these men for the specific deed of "makynge sale of Iustice, ryght and lawe," a crime completely unmentioned in Fabyan's account (102).[29] Later in his work Fabyan describes how Mowbray joined Thomas of Wudstocke, Duke of Gloucester, in 1397 as an ally in the planning of a second rising against Richard, but how Mowbray later, "fearyng the sequel of the matter," decided to reveal the scheme to King Richard.[30] Baldwin, however, presents Mowbray as Richard's secret

28. Throughout "Mowbray," Baldwin mistakenly identifies Henry Bolenbroke (or Bolingbroke) as Earl rather than Duke of Hereford.

29. Fabyan, *Chronicle*, sig. 3B5r. Unlike Baldwin, Fabyan describes no specific crime committed by Richard's counselors, writing only that they "misled" the king.

30. Ibid., sig. 3C4r.

ally from the beginning of this plot and as a man determined from its first moments to betray his unsuspecting co-conspirators to the king. Finally and most remarkably, Baldwin departs from Fabyan's account altogether for his presentation of the dispute between Mowbray and Henry Bolenbroke and all the events that followed it. Fabyan's claim that it was Mowbray rather than Bolenbroke who complained of Richard's misrule of the realm would, of course, not suit Baldwin's portrait of Mowbray as King Richard's creature; Baldwin therefore abandons Fabyan's narrative at this point and replaces it with the account found in Hall's *Union*, which asserts that it was Bolenbroke who spoke out against Richard's misgovernment and Mowbray who denounced Bolenbroke to the king.[31]

Baldwin alters his source material in order to shape the historical Mowbray's career into an exemplum designed to dissuade current magistrates from placing their queen's wishes above the ideal of justice for all in the realm. Through a narrative offering readers both positive and negative examples of proper magisterial behavior, Baldwin seeks to convince Queen Mary's (and, later, Queen Elizabeth's) chief officers that their true duty lies not in offering unquestioning obedience to the ruler's desires but in challenging, opposing, and even actively resisting any royal command that threatens the existence of justice in England.

In "Mowbray," Baldwin presents strict devotion to monarchical will as nothing less than a product of pernicious sin and "vyce." Baldwin's Mowbray describes the unquestioning subservience he offered King Richard during his lifetime as a moral failing, an act born solely of "self loue." It was a proud desire to remain in his high place about his monarch, Mowbray admits, that led him to curry favor with Richard by offering unqualified "assent" even to his unjust and immoral whims (102–4). "To thende I might enjoye / The kinges good wyll I made his lust my lawe," Mowbray confesses,

> And where of late I laboured to destroye,
> Such flateryng folke as thereto stoode in awe,
> Nowe learned I among the rest to clawe:
> For pride is suche, yf it be kindely caught,
> As stroyeth good, and styrreth vp every nought. (103)

Recalling the acts of oppression, robbery, and fraud he willingly executed in Richard's service, Mowbray's spirit warns current magistrates that "vyce, onely vyce, with her stoute strengthles arme, / Doth cause the harte to euyll to enclyne" (102). If a magistrate commits immoral acts, the true motive for such behavior can only be vice. No claim of principled obedience to the

31. Hall, "Introduction," in *Union*, fol. 3r–v; see also *Mirror*, 110.

prince could ever justify the commission of sinful acts, even those undertaken on the monarch's direct command.[32]

In fact Baldwin's tragedy contends that officers who commit a sin on behalf of their prince harm not only their own moral health but that of their monarch as well. Baldwin paints his poem's King Richard as an undeniably corrupt ruler; nevertheless, he shapes "Mowbray" to place the blame for Richard's corrupt practices not so much on Richard himself as on the king's supine counselor Thomas Mowbray. Baldwin presents Richard to readers not as a reprobate but as an immature, "fonde" ruler, a young man dangerously susceptible to the impulses of "wanton youth" and thus one strongly in need of proper guidance (102). When Mowbray elected to make Richard's "lust" his "lawe" and to affirm even Richard's most immoral whims, he robbed his monarch of proper moral instruction and led him into the disastrous belief that his every desire was "a lawfull matter" (103). The result, Mowbray recalls, was the fall of his uncounseled, unrestrained king into depravity and crime. Mowbray's ghost castigates his earlier passive acceptance of Richard's illicit desires, describing this practice not as an expression of laudable obedience but as "flattery," that most execrated of all forms of courtly speech. "My duty bounde me to have tolde, / My prince his fault, and wylde him to refrayne," Mowbray confesses (105); by neglecting this duty, Mowbray "abused [Richard's] wanton youth" and allowed his king to stray into the pernicious behavior that would lead to his eventual "payne" (102, 105). Only by seeking to impose his own will on the monarch when he or she errs, Baldwin asserts, does a high royal officer truly serve his prince. Any officer who abandons that duty in the name of strict obedience to the prince's will does not truly serve his monarch but merely helps his prince to moral corruption.

The ruler and his or her erring magistrate, the poem further warns, will not be the only ones to suffer from a contemporary officer's unquestioning obedience to royal desire. Rather, such behavior harms each and every subject through its swift debilitation of equitable justice in the realm. When he has Mowbray confess that he made his king's "lust my lawe" and that he held Richard's every desire to be "a lawfull matter," Baldwin conveys the threat that strict obedience to royal will offers to the very concept of the impartial rule of law. Despite the circulation in mid-Tudor England of Henrician paeans to the absolute authority of the English monarch, the mainstream of political thought at this time held that monarchs and subjects alike were bound by the dictates of common and statute law. It was English law, Tudor

32. Compare the similar warning issued in the *Memorial-Mirror* tragedy "The infamous ende of Lord Iohn Tiptofte Earle of Wurcester, for cruelly executing his princes butcherly commaundementes" (197–202).

lawyers and legislators asserted, that established royal authority itself, defining the specific prerogative power enjoyed by the monarch and specifying the authority of law over such power.[33] By allowing their monarch the means to act even on illicit desires, magistrates render powerless the traditional legal protections enjoyed by English subjects and thus allow absolutism to enter into the nation. Such absolutism, in Baldwin's view, necessarily leads to tyranny, as the unrestrained monarch, convinced by his or her counselors that each of his or her whims is by its very nature a "lawfull matter," comes to act solely upon impulse and "lust." Under such conditions, the country cannot but fall into "ruyne" (103–4).

To dissuade officers from helping their prince to extralegal power, Baldwin crafts "Mowbray" to assert that any unjust power officers grant to their prince will be used ultimately to harm those magistrates who helped their monarch achieve it. At the end of the poem Mowbray bitterly reveals how King Richard made him the victim of precisely the sort of cruel treatment that Mowbray had earlier helped Richard mete out to others. After unjustly denouncing Henry Bolenbroke in hopes of gaining reward, Mowbray learned that Richard had decided to condemn Mowbray himself to impoverishment and exile. Richard banished his former servant not for any specific crime (Mowbray, after all, had undertaken his acts of injustice on Richard's own command) but solely so that he might seize Mowbray's lands and enrich himself at Mowbray's expense. Baldwin portrays Mowbray's spirit as suffering even after death from his memories of Richard's treachery, his pain made worse by his knowledge that he himself was instrumental in undermining the impartial system of justice that once might have allowed him protection from the depredations of his prince (107). Mowbray thus concludes his mournful narrative by urging Baldwin to warn England's chief magistrates ("princes") never to follow his own tragic lead. Those who seek to please the monarch by indulging in sin, crime, and vice on his or her behalf, Mowbray warns, will only find "attaynt" similar to his for their crimes (109).

Instead of championing the idea of an officer's absolute devotion to the monarch, then, Baldwin urges magistrates to devote themselves first and foremost to the protection of justice for all in the realm, even if such protection entails active resistance to the ruler. In the early stanzas of his poem, Baldwin has Mowbray recount the central role he played in the Lords Appellant's rising against Richard's corrupt favorites. Before the rising, Mowbray recalls, Richard had created him "Marshall of the realme." It was specifically in his "estate" of Earl Marshal, Mowbray continues, that

33. Dunham, "Regal Power and the Rule of Law"; Baumer, *Early Tudor Theory of Kingship*, 184–85; Elton, "Rule of Law," 268–69.

> The Piers and people ioyntly to me came,
> with sore complaynt against them that of late
> Made offycers, had brought the king in hate
> By makynge sale of Iustice, ryght and lawe,
> And lyuyng nought, without all dreede and awe.
>
> I gaue them ayde these euyls to redresse,
> And went to London with an army strong,
> And caused the king against his wyll oppresse
> By cruell death, all suche as led him wrong. . . .
>
> These wicked men from thus the king remoued,
> who best vs pleased, succeded in theyr place:
> For whiche both kyng and commons muche vs loued
> But chiefly I with all stoode high in grace,
> The kyng ensued my rede in euery case. (102–3)

Baldwin in no way condemns this rising, even though it violates all received notions of the proper duty of a subject toward his prince. Instead he emphasizes the purity of its motives and its laudable role in the return of justice and order to the realm. Baldwin presents Mowbray's sole purpose in rising against royal authority as a selfless desire to counter Richard's officers' debilitation of "Iustice, ryght and lawe." Furthermore, Baldwin suggests to readers that Mowbray led this rising not as a private subject but as "Marshall of the realme," that is, as one of the great officers of England.[34] Finally, Baldwin stresses that Mowbray undertook his bold action solely on behalf of the English people: it was only the joint appeal of the "Piers and people" that spurred Mowbray to rise against Richard's pernicious officers (102). Through his account of Mowbray's rising, Baldwin exemplifies his conviction that it is the paramount duty of a high magistrate to protect justice and to "helpe other" in the realm (64). Active resistance to sustained monarchical injustice is not rebellion if it is undertaken by a high officer for the purpose of helping all other men and women; rather, Baldwin's poem implies, it is the proper response of a dutiful magistrate to the "euyls" that arise whenever injustice, whether caused directly by the monarch or indirectly by his or her refusal to discipline corrupt officers, is allowed to reign unchecked in the kingdom.

Included among those such a rising will help, Baldwin suggests, is the erring prince himself or herself. If unquestioning obedience to royal will harms the monarch, limited, principled opposition to a ruler's unjust desires will in the long run aid rather than harm him or her. Baldwin seeks to convince

34. Through his portrait of Marshal Mowbray's dutiful defense of the people against royally sanctioned depredations, Baldwin adapts to England's system of crown officers the teachings of Calvin concerning the duty of popularly elected magistrates to "withstand" unjust rulers. See Lucas, "Let none such office take."

readers of this claim by portraying King Richard, once he is returned to his senses in the wake of the Appellants' rising, as one of the chief *supporters* of Mowbray's act of defiance. Richard "loued" Mowbray, the poem insists, precisely for saving him from the temporary depravity into which he had sunk and for leading him once more to reasonable, well-counseled rule of the land (103). For Baldwin, the return of peace and justice to the realm and of virtue to the prince is worth any upheaval caused by principled resistance to an erring monarch.

Through "Mowbray," Baldwin seeks to move magistrates to resist the dual temptation to "flatter" their queen through passive acceptance of her illicit desires and to allow her unjustly to augment her power above that established by tradition and law. When the monarch strays into error, high officers must hold among their chief tasks the telling of their "prince [her] fault," even at the risk of incurring royal disfavor (105). If such admonition does not work, magistrates must resist monarchical injustice with stronger measures, even to the point of actively resisting the monarch's will. It is only through opposition and even resistance to the ruler's illicit wishes, Baldwin's poem teaches, that officers can preserve justice, protect their countrymen, aid their queen, and indeed save their own lives. Baldwin's call to officers to employ limited, principled resistance if necessary was a daring message to communicate in Tudor England, even obliquely; it was one that Baldwin and many others felt it vital to convey, however, no matter the risks, in what were for many the dark, anxious days of Mary's early reign.

"Kyng Richarde the Seconde": Law, Justice, and the Fragility of Monarchical Power

The final tragedy examined in this chapter, Sir Thomas Chaloner's "Howe kyng Richarde the seconde was for his euyll gouernaunce deposed from his seat, and miserably murdred in prison," stands as perhaps the boldest attempt by a *Memorial* author to forestall royally sanctioned abuse of justice. Chaloner directs the lessons of his poem specifically to English "Kynges," a group that in 1554, of course, numbered only one reader of Chaloner's tragedy, Queen Mary herself (112, 118).[35] Through a corrosive examination of the foundations of monarchical power, Chaloner seeks to lead his queen to accept that the true basis for her authority is the consent of the English people to her governance. If she refuses to respect the traditional rights and legal protections of her subjects, she will lose that consent and bring about only her own suffering, deposition, and even death.

35. The only other candidate, Mary's husband, Philip of Spain, did not read English.

In the poem King Richard II returns from the dead to present his tragic career as an exemplary warning to all English rulers.[36] During his time in power, Richard was a king who "ruled all by lust, / That forced not of vertue, ryght, or lawe" (113). Devoting himself solely to the satisfaction of his own desires, Richard did not scruple to rob his people, impoverishing them by means of unjust subsidies, forced loans, blank charters, and other illicit documents. If any counselor attempted to tell Richard his "fault," he simply had that person exiled or killed (114). Suffering under Richard's pernicious rule, the nobles and commoners of England alike soon came to "sore detest" their prince. The king, however, remained deaf to his subjects' increasing rancor. He was thus caught completely by surprise when, after departing for Ireland, he learned that his lieutenant in England, Edmund, Duke of York, and members of the Percy family had withdrawn their obedience to him and had invited the exiled Henry Bolenbroke back into the realm. With Bolenbroke offering armed defiance to England's hated ruler, even Richard's most trusted servants quickly abandoned their master. Bereft of all support, Richard was seized, imprisoned, and forced to yield his crown. Soon after, England's new king, Henry IV, had Richard murdered in his prison cell, an act that even Richard's ghost admits brought to a fittingly "lawles" end an English monarch who had himself done so much to debilitate justice in the realm (118).

In his tragedy Richard identifies a range of vices in which he indulged during his time as England's prince. He insists, however, that only one of these, his abuse of "ryght and law," led him to his terrible end. Far from a unique occurrence in English history, Richard warns, a fate such as his is what awaits any English monarch who dares to indulge in acts of injustice. "Happy is the prince that hath in welth the grace / To folowe vertue, keping vices vnder," Richard exclaims at the opening of his poem,

> But wo to him whose will hath wisedomes place:
> For who so renteth ryght and law a sunder
> On him at length loe, al the world shall wunder,
> Hygh byrth, choyse fortune, force, nor Princely mace
> Can warrant King or Keysar fro the case. (111)

Here and elsewhere Chaloner's Richard asserts a direct causal link between sustained monarchical abuse of "ryght and law" and the downfall of the prince who engages in it. For a ruler, "lawles life, to lawles deth ey drawes,"

36. Chaloner draws upon both Fabyan's and Hall's chronicles for the historical details of his tragedy. Except where noted, Chaloner generally follows closely the accounts of Richard's crimes and subsequent suffering found in his sources.

Richard warns; it is only if English "Kynges be rulde and rule by right" that they can ever hope to escape the sort of misery he himself was forced to endure (118).

To move his queen to accept his poem's asserted link between just behavior and sustained monarchical power, Chaloner first works to undermine any belief she may have in the safety and strength of her royal station. Chaloner excludes from his exemplum all the well-worn claims of royal might and divine protection for the ruler that informed Tudor propaganda; instead, he depicts the tragically ephemeral nature of royal authority and the fundamental status of even the prince as weak and unprotected human flesh. Chaloner begins this project even before his poem commences. In the prose passage preceding "Kyng Richarde the seconde," Chaloner bids Baldwin (and, by extension, all readers) to imagine his ghostly speaker not as a proud monarch restored after death to the dignity of his royal station but as a naked, mutilated corpse, a figure of horrific abjection, "al to be mangled, with blew woundes, lying pale and wanne al naked vpon the cold stones in Paules church, the people standing round about him, and making his mone" (111).[37] In a collection filled with tragic speakers, Chaloner's Richard stands as one of the most tragic of them all, precisely because of the terrible gap between his former exalted station and the profoundly degraded state in which Chaloner presents him. Chaloner constructs this disturbing image of England's former ruler as a means to shock the queen into reflecting critically on the true nature of royal power and royal security. In response to the sort of Marian propaganda that presented Sir Thomas Wyatt's recent defeat as clear evidence that rebels could never succeed against an English sovereign, Chaloner's poem offers Richard's mangled body and his "blew woundes" as undeniable historical evidence of the English prince's fragile hold on power and of his or her tragic susceptibility to the violence of those who would take up arms against their monarch.

Chaloner continues in the text of the poem itself to move his chosen audience to such reflections, particularly when he has his fallen protagonist directly beseech princely readers to learn from his abject, brutalized condition just how vulnerable the prince is to suffering and how tenuous is his or her hold on royal power. "Beholde my hap," Richard urges England's "rulers,"

> see how the sely route
> Do gase vpon me, and eche to other saye:
> Se where he lieth for whome none late might route,

37. The claim that Richard's naked body was cast upon the steps of Saint Paul's Cathedral after Richard's murder is Chaloner's own invention. Historically, Richard's corpse was covered in lead and displayed with honor in Saint Paul's. See Hall, "Henry IV," fols. 14v–15r.

Loe howe the power, the pride, and riche aray
Of myghty rulers lightly fade away.
The Kyng whych erst kept all the realme in doute,
The veryest rascall now dare checke and lowte:
What moulde be Kynges made of, but carayn [carrion] clay?
Beholde his woundes, how blew they be about,
Whych whyle he lived, thought neuer to decay. (112)

The familiar attributes of royal station—"the power, the pride, and riche aray" of the monarch—have no force in and of themselves to protect the prince. Instead, each of these can be stripped from any sovereign as easily as Richard's own power and symbols of rule were taken from him. Neither royal might nor royal station is an essential attribute of one who wears the crown; each may at any moment "lightly fade away," leaving the monarch bereft of all but the weak and easily wounded "carayn clay" into which he or she was born.

Princely power is ephemeral precisely because such power is never truly the prince's at all. Chaloner shapes "Kyng Richarde the seconde" to persuade his queen that the true foundation of monarchical authority rests not on a prince's "high byrth, choyse fortune, force, [or] Princely mace" but solely on the willingness of the people to consent to the monarch's rule (111). If the people withdraw that consent, the monarch will have no one to fulfill his or her commands and thus no power beyond that of his or her own person. In his account of Richard's abandonment by his Lord Steward, Thomas, Earl of Worcester, Chaloner offers Mary an image of the disturbing ease with which even her closest sworn officers can leave her control once they decide to withdraw their obedience to her. Richard bitterly recalls how his chief household servant, Worcester, brought to an end his years of loyalty simply by breaking his staff of office and departing from the court (115).[38] God did not intervene to punish Worcester's disobedience, nor did Worcester in any way suffer from his act. Indeed, far from reviling Worcester as a traitor, every one of Richard's household servants chose to follow Worcester's lead and withdraw his own loyalty from the king. "See princes," Richard cries out, "see the power wherof we boste, / Whome most we trust, at nede do vs betray" (115). The "power wherof [monarchs] boste," princely readers are to learn from Richard's abandonment by his household officers, is only lent to rulers by those who choose (whether willingly or under threat of punishment) to obey their commands. While he may rage in his anguish at his servants' renuncia-

38. Chaloner suppresses in his poem any recognition that Worcester was a member of the Percy family in order to portray his renunciation of loyalty to his prince as motivated by the spur of moral outrage rather than by that of family allegiance.

tion of their duty to their prince, Richard nevertheless cannot deny the bitter truth that the choice to serve or to leave him was always his officers' own to make, just as it was that of all other subjects in his realm.

To enjoy lasting power in England, monarchs must always strive to ensure that their subjects remain willing to grant them their obedience. The chief means to accomplish this end is for the ruler to respect the laws and to uphold at all times the rights of the English people. If a prince refrains from acts of injustice and strives to protect "ryght and law" in the realm, the people as a whole will happily serve their ruler and keep him or her in authority. If the monarch refuses to respect the rights and legally defined privileges of the people, however, the people will similarly refuse to respect the "rights" and privileges of the monarch, and it will be the prince and not those under him or her, Chaloner's poem warns, who will ultimately suffer most from such a break in established political decorum.

Chaloner, in fact, uses "Kyng Richarde the seconde" to move monarchs to understand their interaction with their subjects in terms of a tacit contract between ruler and ruled. Richard suggests the existence of such a compact when he reminds princes of the "rules" of political behavior and the misery that awaits princes who break them. "Realmes haue rules, and rulers haue a syse [i.e., a proper limit to their actions]," Chaloner's Richard warns, "Which if they kepe not, doubtles say I dare / That eythers gryefes the other shall agrise [i.e., afflict] / Till the one be lost, the other brought to care" (113). Both ruler and subjects alike shall suffer if a monarch refuses to keep within the established "syse" of his or her political actions. Only if England's princes respect the "rules" of proper social interaction will the people accept their governance and live in order and happiness under them, granting them the power that comes only from the people's consent to their rule. Of course, for Chaloner the proper scope of a monarch's actions toward his or her people is established by English law and by the canons of justice in the realm, and it is only through the proper and lasting respect for those boundaries that any monarch may remain long on the throne.

Indeed, as both Chaloner and Queen Mary knew, such an agreement by English monarchs to abide by the "rules" of law and justice was not an unspoken promise at all, but one of the key components of any prince's rise to royal power in early modern England. Since the fourteenth century, all candidates for the throne swore at their coronations a multipart oath "in sight of all the people" to behave justly toward their subjects. The first part of this oath was the monarch's solemn promise to "graunt and keepe to the people of Englande the Lawes and customes to them as olde rightfull and devoute kinges graunted" and to recognize and to defend all "such lawes as . . . shalbe chosen by [the] people" during the monarch's reign. Each would-be ruler then swore to "make to be done . . . rightfull Justice in all [his or her] domes and iudgementes," promising, in other words, to uphold precisely the conditions Chaloner asserts to be the sine qua non of lasting monarchical rule.[39] At the height of Wyatt's rebellion, Mary herself had put her subjects in mind of her pledge to respect the laws of the nation, declaring in her famous Guildhall speech that her coronation had effectively wed her "to the realme, and to the lawes of the same."[40] In the face of what seemed Mary's increasing willingness in the months after Wyatt's defeat to supersede English law to satisfy her own desires, and in the face of what many saw as the uncertain future for English law and English rights under the joint rule of Queen Mary and King Philip, Chaloner's "Kyng Richarde the seconde" recalls to Mary the pledges she made at her coronation and implores her always to uphold the laws and to further justice in the realm. If she forgoes her pledge to respect and protect English laws and English rights, Chaloner's exemplary poem warns, the "contract" between her and her people will be broken, and the result will be nothing less than an end for England's current monarch every bit as swift and brutal as that of her predecessor Richard II.

Although they present readers with numerous images of armed resistance in the face of sustained monarchical misrule, the *Memorial* authors did not craft poems such as "Tresilian," "Mowbray," and "Kyng Richarde the seconde" as calls to revolution. Rather they created them first and foremost as attempts to forestall the sort of civil dissension described in their narratives, as works designed to spur England's governors to eschew any attempt to increase royal power at the expense of justice and thus to avoid the upheavals that would inevitably (so they believed) follow such a move. Chancellor Gardiner's decision to prohibit publication of *A Memorial of suche Princes* ensured that the authors' admonitions never reached their intended audiences. It was only after Mary's death, in the first year of Elizabeth's reign, that Baldwin found means to bring the poems of *A Memorial of suche Princes* before the reading public (1559). By that time the immediate topical "moment" of these tragedies had passed, and it was for this reason that Baldwin offered the newly titled *Mirror for Magistrates* to Elizabethan officers not as a text engaged specifically with the concerns of Mary's early reign but as a collection of more general political exempla profitable for magistrates of any period.

39. Legg, *English Coronation Records*, 230. Although the text of Mary's coronation oath has not survived, there is no record of any departure from the traditional oath followed (with one exception) since the fourteenth century. See Hoak, "Coronations," 149.

40. Grafton, *Grafton's Chronicle*, 2:539.

In 1563, however, Baldwin began to prepare a new volume of political poetry for the press, one that would be joined to the 1559 *Mirror* and that would offer warnings composed specifically for the Elizabethan "nobilitye and all other in office" (63). How Elizabeth's officers would respond to such a work was for Baldwin an unanswered question. Would the queen's Councilors follow the lead of their Marian predecessors and prohibit a text whose poems might touch, even allusively, upon contemporary "princes cheefe affayres," or would they tolerate its poems' words of counsel, admonition, and even protest as long as they were offered in oblique, literary form (246)? The uncertain future of political literature in Elizabeth's reign forms the primary focus of William Baldwin's several contributions to the *Seconde Parte of the Mirrour for Magistrates*, the 1563 compendium of Elizabethan and Marian poems appended to the original gathering of *Mirror* tragedies. It is to these works that we now turn.

CHAPTER SIX

The Seconde Parte of the Mirrour for Magistrates and the Future of Political Literature in Elizabeth's Reign

The Seconde Parte of the Mirrour for Magistrates (the gathering of poems and prose links first appended to the original selection of *Mirror* poems in 1563) is a curious collection of writings. While presented as a unified volume compiled seven days after the tragedies of the first edition were composed, its contents are actually extremely disparate in age, content, and tone. Although its first half was constructed in the Elizabethan period, its second half is certainly Marian in origin. These two sections were grafted together and printed without notice of their disparity, as a result leaving comments appropriate to Elizabeth's rule (such as references to the government's opposition to expressions of Catholic doctrine) sitting uncomfortably with passages appropriate only to Mary's reign (such as a long discussion of Philip's and Mary's right to rule). Some of the tragedies of the *Seconde Parte* are by original *Memorial* authors, others are by new men solicited by Baldwin and Ferrers, and still others are by men connected to the project only through its Elizabethan printer, Thomas Marshe. Even the auditors who discuss the poems in the prose sections change in the middle of the work from an Elizabethan company of "frendes and furderers" (but not authors) to a Marian group of men who are either actual or possible authors of *Mirror* tragedies (243).[1]

The *Seconde Parte* introduces several concerns to the *Mirror* not found in the 1559 edition, including a newfound focus on social rather than strictly political problems and an increased interest in the specific literary art of the individual tragedies. Foremost among the concerns of this text, however, is the question of the proper role for, and even the possibility of, controversial

1. See the appendix.

political poetry in the new Elizabethan age. Baldwin crafts several of his contributions to the *Seconde Parte* as means to raise and respond to precisely this question. In the tragedies "How Sir Anthony Wudvile Lorde Rivers [was] causeles imprisoned, and cruelly murdered" and "Howe Collingbourne was cruelly executed for making a foolishe rime," and also in the prose link that precedes the Collingbourne poem, Baldwin offers Elizabethan magistrates and poets alike an oblique series of appeals. Through them, Baldwin seeks to urge Elizabeth's high officers to accept the independent, politically engaged poet as a beneficial and necessary counselor in public affairs. At the same time, he also exhorts his fellow poets to continue to publish works of admonition and protest, even in the face of possible personal danger. Through the tragedy "Collingbourne" in particular, Baldwin offers magistrates and authors a model of an implicit contract that they might share for producing and receiving any future political verse. His goal in that work and others is to urge English officers and writers alike to create social conditions that will allow politically interventionary literature not only to be tolerated in the new Elizabethan age but also to take a key place in the English political system.

"Sir Anthony Wudvile Lorde Rivers," Sackville's "Induction," and the Question of Censorship

Baldwin registers the uncertain future for public political commentary under Elizabeth in the very first tragedy of the *Seconde Parte*, "How Sir Anthony Wudvile Lorde Rivers [was] causeles imprisoned, and cruelly murdered." At the beginning of this poem, Rivers's ghost appears before Baldwin to complain that he was never allowed a chance to speak when the original collection of *Memorial-Mirror* tragedies was compiled. According to the poem, Rivers "long attended for my turne / To tell my tale" while the original tragedies of the collection were composed (246). It was with shock, therefore, that Rivers watched the *Memorial-Mirror* poets suddenly disperse after narrating the death of King Edward IV, leaving Rivers and others who met their deaths under the next two monarchs, Edward V and Richard III, unable to tell their life stories. Rivers spent his long wait (seven days, according to the conceit of the text itself; nine years, according to the actual time elapsed between the composition of the first poems and the printing of the *Seconde Parte*) searching for the reason why the authors never continued with their literary project. Upon considering both the oddly abrupt end to the first edition of the collection and what seemed to be the subsequent complete abandonment of the *Mirror* project, Rivers found himself driven to a single melancholy conclusion: that the *Mirror* had suffered the fate of all other literary endeavors that dared to touch honestly on contemporary political affairs, namely, complete suppression, by means of either official prohibition or an act of fearful self-censorship imposed by the authors themselves. It seemed to him only logical, Rivers explains, to assume that censorship (either actual or anticipated) led to the authors' sudden silence,

> For hytherto slye wryters wyly wittes
> Which have engrossed princes cheefe affayres,
> Have been lyke horses snaffled with the byttes
> Of fansye, feare, or doubtes full diepe dispayres,
> Whose raynes enchayned to the chefest chayres,
> Have so ben strayned of those that bare the stroke
> That truth was forst to ch[e]w or els to choke. (246–47)

Authors who seek to compose works of honest political commentary, Rivers insists, live constantly in fear of retribution from "princes" who feel "the stroke" in seeing their own transgressions on display. No matter how "slye" such authors might be in couching their commentary in indirect, seemingly inoffensive form, guilty rulers always force them to choke back any unpalatable truth they seek to display. The constant threat of official retribution for their words allows politically minded authors only two courses of action: either to "leade awry" readers by lying about the nature of erring officers' immoral actions or to bury the truth in enforced silence (247).

Rivers's lament for the travails of past political literature touches allusively on the difficulties faced by the *Memorial-Mirror* authors themselves in the previous reign, when Mary's Lord Chancellor ordered the first version of *A Mirror for Magistrates*, the *Memorial of suche Princes*, destroyed.[2] Through Rivers's comments, Baldwin suggests the reason why Mary's officers suppressed the *Memorial*: its poems allusively "engrossed" contemporary "princes cheefe affayres" and thus provoked the wrath of political leaders who could not tolerate the admonishment they offered. Rivers's words also explain why Baldwin waited nearly ten years before printing a new collection of political verse to add to the Marian poems of the 1559 *Mirror*. Baldwin, the poem implies, thought it "better therefore not to wryte at all / Than stayne the truth" by composing works that could find publication only at the cost of hiding the faults of those in power (247).

Baldwin uses "Rivers" to defend his choice of public silence after the suppression of the *Memorial* and to indict those who turned their talents to defending the "crimes" of Mary's officers. In the poem Rivers implies that it is far worse for an author to turn his rhetorical skill to the support of wicked

2. Baldwin alerts readers to the suppression of the *Memorial* in his dedicatory epistle to the *Mirror* (66).

rulers than it is for him merely to withhold comment on their crimes. Those who take up their pens to defend evil officers help to advance those crimes, and thus make themselves partners in the officers' sins. "What harme may hap by helpe of lying pennes," Rivers declares,

> How wrytten lyes may lewdly be maynteyned.
> The lothly rytes, the divilysh ydoll dennes
> With gyltles blud of vertuous men bestayned,
> Is such a proofe as all good hartes haue playned.
> The taly groundes of storyes throughly tryes,
> The deth of martyrs vengeauns on it cryes. (247)

The "helpe of lying pennes" assists the wicked in their misdeeds. Therefore, to avoid participating in sinful acts, authors must never support the pernicious actions of erring rulers. If the highest of the realm will not tolerate moral admonishment, it is better to abandon one's poetic vocation and remain silent, the poem implies, than it is to turn one's talent to the service of a corrupt government. In his reference to "divilysh ydoll dennes" and "martyrs," Baldwin elliptically indicts those writers who employed their pens in the support of Mary's religious policies after the death of Edward VI. Those authors who defended in print the actions of Mary's government (particularly, Baldwin implies, its execution of Protestants) aided the queen and her Catholic officers in bringing idolatry and murder into England. God will wreak "vengeauns" upon such mercenary writers, the poem obliquely warns, just as surely as he punished the wicked men who once employed them.

Rivers creates something of a crescendo in his lament for the fate of truth-telling political literature in England. Yet after more than fifty lines on the dangers facing those who seek to publish controversial works of political comment, he makes an unexpected turn, abruptly claiming that none of these dangers in fact had anything to do with the delay Baldwin endured between releasing the first and second set of *Mirror* tragedies. Rivers now knows that Baldwin and his fellow authors let "my story fall" not for political reasons but for literary ones: they ended their project at Edward IV's reign, Rivers insists, solely because they wanted to allow a "pause" for "the readers ease" between the first collection of tragedies and the second. Here Rivers leaves behind his earlier allusions to Mary's reign and the suppression of the *Memorial* and returns to the fiction that the two sections of the *Mirror* were both Elizabethan in origin and compiled within one week of each other. Gone from Rivers's monologue is any suggestion of the threats of official retribution that stymied Baldwin in his desire to publish new *Memorial* tragedies under Mary. Instead, Rivers exclaims, "highly it dyd me please" to learn that it was Baldwin's concern for his readers' stamina and not a threat of persecution from Elizabeth's government that led him to decide if and when he would continue his *Mirror* project (247).

Baldwin introduces this sudden turn from the political to the literary to sound a note of cautious optimism for authors writing in Elizabeth's reign. This section of "Rivers" offers implicit praise to the new Elizabethan government for allowing the authors of *A Mirror for Magistrates* to do what (according to the poem) had never been done before: to publish works of honest commentary on "princes cheefe affayres." Still, Baldwin dampens the sense of optimism in this passage by prefacing it with the gloomy history of political censorship that precedes it and by following it with a suggestion that further hostility toward the *Mirror* poets is yet to come from offended private individuals who will "brall" and "mumble" against the authors upon reading the text (248).

In fact, at the time he was composing "Rivers," Baldwin had good reason to remain uncertain about the ability of authors to publish future works of topical political commentary under the new Elizabethan regime. While Elizabeth's government had indeed allowed the publication of the once prohibited poems of the *Memorial* (under the title *A Mirror for Magistrates*), this decision had not been much of a test of the government's tolerance of controversial political verse. The admonitory poems of the 1559 *Mirror* spoke chiefly to problems specific to the reign of Queen Mary, problems that had disappeared in the previous year with the end of the Marian regime. The *Seconde Parte of the Mirrour for Magistrates*, by contrast, would include newly composed works of political admonition that could well be suspected of touching allusively on the doings of Elizabeth and her officers. How *these* poems would be received was, at the time of the writing of "Rivers," still unclear. Despite being more tolerant of political expression than Mary's regime had been, Elizabeth's government still maintained mechanisms of censorship, among them a system of licensing that entailed preapproval of printed works by the queen, six or more Privy Councilors, or two or more Elizabethan bishops (including at least one archbishop); a ban on all unauthorized plays touching on religion or state policy; and an announced policy of allowing only "men of authority" to speak publicly on government affairs.[3] There was no established body of rules by which the government would decide whether or not to grant a license for a work, nor was there a clear sense of how severely any individual author might be punished for his words. The extent of any writer's ability to publish works that touched on government policy in Elizabethan England was thus still uncertain, and the extent to

3. Loades, *Politics, Censorship and the English Reformation*, 105; Hughes and Larkin, *Tudor Royal Proclamations*, 2:115–16.

which authors could speak freely without fear of retribution still relatively unknown. Baldwin confronts just this ambiguous state of affairs in the prose link between Thomas Sackville's contributions to the collection (Sackville's "Induction" and "The complaynt of Henrye duke of Buckingham") and his own tragedy "Howe Collingbourne was cruelly executed for making a foolishe rime." Here Baldwin indirectly urges magistrates to confirm or deny once and for all the possibility of autonomy for authors who seek to compose works of political admonition in the Elizabethan era.

In "The Induction," the first of his two linked poems of the *Seconde Parte*, Thomas Sackville describes a dream vision in which he follows a personified figure of Sorrow down to the underworld to encounter (in the manner of Aeneas in Book 6 of the *Aeneid*) numerous allegorical figures and fallen "Prynces of renowne" (316). Among these is King Richard III's erstwhile ally Henry, Duke of Buckingham, whose first-person narrative forms the second of Sackville's two poetic contributions to the collection.

In the prose link following Buckingham's tragedy, an anonymous auditor praises Sackville's two poems for their artistry, yet expresses doubts about whether they should be printed in the form in which they were composed. In particular the auditor fears that Sackville's setting will raise unwanted difficulties for the *Mirror* authors: "But where as [Sackville] faineth to talke with the princes in hel, that I am sure will be mislyked, because it is moste certayne, that some of their soules be in heauen. And although he herein do follow allowed Poetes, in theyr discription of Hel, yet it sauoreth so much of Purgatory, whiche the papistes haue digged thereout, that the ignorant maye therby be deceyued" (346).

To modern eyes, the speaker's concerns seem excessive. Sackville's journey to the underworld is modeled not on Christian conceptions of hell but on the underworld portrayed in Virgil's pre-Christian *Aeneid*. In the poem Sackville clearly identifies his hell as Virgil's, declaring Pluto to be its king, taking all the allegorical figures that inhabit it from the *Aeneid*, and locating its entrance at Lake Avernus.[4] There seems little to support the speaker's fear that some may construe the poem to be a covert affirmation of the Catholic doctrine of purgatory. Yet while the speaker's fears of misinterpretation may today seem exaggerated, they were at the time not unfounded, for they arose out of the particularly volatile religious context in which Elizabethan sections of the *Seconde Parte* were composed and printed. In the very year of the printing of the *Seconde Parte*, Convocation declared "the Romish doctrine concerning Purgatory" to be a belief "perniciously repugnant to the word

4. On the depth of Sackville's debt to Virgil, see Swart, *Thomas Sackville*, 52–57.

of God," while the 1563 Parliament had shown itself to be virulently anti-Catholic.[5] The suggestion of Roman Catholic doctrine in a publicly disseminated printed text may indeed have been "misliked" by Elizabeth's officers, particularly since the person who would be suspected of such dissemination, Thomas Sackville, was the son of one of Elizabeth's Privy Councilors and a man whose own religious allegiance was at least somewhat questionable.[6]

In answering this speaker, Baldwin seems, surprisingly, to misunderstand his concerns. Baldwin's reply to the fear of unwanted reader response is to speak only of authorial intention: Sackville did not mean for his hell to be understood as purgatory, Baldwin explains. In fact, Sackville's hell, according to Baldwin, represents neither the pagan underworld nor Roman Catholic purgatory but in reality "the Graue, wherin the dead bodies of al sortes of people do rest till tyme of the resurrection. And in this sence is Hel taken often in the scriptures, & in the writynges of learned christians. And so (as [Sackville] himselfe hath tolde me) he meaneth, and so would haue it taken" (346). Far from alluding to Catholic doctrine, Baldwin insists, Sackville embeds in his classical setting an image of a familiar Protestant conception of the afterlife, one conveyed so covertly that not even Sackville's own "frendes" are able to detect it.

Baldwin's assertion of Sackville's intention says nothing about the possibility of readerly misinterpretation. His odd attempt to align Sackville's Virgilian underworld with Protestant doctrine seems strained, too, producing an interpretation of the text as inappropriate as the imagined Catholic one of the "ignorant." Baldwin offers no textual proof to suggest that Sackville created his hell with "the Graue" in mind, nor does he attempt to reconcile this interpretation with the obviously classical features of Sackville's setting. In fact his insistence on the Protestant orthodoxy of Sackville's use of the term "hell" in his Virgilian poem seems only to highlight the doubtfulness of his assertion.

Leaving readers to swallow their skepticism on this point, the *Mirror* now adds a third opinion—a new speaker, who insists that Baldwin and the first interlocutor worry too much about the meaning of what is, after all, "a Poesie and no diuinitye." Sackville's poems should be printed as they stand, he argues, for poetry is an autonomous realm, and literary works should be

5. See Article 22 of the Thirty-nine Articles (Heylyn, *Ecclesia Restaurata*, 2:448).

6. Sackville's mother had been arrested in 1561 for attending Mass, while Sackville himself made a strange journey to Rome late in 1563 and attempted to return with a note from the pope to Queen Elizabeth (Swart, *Thomas Sackville*, 9–12). Furthermore, government suspicions about covert messages in Sackville's poems would not have been unwarranted, since Sackville had already established a reputation for composing allusive political commentary through his and Thomas Norton's topical tragedy *Gorboduc* (see James and Walker, "Politics of *Gorboduc*").

judged only by the laws of literary art. There is simply nothing to worry about, for by the laws of poesie "it is lawfull for poetes to fayne what they lyst, so it be appertinent to the matter" (346).

Baldwin, in his reply, seems to misunderstand this person as well. Where the new speaker invokes the laws of literary decorum, Baldwin hears reference only to the laws of the nation. "Where you say a poet may faine what he list," Baldwin replies, "in deede my thynke [i.e., methinks] it should bee so, and ought to be well taken of the hearers: but it hath not at al times been so allowed." Baldwin turns the speaker's words away from the internal rules of composition to external laws of political regulation: the "hearers" to whom he refers are government officers, and to prove the past inability of poets to "fayne what they lyst" under regimes that restrict poetic expression, he proposes to read the tragedy of "one called Collingborne," a fifteenth-century poet who "was cruelly put to death for makyng of a ryme" (346).

The odd and frequently illogical trajectory of this conversation seems initially baffling. It may be understood, however, if readers approach this exchange not as raw reported discourse but as an artfully constructed indirect address to the collection's most important readers, the "nobilitye and all other in office" (63). The exchange raises, but does not answer, its questions about Sackville's poems in order to suggest to Elizabethan magistrates that such questions are, for poets, as yet unanswerable. The first speaker's words show how, under censoring regimes, even the authors of seemingly uncontroversial literary creations (such as Sackville's classical "Induction") live in constant fear of unexpected misconstructions that could call down punishment upon them. By publishing the speaker's question of whether Sackville's poem should be presented to licensers as it was written, Baldwin indirectly urges Elizabethan officers to acknowledge that fear among authors and to answer for themselves the series of questions that it provokes. Will those officers charged with controlling public discourse punish a poet if his poem is misinterpreted by "ignorant" readers, even if the poet did not mean for his work to be construed as it was? Will magistrates accept a poet's own interpretation of his poem as politically or religiously inoffensive, even when that explanation (such as the one Baldwin proffers in the prose link) seems formulated only in response to the charges of unorthodoxy brought against it? And finally, is it indeed "lawfull for poetes to fayne what they lyst" in works of imaginative literature, or will government surveillance and suspicious readers force poets into the lies and timorous self-censorship that, as "Rivers" allusively recalled, exacerbated the misery of Mary's reign?[7]

7. Andrew Hadfield was the first to notice the questioning form of this prose link. See Hadfield, *Literature, Politics and National Identity*, 103.

"Collingbourne" and the Public Role of the Political Poet

In the tragedy that follows this exchange, "Howe Collingbourne was cruelly executed for making a foolishe rime," Baldwin continues to pose such questions, but he also proposes answers to them. "Collingbourne" is informed by Baldwin's uniquely interventionary poetics, a poetics based on the fundamental assumption that works of political admonition and protest are of the greatest importance to the well-being of both officers and the commonwealth. Baldwin shapes "Collingbourne" to assert this importance indirectly and to describe the conditions necessary for the optimal production and reception of such literature. In fact, though couched in the elliptical form of a negative exemplum, "Collingbourne" can be read as presenting the terms of a sort of contract between poets and officers, one designed to create the conditions that would allow interventionary political verse a key place in the English political decision-making process.

According to Fabyan's chronicle (the source from which Baldwin derives Collingbourne's story), the historical William Collingbourne was executed in 1484 for "sondry treasons" committed against Richard III on behalf of Henry of Richmond, and only secondarily for composing a couplet—"the catte, the ratte, and louel our dogge. / Ruleth all englande vnder a hogge"—that allusively satirized Richard's chief henchmen (William Catesby, Richard Ratcliffe, and Francis Lovell) and Richard himself, whose badge was the boar.[8] In the *Mirror*, Baldwin reshapes Fabyan's account for his own purposes, making Collingbourne a poet whose sole crime was the production of satirical, allusive verse.

At first "Collingbourne" seems to renew the sense of doubt that suffused the initial stanzas of "Rivers." In a surprising opening, Collingbourne's ghost returns from the grave to warn Baldwin and the other *Mirror* authors against composing precisely the sort of topical verse that fills their collection. In tyrannous times, Collingbourne warns, all attempts at political commentary are suspected and "misliked." Wicked rulers prejudge as offensive all matter alluding critically to their actions, no matter how carefully hidden it might be: "Touche covertly in termes, and then you taunt," is Collingbourne's description of how corrupt governors understand criticism, even criticism presented in indirect form (347). Fearing that the officers of Elizabeth's England are similar to those of Richard III's reign, Collingbourne beseeches Baldwin to abandon the *Mirror* project as one too dangerous to continue:

8. Fabyan, *Chronicle*, sig. 3R1r. Hall's chronicle also speaks of Collingbourne, but Hall offers a version of Collingbourne's couplet that differs from Fabyan's and Baldwin's (Hall, "Richard III," in *Union*, fol. 18r).

Ceas therfore Baldwyn, ceas I thee exhort,
Withdrawe thy pen, for nothing shalt thou gayne
Save hate, with losse of paper, ynke and payne.
Fewe hate theyr sinnes, all hate to heare them touched,
Howe covertly so ever they be couched.

"Thy entent I knowe is godly, playne, and good," Collingbourne continues, "to warne the wyse, to fraye [frighten] the fond fro yll." He assumes, however, that good intentions will be of no importance to those in power; in reading the tragedies of the *Mirror*, they will simply "to the wurst . . . all thinges construe" (349).

Collingbourne's initial admonition *against* interventionary verse has led to confusion among *Mirror* critics. Andrew Hadfield, for one, finds the tragedy perplexing. In his study of the poem in *Literature, Politics and National Identity*, he notes that a work written by William Baldwin should champion the production of political poetry, but concludes that "Collingbourne" can be read only as counseling poets to "stay aloof from politics."[9] Finding his understanding of "Collingbourne" to be irreconcilable with his understanding of the political nature of other *Mirror* tragedies, Hadfield concludes that the poem must have been designed to signify the exact opposite of what it actually says.[10]

Hadfield is correct to identify the poem as one that works by indirection; his characterization of its signifying practice, however, is too extreme. Far from asserting that in the Elizabethan period "there is no suitable audience for an intersubjective, political communication to function successfully," this section of "Collingbourne" instead poses that statement as a question to the nation's governors.[11] Baldwin specifies a particular audience for Collingbourne's opening admonition: not all politically minded poets but only those who "purpose to rehearce / By any arte what *Tyrantes doynges* are" (347).[12] This qualification is designed to move magistrates to ask themselves whether Collingbourne indeed has such an audience in Elizabethan times. Are the actions of Elizabethan magistrates "Tyrantes doynges"? Do Elizabethan poets live in a period of tyranny, as Collingbourne assumes they must? In particular, do they face "tyrannical" punishments for their words, as Collingbourne did in Richard III's reign, or have Elizabeth's magistrates eschewed that wicked practice? Baldwin's opening attempts to compel magistrates to take one of two positions on the question of how much free expression should be

9. Hadfield, *Literature, Politics and National Identity*, 105.
10. Ibid., 107.
11. Ibid., 105.
12. Emphasis added.

allowed in printed works: either they choose to censor and to punish authors for their words and thus to engage in the tyrannical practices of Richard III and his officers, or they choose to tolerate those authors' works and thus to present themselves as enlightened men. Any understanding of censorship as sound political policy is simply excluded from the poem.

The questions obliquely posed here are for Baldwin urgent ones, as he ascribes great importance to the ability—indeed the necessity—of politically minded poets to speak freely to those in power. In Baldwin's bold conception, poets are properly the guardians of the moral health of the nation's rulers and thus, by extension, of the nation. They must be allowed the freedom to admonish and even to rebuke high officers, for the well-being of the commonwealth is dependent on their ability to exert moral "controll" over magisterial behavior.[13]

Baldwin's formulation of the power that political poets should hold over the behavior of English officers seems stunningly presumptuous, yet its logic has been implicit throughout the pages of the *Mirror*. Its rationale is articulated most clearly in Baldwin's prefatory dedication to the collection, which asserts that the morality of a nation's people is dependent on the ethical fortitude of those in office. Such are the temptations to abuse power and high place that even the most upright of officers cannot fully be trusted to resist their lures. It is therefore necessary that some "provision" be made to ensure "that officers be forced to do their duties" (63). But who might best compel magistrates to carry out their obligations? In "Collingbourne," Baldwin nominates the independent public poet for this role. More traditional candidates, he implies, are either untrustworthy or ineffective. Thus, while the nation may first look to the monarch to fulfill the duty of supervising his or her officers, the *Mirror* in general and "Collingbourne" in particular cast overwhelming doubt on the monarch's ability to serve this function. From the "raging" Richard II of the first poem of the collection to the "Tyraunt" Richard III of "Collingbourne," the *Mirror* presents almost every one of its portrayed monarchs as at best ethically unreliable and at worst the very fount of corruption in his own government.

Similarly, Baldwin exposes the weakness of the other familiar candidate for moral supervisor, the court preacher. In the Edwardian period, evangelical preachers at court understood it to be their duty to admonish English magistrates in their sermons, even to the point of direct, open rebuke.[14] Yet

13. In the section in which Collingbourne impersonates the voice of a typical tyrant, the very first words of the tyrant to poets are "controll vs not" (*Mirror*, 347).

14. This duty is perhaps described most explicitly in the first sermon (preached March 8, 1549) of Latimer's *Seven Sermons before Edward VI*, 22–26.

if he could easily recall how the evangelical preachers at Edward's court had fearlessly devoted themselves to rebuking the nation's leaders, Baldwin could also remember that, at least according to the hindsight of those who suffered from the collapse of Dudley's regime and the accession of Mary I, the admonitory messages of those churchmen had little practical effect. Preachers of the Edwardian period loudly lamented how few of the chief men of Dudley's government heeded their corrective sermons.[15] In the voice of the "wycked sorte" of ruler, Collingbourne's ghost confirms the ease with which pernicious officers dismiss churchmen's warnings:

> Rude preachers . . . dare threaten vs plages & rods,
> And blase the blots whereby we stayne our state:
> But nought we passe what any such do prate.
> Of course and office they must say theyr pleasure,
> And we of course must heare and mend at leasure. (348)

Sinful officers will listen patiently to promises of some future punishment but will feel no impetus to "mend" until it suits their own purposes. In Baldwin's view, as long as churchmen can offer no specific threat of immediate punishment, their admonitions remain ineffective.

The politically interventionary poet working in the public sphere succeeds where the others fail precisely through his unique role as an independent, widely heard voice. First, as a political actor outside the actual government, he is not subject to the pitfalls of high place encountered by the monarch and his officers. With no direct participation in government affairs, the poet has no temptation to become a "flatterer [or] bolsterer of vyce" for political advancement; he speaks only what is best for all, because his sole reward is whatever general benefit his counsel brings to the commonwealth (352).[16]

Second, the independent poet is in constant contact with the people at large: he knows what they "grudge at" and has the skill to articulate and to present the causes of their dissatisfaction. The public poet, in Baldwin's telling, is vox populi; he alerts rulers to discontent so that they may alter

15. For instance, John Knox denounced Dudley and his men for listening to but failing to act upon the court sermons of Edward's last months: "What reverence and audience was given unto Preachers thys last Lent [1553]," Knox complained in 1554, "by such as then wer in authority: their own countenaunces declared, assuredly even such as was geven to Jeremy. Thei hated such as rebuked their vice, and stubbornely they sayd: We wyll not amend" (Knox, *Admonition*, sig. B3r).

16. Baldwin never considers the possible existence of a virtuous court poet of the sort that Ben Jonson imagined himself to be. In the *Mirror*, poets employed by the government appear only as flatterers. Thus in "Collingbourne," when Baldwin speaks of the moral epigrammatist Martial, who lived as a client of the Roman emperor Domitian, he characterizes him solely as one who was "forst" to flatter "Ceasars faultes" (*Mirror*, 347).

their harmful actions and thereby lessen the people's "hate" (359, 357).[17] It is this reasoning which informs Collingbourne's claim that his couplet was designed only to "wyshe [Richard and his officers] safetye." As "al men dyd lament" the harmful actions of their rulers, "therfore [I] made the rymes," Collingbourne explains, "to warne withal the careles of theyr crymes" (350). Collingbourne merely put into words the people's anger in an attempt to inform his rulers of the potentially dangerous discontent their own policies were creating.[18]

Third, through the wide dissemination of his verse, the poet who publishes his work to the general public is able to spur officers to amendment in a way the court preacher never could. In the voice of the tyrannous ruler, Baldwin describes the unique ability of such widely read poetry to catch the attention of misbehaving officers:

> But when these pelting poetes in theyr rymes
> Shall taunt, and iest, or paynt our wicked wurkes,
> And cause the people knowe, and curse our crymes,
> This ougly fault, no Tyrant lyves but vrkes. (348)

Unlike the court preacher, the public poet brings to bear upon erring rulers the pressure of a wide public awareness of their misdeeds. His poetry focuses popular anger and produces an anxiety in officers that such anger will explode into active resistance if they continue in their wrongful behavior. The threat of immediate physical harm provides precisely the goad to amendment that the court preacher's more general warnings lack.

It is noteworthy that Baldwin's theory of the value of public political poetry does not resemble prominent modern explanations of the function of early modern literature written under censorship. While Annabel Patterson, for instance, has argued that Baldwin believes that works of protest should serve a "safety valve" function designed to defuse popular anger by releasing it through relatively safe means of expression, in fact Baldwin locates the value of oppositional political literature in its ability to *concentrate* such anger and thereby to force specific changes in national policy.[19] Baldwin's theory, furthermore, does not construe literature as a medium through which to "stage"

17. In England this sense of the citizen poet as the voice of the people goes back at least to the medieval period. John Gower, for instance, conceives of the role of the poet in this way in *Vox Clamantis* and in other works (Ferguson, *Articulate Citizen*, 72–73).

18. That Collingbourne's poem failed, this stanza further suggests, was due in large part to the fact that Collingbourne mixed his laudable goal of communicating the anger of the people with a baser desire "to shewe my wyt, howe wel I could invent" (*Mirror*, 350). The result was his creation of a couplet whose flashy satirical aplomb worked to undercut its admonitory function.

19. Patterson, *Censorship and Interpretation*, 13–14.

social problems in order to come to an understanding of them. In keeping with his functional theory of magisterial and national morality, Baldwin's logic assumes that all the nation's problems are already comprehensible to "wise" poets and remediable if only such poets can "force" magistrates to solve them by the means the poets' works suggest.

Baldwin's beliefs are in fact best explained not by theories derived from later-sixteenth-century literary endeavor but by those designed to interpret acts of political opposition contemporaneous to the *Mirror*, in particular the several localized, "quasi-violent" uprisings over national policy in early and mid-Tudor England. In his study of such rebellions in Henry VIII's reign (which include the protests against the so-called Amicable Grant [1525], the Lincolnshire uprising [1536], and the Pilgrimage of Grace [1536–37]), Mervyn James argues that limited protests of this kind were chiefly admonitory and communicative, not revolutionary, in function. They sought not to overthrow the monarch or existing sociopolitical hierarchies but rather to register opposition among a cross-section of the king's subjects to specific instances of misgovernment. In their show of resistance to particular political policies, the protesters "called the prince to self-examination and [to] the correction of misrule," sending a message to the central government "that the very ideology of 'obedience' on which its authority rested could be brought into question by policies that threatened the material and moral disruption of the regional societies over which it presided."[20]

The *Mirror* itself portrays just such a protesting rebellion as those that James studies. In the poem "Jack Cade," Henry VI is portrayed as a king who refused to police the behavior of his officers. Cade easily drew numerous followers to his revolt, precisely because the people found no way other than violent confrontation to attract the attention of their unresponsive monarch. Only after Cade and his men defeated the royal army did Henry and his officers attempt "the peoples grudge [to] abate"; after his defeat, "where the king would nothing heare before," Cade recalls, "Nowe was he glad to send to know my minde" (174). It was only after this violent confrontation that Henry learned "the peoples grudge" and sought to ameliorate the problems of the realm by imprisoning his most pernicious magistrates. While the prose link following "Jack Cade" suggests that the *Mirror* authors are unable to

20. James, *Society, Politics and Culture*, 4, 192. While often referred to as "popular" rebellions (to distinguish them from the frequent rebellions of high nobles that marked the fifteenth century), these revolts were not "popular" in the sense of being composed only of poor commoners; they were in fact often led by members of the gentry or even minor noblemen. They frequently ended in submission to the government rather than in defeat on the battlefield once their participants thought their grievances would be redressed (ibid., 192–93).

sanction Cade's rebellion (not the least because Cade himself—unlike his followers—rebelled chiefly out of personal ambition), it nevertheless declares that even if rebellions are the devil's work, "yet God alwayes vseth them to his glory, as a parte of his Iustice. For whan Kynges and chiefe rulers, suffer theyr vnder officers to mysuse theyr subiectes, and wil not heare nor remedye theyr peoples wronges whan they complayne, than suffreth GOD the Rebell to rage, and to execute that parte of his Iustice, whiche the parcyall prince woulde not" (178).[21]

James in fact notes that Lydgate's *Fall of Princes* and the *Mirror for Magistrates* articulate beliefs concerning the rulers' responsibility for disorder that are similar to those that guided these uprisings. Yet whereas James sees only a coincidence of political "commonplaces" shared by the rebels and the *Mirror* authors, Baldwin conceives of interventionary verse as a direct *substitute* for the sort of limited revolts James describes. Like the armed protests, topical verse provides a "means whereby a profound sense of disagreement with the king's policies, and of injustice at supposed injuries inflicted by his agents on individuals, could receive expression."[22] It supersedes these protests in effectiveness precisely because it offers their communicative function without, crucially, their actual physical violence. If the political verse that Baldwin champions could be produced and received freely, it could serve the politically communicative purpose of the limited protests but also forestall the dangerous rifts in the social order that inevitably attended them. This idea is stated most clearly by one of the auditors in the prose link that follows "Collingbourne." This person speaks of the "great commodities" Richard and his men could have gained had they allowed political poets to address them. The first of these, he notes, would have been the ability to know "what the people myslyked and grudged at," a knowledge that would have allowed Richard and his officers to "have found meane . . . to have stayed the peoples grudge: the forerunner commonly of Rulers destructions" (359).

Baldwin's theory of the function and value of publicly disseminated political verse challenges the very logic of Tudor censorship, turning on its head the government's understanding of protest literature. As David Loades notes, the theory behind the government censorship of oppositional writings in Tudor England was based on the perceived need "to protect society from its own disruptive instincts." Tudor authorities understood works critical of

21. Cade's rebellion began to fail, according to the poem, only when it lost its communicative function and turned into a vehicle to satisfy Cade's own immoral "desier" for power and riches beyond his social station (174).

22. James, *Society, Politics and Culture*, 193.

official behavior to be directed foremost toward the people and designed to cause unrest. It was necessary to suppress such literature, they believed, because it created popular discontent and encouraged disobedience.[23] Baldwin's implicit argument against political censorship completely counters these assumptions. Interventionary public verse in Baldwin's formulation is not a threat to good order but a means of ensuring it. Such literature is addressed primarily to erring rulers, and it is designed ultimately to ameliorate popular discontent, not to exacerbate it. Thus censorship of politically admonitory literature (at least that written by "godly, playne, and good" writers) is a *cause* of disorder in the realm, not the weapon against it that Tudor authorities imagine it to be.

The gap between Baldwin's understanding of the role of protest literature and that held by England's officers informs the shape and tone of "Collingbourne." The poem balances its author's confident awareness of an important mechanism for social harmony with his frustrated conviction that the realities of English political life have up to now thwarted that mechanism's success. As the author of the poem "The infamous ende of Lord Iohn Tiptoft Earle of Wurcester, for cruelly executing his Princes butcherly commaundmentes," and Baldwin in "Lorde Rivers" complain, politically minded writers are often too frightened to speak of their ruler's misdeeds, while officers are frequently impervious to even the most beneficial admonition or rebuke (197–99, 246–47). Self-censorship and governmental persecution of authors thus strangle most attempts to produce topical, interventionary literature.

Baldwin uses "Collingbourne" to argue covertly yet pointedly for a reshaping of the conditions of literary production and reception in England. "Collingbourne" offers to authors and officials alike an obliquely proposed set of guidelines designed to make free-speaking political comment a central component of the English political system. In Baldwin's plan, both authors and officers must remain within certain boundaries when respectively composing and receiving political verse. If the poets whom Baldwin describes agree to adhere to certain ethical standards and to present their commentary only in oblique, inoffensive forms, officers must tolerate their work and accept it in the spirit in which it is offered. Baldwin's guidelines for authors and magistrates stand as the terms of an implied contract. By adopting Baldwin's prescriptions, both sides will gain a means of communication that will help to ensure the future happy state of the commonwealth.

23. Loades, *Politics, Censorship and the English Reformation*, 97.

The Poet as Officer

Although the terms of this "contract" are scattered throughout "Collingbourne," most of Baldwin's description of the proper parameters for political verse are contained in a long, seemingly digressive discussion of the ancient Greek ideal of the "perfect Poete." In setting forth these supposedly classical pronouncements (which are described in terms of the attributes of Pegasus), Baldwin presents the qualities and literary skills necessary for those who would presume to offer counsel, admonition, and even words of protest to the highest in the land. Baldwin describes these prescriptions for his "perfect Poete" as the duties of the "Poetes office." His choice of terms for the poet's vocation is significant, for "office" conveys a sense of quasi-governmental status and implies that the poet, while remaining independent of the central government, nevertheless properly has his own "official" duties to execute in the English political sphere (352–53).

Under Baldwin's plan, "official" political poets are to be an elite body made up of the most wise and ethical men in the nation. They will be "chaste and vertuous" and have only "regarde of truth" as their guide. Such men, he assures readers, will be utterly dependable; they will never be tempted or coerced into harmful flattery. In Baldwin's conceit, they will be like Pegasus "bred out of Medusaes blud . . . / Who to her power the Ocean god wythstoode": in other words, those who will hold the poet's office will resist magisterial pressure on their judgment just as Medusa (from whose blood, according to Ovid, Pegasus sprang) withstood Neptune mentally even while assaulted by lascivious enticements and physical coercion (353).[24] The "official" poets will be educated in both political and philosophical wisdom: continuing in his conceit of Pegasus, Baldwin writes that the perfect poet is one who can "flye to heaven, thereto to feede and rest: / He must have knowledge of eternal thynges, / Almighty Iove must harber in his brest" (354). While Andrew Hadfield reads this passage as directing authors to compose Neoplatonic (and thus abstract and uncontroversial) literature, it is noteworthy that Baldwin himself says nothing of such expected Neoplatonic elements as divine *furor*, the Platonic ladder, or the poetic creation of a "second nature."[25] The poet's soul, in Baldwin's telling, does not ascend to *dwell* with God; rather it "rest[s]" there, and then returns to earth informed and given grace by its heavenly knowledge. Thus, in the next stanza, Baldwin reiterates the chief concern for those who would hold the "Poetes office," the well-being of

24. See Ovid, *Metamorphoses*, 106. Baldwin chooses to compare the attributes of the poet's office to those of Pegasus because Pegasus was, according to myth, the creator of the Hippocrene stream.

25. Hadfield, *Literature, Politics and National Identity*, 105.

the commonwealth. He directs his poet to "trauayle farre to viewe the trades of men" in order to pen "thynges notable" and, most important, to reprove "vyces sharpely now and then." Rather than ask them to abandon the world, Baldwin uses this passage to urge poets to educate themselves in "eternal thynges" so that they may be the spiritual as well as the political guardians of their rulers (354). The key line in this reading is "Almighty Iove must harber in his brest"; the poet must have knowledge of heavenly things so that he will bring God's grace to his work, part of which is to make "sprynges of grace" flow in others (353).[26]

Far from turning away from earthly matters, one of the chief tasks of poets, according to Baldwin, is to serve as political analysts for those in office. It is properly the poets' duty to seek out and to expose the "darke causes and obscure" of misery in the realm, especially if they are to be traced to the policies of those in power (353). Baldwin here seems to model his poet on the Edwardian political pamphleteers who, until they were silenced in Mary's reign, understood it as their task to communicate to their rulers in public, printed form what they believed to be the political and economic causes of problems in the commonwealth. These writers, we may recall, were emboldened to publish their views after Protector Somerset's government created conditions that allowed open expression by loosening earlier censorship laws. Only a similar climate of tolerance, Baldwin implies, will allow free-speaking poets in Elizabeth's reign to fulfill a similar function.[27]

In Baldwin's formulation, the proper political poet will be not only wise enough to find the roots of social problems but also courageous enough to publish his findings openly, even if they indict the highest of the realm. "No byt nor reyne his tender Iawes may twight," Baldwin declares; "No power or fansie" (government threats or fearful acts of self-censorship) can or will prevent him from composing and printing his admonitory verse (353). In fact, Baldwin makes principled disobedience a *duty* for poets writing under a "tyrannical" regime. The "perfect Poete" will consider it no crime to flee unjust persecution if his poems cause offense; he will "be swyft when touched tyrants chafe, / To gallop thence to kepe his carkas safe" (354).[28] Baldwin's

26. Thus, in the prose link succeeding "Collingbourne," the auditor who speaks of the commodities Richard and his officers would have received from political literature names two: the practical benefit of learning the people's "grudge" and also the spiritual benefit of recognizing the dangerous consequences of their sins, "whyche call continually for Gods vengeance, which never fayleth to fall on theyr neckes sodaynely and horriblye, vnles it be stayed with harty repentaunce" (359). It is the duty of the poet to protect the "safetye" of his rulers' souls as well as their authority.

27. See Ferguson, *Articulate Citizen*, 157–58, 200–207.

28. Baldwin's words evoke memories of the numerous evangelical authors who fled overseas rather than conform to the policies of Mary's government that they opposed.

justification of principled disobedience is based on the same rationale that justified the limited Tudor rebellions: if poets withdraw obedience from the rulers, it is only because they have been forced to do so by their rulers' own misdeeds (which include the unjust persecution of well-meaning authors). Of course the poem implies that if Elizabethan officers "ratifie" the rights of poets to speak freely on political affairs, such disloyalty will never have to occur (359).

The Poetics of Public Protest

Baldwin not only lays out prescriptions for the ethical character of his proposed "official" poet but also prescribes for him quite strict guidelines for the proper construction of his poems. Baldwin's statements on literary production in "Collingbourne" stand as a poetics for any future protest literature, describing for those who would admonish rulers the safest and most effective methods for offering correction.

Above all, Baldwin insists, the poet who would address government officers must convey critical messages only in indirect form. He must handle their affairs covertly: his works must be pointed in their topical messages but must name "no man outryght" (351). Although Baldwin does not make his reasoning explicit, readers can deduce the benefits of indirect presentation. First, a work that presents controversial matter only indirectly may come to be read even by those who might otherwise immediately reject a work of reproof directed expressly to them. We may recall Roger Ascham's description of how those in power frequently refuse straightforward works of beneficial counsel simply because they assume they will be offensive and insulting. Too often officials "are so ware [in receiving such works], that commonly they wil complaine of theyr hurt before they feele harme." Topical commentary presented covertly can deflect this initial hostility, drawing officers into reading works of counsel before they can realize their true purpose.[29]

Second, an elliptical presentation protects the poet by allowing him to efface his guiding role in "controlling" his readers. Rebuking the actions of leaders allusively rather than directly allows officers themselves to apply the moral of a poem to their behavior, and thus to judge their actions on what appears to be their own initiative. A poet who writes pointed, topical reproof while seeming only to indict general vices or the vices of men in the past can (it may be hoped) escape a charge of direct affront to those whom he targets. By this means, the cause of any sense of offense an officer perceives is shifted

29. Ascham, *Report*, 160. For Baldwin's construction of the prefatory materials of the *Memorial* to entice readers who might otherwise be resistant to his message, see chapter 1.

from the content of the work to the reader himself: it is understood as the effect not of pointed words but of a guilty conscience. This, of course, is the very guiding principle of the form of the *Memorial*, whose strongly topical tragedies are usually presented overtly as mere historical rehearsals of past political crimes, general rather than topically specific works that may be applied by any reader who sees a coincidental image of his or her own actions in them.

Just as he must shape the *content* of his works to deflect any perception of insult, so too must the poet construct their literary form in a manner calculated to produce amendment, not anger. "A poet," Baldwin advises, "must be plesaunt, not to[o] playne"; in composing even works of covert correction, he must "myxe [his] gall with spyce" (351-52). Baldwin exemplifies the need for a "plesaunt" presentation through the negative example of Collingbourne's career. Collingbourne's couplet, which referred to Richard III as "a Hog," was too "sharp," too blatantly confrontational (349). Baldwin describes it as a "foolishe rime" precisely because its strongly satiric tone produced only offense. Would-be poetic "officers" are to learn from Collingbourne's mistakes that "whan they touch thinges which they wish amended[,] / To sause them so, that fewe nede be offended" (352). If a poem's artistic delight outweighs the offense of its matter, its form can save its author from punishment, moving an official to "wink" even at the most transgressive elements in the work.

Most important, Baldwin argues that affective literary form can not only protect the poet but also persuade potentially resistant readers in a manner no other kind of discourse can. "Collingbourne" presents two distinct theories of the use of literary affect in moral persuasion, one applicable to general audiences and one specifically for persons strongly confirmed in their errors. The first is a variation on the Horatian poetic of mixed instruction and delight. Baldwin claims that poets who "myxe theyr sharpe rebukes with myrth" will not merely avoid producing a sense of immediate insult in their readers but actually spur those readers more quickly to amendment. Baldwin's debt to Horace is reflected in his reference to Horace's satires as models of well-made poems, works able to move non-tyrannical magistrates through indirect counsel and literary delight:

> Belyke no Tyrantes were in Horace dayes,
> And therefore Poetes freely blamed vyce.
> Witnes theyr Satyr sharpe, and tragicke playes,
> With chyefest Prynces chyefly had in pryce.
> They name no man, they myxe theyr gall with spyce. (351)

Works constructed in this way can "pearce, not causyng any payne, / Saue such as followeth euery kyndly byrth, / Requyted strayte, with gladnes of the gayne" (352). The poet still touches readers to the core with his necessary "sharpe rebukes," but in such a way that the only pain they will feel is perhaps a sense of guilt about their misdeeds, followed immediately by a sense of "gladnes" in being led away from their sins (352).

The second theory is for works composed to move hardened sinners. For addressing these readers, Baldwin recommends nothing less than the use of literature as a weapon of psychological violence. Continuing here in his conceit of the poet as Pegasus, Baldwin asserts that a poet's

> hooves must also plyant be and strong,
> To ryve the rockes of lust and errors blynde,
> In brayneles heades, that alway wander wrong:
> These must he bryse wyth reasons playne and kinde,
> Tyll sprynges of grace do gushe out of the minde.
> For tyl affections from the fond be dryven,
> In vayne is truth tolde, or good counsayle geuen. (353)

The essentially good and reasonable spirits of those confirmed in error lie powerless under the weight of accumulated sins, which, like barren rocks, stop up their "sprynges of grace." Persons in this condition are like Richard III and his officers: they have lost the ability to reason for themselves and thus will not believe even the wisest of counsel.[30] The poet must mount an assault on such officers in which psychological pressure, expressed as physical violence, compels receptivity. Baldwin's language is explicitly that of violence: the poet must "bryse" (bruise) the affections of those who have embraced wickedness and "ryve" (crack, rend) their prejudices in order to re-create such rulers as persons fit to receive the poet's messages.[31]

The psychological violence Baldwin urges appears to be innovative in English literary theory. Certainly it is a departure from the *Mirror* authors' formal model, Lydgate's *Fall of Princes.* In that work Lydgate asserts that the function of political-moral poetry is to bring its readers to "order and harmony" through beautiful eloquence and rhetorical flourish. Lydgate's figure

30. Baldwin portrays an image of these men in the figure of the tyrant whom Collingbourne mimics. Collingbourne's tyrant admits that he and his fellows have lost all sense of reason: they do not believe that fortune will ever turn against them, that ambition is a sin, that their own "faultes" will cause their downfall, or that God or man can ever harm them (347–48).

31. If the reasons he offers are "playne and kinde," their presentation is not. While the "reasons" must be recognizable and convincing, "a poet must be pleasant, not to[o] playne" in his form. Such is the model of the *Mirror*, which presents the "reasonable" political and providential consequences of sin through the allusive form of imaginative literary setting.

for the political poet is Amphion, who brought concord to the citizens of the new city of Thebes through the eloquence of charming song.[32] Instead the precedent for the *Memorial-Mirror* authors in constructing their tragedies would seem to be Nathan's topical fable of rebuke presented before King David. Through the fabular form of a story about a poor man whose only sheep was taken from him by a rich neighbor, Nathan lured King David into indignation against crimes that covertly mirrored David's own. The horror produced when David recognized his own actions in Nathan's fable wrenched the sinning king free from his ruling passions, turning him to reform and repentance in precisely the manner sought by the *Mirror* authors for the rulers of their own time.[33]

Baldwin's poetics presents allusive, affective literature as the best means of communication for independent poets, one that can allow their messages to be read by those who would be hostile to them, protect authors from the charge of direct insult to officers, and more powerfully than any other discursive form persuade rulers to change their behavior. While his description of the "perfect Poete" and his office teaches would-be political authors how to live and write, it speaks as well to officers, promising them that those who presume to guide them will write only in this way. Officers who agree to tolerate public political verse will not need to fear that poets allowed free expression will abuse their privilege through railing, open rebuke, or unreliable counsel. Rather, Baldwin's poets will promise to show deference to their rulers' place and honor by offering their pointed, free-speaking counsel only in the less confrontational medium of allusive literary form.

Official Tolerance and the Poet's "Auncient Liberties"

If he asks poets to concede the necessity of keeping their verse within the ethical and stylistic bounds that "Collingbourne" sets for them, Baldwin also asks Elizabethan officers themselves to make concessions by imposing constraints on government policies limiting free speech and on their own individual responses to well-intended political poetry.[34] The constraints that Baldwin proposes are audacious: under his plan there must be no state cen-

32. Ebin, *Illuminator, Makar, Vates*, 39–44.

33. Samuel 12.

34. Baldwin never addresses the question of whether tolerance of literary-political expression may allow political poetry written for impure motives to be composed along with the verse written for rulers' benefit. All the base poets whom he discusses are creatures of wicked governors and thus already have the necessary "liberty" to compose and publish their lies. He does not seem to anticipate the problem of the later oppositional authors (such as English Catholics) who would protest Elizabethan policies on grounds Baldwin would never accept.

sorship in Elizabethan England, no punishment of authors who may offend, and in fact no attempt to enforce English law against poets or their work.

Through "Collingbourne," Baldwin asks officers to surrender their power to control the content of a poet's work and to acknowledge instead a set of "auncient liberties" that protects poets from any individual government's restrictions on freedom of written expression (354). Baldwin does not present these privileges as innovations, as new guidelines developed by him to allow poets respite from Tudor censorship laws. Instead he claims that they predate any English laws on control of the press. They are of ancient origin, "graunted [to poets] of elde" and long recognized by numerous governors since the classical period. Even the highest Roman officers, Baldwin claims, allowed poets to address them freely, provided their commentary was presented in indirect form. In Horace's day, "Poetes freely blamed vyce. / Witnes theyr Satyr sharpe, and tragicke playes, / With chyefest Prynces chyefly had in pryce" (347, 351).[35]

Furthermore, Baldwin inserts these ancient liberties into the context of specifically English customs and legal practices. To urge their "reinstatement" in Elizabeth's reign, Baldwin aligns poetic privileges with the more general rights and privileges enjoyed by citizens under the English common law—that revered set of precedents and customary rights that was understood to champion and to protect the "lives, liberties, and estates of Englishmen" against arbitrary, oppressive decisions by the nation's governors.[36] In order to connect the supposedly universal liberties of poets with the liberties of English subjects, Baldwin implies the customary nature and legal force of these poetic rights in England. He represents Collingbourne as having not so much requested liberty of speech from King Richard as having merely expected it as an unquestioned privilege:

> I thought the Poetes auncient liberties
> Had bene allowed plea at any barre.
> I had forgot howe newefound tyrannies
> Wyth ryght and freedome were at open warre,
> That lust was lawe, that myght dyd make and mar,
> That with the lewde save this no order was,
> *Sic volo, sic iubeo, stet pro ratione voluntas.* (354–55)

35. On the topical nature of Horace's satires, see Rudd, *Satires of Horace*, 132–59.

36. Burgess, *Politics of the Ancient Constitution*, x. On the power of the language of "customary" protections and legal practices in the political debates of Elizabethan England, see Kelley, "Elizabethan Political Thought," 67–72; and, for a more general discussion, J. G. A. Pocock, *Ancient Constitution*, 30–55. The language of customary rights and liberties was often on the lips of the protesters whom Mervyn James studies. They used the rhetoric of ancient privilege and common law reasoning against the disruptive innovations of particular regimes.

Even though he knew Richard and his officers to be vicious men, Collingbourne never imagined that they or any others could go so far in their wickedness as to deny him the fundamental customary protections of the "Muses freedoome" (347). The liberties, in his telling, should have the status of common law protections in courts of law: they should be "allowed plea at any barre" and, if any government denies their validity, that denial should be understood as evidence of a larger assault on all freedoms of English citizens. According to Baldwin's logic, an England in which poets cannot speak freely must be one in which "lust [is] lawe"; thus, the poem implies, only by recognizing the ancient liberties as legally valid (and thereby giving up their ability to prosecute offending poets) can Elizabethan magistrates show themselves to be the protectors, not the enemies, of the law and all the traditional rights of Englishmen (355).

While Baldwin could expect an appeal to the common law tradition to have persuasive force, he augments its power by adopting a rhetoric for promoting the "auncient liberties" calculated to appeal with particular strength to English officers. In his appeal for the recognition of the poet's privileges, Baldwin echoes the words of the Speaker of the House of Commons in requesting the traditional "liberties and priviledges" of members of Parliament. At the beginning of every new Parliament,

> The speaker requireth certaine requests of the prince in the name of the commmons, first that his majestie would be content that they may use and enjoy all their liberties and priviledges that the common house was wont to enjoy. Secondly that they might franckely and freely saye their mindes in disputing of such matters as may come in question, and that without offence of his Majestie. Thirdly that if any should chaunce of that lower house to offend or not to do or say as should become him . . . [t]hat [the Members of Parliament themselves] might (according to the ancient custome) have the punishment of them. . . . All which he promiseth in the commons names that they will not abuse, but have such regarde as most faithfull, true and loving subjectes ought to have to their prince.[37]

Just as the Speaker requests that members may find the House of Commons a place where they can "franckely and freely saye their mindes," so Baldwin obliquely asks Elizabethan officers to preserve the discursive "site" of literature as a similarly unfettered forum for open expression. Baldwin speaks of "free Hellicon, & franke Pernassus hylles," adopting the phrasing of the Speaker and, significantly, the adjectives George Ferrers applied in

37. Sir Thomas Smith, *De Republica Anglorum*, 80–81. This work was composed between 1562 and 1565, roughly the same period as the Elizabethan poems of the 1563 *Mirror*.

"Robert Tresilian" to the reforming Parliament called by the Lords Appellant (347, 78).[38] Furthermore, just as "ancient custome" exempts Parliamentarians from retribution from the crown by reserving the punishment of offending members to Parliament itself, so too, Baldwin suggests, must the "auncient liberties" be understood as protecting the poet from similar royal persecution when fulfilling his duties.[39] By adopting the traditional language of the great body of representatives of the monarch's subjects, Baldwin seeks to confer a sense of an authorized advisory status on political authors similar to that long granted to Parliament.

Throughout "Collingbourne," Baldwin argues strongly against any attempt to punish poets for political verse; he is most forceful, however, in denouncing one particular form of attack on literary writers: prosecution for treason. An accusation of treason was the most dangerous charge a poet could face in mid-Tudor England, and among its possible penalties were mutilation and death.[40] Baldwin insists that magistrates must come to understand treason law as inapplicable to interventionary poets. The statute in force at the time Baldwin composed "Collingbourne" declared it to be an act of treason if "any person . . . by any writing, printing, overt deed or act" denied the queen's right to the throne, or by "express words" sought the overthrow or death of the queen.[41] A charge based on these terms, Baldwin suggests, is totally inappropriate to the sort of verse he and like-minded authors construct. By definition, the poet whom Baldwin describes never counsels harm to rulers. "Traytours but seeke to bryng mans lyfe to ende," Collingbourne explains, when all Baldwin's poet seeks to do is "wyshe [his rulers] safetye" (356).[42]

38. In opening the 1563 Parliament, the Speaker of the House requested "that the Assembly of the Lower House may have frank and free Liberties to speak their minds, without any Controulment, Blame, Grudge, Menaces or Displeasure, according to the old antient Order" (Neale, "Commons' Privilege," 286). In a sermon of 1549 Hugh Latimer similarly spoke of the "lyberty" of men to speak "franke, and fre," in the Commons without danger of retribution. Latimer told his audience that he knew "of olde the manner" of free speech enjoyed by that body (Latimer, *Seven Sermons*, 144).

39. While the suggested parallel reflects Baldwin's belief that officers must "wink" at poets who overstep their bounds, he does not propose any mechanism for poets to be punished by their fellow poetic "officers." Baldwin seems to conceive of only well-meaning poets who, if they transgress, do so solely out of faulty ability, not out of impure intent. They will not need to be punished, for they will learn from their mistakes and amend themselves.

40. Loades, *Politics, Censorship and the English Reformation*, 103.

41. *1 Eliz. cap. 5*, in Prothero, *Select Statutes*, 23–24.

42. Thus Baldwin urges poets "to teach also subiectes to take heade / They meddle not with Magistrates affayres, But praye to God to mende them if it nede" (352). The next line separates poets from the general category of "subjects," making poets, not the people, the ones to oppose official misbehavior and to present popular grievances.

Furthermore, allusive political poetry is not an *act* of any sort and thus cannot be an act of treason. Imaginative verse works by "metafors": it has no "overt" political message but signifies differently to different readers. On the basis of its ambiguous and multiply interpretable nature, Collingbourne defies Baldwin (and thus, implicitly, magisterial readers) to find any indisputable way to construe a poem such as his as treason: "I praye you nowe what treason fynde you here? . . . / There is no worde agaynst the prynce or state, / Nor harme to them whom al the realme dyd hate" (357). In his rhyme, Collingbourne played on three officers' names and on Richard's badge of the boar. His only declarative statement, he insists, was that Richard and his men "rule[d] al England" (349). Surely this cannot be construed as an act of "harme": "What, is it treason in a riming frame / To clyp, to stretche, to adde, or chaunge a name? / And this reserved, there is no rime or reason, / That any craft can clowt to seeme a treason" (357). Collingbourne's poem proved insulting in its implications, but how can one fix tone or perceived allusiveness when a work is imaginative and elliptical in form? In Baldwin's formulation, there is simply no treasonable offense in imaginative verse that one may prosecute.

Baldwin therefore asks officers to treat any future instance of inadvertently offensive verse as "trespas smal," not as sedition: its transgression is a mistake in decorum, not a treasonous act (352). But what if a poem offers insult that simply cannot be overlooked? If a zealous but clumsy poet oversteps his limits in his reproof, Baldwin urges officers to take into consideration that "Wordes sometyme beare more than the hart behiteth": that even well-meaning political commentary may cause unintended offense (355). If those in power feel it incumbent upon them to bring an author to account for his words, Baldwin asks them to allow the poet an escape route, one designed to provide the poet the chance to deny any allusions perceived in his work, no matter how obvious those allusions are or how unlikely his denial. One of the "auncient liberties," Collingbourne claims, is the right to contest any officers' reading of a poem as offensive:

> But wyth the learnde whom lawe and wisdome lead
> Although through rashenes Poetes hap to rayle,
> A plea of dotage may all quarels quayle:
> Their libertyes theyr wrytinges to expounde,
> Doth quyt them clere from faultes by Momus founde. (355)

"Dotage" is a plea of temporary lack of judgment: it explains the poet's transgressions as lapses in discretion, not as evidence of evil intent. Baldwin asks officers to recognize poets as the final, unquestionable arbiters of their own meaning, even if the explanations of their poems seem produced solely to escape punishment:

> The authours meanyng should of ryght be heard,
> He knoweth best to what ende he endyteth:
> Wordes sometyme beare more than the hart behiteth [intends].
> Admyt therefore the authours exposicion,
> Yf playne, for truth: if forst, for his submission. (355)

Andrew Hadfield, construing "of ryght" to mean something like "correctly, by its unalterable meaning," takes these lines to suggest that Collingbourne appeals to "authorial omniscience" to avoid "confusion" in interpretation.[43] Instead, "of ryght" here means "according to the poet's right to do so": that is, Collingbourne insists that it is a right of the poet to have final determination of the meaning of his verse. In fact the possibility of confusion in interpretation is key to Baldwin's poetics. Far from arguing here that originary authorial intention is primary in fixing the meaning of a work, this passage urges officers to accept any interpretation an author might make of his own creation, whether or not that interpretation has anything to do with the author's original intention.

Baldwin's insistence on the author's authority in interpretation is thus fundamentally situational in its logic: he does not claim that the poet can be relied on accurately to articulate his poem's intentional meaning, but asserts instead that the poet's explanation must be accepted even if it seems obvious to officers that this interpretation does not reflect the probable intended meaning of the words. Thus, Baldwin argues, if a poet under duress renders an "exposicion" of his poem as inoffensive, magistrates should treat that explanation as the inarguable, final one, no matter how different it is from their own interpretation. If the explanation is believable and "playne," Baldwin directs the magistrate to accept it and admit that his offended response was mistaken or excessive. If the poet's interpretation is unlikely, convoluted, or "forst," the officer should nevertheless accept that explanation as well, for it is the poet's way of indirectly "submitting," of showing respect to political authorities by "unsaying" that which had caused offense.[44] For a poet to deny

43. Hadfield, *Literature, Politics and National Identity*, 105.

44. Furthermore, the phrase "to what end" suggests not that the poet knows best the absolute meaning of his individual words but rather that he knows best their intended goal. Collingbourne's explanation that he wrote only to wish Richard and his men "safetye" should be accepted, the poem argues, no matter what Catesby initially assumed about the intent of Collingbourne's couplet.

the significance of his own handiwork—particularly when the interpretation he denies was actually the one he intended—should be punishment enough; after all,

> Of slaunderers iust lawes requyre no more
> Save to amend that seemed euel sayd:
> Or to vnsaye the slaunders sayd afore,
> And aske forgeuenes for the hasty brayd:
> To Heretykes no greater payne is layed
> Than to recant theyr errours or retract:
> And wurse than these can be no wryters acte. (355–56)

Slanderers are allowed to take back words that seemed evil, and even heretics may simply recant. Therefore, well-meaning poets should be allowed all the more to "vnsaye" perceived offensive meanings and to remain unharmed for their verse. They are counselors, not rebels; to impose any restrictions or punishments on them for their speech jeopardizes their ability to fulfill their duties. Just as under Baldwin's plan erring officers will not be purged from their places but allowed to amend, so clumsy poets must not be turned out of their own "office" but allowed the same chance at reform.[45]

Baldwin ends "Collingbourne" with two final elliptical appeals to the poets and officers of the new Elizabethan regime. Once again seeming directly to address Baldwin, Collingbourne exhorts him "boldly to the good / Rebuke thou vice, so shalt thou purchase thankes," while "as for the bad thou shalt but move his mood, / Though plesantly thou touch his sinfull prankes." His warning works once again to position English officers, this time in their final responses to the work. Magistrates can be "good," it suggests, only if they agree to Baldwin's proposed guidelines for reader response. If they continue to censor or punish writers of political protest as offensive, however, they will merely show themselves to be among "the bad." Baldwin then directs the last three lines of the poem to the other participants in his implied contract. "Warne poetes," Collingbourne implores, "therfore not to passe the bankes / Of Hellicon, but kepe them in the streames, / So shall their freedome save them from extreames" (358). If poets stay within the boundaries of allusive and imaginative verse, they will remain safe, and their work will be tolerated by those new, enlightened officials of Elizabeth's reign, who will "ratifie" their

45. Baldwin seeks something of the same effect in the prose link after Sackville's poems. His Protestant explanation of Sackville's hell seems "forst" and formulated specifically as an ad hoc response to a possible charge of unorthodoxy. Baldwin's explanation—put forth as Sackville's own explanation of his meaning—"unsays" in advance any perceived unorthodox significance in Sackville's classical hell, allowing his poem to remain free from both self-censorship (the reediting the first speaker urges) and outside persecution on the basis of perceived Catholic allusions.

proposed "liberties" and accept the interpretive guidelines Baldwin offers them (359). After the pessimism of the first lines of "Anthony Lord Rivers," a pessimism born from that poem's retrospective analysis of the conditions of Mary I's censoring reign, "Collingbourne" offers tentative hope that a new, enlightened commonwealth may come to pass, in which peace and order reign precisely because governors allow "official" poets to play a dominant role in "princes cheefe affayres."

Conclusion: The *Mirror* and Its Legacy

Despite the fervor with which he composed his poetic contributions to the *Seconde Part of the Mirrour for Magistrates*, William Baldwin nevertheless betrays elsewhere in the 1563 *Mirror* a growing weariness with his now decade-old and still unfinished project. In the dedicatory epistle to this edition, Baldwin confesses his initial reluctance to compile the new volume of *Mirror* tragedies he now presents to readers. Since publishing the 1559 *Mirror*, Baldwin declares, "I have bene called to an other trade of lyfe," that of a minister. It was only because Henry Lord Stafford "hath not ceassed to call vpon me" to publish the remaining *Mirror* poems, he insists, that he ever returned to his *Mirror* project at all (66). As evidence for his reluctance to continue any further with this endeavor, Baldwin notes that he himself has contributed relatively little to the 1563 gathering of tragedies, and he suggests that while he may someday serve as editor for a future and final volume of *Mirror* poems, he himself will not compose any new tragedies for it (66).

Baldwin's weary tone in the 1563 dedication complements the larger air of disappointment that suffuses many of the prose passages of the *Seconde Parte*. In the Marian section of this volume Baldwin complains that many of the poems he has received from would-be contributors are simply unfit to be considered for his *de casibus* tragedy collection. Baldwin testily dismisses these works as "rabets," a term denoting tragedies so hurriedly and poorly composed that they are simply "not wurth the readinge" (421). Baldwin reveals a similar sense of unhappiness in the Elizabethan section of the *Seconde Parte*. There he portrays George Ferrers as echoing Baldwin's own denunciation of the numerous "swift feble Rabettes" that Baldwin has received from commissioned *Mirror* contributors. Baldwin then has Ferrers complain about those men he labels "Olyphantes," dilatory authors who had promised Baldwin tragedies but who never made good on their pledges (244). Remarkably, Baldwin does not even spare several of the poems he *includes* in his *Seconde Parte* from condemnation. Rather than pass over the worst of the *Seconde Parte* tragedies without comment, Baldwin records his auditors' often pointed criticism of these works, criticism that is hardly mitigated by the halfhearted and often seemingly ironic words of defense he offers for each faulty piece.[1]

If Baldwin himself grew increasingly disenchanted with his ongoing *Mirror* project, he was perhaps the only person in early modern England to do so. Baldwin passed away in September 1563, and it is thus likely that he ended his life with no inkling of the astonishing popularity, influence, and admiration his collection was to enjoy over the next six decades. Far from presenting itself to later Tudor and Stuart readers as outdated, wearisome, or flawed, each new edition of the *Mirror* earned only praise from its admirers and inspired numerous authors unconnected with the original *Mirror* project to adopt its literary form for their own political, moral, and artistic purposes.[2]

The first known imitator of the *Mirror*, Thomas Jenye, took Baldwin's collection as a model for composing his own trenchant political commentary. Two years after publication of *The Seconde Parte of the Mirrour for Magistrates*, Jenye, a servant of Queen Elizabeth's representative to the Scottish court, Thomas Randolph, created "Maister Randolphe['s] Phantasey," a two-part poem cast as the beginning of a new, specifically Scottish *Mirror for Magistrates* (1565). In a Sackville-like induction to his work, Jenye surveyed current Scottish affairs and castigated contemporary Scottish political leaders. He then presented Scotland's Queen Mary as appearing in a vision to confess her numerous political and moral crimes.[3] Jenye's manuscript, which circulated anonymously in Scotland in 1566, caused an immediate sensation. Mary angrily suppressed the work and ordered Randolph, whom she believed to be the true author of the poem, expelled from her country. So great was the Scottish queen's fury that Queen Elizabeth herself was forced to intervene in the matter, sending a letter to her cousin promising punishment for the author of "Maister Randolphe['s] Phantasey" once his identity might

1. See *Mirror*, 244, 297, 391, 421.

2. See, however, Joseph Hall's satire *Virgidermiarum Sixe Bookes* (1597), which denounces the *de casibus* tragedy genre as a whole (Trench, *"A Mirror for Magistrates,"* 79–80).

3. Jenye, "Maister Randolphe['s] Phantasey: a breffe calgulacion of the procedinges in Scotlande from the first of Julie to the Last of Decembre [1565]." Jenye's chief influence in this poem is the work of Thomas Sackville, though he incorporates into his poem phrases and imagery from numerous other *Mirror* tragedies as well.

be discovered.[4] Jenye was but the first (and most controversial) of many subsequent poets who adopted the *de casibus* tragedy form of the collection as a vehicle for commenting on current political events or for judging the deeds of contemporary political figures. Over the next six decades those presented as speakers of their own *Mirror*-like tragedies included Sir Nicholas Bacon, Sir Nicholas Throckmorton, Henry Lord Darnley, Queen Mary Stuart, Anthony Babington, the Earl of Essex, and James, Earl of Morton.[5]

Other poets, particularly in the 1570s, seized upon the admonitory power of Baldwin's collection for general rather than strictly political calls to morality. Collections such as Richard Robinson's *Rewarde of Wickednesse* (1574), Anthony Munday's *Mirrour of Mutabilitie, or Principall Part of the Mirrour for Magistrates* (1574), George Whetstone's *Rocke of Regard* (1576), and Thomas Blener Hasset's *Seconde Part of the Mirrour for Magistrates* (1578) sought to spur Englishmen and women to forswear vice by employing the powerfully persuasive form of exemplary tragic narrative. Drawing on stories from the Bible, classical and continental tales, the ancient British past, and recent works of anti-Catholic propaganda, the authors presented their readers with numerous narratives detailing the dangers of sin and the multitude of punishments awaiting the wicked. Most directed their works to a large general readership rather than to men solely of the magisterial classes. Numerous other authors at this time, equally zealous in their desire to reform the morals of English society, composed works that abandoned the *de casibus* tragedy style of Baldwin's collection while preserving its didactic, admonitory focus. Such men often prominently employed the word "mirror" in their own works' titles in order to link their exhortations to virtue to the widely revered poems of *A Mirror for Magistrates*.[6]

It was, however, the sheer emotional power of Baldwin's chosen form of confessional tragic complaint that attracted most of those who sought to emulate the style of the *Mirror*. From Thomas Churchyard's "Sir Simon Burlies Tragedy" in the 1570s to the explosion of the numerous lengthy, impassioned, and highly polished historical complaints of the 1590s and early 1600s, poets found the tragic narrative form of the *Mirror* a powerful vehicle for their set pieces displaying complex, moving, and intensely personal expressions of anguish and regret. Michael Drayton, Thomas Middleton, and a number of lesser-known men turned their hand at this time to composing narratives in the style of the *Mirror*, while many more, though innovating upon the spe-

4. *Calendar of State Papers relating to Scotland*, 2:281, 284, 287.
5. For a study of many of these works, see Craun, "The *De Casibus* Complaint."
6. For these works, see Zocca, *Elizabethan Narrative Poetry*, 36–93.

cifically *de casibus* style of Baldwin's work, drew on its general tragic model for their own poetic laments.[7] Of course, as scholars have long recognized, the *Mirror* also exerted an important influence on the development of English dramatic tragedy and on English history plays in the late Elizabethan period. In particular, its poems' dynamic presentation of English history through the voices of actual historical characters helped to guide playwrights away from the morality play trappings and stilted classical forms of earlier historical dramas to the rich interplay of characters in realistic settings that marked later Elizabethan historical productions. Furthermore, its use of English history to touch upon controversial political subjects provided playwrights with a compelling model on which they might shape their own plays to confront in indirect literary form the ongoing political problems of their own time.[8]

While the numerous literary imitations and evocations of the *Mirror* attest to its influence on Elizabethan poets and playwrights, the continuing impact of the work on those who Baldwin hoped would remain its primary audience, the officers of England, has been less well documented. Evidence suggests, however, that Baldwin's collection remained admired and widely read among several generations of Elizabethan and Jacobean officers. The reverence for his work among men destined to take a role in the political life of England was first noted in 1560, when Jasper Heywood observed that the *Mirror* had achieved "eternall fame" at the Inns of Court, the home of many of those who then filled and would continue to fill the offices of Elizabeth's government. Two decades later John Stubbs simply referred to the *Mirror* in his notorious *Gaping Gulf* as "our English book of fallen magistrates," a phrase he used with the expectation that readers of his polemic would be so well acquainted with Baldwin's text that they would recognize it by this shorthand reference alone.[9] Even as late as 1611 George Chapman presented the *Mirror* to theatergoers as the habitual reading matter of England's most serious and sober officers.[10]

7. For these works, see, among others, Craun, "The *De Casibus* Complaint"; Zocca, *Elizabethan Narrative Poetry*, 30–93; Trench, *"A Mirror for Magistrates,"* 98–135; Dubrow, "A Mirror for Complaints"; and Schmitz, *Fall of Women*. Several of these imitations were added to new editions of the *Mirror* itself; for these poems, see Lucas, "Hall's Chronicle and *A Mirror for Magistrates*."

8. For the influence of the *Mirror* on early Elizabethan drama, see Winston, "National History to Foreign Calamity." The general influence of the *Mirror* on later Elizabethan dramatic works remains understudied. For a recent discussion of the subject, see Budra, *"A Mirror for Magistrates" and the* de casibus *Tradition*, 73–93.

9. *The Seconde Tragedie of Seneca entituled Thyestes*, sig. *7v; Berry, *John Stubbs's Gaping Gulf*, 54.

10. In his comedy *May-Day*, Chapman has one of his play's young madcaps cite the fact that the elderly officer Lorenzo has read "the *Mirror of Magistrates*" as evidence of the former life of high seriousness from which this now comically love-besotted magistrate has fallen. See Chapman, *May-Day*, 39.

What the *Mirror* offered Elizabethan and Jacobean governors was an image of the English magistrate as a man of enormous power, fierce independence, and awesome responsibility. The dedicatory epistle of the *Mirror* cast such officials as nothing less than God's deputies on earth, men worthy (when they acted dutifully) of bearing the name "gods" themselves (67). The *Mirror* taught English officials that they were first and foremost protectors of the people, officers enjoined by divine commandment to "helpe other" and to protect against all forms of injustice, even those undertaken by the monarch himself or herself. Through its strong emphasis on magisterial independence from strict royal control and on the duty of the officer to challenge his monarch's errors, the *Mirror* served as a compelling intellectual basis for what Patrick Collinson has called the "monarchical republic" model of governance, that de facto system of "two governments," magisterial and monarchical, that ruled England together in the first half of Elizabeth's reign.[11] Even later in the Elizabethan period, during what John Guy terms the "drift to authoritarianism" that marked the 1580s and 1590s, the *Mirror* continued to hold out to English officers an image of strength, independence, and the duty of resistance to monarchical injustice that may well have helped later to inspire the growing assertion of parliamentary rights and personal liberties that marked the reigns of Elizabeth's successors.[12] Much work remains to be done on the legacy, poetical and political, of *A Mirror for Magistrates*. Nevertheless it is clear that this work, through its long life, pervasive influence, and wide readership, played an important role in shaping the intellectual culture of Elizabethan and Jacobean England. Long after its original topical moment had passed, long after its mid-Tudor language had begun to appear old-fashioned, even long after new works of *de casibus* tragedy came into print to rival it, Baldwin's evocation of Edwardian social values, Marian resistance theory, and the early Elizabethan hope for freedom of speech for poets spoke eloquently and influentially to each new generation of early modern readers.

11. Collinson, "Monarchical Republic"; see also Lucas, "Let none such office take."
12. Guy, "Tudor Monarchy and Its Critiques," 99.

Appendix: The Growth and Development of William Baldwin's *A Mirror for Magistrates*

The history of William Baldwin's *A Mirror for Magistrates* is one of the most confused, controversial, and error-filled subjects in all of Tudor literary studies. Inaccuracies first advanced decades ago still find their way into contemporary *Mirror* criticism, and there has yet to be written a fully accurate account of the genesis of Baldwin's long-lived and influential work. To begin to rectify this situation, I offer here both a history and a prehistory of Baldwin's *Mirror* project, one that provides known facts as well as some necessarily speculative suggestions about its growth and development.

The two-part text published in 1563 as *A Myrrovr for Magistrates* and *The Seconde Parte of the Mirrour for Magistrates* draws on no fewer than five previous literary ventures for its contents. These are (1) *A Memorial of suche Princes*, (2) The "second parte" of *A Memorial of suche Princes*, (3) The "thyrde volume" of *A Memorial of suche Princes*, (4) Thomas Sackville's "A Memorial of suche Princes," and (5) *A Myrrovre for Magistrates* (1559). In this appendix I examine evidence for the date and the contents of each of these, ending with a consideration of the last text Baldwin had a hand in editing, *The Seconde Parte of the Mirrour for Magistrates* (1563).

A Memorial of suche Princes

Date: As we have seen in chapter 1, the Marian printer John Wayland conceived of *A Memorial of suche Princes* as a specifically British continuation of John Lydgate's *Fall of Princes*. Wayland assigned the work to William Baldwin sometime in early 1554, after assuming control of Edward Whitchurch's former print shop. Although it is unknown when the first *Memorial* poems were composed or when the last were completed, the evocation in the poem "William Duke of Suffolk" of Prince Philip's kingly titles, bestowed on him shortly before his July 1554 marriage to Queen Mary, suggests that *Memorial* poems were still being written or at least revised in that month (165).

Evidence suggests that the printing of the joint *Fall-Memorial* volume began no later than September 10, 1554. This *terminus ad quem* is indicated by a comment in the printer's note found on the verso of the original title page, in which Wayland informs readers that his edition of Lydgate's work is not as textually accurate as he would like it to be but that readers will "fynde it as clere as any other heretofore set fourth" (5). On September 10, 1554, Richard Tottel released his own edition of Lydgate's *Fall*, an edition based on a copy text far superior to Wayland's. As W. A. Jackson first noted, Wayland's claim that his corrupt edition is as clear as any "heretofore set fourth" would be groundless if Tottel's version were already in print.[1] In Jackson's view, Wayland's words suggest that the printer's note (which was likely printed at the same time as the internal *Memorial* title page, after the printing of the *Fall* was completed and work on the *Memorial* had begun) came into print before Tottel's edition appeared before the public. If Jackson is correct, the printing of the *Fall-Memorial* volume would have commenced sometime in the summer of 1554, and the suppression of the *Memorial* consequently would have occurred in late summer or early fall of that year.[2] Even if Wayland wrote his printer's note after September 10, 1554 (choosing simply to ignore the superior nature of Tottel's text), the *Memorial* certainly had to have come into print before January 1555, for the letters patent that Wayland reproduced on the verso of the *Memorial* title page refer to Queen Mary as the "Supreme Head" of the English church, a designation she officially abandoned on January 3, 1555. Following the abolishment of the "Supreme Head" designation, the loyal Catholic Wayland quickly removed mention of it from all subsequent printings of his letters patent, beginning with the copy included in John Elder's *Copie of a Letter*, a newsletter whose text bears the date January 1, 1555.[3]

1. Jackson, "Wayland's Edition," 157.

2. Printing of the *Fall of Princes* section of the joint *Fall-Memorial* volume may have begun while the *Memorial* was still being composed, since it would have taken at minimum nearly a month (working at full speed and with four presses dedicated to the Lydgate project) and probably much longer for Wayland's workers to print the enormous text of the *Fall of Princes*. For a detailed analysis of the printing of the *Memorial*, including the evidence for the dates of its printing and suppression, see Lucas, "Suppressed Edition."

3. See ibid., 40–41.

Contents: Only two fragments of the *Memorial* have survived into modern times, the original title page of the collection and one leaf of its text. Despite the meager remains of the actual *Memorial*, scholars have uniformly held the 1559 *Mirror for Magistrates* to be a lightly edited new version of this lost text. Their understanding of the correspondence between the *Mirror* and the *Memorial* rests on comments by Baldwin in *A Mirror for Magistrates*, the relationship between the surviving *Memorial* leaf and its counterpart in the *Mirror*, and the language appropriate to *A Memorial of suche Princes* which suffuses *A Mirror for Magistrates*:

In his dedicatory epistle to the 1559 *Mirror*, Baldwin notes that

> the wurke was begun, & part of it printed .iiii. yeare agoe, but hyndred by the lord Chauncellor that then was. . . . Whan I first tooke it in hand, I had helpe of many graunted, & offred of sum, but of few perfourmed, skarce of any: So that wher I entended to have continued it to Quene Maries time, I have ben faine to end it much sooner: yet so, that it may stande for a patarne, till the rest be ready: which with Gods grace (if I may have anye helpe) shall be shortly. (66)

In this passage Baldwin draws a direct tie between the text he is issuing as *A Mirror for Magistrates* and the collection that was "hyndred" in 1554.[4] The close correspondence between the surviving leaf of the *Memorial* and its counterpart in the *Mirror* confirms the connection Baldwin draws between the two texts. The matter contained in the *Memorial* leaf is reprinted with only small changes in the 1559 *Mirror*. Furthermore, the running title on this extant leaf, "A briefe memorial of Unfortunate Englysh princes," corresponds to the inner title of the 1559 *Mirror*, "A Briefe Memorial of sundrye Vnfortunate Englishe men" (68).[5] Finally, key elements of the preface to *A Mirror for Magistrates* (the long prose passage following the Elizabethan dedicatory epistle) are appropriate only to the 1554 *Memorial* and not to the 1559 *Mirror*. Baldwin, for instance, describes at the opening of this preface how "the Printer had purposed with hym selfe to printe Lidgates booke of

4. Although the terms "begun" and "part of it printed" at first glance suggest that the *Memorial* may have contained fewer tragedies than the 1559 *Mirror*, the "wurke" of which Baldwin speaks in this passage is not the 1559 *Mirror* but his as yet incomplete project for a collection of tragedies stretching from Richard II's reign "to Quene Maries time." It was this grand project that was "begun" by *A Memorial of suche Princes*, not the text of the 1559 *Mirror* itself. Baldwin appears to have reckoned dates by the old style that began the new year on March 25. The only one of Baldwin's works to be dated by month and year both is dated in that manner (see the first edition of Baldwin's *Treatise of Morall Phylosophie*, dated January 20, 1547 [i.e., January 20, 1548]). If Baldwin is strictly accurate in dating the suppression of the work as four years previous to the time of his dedication, it suggests that the *Mirror* was ready for printing before March 25, 1559 (1558 in the old style).

5. Compare *Mirror*, plates 6 and 7, and pages 68, 119–25.

the fall of Princes" (68). Baldwin's comment obviously refers to John Wayland, printer of the 1554 joint *Fall-Memorial* volume, and not to Thomas Marshe, printer only of the 1559 *Mirror*. Later George Ferrers declares that he will make the tragedy of Robert Tresilian the first poem of the collection, defending his choice by saying that "althoughe [Tresilian] be no great prince, yet . . . he had a princelye offyce" (71). Since Tresilian had been chief justice of England, Ferrers's apology for beginning the text with a magistrate rather than a "prince" makes little sense in the context of a work titled *A Mirror for Magistrates*. It makes sense only in the context of a work originally titled *A Memorial of suche Princes*. Indeed, the language of "princes" rather than magistrates suffuses all but the dedicatory epistle of *A Mirror for Magistrates*, pointing to the origin of this text's contents in a work titled *A Memorial of suche Princes*.

For reasons such as these, scholars have accepted the 1559 *Mirror* as a lightly edited version (with a new title and dedicatory epistle added) of the suppressed *Memorial*. The one major difference between the *Memorial* and the *Mirror* appears to be the absence of the poem "Humfrey Duke of Gloucester" from the latter text.[6] This tragedy is mentioned in the table of contents of the *Mirror* but is not contained in the *Mirror* itself. Usually printers create tables of contents only after the text of a newly printed work is complete. They derive their tables from the completed text itself, drawing from it the names of its sections and the folio numbers of the leaves on which those sections begin. The fact that the index of the 1559 *Mirror* lists a poem that was never printed in the collection indicates that this table was based not on the finished 1559 *Mirror* itself but on an independent list of tragedies drawn up before printing was completed (a supposition further strengthened by the odd alternate titles this table lists for the poems of the collection) (522–23).[7] Since there is no bibliographical indication that Baldwin ever meant to include "Humfrey Duke of Gloucester" in the 1559 *Mirror*, it seems that the list of poems followed by the compiler of the index

6. Feasey, Campbell, and others who have followed them argue that "Edmund Duke of Somerset" and "Elianor Cobham" were also part of the original *Memorial*. Neither of these works, however, appears to have been part of that collection. See Feasey, "Licensing of *A Mirror for Magistrates*"; Campbell, "Humphrey Duke of Gloucester"; and the discussion of "Somerset" and "Cobham" in this appendix.

7. The confusion of the table's compiler over the absence of the "Gloucester" poem from the completed *Mirror* text is revealed by the fact that there are no folio numbers recorded for the succeeding two tragedies. Evidently, on the basis of the list of tragedies he had at hand, the compiler expected the poem to be included in the *Mirror*. In its absence he left off listing folio numbers in the table for the next two poems in case it might later be inserted into the text.

was derived not from the 1559 *Mirror* but from the table of the work on which the 1559 version was based, *A Memorial of suche Princes.*[8] If this is the case, it reveals that "Humfrey Duke of Gloucester" was part of the original *Memorial* but was excluded from the allowed version of this text, *A Mirror for Magistrates.*

In light of the allusive import of "Humfrey Duke of Gloucester," a reluctance on Baldwin's part to include this tragedy in his text is understandable. As we have seen, "Humfrey Duke of Gloucester" offers sharp, indirect criticism of Queen Mary for her role in Edward Seymour's downfall, criticism that may well have made "Gloucester" the very *Memorial* poem Chancellor Gardiner found most offensive. Even after Mary's death, Baldwin could have feared that its unflattering allusive characterization of a Tudor monarch (the current queen's sister) might lead Elizabethan officers to follow the lead of their Marian predecessors and deny Baldwin permission to publish his work. It may be for this reason as well that "Gloucester" did not appear in any *Mirror* edition until that of 1578.[9]

The "Second Parte" and "Thyrde volume" of *A Memorial of suche Princes*

Date: Despite the trouble that greeted the first version of *A Memorial of suche Princes*, Baldwin still clung to his dream of publishing a collection of specifically British poems in the manner of Lydgate's *Fall of Princes.* Within two years after the suppression of the *Memorial*, Baldwin began to commission

8. Baldwin, in fact, signals the absence of the poem "Humfrey Duke of Gloucester" from the *Mirror* when he portrays Ferrers as remarking that he will "at leasure" declare Duke Humfrey's and his wife's tragedies. Ferrers's promise to "declare" Gloucester's tragedy rather than compose it suggests that he has already written such a poem. His promise to do it "at leasure" further suggests that he will relate this tragedy not in the current text but at a later time (161).

9. "Humfrey Duke of Gloucester" was announced in the table of contents of the 1571 edition but not published until the 1578 *Mirror* (526–28). In the second stanza of "Gloucester," Duke Humfrey urges Baldwin to make his life "a mirrour of Magistrates all" (445). This phrase may have supplied Baldwin with the inspiration for the new title he bestowed on the 1559 version of *A Memorial of suche Princes.* However, it may instead be a phrase Ferrers added to his poem in Elizabeth's reign. According to the table of contents of the 1571 edition, Marshe had secured at least the promise of Ferrers's poem "How Dame Elianor Cobham Duchesse of Glocester for practising of witchcraft and Sorcery, suffred open penance, and after was banished the realme into the yle of Man," a tragedy that was not printed until the canceled edition of the 1578 *Mirror* (*STC* 1252.5). Unlike "Humfrey Duke of Gloucester," "Elianor Cobham" appears to be Elizabethan in origin and to have had no topical purpose. Instead Ferrers seems to have set out in this tragedy to rework the fifteenth-century ballad "The Lament of the Duchess of Gloucester" (see Robbins, *Historical Poems*, 176–80). If he wrote "Elianor Cobham" in the 1560s or early 1570s, Ferrers of course may have edited "Humfrey Duke of Gloucester" at this time as well.

new works for a planned two-volume *de casibus* tragedy project he called informally the "second parte" and "thyrde volume" of the *Memorial.* The "second parte" would cover tragedies of Edward V's and Richard III's reigns, and the "thyrde volume" would handle the falls of figures stretching from Henry VII's time "to the ende of this king & Queenes raigne" (387). Baldwin compiled the best of the poems he received in a single manuscript and linked the tragedies through prose passages similar to those of the *Memorial* (243).[10] He intended this manuscript for private circulation rather than for printing, a fact indicated by his use of its pages to gather into one continuous collection all the poems he planned later to allocate to three separate texts, the "second part," the "thyrde volume," and the previously compiled "fyrst parte" of the *Memorial.*

The death of Thomas, Lord Vaux, in late September or early October 1556 sets a terminal date for the beginning of Baldwin's solicitation of new *Memorial* poems, since Baldwin records that he had issued an invitation to Vaux to compose at least one poem for the "second parte" (297). It is not known when Baldwin compiled his manuscript of poems intended for the second and third parts of the *Memorial.* A clue may lie, however, in the prose passage following Thomas Churchyard's "Howe Shores wife, Edwarde the fowerthes concubine, was by king Richarde despoyled of all her goodes, and forced to do open penance." There Baldwin represents several of his auditors as urging him to "procure Maister Churchyarde to vndertake and to penne as manye moe of the remaynder [of the tragedies] as myght by any meanes be attaynted at his handes" (387). If these words imply a certain knowledge that Churchyard was in England at the time the manuscript was compiled, the comment fixes the latest date for the compilation of the manuscript as June 1557, the month before the veteran solider Churchyard left England to spend the rest of Mary's reign fighting in France.[11]

10. In this new *Memorial* manuscript, Baldwin dropped the conceit that he and his fellow authors composed their poems extemporaneously and recited them to one another. Instead of describing a company of authors, Baldwin now represented himself as reading the works of other men to a gathering of potential contributors to his post-suppression *de casibus* tragedy project (387).

11. Woudhuyson, "Vaux," 222; Lyne, "Churchyard," 688. England's forces departed for France on July 5, 1557 (Loades, *Reign of Mary Tudor,* 312). Churchyard did not return from the French wars until 1559. Although some have attempted to connect his name with the anonymous poems of the suppressed *Memorial of suche Princes,* Churchyard could not have been among the original group of *Memorial* authors. He had spent all of 1553 and 1554 on the continent as a soldier of fortune serving in the imperial army (Lyne, "Churchyard," 688). Although the *Oxford Dictionary of National Biography* dates Churchyard's return to England as 1555, it is more likely that Churchyard remained on the continent until February 1556, when the Treaty of Vaucelles ended imperial-French hostilities in Flanders.

Contents: We know of Baldwin's private Marian manuscript only through the section of it printed in the 1563 *Seconde Parte of the Mirrour for Magistrates*, a fragment comprising Thomas Churchyard's "Shore's Wife" (destined for the "second parte"), Humphrey Cavell's poem "The wilfull fall of Blacke Smyth, and the foolishe ende of the Lord Awdeley" (intended for the "thyrde volume"), and George Ferrers's "Edmund Duke of Somerset" (to be added to the original collection of suppressed *Memorial* tragedies).[12] Baldwin claims in this surviving fragment that he has gathered enough tragedies of the "second parte" to make a "handsum volume" (387). With the exception of "Shore's Wife," however, the contents of the Marian tragedies designed for the "second parte" are unknown, since Baldwin replaced them with Elizabethan works once he returned to this manuscript in 1563.[13]

Besides the new poems and prose passages linking them, Baldwin included at the end of this Marian manuscript a lengthy oration by an unnamed auditor denouncing rebellion and defending Mary's status as queen regnant. This anonymous speaker's lengthy effusion seems on its face to contradict much of the content of the original *Memorial*, including the endorsement of active, principled resistance Baldwin himself offers in "Mowbray." In the manner of his earlier attempts to deflect the suspicions of hostile readers of the *Memorial* (see chapter 1), Baldwin seems to have included this passage in his manuscript chiefly to combat assumptions that his proposed new volumes of historical *de casibus* tragedies would contain covert politically controversial matter. Nevertheless, Baldwin could not resist building in to this politic expression of loyalty several passages that, in the context of the original *Memorial*, can only be read ironically (such as the speaker's suggestion that by virtue of her sex alone Queen Mary cannot help but be a mild and good ruler, one who causes "iustice to be mynistred according to gods lawes," who stands as a "terror to al other princes," and who always hearkens to the counsel of "godly . . . heades") (420). Furthermore, while he does not countenance rebellion in this manuscript, Baldwin nevertheless cannot bring himself to recommend to readers absolute devotion to erring princes. Instead, in a carefully worded speech he urges subjects in his own voice to follow "all good lawes" but to disobey any unjust royal command (421).

Despite his manuscript's overt expression of political orthodoxy, Baldwin

12. The Marian fragment of *The Seconde Parte of the Mirrour for Magistrates* begins with Churchyard's "Shore's Wife" (373). Its Marian provenance is indicated by its reference to "this king & Queenes raigne" and one auditor's defense of Philip and Mary against certain of their detractors (387, 420).

13. It is possible, however, that Baldwin wrote "Lord Rivers" in Mary's reign and inserted those stanzas that glance back at his troubles under Mary only at a later time.

was never able to bring his "second parte" of *A Memorial of suche Princes* before the public in Mary's reign. No part of this Marian manuscript would see publication until the 1563 *Seconde Parte of the Mirrour for Magistrates.*

Thomas Sackville's "Memorial of suche Princes"

Date and Contents: Only two poems were ever composed for Thomas Sackville's planned single-author version of *A Memorial of suche Princes,* namely, Sackville's famous "Induction" and his "Complaynt of Henrye duke of Buckingham." Baldwin included both works in the Elizabethan section of *The Seconde Parte of the Mirrour for Magistrates* (1563). In the prose passage preceding these linked poems, one among Baldwin's "frendes and furderers" asks why Sackville has taken the unusual step of writing an induction to Buckingham's tragedy. In reply Baldwin explains that

> after [Sackville] vnderstoode that some of the counsayle would not suffer the booke to be printed in suche order as we had agreed and determined, he purposed with him selfe to haue gotten at my handes, al the tragedies that were before the duke of Buckinghams, Which he would haue preserued in one volume. And from that time backeward euen to the time of William the conquerer, he determined to continue and perfect all the story him selfe, in such order as Lydgate (folowing Bocchas) had already vsed. And therfore to make a meete induction into the matter, he deuised this poesye: which in my iudgement is so wel penned, that I woulde not haue any verse therof left out of our volume. (297–98)

Baldwin reveals in this passage that Sackville's "Induction" was never meant for the "second parte" of the *Memorial* at all. Rather it was a product of Sackville's intention to create his own single-author *Memorial of suche Princes.*[14]

As Baldwin explains, Sackville's decision to compose his own *de casibus* tragedy collection came about only after he learned from Baldwin that "some of the counsayle would not suffer the booke to be printed in suche order as we had agreed and determined" (297). Scholars have usually understood Baldwin's words to refer to the 1554 suppression of the original *Memorial;* they appear more likely, however, to refer to Baldwin's failure to receive permission to print the "second parte" of the *Memorial.* "The booke" whose

14. The existing autograph manuscript of Sackville's "Induction" and "Henrye Duke of Buckingham" shows that Sackville conceived of the two poems as a single unit. The "Induction," in other words, was meant all along to precede "Henry Duke of Buckingham" and to begin Sackville's new collection of *de casibus* tragedies, poems whose speakers would direct their words not to Baldwin but to Sackville himself. For this manuscript, see Hearsey, *Complaint of Henry Duke of Buckingham.* Baldwin's reference to Sackville's use of Lydgate's text rather than Baldwin's own as his model may suggest that Sackville consciously set out to avoid the allusive and politically contentious purposes to which Baldwin had turned his own collection.

contents Baldwin and his Elizabethan audience discuss in this passage is not the suppressed *Memorial* but the revised manuscript that would form the basis of the *Seconde Parte of the Mirrour for Magistrates*. This is the "booke," the context suggests, that encountered trouble with Marian authorities similar to that facing the original *Memorial*. Baldwin's specific description of the suppression of the *Memorial* in the dedicatory epistles of both the 1559 and 1563 *Mirror for Magistrates* adds weight to this assumption. In those epistles Baldwin clearly notes that it was a single figure alone, the Lord Chancellor, who prohibited *A Memorial of suche Princes* under Mary. In this prose link, by contrast, he describes not Chancellor Gardiner but several unnamed Councilors as those who would not "suffer the booke to be printed in suche order as we had agreed."

Although the reason why Mary's Councilors would not allow Baldwin's scheme for a new printed *de casibus* tragedy collection is unknown, Baldwin's identification of the "order" of the collection as the element that caused trouble for it may suggest that the Councilors objected not to the content of Baldwin's collection but to its proposed chronology. If Baldwin or his intended printer had explained to these men the full scope of Baldwin's post-suppression *Memorial* project, it would not be surprising that a number of them would find such a scheme potentially too controversial for publication. After all, Baldwin sought to offer poems in his planned two-volume continuation of the *Memorial* that would relate the falls not only of prominent political figures of the past but also those of even "this king & Queenes raigne" (387). Given the uncomfortable intrusion into contemporary politics that such a scheme would have entailed, it could well have been the chronological "order" of Baldwin's project alone that led to the Councilors' refusal to allow it. This supposition receives circumstantial support from Sackville's own scheme for his planned collection of *de casibus* tragedies. Rather than work forward toward the Tudor era in his collection, Sackville planned to work backwards in time from Richard III's reign to that of William the Conqueror (298). Such a chronology seems counterintuitive (why not begin with the Norman invasion and work forward?), unless it were one forced on Sackville by a government that had shown itself hostile to any *de casibus* tragedy collection that sought to move forward in history rather than backwards into England's distant past (297).[15]

15. Baldwin's use of the word "order" to mean "manner or style" later in this passage, however, may suggest that the difficulties his collection faced from Mary's Councilors lay not in its chronology but in its very literary form (a politically admonitory *de casibus* tragedy collection cast in the voices of English historical figures). If this is true, it would suggest that Sackville never intended to publish his private collection of *de casibus* tragedies, since he knew from Baldwin's experience that their form alone would incur displeasure if they were brought into print.

The date of Sackville's assumption of the *Memorial* project is unknown, though circumstantial evidence from Sackville's surviving autograph manuscript of his poems suggests a time late in Mary's reign, in the last half of 1557 or thereafter. Among the unused stanzas Sackville jotted down at the end of his manuscript of the "Induction" and "Henry Duke of Buckingham" are several meant to convey the daunting nature of writing a poetic record of the falls of England's mighty (544–47). In one Sackville exclaims:

> Not surrea [i.e., Surrey] he that hiest sittes in chair
> of glistering fame for ay to live and raighn
> not his proud ryme that thunders in the aier
> nor al the plaints wherin he wrote his pain
> when he lay fetterd in the fyry chain
> of cruell love. they cold no whit suffyse
> texpresse thes plaints in ful. (545)

Given that up until the publication of Tottel's *Songes and Sonnettes* (June 1557) Surrey's love lyrics were known only to a relatively few readers at court, and given that there is no evidence that Sackville himself was at court during Mary's reign, Sackville's reference to the high and everlasting "fame" that Surrey has achieved for his love poetry and for the "thundering" verse of his *Aeneid* translation would seem to be appropriate only to the period after the publication of Surrey's translation of Book 2 of the *Aeneid* and the printing of Tottel's miscellany, both of which occurred in 1557. This would set a date after June 1557 but before November 1558 (the last month in which Mary's Privy Council could have prohibited Baldwin's collection) for the beginning of Sackville's aborted *Memorial* project.

Such a late start to Sackville's project in Mary's reign could help to answer one of the most baffling questions in all of *Mirror* scholarship: why Baldwin announced the inclusion of George Ferrers's poem "Edmund Duke of Somerset" in the text of the 1559 *Mirror* (and even left a gap of ten leaves in the foliation of the text in order to accommodate it) but never actually published the work. The answer would be that Baldwin had given "Somerset" to Sackville as part of the post-suppression manuscript he had lent him (comprising the poems of Edward V's and Richard III's reigns that, with the tragedies of the original *Memorial*, Sackville would have "preserued in one volume"), and Sackville still had not returned it to Baldwin by the time the 1559 *Mirror for Magistrates* appeared (298). When he did receive this manuscript once again (or shortly thereafter), Baldwin received as well Sackville's own two poems, the only works Sackville completed for his intended "Memorial of suche Princes." Recognizing the artistic quality of Sackville's endeavors, Baldwin gladly inserted them into the Elizabethan manuscript he was preparing for

The Seconde Parte of the Mirrour for Magistrates, thus preserving the sole contents of Sackville's short-lived *de casibus* tragedy project.[16]

A Myrrovre for Magistrates (1559)

Date: The printer Thomas Marshe received a license to print *A Mirror for Magistrates* sometime between Elizabeth's accession and July 10, 1559 (8).[17] In the *Mirror*, Baldwin credits Henry, Lord Stafford, for helping to get the work perused and licensed by Elizabethan authorities. At first glance Stafford seems an odd champion for a collection that received so much trouble from Marian authorities, for Stafford had become a confirmed religious conservative under England's Catholic queen. Stafford, however, was a devoted student of history, literature, and, in particular, the deeds of his ancestors, all important elements of the poems of *A Mirror for Magistrates*.[18] Furthermore, despite his later conservatism, Stafford had been in Edward VI's reign an outspoken supporter of religious reform and a fervent admirer of Edward Seymour, Duke of Somerset. Stafford is said to have been frequently at court under Edward, and it may have been at that time that he became acquainted with Baldwin, sharing with the author of the *Treatise of Morall Phylosophie* a love of learning and poetry that allowed them both later to transcend the religious differences that eventually grew between them.[19]

Contents: For the contents of this work, see the foregoing discussion of *A Memorial of suche Princes*.

A Myrrovr for Magistrates (1563) and *The Seconde Parte of the Mirrour for Magistrates* (1563).

Date and Contents: Between July 22, 1562, and July 22, 1563, Thomas Marshe received a license to print a new edition of *A Myrrovre for Magistrates* and

16. The annotations in Sackville's copy of Fabyan's chronicle (preserved in the J. Pierpont Morgan Library) show that Sackville had gone as far as commencing research into early Norman England before abandoning his "Memorial" project. The year in which Sackville gave up on his own *de casibus* project is unknown. We can say with confidence only that by 1563 he had forever abandoned his plans.

17. Marshe's payment for the license appears in the stationer's register for the period July 10, 1558–July 10, 1559. Baldwin, however, notes in the 1563 edition that the work was licensed in the first year of Elizabeth's reign, making the date sometime in November 1558 or after (66).

18. Stafford was a direct descendent of Henry, Earl of Northumberland, whose story is told in the 1559 *Mirror*, as well as a distant relation of several other figures in the collection.

19. For Stafford's admiration of Seymour and his religious reforms, see Stafford's preface to his translation of Edward Fox's caesaropapist tract *The True Dyffere[n]s between ye regall power and the Ecclesiasticall power*. See also Davies, "Stafford."

with it a companion volume titled *The Seconde Parte of the Mirrour for Magistrates*. According to Baldwin, after publication of the 1559 *Mirror*, Lord Stafford asked him to bring all of the remaining unpublished *Mirror* poems into print (66). Baldwin decided to go beyond Stafford's request. Instead of merely publishing the Marian poems he had collected in the "second parte" and "thyrde volume" manuscript, Baldwin and Marshe sought out new, Elizabethan tragedies to replace some or all of the older Marian tragedies Baldwin had collected in the wake of the suppression of the *Memorial*. The two poems Baldwin composed for this section both contain matter that appears to date from Elizabeth's reign (in particular their angry, backward glances at life for poets in Marian England), while the *Seconde Parte* makes it clear that John Dolman's "Lord Hastings" and Frauncis Segars's "Richard Duke of Gloucester" (the other two Elizabethan poems of this section) were obtained by the printer Marshe specifically for the 1563 *Mirror* (244).[20] Baldwin also rewrote prose passages in the Marian manuscript to reflect Elizabethan concerns.[21]

Baldwin appears to have been in the process of editing his Marian manuscript of tragedies when he died in September 1563. This is the only way to explain why *The Seconde Parte of the Mirrour for Magistrates* contains in its first half works that are clearly Elizabethan in origin and in its second pieces that clearly date from Queen Mary's reign (see chapter 6 and the discussion in this appendix of the "second parte" and "thyrde volume" of the *Memorial*). Faced with only a partially revised manuscript for the *Seconde Parte*, Marshe seems to have decided in the wake of Baldwin's death to print without comment what he had before him rather than to scrap the whole project, leaving centuries of readers to puzzle over the oddly hybrid nature of this text.

The revisions to the first section of *The Seconde Parte of the Mirrour for Magistrates* were Baldwin's last contribution to *A Mirror for Magistrates*. Even though his text lived on for decades beyond his death, there is no reliable evidence to suggest that any of its subsequent editions were edited by men connected with the original *Memorial-Mirror* project.

20. Marshe had printed Dolman's first work in 1561; his connection to the well-known author and translator Segars is less clear (see *Mirror*, 44–46).

21. See chapter 6.

Bibliography

Aesquillius, P. [pseud.]. *Ein Sendbrieff P. Aesquillii von dem tode Pauli des dritten Babsts dieses namens*. Translated by Matthias Flacius Illyricus. Magdeburg, [1550?].

Alford, Stephen. *Kingship and Politics in the Reign of Edward VI*. Cambridge: Cambridge University Press, 2002.

Alsop, J. D. "The Act for the Queen's Royal Power, 1554." *Parliamentary History* 13, no. 3 (1994): 261–76.

Ascham, Roger. *Report of the Affaires and State of Germany* [1553]. In *English Works*, edited by William Wright, 121–69. Cambridge: Cambridge University Press, 1904.

Ayre, John, ed. *Prayers and Other Pieces of Thomas Becon*. Cambridge, 1844.

Baldwin, William. *Beware the Cat: The First English Novel*. Edited by William Ringler and Michael Flachmann. San Marino, Calif.: The Huntington Library, 1988.

———. *The Funeralles of King Edward the sixt: Wherin are declared the causers and causes of his death*. London, 1560. *STC* 1243.

———. *A Treatise of Morall Phylosophie*. London, 1547 [January 1548]. *STC* 1253.

Bale, John. *Scriptorum Illustrium maioris Brytanniae . . . Catalogus*. 2 vols. Basel, 1557–1559.

Baskerville, E. J. *A Chronological Bibliography of Propaganda and Polemic Published in English between 1553 and 1558*. Philadelphia: American Philosophical Society, 1979.

Baumer, Franklin. *The Early Tudor Theory of Kingship*. New Haven: Yale University Press, 1940.

Beer, Barrett. *Northumberland: The Political Career of John Dudley, Earl of Warwick and Duke of Northumberland*. Kent, Ohio: Kent State University Press, 1973.

Bergenroth, G. A., Don Pascual de Gayangos, Martin Hume, and Royall Tyler, eds. *Calendar of State Papers, Spanish*. 13 vols. London: HMSO and Longman, 1862–1964.

Berkman, James. "Van der Delft's Message: A Reappraisal of the Attack on Protector Somerset." *Bulletin of the Institute of Historical Research* 53, no. 128 (1980): 247–52.

Bernard, G. W. "The Downfall of Thomas Seymour." In *The Tudor Nobility*, edited by G. W. Bernard, 212–40. Manchester: Manchester University Press, 1992.

Berry, Lloyd, ed. *John Stubbs's Gaping Gulf with Letters and Other Relevant Documents*. Washington, D.C.: Folger Shakespeare Library, 1968.

Betteridge, Tom. *Literature and Politics in the English Reformation*. Manchester: Manchester University Press, 2004.

Billington, Sandra. *Mock Kings in Medieval Society and Renaissance Drama*. Oxford: Clarendon Press, 1991.

Bindoff, S. T., ed. *The History of Parliament: The House of Commons, 1509–1558*. 3 vols. London: Secker and Warburg, 1982.

———. *Ket's Rebellion 1549*. London: Historical Association, 1949.

Binns, J. W. *Intellectual Culture in Elizabethan and Jacobean England: The Latin Writings of the Age*. Leeds: Francis Cairns, 1990.

Birchenough, Edwyn. "The Prymer in English." *The Library*, 4th ser., 18, no. 2 (1937): 177–94.

Blayney, Peter. "The Site of the Sign of the Sun." In *The London Book Trade: Topographies of Print in the Metropolis from the Sixteenth Century*, edited by Robin Myers, Michael Harris, and Giles Mandelbrote, 1–20. New Castle, Del.: Oak Knoll Press, 2003.

Blazer, Phyllis. "The Life of Sir Thomas Chaloner." Ph.D. diss., SUNY Buffalo, 1978.

Bond, Roland, ed. *"Certain Sermons or Homilies" (1547) and "A Homily Against Disobedience and Wilful Rebellion" (1570)*. Toronto: University of Toronto Press, 1987.

Brewer, J. S., et al., eds. *Letters and Papers, Foreign and Domestic, of the Reign of King Henry VIII*. 21 vols. London: HMSO, 1862–1932.

Brigden, Susan, ed. "The Letters of Richard Scudamore to Sir Philip Hoby, September 1549–March 1555." In *Camden Miscellany 30*, 67–148. Camden Society, 4th ser., 39. London: Royal Historical Society, 1990.

———. *London and the Reformation*. Oxford: Clarendon Press, 1989.

———. "Thomas Cromwell and the 'Brethren.'" In *Law and Government under the Tudors*, edited by Claire Cross, David Loades, and J. J. Scarisbrick, 31–50. Cambridge: Cambridge University Press, 1988.

Brodugan, Nicholas. *An Epitome of the Title that the Kynges Maiestie of Englande, hath to the soueraigntie of Scotlande*. In Murray, *The Complaynt of Scotlande*, 247–56.

Brown, Michael. *James I*. Edinburgh: Canongate Academic, 1994.

Budra, Paul. *"A Mirror for Magistrates" and the* de casibus *Tradition*. Toronto: University of Toronto Press, 2000.

Bullinger, Heinrich. *An Holsome Antidotus*. Translated by Jean Veron. London, 1548. *STC* 4059.

Burgess, Glenn. *The Politics of the Ancient Constitution*. University Park: Pennsylvania State University Press, 1992.

Bush, M. L. *The Government Policy of Protector Somerset*. London: Edward Arnold, 1975.

The Byble in Englyshe. Paris and London, 1539. *STC* 2068.

The Byble, that is to say, al the Holy Scripture. Edited by Edmund Becke. London, 1551. *STC* 2088.

Byrom, H. J. "John Wayland—Printer, Scrivener, and Litigant." *The Library*, 4th ser., 11, no. 3 (1931): 312–49.

Calendar of the Patent Rolls, Philip and Mary. 4 vols. London: HMSO, 1936–1939.

Calendar of the Patent Rolls Preserved in the Public Records Office: Edward VI. 6 vols. London: HMSO, 1924–1929.

Calendar of State Papers, Foreign Series, of the Reign of Elizabeth. 23 vols. London: HMSO, 1863–1950.

Calendar of State Papers relating to Scotland and Mary, Queen of Scots, 1547–1603. 13 vols. Edinburgh: HMSO, 1898–1969.

Calvin, John. *Certaine Homilies of M. Ioan Calvine conteining Profitable and Necessarie Admonitio[n] for this Time, with an Apologie of Robert Horn*. [Wesel?], 1553. *STC* 4392.

Campbell, Lily. *Collected Papers of Lily B. Campbell*, edited by Louis Wright. New York: Russell and Russell, 1968.

———. "Humphrey Duke of Gloucester and Elianor Cobham his Wife in the *Mirror for Magistrates*." *Huntington Library Bulletin* 5 (1934): 119–55.

———, ed. *The Mirror for Magistrates: Edited from Original Texts in the Huntington Library.* Cambridge: Cambridge University Press, 1938.

———, ed. *Parts Added to the Mirror for Magistrates by John Higgins and Thomas Blenerhasset*. Cambridge: Cambridge University Press, 1946.

———. *Shakespeare's "Histories": Mirrors of Elizabethan Policy*. San Marino, Calif.: The Huntington Library, 1947.

Cancellar, James. *The Pathe of Obedience, Righte Necessarye for all the King and Quenes Maiesties Louing Subiectes*. London, 1556. *STC* 4564.

Cavendish, George. *Metrical Visions*. Edited by A. S. G. Edwards. Columbia: University of South Carolina Press, 1980.

"Certayne brife notes of the controversy between the dukes of Somerset and the duke of Nor[t]humberland," edited by Simon Adams, Ian Archer, and G. W. Bernard. In *Religion, Politics, and Society in Sixteenth-Century England*, edited by Ian Archer et al., 123–36. London: Royal Historical Society, 2003.

Certayne Questions Demaunded and Asked by the Noble Realme of Englande, and of her True Naturall Chyldren and Subiectes of the Same. [Wesel?], n.d. *STC* 9981.

Chaloner, Sir Thomas. "Deploratio acerbae necis heroidis praestantissimae D. Janae Grayae." In *De Republica Anglorum Instauranda Libri Decem*, edited by William Malim, sigs. T4v–T6r. London, 1579. *STC* 4938.

Chapman, George. *May-Day: A witty comedie diuers times acted at the Blacke Fryers.* London, 1611. *STC* 4980.

Christmas, Henry, ed. *Select Works of John Bale*. Cambridge, 1849.

Collinson, Patrick. "The Monarchical Republic of Queen Elizabeth I." In *Elizabethan Essays*, 31–57. London: Hambledon Press, 1994.

Cooper, J. P. *Propaganda and the Tudor State: Political Culture in the Westcountry.* Oxford: Clarendon Press, 2003.

Cooper, Thomas. *Coopers Chronicle*. London, 1560. *STC* 12148.

Corbett, Margery, and Ronald Lightbown. *The Comely Frontispiece: The Emblematic Title-Page in England, 1550–1660*. London: Routledge and Kegan Paul, 1979.

Courthope, W. J. *A History of English Poetry*. London, 1897.

Craun, Edwin. "The *De Casibus* Complaint in Elizabethan England, 1559–1593." Ph.D. diss., Princeton University, 1971.

Crowley, Robert. *An Epitome of Cronicles*. London, 1559. *STC* 15217.5.

———. "Philargyrie of greate Britayne by Robert Crowley," edited by John N. King. *English Literary Renaissance* 10, no. 1 (1980): 47–75.

Dasent, J. R., et al., eds. *Acts of the Privy Council of England.* New Series. 46 vols. London, 1890–1949.

Davies, Catherine. *A Religion of the Word.* Manchester: Manchester University Press, 2002.

Davies, C. S. L. "Stafford, Henry, Tenth Baron Stafford (1501–1563)." In Matthew and Harrison, *The Oxford Dictionary of National Biography*, 52:50–51.

Dickens, A. G., ed. "Robert Parkyn's Narrative of the Reformation." In *Reformation Studies*, 247–83. London: Hambledon Press, 1982.

Dubrow, Heather. "A Mirror for Complaints: Shakespeare's *Lucrece* and Generic Tradition." In *Renaissance Genres: Essays on Theory, History, and Interpretation*, edited by Barbara Lewalski, 399–417. Cambridge: Harvard University Press, 1986.

Duffy, Eamon. *The Stripping of the Altars: Traditional Religion in England, 1400–1580.* New Haven: Yale University Press, 1992.

Dunham, William. "Regal Power and the Rule of Law: A Tudor Paradox." *Journal of British Studies* 3, no. 2 (1964): 24–56.

Dutton, Richard. *Licensing, Censorship and Authorship in Early Modern England.* Houndmills: Palgrave, 2000.

Ebin, Lois. *Illuminator, Makar, Vates: Visions of Poetry in the Fifteenth Century*. Lincoln: University of Nebraska Press, 1988.

Elder, John. *The Copie of a letter sent in to Scotlande, of the . . . marryage of the moste Illustre Prynce Philippe . . . to the moste excellente Princes Marye Quene of England.* London, 1555. *STC* 7552.

Elton, G. R. *Reform and Reformation: England, 1509–1558*. Cambridge: Harvard University Press, 1977.

———. "The Rule of Law in Sixteenth-Century England." In *Studies in Tudor and Stuart Politics and Government* (3 vols.), 1:260–84. Cambridge: Cambridge University Press, 1974.

———. *The Tudor Constitution: Documents and Commentary*. Cambridge: Cambridge University Press, 1960.

Englehardt, Tom. *The End of Victory Culture: Cold War America and the Disillusioning of a Generation*. New York: Basic Books, 1995.

Esquillus, Publius [pseud.]. *Wonderfull newes of the death of Paul the .iii.* Translated by William Baldwin. London, [1552?]. *STC* 10532.

Evenden, Elizabeth. "The Fleeing Dutchmen? The Influence of Dutch Immigrants upon the Print Shop of John Day." In *John Foxe at Home and Abroad*, edited by David Loades, 63–78. Aldershot: Ashgate, 2004.

———. "The Michael Wood Mystery: William Cecil and the Lincolnshire Printing of John Day." *Sixteenth Century Journal* 35, no. 2 (2004): 383–94.

Fabyan, Robert. *The Chronicle of Fabyan*. London, 1542. *STC* 10662.

Farnham, Willard. *The Medieval Heritage of Elizabethan Tragedy*. Berkeley: University of California Press, 1936.

———. "The *Mirror for Magistrates* and Elizabethan Tragedy." *Journal of English and Germanic Philology* 25, no. 3 (1926): 66–78.

Feuillerat, Albert. *Documents Relating to the Revels at Court in the Time of King Edward VI and Queen Mary*. Louvain: A. Uystpruyst, 1914.

Feasey, Eveline. "The Licensing of the *Mirror for Magistrates*." *The Library*, 4th ser., 3, no 3 (1922): 177–93.

Ferguson, Arthur. *The Articulate Citizen and the English Renaissance*. Durham, N.C.: Duke University Press, 1965.

Ferrers, George, ed. and trans. *The Boke of Magna Carta with diuers other statutes . . . translated into Englyshe*. London, 1534; *STC* 9272.

Fleay, F. B. *A Biographical Chronicle of the English Drama, 1559–1642*. 2 vols. London, 1891.

Fox, Edward. *The True Dyffere[n]s between ye regall power and the Ecclesiasticall power*. Translated by Henry, Lord Stafford. London, 1548. *STC* 11220.

Foxe, John. *The First Volume of the Ecclesiastical History, contayning the Actes and Monuments of thinges passed in euery kinges time*. London, 1576. *STC* 11224.

Franklin, David. *The Scottish Regency of the Earl of Arran: A Study in the Failure of Anglo-Scottish Relations*. Lewiston, N.Y.: Edwin Mellen, 1995.

Froissart, John. *Here Begynneth the Thirde and Fourthe Boke of Sir Iohn Froissart of the Cronycles*. London, 1525. *STC* 11397.

Gammon, Samuel. *Statesman and Schemer: William, First Lord Paget, Tudor Minister*. Hamden, Conn.: Archon Books, 1973.

Geller, Sherri. "What History Really Teaches: Historic Pyrrhonism in William Baldwin's *A Mirror for Magistrates*." In *Opening the Borders: Inclusivity in*

Early Modern Studies, edited by Peter Herman, 150–84. Newark: University of Delaware Press, 1999.

Gibbons, Geoffrey. *The Political Career of Thomas Wriothesley, First Earl of Southampton, 1501–1550, Henry VIII's Last Chancellor*. Lewiston, N.Y.: Edwin Mellen, 2001.

Grafton, Richard. *An Abridgement of Chronicles*. London, 1562. *STC* 12151.

———. *Grafton's Chronicle*. Edited by Henry Ellis. 2 vols. London 1809.

Green, Lawrence. "Modes of Perception in the *Mirror for Magistrates*." *Huntington Library Quarterly* 44, no. 2 (1981): 117–33.

Gresham, Stephen. "William Baldwin: Literary Voice of the Reign of Edward VI." *Huntington Library Quarterly* 44, no. 2 (1981): 101–16.

Gunn, Steven. "The French Wars of Henry VIII." In *The Origins of War in Early Modern Europe*, edited by Jeremy Black, 28–51. Edinburgh: John Donald, 1987.

Gutierrez, Nancy. "William Baldwin." In *Sixteenth Century Nondramatic Writers: First Series*. Vol. 132 of *The Dictionary of Literary Biography*, edited by David Richardson, 19–26. Detroit: Gale Research, 1993.

Guy, John. "Tudor Monarchy and its Critiques." In *The Tudor Monarchy*, edited by John Guy, 78–109. Oxford: Oxford University Press, 1997.

———. *Tudor England*. Oxford: Oxford University Press, 1988.

Hadfield, Andrew. *Literature, Politics and National Identity: Reformation to Renaissance*. Cambridge: Cambridge University Press, 1994.

Hall, Edward. *The Vnion of the Two Noble and Illustre Famelies of Lancastre & Yorke*. London, 1550. Reprint, Menston, U.K.: Scolar Press, 1970.

Ham, R. E., ed. "The Auto-biography of Sir James Croft." *Bulletin of the Institute of Historical Research* 50, no. 121 (1977): 48–57.

Harbison, E. H. *Rival Ambassadors at the Court of Queen Mary*. Princeton: Princeton University Press, 1940.

Harding, Alan. *A Social History of English Law*. Gloucester, Mass.: Peter Smith, 1973.

Harryson, James. *An Exhortacion to the Scottes to Conforme themselfes to . . . Union betweene the Two Realmes of Englande & Scotlande* [1547]. In Murray, *The Complaynt of Scotlande*, 207–36.

Hasler, P. W., ed. *The History of Parliament: The House of Commons, 1558–1603*. 3 vols. London: Secker and Warburg, 1982.

Hearsey, Marguerite, ed. *The Complaint of Henry Duke of Buckingham, Including the Induction: or Thomas Sackville's Contribution to the "Mirror for Magistrates."* New Haven: Yale University Press, 1936.

Hechter, Michael. *Internal Colonialism: The Celtic Fringe in British National Development, 1536–1966*. Berkeley: University of California Press: 1975.

Henry VIII, King of England. *A Declaration, Conteynyng the Iust Cavses and Consyderations, of this Present Warre with the Scottis, wherin alsoo appereth the Trewe & Right Title, that the Kinges most Royall Maiesty hath to the Souerayntie of Scotlande* [1542]. In Murray, *The Complaynt of Scotlande*, 191–206.

Heylyn, Peter. *Ecclesia Restaurata: Or, The History of the Reformation of the Church of England.* Edited by James Robertson. 2 vols. Cambridge, 1849.

Historical Manuscripts Commission. *Seventh Report of the Royal Commission on Historical Manuscripts.* London, 1879.

Hoak, Dale. "The Coronations of Edward VI, Mary I, and Elizabeth I, and the Transformation of the Tudor Monarchy." In *Westminster Abbey Reformed, 1540–1640*, edited by C. S. Knighton and Richard Mortimer, 114–51. Aldershot: Ashgate, 2003.

———. "The Iconography of the Crown Imperial." In *Tudor Political Culture*, edited by Dale Hoak, 54–103. Cambridge: Cambridge University Press, 1995.

———. *The King's Council in the Reign of Edward VI.* Cambridge: Cambridge University Press, 1976.

———. "The King's Privy Chamber, 1547–1553." In *Tudor Rule and Revolution*, edited by Delloyd Guth and John McKenna, 87–108. Cambridge: Cambridge University Press, 1982.

———. "Rehabilitating the Duke of Northumberland." *The Mid-Tudor Polity, c. 1540–1560*, edited by Robert Titler and Jennifer Loach, 29–51. Totowa, N.J.: Rowman and Littlefield, 1980.

Hole, Christina. *Witchcraft in England.* New York: Scribners, 1947.

Holinshed, Raphael, William Harrison, and Richard Stanyhurst. *The Laste Volume of the Chronicles.* Vol. 2 of *The Chronicles of Englande, Scotlande, and Irelande.* London, 1577. *STC* 13568b.

Hooper, John. *A Declaracion of Christe.* Zurich, 1547. *STC* 13745.

Hughey, Ruth, ed. *The Arundel Harington Manuscript of Tudor Poetry.* 2 vols. Columbus: Ohio State University Press, 1960.

Hughes, Paul, and James Larkin, eds. *Tudor Royal Proclamations.* 3 vols. New Haven: Yale University Press, 1964–1969.

Jackson, W. A. *The Carl H. Pforzheimer Library: English Literature, 1475–1700.* 3 vols. New York: privately printed, 1940.

———. "Wayland's Edition of *The Mirror for Magistrates.*" *The Library*, 4th ser., 13, no. 2 (1932–1933): 155–57.

James, Henry, and Greg Walker. "The Politics of *Gorboduc.*" *English Historical Review* 110, no. 435 (1995): 109–21.

James, Mervyn. *Society, Politics and Culture: Studies in Early Modern England.* Cambridge: Cambridge University Press, 1986.

Jenye, Thomas. "Maister Randolphe['s] Phantasey: a breffe calgulacion of the procedinges in Scotlande from the first of Julie to the Last of Decembre [1565]." In *Satirical Poems of the Time of the Reformation* (2 vols.), edited by James Cranstoun, 1:1–29. Edinburgh, 1891.

Jonson, Ben. *Bartholomew Fair.* Edited by E. A. Horsman. Cambridge: Harvard University Press, 1960.

———. *Bartholomew Fair.* Edited by Eugene Waith. New Haven, Yale University Press, 1963.

Jordan, W. K., ed. *The Chronicle and Political Papers of King Edward VI*. Ithaca: Cornell University Press, 1966.

———. *Edward VI: The Threshold of Power*. Cambridge: Belknap Press of Harvard University Press, 1970.

———. *Edward VI: The Young King*. Cambridge: Belknap Press of Harvard University Press, 1968.

Jordan, W. K., and M. R. Gleason. "The Saying of John Late Duke of Northumberland upon the Scaffold, 1553." *Harvard Library Bulletin* 23 (1975): 139–79, 324–55.

"A 'Journall' of Matters of State," edited by Simon Adams, Ian Archer, and G. W. Bernard. In *Religion, Politics and Society in Sixteenth-Century England*, edited by Ian Archer et al., 52–122. London: Royal Historical Society, 2003.

Kelley, Donald. "Elizabethan Political Thought." In *The Varieties of British Political Thought, 1500–1800*, edited by J. G. A. Pocock, 47–79. Cambridge: Cambridge University Press, 1993.

Kelly, Henry A. *Divine Providence in the England of Shakespeare's Histories*. Cambridge: Harvard University Press, 1970.

Kiefer, Frederick. *Fortune and Elizabethan Tragedy*. San Marino, Calif.: The Huntington Library, 1983.

———. "*A Mirror for Magistrates*." In *Sixteenth-Century British Nondramatic Writers: Third Series*. Vol 167, *The Dictionary of Literary Biography*, edited by David Richardson, 116–27. Detroit: Gale Research, 1996.

King, John N. *English Reformation Literature: The Tudor Origins of the Protestant Tradition*. Princeton: Princeton University Press, 1982.

———. *Tudor Royal Iconography: Literature and Art in an Age of Religious Crisis*. Princeton: Princeton University Press, 1989.

Kinghorn, A. M. *The Chorus of History: Literary-Historical Relations in Renaissance Britain, 1485–1558*. New York: Barnes and Noble, 1971.

Knighton, C. S., ed. *Calendar of State Papers, Domestic Series, of the Reign of King Edward VI, 1547–1553*. London: HMSO, 1992.

Knox, John. *An Admonition or warning that the Faithful Christians in London, Newcastel, Barwycke & others, may avoide Gods vengeaunce, both in thys life and in the life to come*. [Wittenburge (i.e., London?), 1554.] *STC* 15059.

———. *A Faythfull Admonition . . . unto the Professours of Gods Truthe in England* [1554]. In *The Works of John Knox* (6 vols.), edited by David Laing, 3:251–330. Edinburgh, 1854.

Langton, Christopher. *A Very Brefe Treatise . . . of Physick*. London, 1547. *STC* 15205.

Latimer, Hugh. *Seven Sermons before Edward VI, On Each Friday in Lent, 1549*. Edited by Edward Arber. Birmingham, 1869.

Legg, Leopold, ed. *English Coronation Records*. Westminster: Constable & Co., 1901.

Leland, John. "Ad Georgium Ferrarium." In *Principum, ac Illustrium Aliquot & Eru-*

ditorum in Anglia Virorum, Encomia, Trophaea, Genethliaca & Epithalamia, 99. London, 1589. *STC* 15447.

Levack, Brian. *The Formation of the British State: England, Scotland, and the Union, 1603–1707*. Oxford: Clarendon Press, 1987.

Levy, F. J. *Tudor Historical Thought*. San Marino, Calif.: The Huntington Library, 1967.

Lewis, C. S. *English Literature in the Sixteenth Century, Excluding Drama*. Oxford: Oxford University Press, 1954.

Loach, Jennifer. *Edward VI*. New Haven: Yale University Press, 1999.

———. "Pamphlets and Politics, 1553–8." *Bulletin of the Institute of Historical Research* 48 (1975): 31–44.

———. *Parliament and the Crown in the Reign of Mary Tudor*. Oxford: Clarendon Press, 1986.

Loades, David. *John Dudley, Duke of Northumberland, 1504–1553*. Oxford: Clarendon Press, 1996.

———. *Mary Tudor: A Life*. Oxford: Blackwell, 1989.

———. *The Oxford Martyrs*. London: Batsford, 1970.

———. *Politics, Censorship and the English Reformation*. London: Pinter, 1991.

———. *The Reign of Mary Tudor*. 2nd ed. London: Longman, 1991.

———. "Thomas Cranmer and John Dudley: An Uneasy Alliance, 1549–1553." In *Thomas Cranmer: Churchman and Scholar*, edited by Paul Ayris and David Selwyn, 157–74. New York: Boydell Press, 1993.

———. *The Tudor Court*. Totowa, N.J.: Barnes and Noble, 1987.

Lucas, Scott. "The Consolation of Tragedy: *A Mirror for Magistrates* and the Fall of the 'Good Duke' of Somerset." *Studies in Philology* 100, no. 1 (2003): 44–70.

———. Conspiracy and Court Revels: Were the 1551–2 Christmas Revels a Plot against Protector Somerset?" *Medieval and Renaissance Drama in England* 10 (1997): 19–46.

———. "Coping with Providentialism: Trauma, Identity, and the Failure of the English Reformation." In *Images of Matter: Essays on British Literature of the Middle Ages and Renaissance*, edited by Yvonne Bruce, 255–73. Newark: University of Delaware Press, 2005.

———. "Diggon Davie and Davy Dicar: Edmund Spenser, Thomas Churchyard, and the Poetics of Public Protest." *Spenser Studies* 16 (2002): 151–65.

———. "Hall's Chronicle and *A Mirror for Magistrates*: History and the Tragic Pattern." In *The Oxford Handbook of Tudor Literature*, edited by Mike Pincombe and Cathy Shrank. Oxford: Oxford University Press, 2009.

———. "'Let none such office take, save he that can for right his prince forsake': *A Mirror for Magistrates*, Resistance Theory and the Elizabethan Monarchical Republic." In *The Monarchical Republic of Early Modern England: Essays in Response to Patrick Collinson*, edited by John McDiarmid, 91–107. Aldershot: Ashgate, 2007.

———. "The Suppressed Edition and the Creation of the 'Orthodox' *Mirror for Magistrates.*" *Renaissance Papers 1994* (1995): 31–54.

Luther, Martin. *A Faythfull Admonycion of a Certen Trewe Pastor and Prophete*. Strasburg, 1554. *STC* 16980.

Lydgate, John. *The Fall of Prynces. Gathered by Iohn Bochas, fro[m] the begynnyng of the world vntyll his time, translated into English by Iohn Lidgate Monke of Burye. wherunto is added the fall of al such as since that time were notable in Englande: diligently collected out of the Chronicles*. London, [1554]. *STC* 3177.5.

———. *The tragedies, gathered by Ihon Bochas, of all such Princes as fell from theyr estates throughe the mutability of Fortune since the creacion of Adam, vntil his time: wherin may be seen what vices bring menne to destruccion, wyth notable warninges howe the like may be auoyded. Translated into Englysh by Ihon Lidgate, Monke of Burye*. London, [1554]. *STC* 3178.

Lyne, Raphael. "Churchyard, Thomas (1523?–1604)." In Matthew and Harrison, *The Oxford Dictionary of National Biography*, 11:687–90.

MacCulloch, Diarmaid. *The Boy King: Edward VI and the Protestant Reformation*. New York: Palgrave, 1999. Also published as *The Tudor Church Militant*. London: Allen Lane, 1999.

———. "Kett's Rebellion in Context." In *Rebellion, Popular Protest and the Social Order*, edited by Paul Slack, 39–62. Cambridge: Cambridge University Press, 1984.

———. "Kett's Rebellion in Context: A Rejoinder." In *Rebellion, Popular Protest and the Social Order*, edited by Paul Slack, 68–76. Cambridge: Cambridge University Press, 1984.

———. *Thomas Cranmer*. New Haven: Yale University Press, 1996.

———, ed. and trans. "The *Vita Mariae Angliae Reginae* of Robert Wingfield." In *Camden Miscellany 28*, 181–301. Camden Society, 4th ser., 29. London: Royal Historical Society, 1984.

Marcus, Leah. *Puzzling Shakespeare: Local Reading and Its Discontents*. Berkeley: University of California Press, 1988.

Maslen, R. W. "William Baldwin and the Politics of Pseudo-Philosophy in Tudor Prose Fiction." *Studies in Philology* 97, no. 1 (2000): 29–60.

Matthew, H. C. G. and Brian Harrison, eds. *The Oxford Dictionary of National Biography*. 60 vols. Oxford: Oxford University Press, 2004.

Mayer, T. F. "On the Road to 1534: The Occupation of Tournai and Henry VIII's Theory of Sovereignty." In *Tudor Political Culture*, edited by Dale Hoak, 11–30. Cambridge: Cambridge University Press, 1995.

McCaffrey, Wallace. *The Shaping of the Elizabethan Regime*. Princeton: Princeton University Press, 1968.

McCann, I. Lisa, and Laurie Pearlman. *Psychological Trauma and the Adult Survivor*. New York: Brunner/Mazel, 1990.

McKerrow, R. B., and F. S. Ferguson. *Title-page Borders used in England and Scotland, 1485–1640*. Oxford: Bibliographical Society, 1932.

Metzger, Marcia. "Controversy and 'Correctness': English Chronicles and the Chroniclers, 1553–1568." *Sixteenth Century Journal* 27, no. 2 (1996): 437–51.
———. "Failure and Success? Mary, Elizabeth and the Printing Industry in England, 1553–1568." Ph.D. diss., Washington University, 1993.
Millar, Gilbert. *Tudor Mercenaries and Auxiliaries, 1485–1547*. Charlottesville: University of Virginia Press, 1980.
Miller, Clarence, ed. *The Praise of Folie by Sir Thomas Chaloner*. Early English Text Society, original series, 257. London: Oxford University Press, 1965.
Miller, Helen. *Henry VIII and the English Nobility*. Oxford: Blackwell, 1986.
Mills, Jerry Leith. "Recent Studies in *A Mirror for Magistrates*." *English Literary Renaissance* 9, no. 2 (1979): 343–52.
Mosser, François. "L'Art de la poesie historique dans la *Mirror for Magistrates*." *Études Anglais* 40, no. 2 (1987): 129–41.
Mumby, Frank. *Publishing and Bookselling: A History from the Earliest Times to the Present Day*. London: J. Cape, 1930.
Murdin, William, ed. *A Collection of State Papers Relating to Affairs in the Reign of Queen Elizabeth from the Year 1571 to 1596*. London, 1759.
Murphy, John. "The Illusion of Decline: The Privy Chamber, 1547–1558." In *The English Court: From the Wars of the Roses to the Civil War*, edited by David Starkey, 119–46. London: Longman, 1987.
Murray, James, ed. *The Complaynt of Scotlande*. London, 1872.
Neale, J. E. "The Commons' Privilege of Free Speech in Parliament." In *Tudor Studies: Presented by the Board of History in the University of London to Albert Frederick Pollard*, edited by R. W. Seton-Watson, 257–86. London: Longmans, 1924.
Niccols, Richard. *A Mirour for Magistrates*. London, 1610. *STC* 13446.
Nichols, J. G. ed. "Autobiographical Anecdotes of Edward Underhill." In *Narratives of the Days of the Reformation*, edited by J. G. Nichols, 132–76. London, 1859.
———, ed. *The Diary of Henry Machyn*. London, 1848.
———, ed. *The Chronicle of Queen Jane and of Two Years of Queen Mary*. London, 1850.
———, ed. *The Chronicle of the Grey Friars of London*. London, 1851.
———, ed. *The Legend of Sir Nicholas Throckmorton*. London, 1874.
Norbrook, David. *Poetry and Politics in the English Renaissance*. 2nd edition. Oxford: Oxford University Press, 2002.
Ochino, Bernardino. *A Tragoedie or Dialoge of the Vnjuste Primacie of the Bishop of Rome*. London, 1549. *STC* 18770.
Ovid. *Metamorphoses*. Translated by Rolfe Humphries. Bloomington: Indiana University Press, 1955.
Page, William, ed. *The Victoria History of the County of Hertford*. 4 vols. Westminster: A. Constable & Co., 1908.
Parry, G. J. R. *A Protestant Vision: William Harrison and the Reformation of Elizabethan England*. Cambridge: Cambridge University Press, 1987.

Patten, William. *The Expedition into Scotland of the most worthily fortunate Prince Edward, Duke of Somerset* [London, 1548]. In *Tudor Tracts, 1532–1588*, edited by A. F. Pollard, 53–157. Westminster: Constable & Co., 1903.

Patterson, Annabel. *Censorship and Interpretation: The Conditions of Writing and Reading in Early Modern England.* Madison: University of Wisconsin Press, 1984.

———. *Reading Holinshed's Chronicles.* Chicago: University of Chicago Press, 1994.

———, ed. *The Trial of Nicholas Throckmorton.* Toronto: Centre for Reformation and Renaissance Studies, 1998.

Peery, William. "Tragic Retribution in the 1559 *Mirror for Magistrates. Studies in Philology* 46, no. 2 (1949): 113–30.

Pocock, J. G. A. *The Ancient Constitution and the Feudal Law.* Cambridge: Cambridge University Press, 1957.

Pocock, Nicholas, ed. *Troubles Connected with the Prayer Book of 1549.* London, 1884.

Pollard, A. F. *England under Protector Somerset.* London: Kegan Paul, 1900.

Pollard, A. W., G. R. Redgrave, F. S. Ferguson, Katherine Pantzer, and W. A. Jackson. *A Short Title Catalogue of Books Printed in England, Scotland, and Ireland, and of English Books Printed Abroad, 1475–1640.* 2nd ed. London: Bibliographical Society, 1976–1991.

Ponet, John. *A Shorte Treatise of Politike Power.* Strasbourg, 1556. *STC* 20178.

Potter, David. "Foreign Policy." In *The Reign of Henry VIII: Politics, Policy and Piety,* edited by Diarmaid MacCulloch, 101–34. New York: St. Martin's Press, 1995.

Prescott, H. F. M. *Mary Tudor.* New York: Macmillan, 1953.

Prothero, G. W. ed. *Select Statutes and Other Constitutional Documents Illustrative of the Reigns of Elizabeth I and James I.* Oxford, 1894.

Reid, R. R. *The King's Council in the North.* London: Longmans, 1921.

Richards, Judith. "Mary Tudor as 'Sole Quene'? Gendering Tudor Monarchy." *Historical Journal* 40 (1997): 895–924.

Ridley, Jasper. *Henry VIII.* New York: Viking, 1984.

Riordan, Michael, and Alec Ryrie. "Stephen Gardiner and the Making of a Protestant Villain." *Sixteenth Century Journal* 34, no. 4 (2003): 1039–63.

Robinson, Hastings, ed. *Original Letters Relative to the English Reformation.* 2 vols. Cambridge, 1846.

Rose-Troup, Frances. *The Western Rebellion of 1549.* London: Smith, Elder, & Co., 1913.

Rudd, Niall. *The Satires of Horace: A Study.* Cambridge: Cambridge University Press, 1966.

Robbins, Russell, ed. *Historical Poems of the XIVth and XVth Centuries.* New York: Columbia University Press, 1959.

Ryrie, Alec. *The Gospel and Henry VIII: Evangelicals in the Early English Reformation.* Cambridge: Cambridge University Press, 2003.

Samson, Alexander. "Changing Places: The Marriage and Royal Entry of Philip, Prince of Austria, and Mary Tudor, July–August 1554." *Sixteenth Century Journal* 36, no. 3 (2005): 761–84.

Scarisbrick, J. J. *Henry VIII*. Berkeley: University of California Press, 1968.

Schmitz, Götz. *The Fall of Women in Early English Narrative Verse*. Cambridge: Cambridge University Press, 1990.

Seneca, Lucius Annaeus. *The Seconde Tragedie of Seneca entituled Thyestes*. Translated by Jasper Heywood. London, 1560. *STC* 22226.

Seymour, Edward, Duke of Somerset. *Edward, Duke of Somerset . . . : To all . . . of the Realme of Scotlande*. London, 1547. *STC* 7811.

———. *An Epistle or Exhortacion, to Unitie and Peace, sent from the Lord Protector . . . to the Nobilitie . . . and al Others the Inhabitauntes of the Realme of Scotlande* [London, 1548]. In Murray, *The Complaynt of Scotlande*, 237–47.

Seymour, William. *Ordeal by Ambition: A Family in the Shadow of the Tudors*. New York: St. Martin's Press, 1972.

Shagan, Ethan. "Protector Somerset and the 1549 Rebellions: New Sources and New Perspectives." *English Historical Review* 114, no. 455 (1999): 34–63.

Shakespeare, Joy. "Plague and Punishment." In *Protestantism and the National Church in Sixteenth-Century England*, edited by Peter Lake and Maria Dowling, 103–23. London: Croom Helm, 1987.

Slavin, A. J. "The Fall of Lord Chancellor Wriothesley: A Study in the Politics of Conspiracy." *Albion* 7, no. 4 (1975): 265–86.

Smith, Alan. *The Emergence of a Nation State: The Commonwealth of England, 1529–1660*. New York: Longmans, 1984.

Smith, G. G. *Elizabethan Critical Essays*. 2 vols. Oxford: Clarendon Press, 1904.

Smith, Sir Thomas. *De Republica Anglorum by Sir Thomas Smith*. Edited by Mary Dewar. Cambridge: Cambridge University Press, 1982.

Stephen, Sir Leslie, and Sir Sidney Lee, eds. *The Dictionary of National Biography*. 22 vols. Oxford: Oxford University Press, 1921–1922.

Stow, John. *Annales*. London, 1592. *STC* 23334.

———. *Annales*. London, 1605. *STC* 23337.

———. *Summarie of Englyshe Chronicles*. London, 1565. *STC* 23319.

———. *A Survey of London*. Edited by Charles Kingford. 2 vols. Oxford: Clarendon Press, 1908.

Strachey, John, ed. *Rotuli Parliamentorum, ut et Petitiones, et Placita in Parliamento*. 6 vols. London, 1767–1777.

Strype, John. *Ecclesiastical Memorials Relating Chiefly to Religion and the Reformation of It, and the Emergencies of the Church of England, under King Henry VIII, King Edward VI, and Queen Mary*. 3 vols. Oxford, 1822.

———. *The Life of the Learned Sir Thomas Smith, Kt*. Oxford, 1820.

Swart, Jacobus. *Thomas Sackville: A Study in Sixteenth Century Poetry*. Groningen: J. B. Wolters, 1949.

Tillyard, E. M. W. "*A Mirror for Magistrates* Revisited." In *Elizabethan and Jacobean*

Studies Presented to Frank Percy Wilson, edited by Herbert Davis and Helen Gardener, 1–16. Oxford: Clarendon Press, 1959.

———. *Shakespeare's History Plays*. London: Chatto & Windus, 1944.

Tomlin, T. E., William Taunton, and John Raithby, eds. *The Statutes of the Realm*. 11 vols. London, 1810–1828.

Trench, W. F. "*A Mirror for Magistrates*": *Its Origin and Influence*. Edinburgh, 1898.

Tuck, Anthony. *Richard II and the English Nobility*. New York: St. Martin's Press, 1974.

Tytler, Patrick. *England under the Reigns of Edward VI and Mary*. 2 vols. London, 1839.

Walker, Greg. *Plays of Persuasion: Drama and Politics at the Court of Henry VIII*. Cambridge: Cambridge University Press, 1991.

Waller, Gary, *English Poetry of the Sixteenth Century*. London: Longman, 1986.

A Warnyng for Englande Conteynyng the Horrible Practises of the Kyng of Spayne. Emden, 1555. *STC* 10024.

Wernham, R. B. *Before the Armada: The Emergence of the English Nation, 1485–1588*. New York: Harcourt, Brace & World, 1966.

Whetstone, George. *The Censure of a Loyall Subiect* [1587]. In *Illustrations of Early English Popular Literature*, edited by J. Payne Collier. 2 vols. London, 1863.

White, Paul Whitfield. *Theatre and Reformation: Protestantism, Patronage and Playing in Tudor England*. Cambridge: Cambridge University Press, 1993.

White, R. S. *Natural Law in English Renaissance Literature*. Cambridge: Cambridge University Press, 1996.

Williams, Neville. *Thomas Howard Fourth Duke of Norfolk*. New York: E. P. Dutton, 1964.

Wilson, Thomas. *The Arte of Rhetorique*. Edited by Thomas Derrick. New York: Garland, 1982.

Winston, Jessica. "*A Mirror for Magistrates* and Public Political Discourse in Elizabethan England." *Studies in Philology* 101, no. 4 (2004): 381–400.

———. "National History to Foreign Calamity: *A Mirror for Magistrates* and Early English Tragedy." In *Shakespeare's Histories and Counter-Histories*, edited by Dermot Cavanagh, Stuart Hampton-Reeves, and Stephen Longstaffe, 152–65. Manchester: Manchester University Press, 2006.

Wolffe, Bertram. *Henry VI*. London: Methuen, 1981.

Woudhuyson, H. R. "Vaux, Thomas, Second Baron Vaux (1509–1556)." In Matthew and Harrison, *The Oxford Dictionary of National Biography*, 56:220–22.

Wriothesley, Charles. *A Chronicle of England during the Reigns of the Tudors, from A.D. 1485 to 1559*. Edited by William Hamilton. 2 vols. London, 1875–1877.

Wyll, Western [pseud.]. *Westerne Will to Camell*. In *The Contention betwyxte Churchyeard and Camell, vpon David Dycers Dreame*, sigs. F2r–G1r. London, 1560. *STC* 5225.

———. *Westerne Wyll, Vpon the Debate betwyxte Churchyarde and Camell.* In *The Contention betwyxte Churchyeard and Camell, vpon David Dycers Dreame,* sigs. C3r–D4r. London, 1560. *STC* 5225.

Zocca, Louis. *Elizabethan Narrative Poetry*. New Brunswick, N.J.: Rutgers University Press, 1950.

Index